"The work of J. B. Lightfoot, along with that of his close collaborators B. F. Westcott and F. J. A. Hort, remains of landmark significance to contemporary New Testament studies. The editors and their assistants are to be thanked and congratulated for their labors in bringing to publication these previously unpublished notes on 2 Corinthians and 1 Peter, along with various essays by and about Lightfoot. These materials will be of interest to all who work on the historical interpretation of these letters and on the history of their interpretation."

David G. Horrell, professor of New Testament studies, director, Centre for Biblical Studies, University of Exeter

"The discovery and publication of previously unpublished commentaries on the New Testament by Joseph Barber Lightfoot is a highly significant event in the history of New Testament scholarship. For a start, these shed valuable light on the reception of the New Testament in the nineteenth century, representing the work of the foremost English scholar of that era whose linguistic and historical skills exhibit a quality of scholarship that few today can match. . . . Ben Witherington, Todd Still and Jeanette Hagen are to be warmly congratulated for their remarkable success in making such a significant voice from the past resound again today."

John M. G. Barclay, Lightfoot Professor of Divinity, University of Durham

"Joseph Barber Lightfoot has been, for me, in many ways the epitome of what the commentator on New Testament and early church texts can and should aspire to. His detailed knowledge of the literature of the time was unsurpassed, and his ability to shed the light of that knowledge on the New Testament writings was without peer. His commentaries on New Testament texts and the early Fathers retain a relevance and a value to this day almost unique for nineteenth-century scholarship. That a fuller publication of his writings is now available in these volumes is a wonderful bonus for those who want to hear these New Testament and early church texts as they were first heard."

James D. G. Dunn, Emeritus Lightfoot Professor of Divinity, University of Durham

"Harnack said it best: Lightfoot was a true liberal for he was 'an independent, free scholar . . . in the absolute sense of the word. He has never defended tradition for the tradition's sake.' We need more liberals like that today!"

Daniel B. Wallace, Dallas Theological Seminary

"Thanks to Witherington and his associates and to IVP for bringing this cache of material from the great J. B. Lightfoot into the public domain. His previously published works have remained important (his multivolume study of the apostolic fathers is essential for these writings), and this hitherto unpublished material will now also likely come to be seen as a valuable resource."
Larry Hurtado, University of Edinburgh

"From Bede, the greatest European scholar of the seventh century, to today's world-class university sharing a world heritage site with a majestic cathedral, creative and careful study has long stood alongside prayer and worship here in Durham. It is therefore fitting that this amazing discovery of Lightfoot's handwritten manuscripts was made by one of the world's leading biblical scholars in the cathedral library. For within these pages, Lightfoot embodies that Durham tradition—outstanding independent scholarship offered humbly in the service of God."
David Wilkinson, Durham University

"The discovery of hitherto unknown exegetical works by J. B. Lightfoot is a rare gift, full of potential for fresh insight both about the man himself (acknowledged worldwide as the leading scholar of his day) and, as he would have wished, about texts which he knew so well and which themselves express the heart of the gospel. Hearty congratulations to finder, editor and publisher on an unexpected and exciting addition to the core library of seminal biblical studies."
N. T. Wright, University of St. Andrews, former Bishop of Durham

"We are greatly in debt to Ben Witherington, Todd Still and their collaborators for bringing this material to light for our day."
Steve Walton, Tyndale House, Cambridge

J. B. LIGHTFOOT

The Epistles of

2 Corinthians and 1 Peter

Newly Discovered Commentaries

THE LIGHTFOOT LEGACY SET

◆

Volume 3

Edited by
BEN WITHERINGTON III
and TODD D. STILL

Assisted by
JEANETTE M. HAGEN

IVP Academic
An imprint of InterVarsity Press
Downers Grove, Illinois

InterVarsity Press
P.O. Box 1400, Downers Grove, IL 60515-1426
ivpress.com
email@ivpress.com

InterVarsity Press® is the book-publishing division of InterVarsity Christian Fellowship/USA®, a movement of students and faculty active on campus at hundreds of universities, colleges and schools of nursing in the United States of America, and a member movement of the International Fellowship of Evangelical Students. For information about local and regional activities, visit intervarsity.org.

All Scripture quotations, unless otherwise indicated, are the author's translation.

Cover design: Cindy Kiple
Interior design: Beth McGill
Images: Joseph Lightfoot, English theologian and Bishop of Durham, Lock and Whitfield (19th century) / Private Collection / © Look and Learn / Elgar Collection / Bridgeman Images.
   recycled paper: © tomograf/iStockphoto
   Glossy insert page images courtesy of Durham Cathedral Library / © Chapter of Durham library

ISBN 978-0-8308-2946-0 (print)
ISBN 978-0-8308-9959-3 (digital)

Library of Congress Cataloging-in-Publication Data
Names: Lightfoot, J. B. (Joseph Barber), 1828-1889, author. | Witherington, Ben, III, 1951- editor. | Still, Todd D., editor.
Title: The epistles of 2 Corinthians and 1 Peter : newly discovered commentaries / J. B. Lightfoot ; edited by Ben Witherington III and Todd D. Still ; assisted by Jeanette M. Hagen.
Description: Downers Grove : InterVarsity Press, 2016. | Series: The lightfoot legacy set ; Volume 3 | Includes index.
Identifiers: LCCN 2016041785 (print) | LCCN 2016042807 (ebook) | ISBN 9780830829460 (hardcover) | ISBN 9780830899593 (eBook)
Subjects: LCSH: Bible. Corinthians, 2nd—Commentaries. | Bible. Peter, 1st—Commentaries.
Classification: LCC BS2675.53 .L54 2016 (print) | LCC BS2675.53 (ebook) | DDC 227.307—dc23
LC record available at https://lccn.loc.gov/2016041785

P	23	22	21	20	19	18	17	16	15	14	13	12	11	10	9	8	7	6	5	4	3	2	1
Y	36	35	34	33	32	31	30	29	28	27	26	25	24	23	22	21	20	19	18	17	16		

Figure 1. J. B. Lightfoot

Rightly understood . . . Joseph Barber Lightfoot, historian and theologian, Christian and bishop, can still become our tutor today.

Martin Hengel, "Bishop Lightfoot and the Tübingen School on the Gospel of John in the Second Century"

There was a peculiar fitness in the time that was selected for the revelation of Messiah to his people. But can we venture a step beyond, and say that we see in the popular mind of the day the germ of a natural development of the Christian scheme? The voice of prophecy had been silent for four centuries, but it was felt to be as the death-like stillness that precedes the hurricane. Hence, men with busy whisperings were anxiously looking for the coming of that great Terrible Day of the Lord which, amidst many horrors, was yet to bring their deliverance.

J. B. Lightfoot, "Lessons of History from the Cradle of Christianity"

For there is a testimony which it is not in the power of historical criticism to grasp, the testimony of the heart which finds in Christianity its deepest aspirations realized and its fondest hopes fulfilled, the testimony of a conscience smitten and pierced, as by a sharp two-edged sword, by the record of His words 'who spake as no man spake,' the testimony of experience which reminds the Christian that in proportion as he has cultivated his best faculties and highest feelings of his nature, the clouds of doubt and difficulty have been dispersed before the 'light of the Spirit which bears witness to his spirit,' and have only gathered again when he has been betrayed into spiritual carelessness or moral ambiguity.

J. B. Lightfoot, "Lessons of History from the Cradle of Christianity"

In an even earlier lecture than that on Lightfoot, to which I have already referred, I described the way in which Lightfoot, Westcott, and Hort divided up the New Testament with a view to writing commentaries on the whole. . . . The Chapter Library at Durham contains a quantity of [unpublished] manuscript material which is interesting in that it shows both how probably the most popular teacher of theology at Cambridge in his time prepared and presented his material, and also how the finished commentaries took shape.

C. K. Barrett

CONTENTS

FOREWORD

In 1978, I (BW3) was in the Durham Cathedral cloister visiting
the Monk's Dormitory that then, as now, served as a display room for important artifacts and manuscripts. It was also something of an archival library. I was a young doctoral student of Charles Kingsley Barrett and had
already come across the name of J. B. Lightfoot on various occasions. Indeed,
I had bought a reprint of his classic Philippians commentary while I was still
in seminary in Massachusetts several years earlier. While perusing the
various display cases, I came across an open notebook that displayed Lightfoot's comments on a notoriously difficult passage in Acts 15, and I wondered
whether there were more of this sort of meticulous exegetical material,
written in Lightfoot's own hand, somewhere else in that library.

Naturally, I was interested, since there were no publications by Lightfoot
that directly dealt with Acts, and certainly no commentaries by Lightfoot
on Acts. I mentioned this discovery to Professor Barrett, who himself was
an admirer of J. B. Lightfoot. In fact, in the early 1970s he had written a
Durham University Journal article in which he praised Lightfoot as ar-
guably the foremost scholar of the New Testament of his era.[1] Somehow,
however, nothing more happened in regard to this matter, and in truth, I
forgot about it.

I mentioned in passing seeing this material some years later to Professor
J. D. G. Dunn, who was then serving as the Lightfoot Professor of Divinity at
Durham University. Still, nothing more came of it. Yes, there was a celebration

---

[1]C. K. Barrett, "Joseph Barber Lightfoot," *Durham University Journal* 64 (1972): 193-204.

of the centennial of Lightfoot's death in 1989, planned and organized by the tireless efforts of Professor Dunn, that produced a fine special issue of the *Durham University Journal*, published in 1990, with various articles about the legacy of Lightfoot.[2] There was even a fine monograph done by G. R. Treloar on Lightfoot as a historian.[3] Although it was clear that Treloar had read and studied some of Lightfoot's unpublished work on Acts, the primary sources had not been completely read or studied, much less published.

On my sabbatical in the spring of 2013, when I was scholar-in-residence in St. John's College at Durham University, I decided to try to see just what Lightfoot materials might still be gathering dust in the cathedral library. I must confess, I was not prepared for what I found. There, in the Monk's Dormitory in a tall bookcase—whose lower compartment was crammed with Lightfoot files, folders, letters, pictures, inkwells and more—sat not only three brown notebooks of Lightfoot's detailed exegetical lectures on Acts numbering over 140 pages, but also a further gigantic blue box full of hundreds of pages of additional Acts materials, including a lengthy excursus on the authenticity of the Stephen speech. But even that was not all.

There was also a whole blue box full of hundreds of pages of Lightfoot's exegetical studies on the Gospel of John, two notebooks on 1 Peter, lectures on 2 Corinthians and finally a further notebook of Lightfoot's reflections on early Judaism. All were in Lightfoot's own hand, all done in great detail and none of it, except the first four or five pages of the introduction to Galatians contained in the first Acts notebook (which Kaye and Treloar excerpted and published in a *Durham University Journal* article in 1990[4]), had ever been published—until now.[5]

---

[2]Professor Dunn edited this special edition of the journal, which includes articles by David M. Thompson on Lightfoot as a churchman, Martin Hengel on Lightfoot's interaction with the Tübingen school on the Gospel of John and the second century, C. K. Barrett on Lightfoot as a biblical commentator, and James D. G. Dunn on the contributions of Lightfoot to church and academy.

[3]G. R. Treloar, *Lightfoot the Historian: The Nature and Role of History in the Life and Thought of J. B. Lightfoot,* Wissenschaftliche Untersuchungen zum Neuen Testament 2.103 (Tübingen: Mohr Siebeck, 1998).

[4]B. N. Kaye and G. R. Treloar, "J. B. Lightfoot and New Testament Interpretation: An Unpublished Manuscript of 1855," *Durham University Journal* 82 (1990): 160-75 (on 171-75).

[5]There are a few other exceptions to this remark: (1) Three articles on Acts, which appear in the appendices to volume one of this series (*Acts of the Apostles: A Newly Discovered Commentary*), were previously published in periodicals and dictionaries but have long since been out of print and are in the public domain, and (2) Lightfoot's essays on the authenticity of the Gospel of John, examining both the external and internal evidence, were published, but not his exegesis of John. These

It is important to say at this juncture that this material would still be unpublished were it not for (1) the capable help of the Durham Cathedral Library staff, especially Catherine Turner (now retired) and Gabrielle Sewell; (2) the hard work of Jeanette Hagen, a recently minted PhD graduate in New Testament from the University of Durham, who did much of the painstaking work reading and transcribing this material; (3) the generosity of Asbury Seminary, Baylor University (through an Arts and Humanities Faculty Development Program Grant administered by the office of the vice provost of research) and Willard J. Still, who helped to pay for the digitalization and transcription of these materials; and (4) our friends at InterVarsity Press, in particular Andy Le Peau, Jim Hoover, Dan Reid and David Congdon, who saw the value of letting this material see the light of day so it might provide valuable help for our understanding of the New Testament, help from an unexpected quarter.[6]

From where exactly did this material come? The answer is from Lightfoot's lecture notebooks. When Lightfoot served as fellow (1851), tutor (1857), Hulsean Professor of Divinity (1861) and Lady Margaret's Professor (1875) at Cambridge University, he gave several series of lectures on Acts, the Gospel of John, 1 Peter and 2 Corinthians (among other subjects). The first Acts notebook, which also includes notes on Galatians, begins with these words— "Lenten Term, 1855." Over time, as he continued to lecture on these great New Testament texts, Lightfoot would revise his lectures, further annotate them, change his mind on a few things and add things.

When Lightfoot became bishop of Durham in 1879, he brought all of his Cambridge work on the New Testament, and much else, with him. This is how these materials eventually came into the possession of the Durham Cathedral Library. Lightfoot had been lecturing on Acts and John and other parts of the New Testament for more than twenty years when he left Cambridge for Durham, and the impression one gets from these unpublished manuscripts is that, having already published commentaries on Galatians (1865), Philippians (1868), and Colossians and Philemon (1875), Lightfoot's views on Acts, John, 2 Corinthians and 1 Peter were mostly

---

essays were first published posthumously by Macmillan in 1893. Baker republished them in 1979 with a fresh introduction by Philip Edgecumbe Hughes under the title *Biblical Essays*. (BW3)
[6]Todd Still joined this ambitious project at the invitation of BW3 in early June 2013. (TDS)

formed by the time he came to Durham. Indeed, one finds in these same
Acts notebooks some of the materials that went into Lightfoot's Galatians
commentary and his fragmentary commentaries on certain Pauline letters
(namely, Romans, the Corinthian and Thessalonian correspondences,
and Ephesians).[7]

In his own lifetime, Lightfoot was a widely recognized expert in the
Pauline corpus, having published landmark commentaries on Galatians,
Philippians, and Colossians and Philemon before beginning his tasks as
bishop of Durham in 1879. It is then something of a surprise that his very
interesting work on 2 Corinthians was never found and published, when
in fact fragments of his work on Romans, 1 Corinthians, Ephesians, and
1 and 2 Thessalonians were published posthumously in a volume titled
Notes on Epistles of St. Paul from Unpublished Commentaries.[8] It is thus a
true windfall that we can now bring to the light of day Lightfoot's work on
2 Corinthians, though sadly it too is fragmentary. What is especially
evident in this commentary is its contradiction of the suggestion that
Lightfoot was almost entirely a historian and not a theologian. While one
may be forgiven for thinking that when reading the first volume in this
series, on the Acts of the Apostles, there can be no excuse after reading the
second and third ones.

But, of course, this was stressed some time ago by C. K. Barrett. Consider this quote from Barrett's well-known essay "J. B. Lightfoot as Biblical
Commentator." After saying that Lightfoot is a master of historical-critical
exegesis, he adds:

> Thus historical exegesis has not only the negative function of saying to the
> modern theologian or moralist, "No, you may not base your proposition on
> that text," but the positive function of providing solid ground for inferences
> relevant to ages long after the original truth was stated. Lightfoot assumes—
> and if the assumption is valid he may be vindicated not only as a philologist
> and a historian but also as a theologian—that the language and the his-
> torical circumstances of Scripture have a quality of universality that gives

---

[7]Lightfoot's comments on these Pauline letters were published posthumously as *Notes on the Epistles
of St. Paul* (London: Macmillan, 1895).

[8]This volume was published by Macmillan in 1895. A very different volume of other materials, essays
and articles was put together as well. See most recently the reprint of some of these key essays,
mostly on Pauline Epistles, in J. B. Lightfoot, *Biblical Essays* (Grand Rapids: Baker, 1979).

them a perennial applicability. . . . There remains for him however an absolute qualitative distinction between the words of Scripture and all other
words, and it is this, together of course with his splendid scholarly equipment,
that places him securely in the line of great biblical expositors, from Origen
and Chrysostom to Calvin to Bengel.[9]

We are also very happy to be able to present Lightfoot's work on a very different epistle indeed, and a non-Pauline one, namely 1 Peter. Lightfoot believed that the two great apostles were indeed Peter and Paul, the former
for the Jews, the latter for the Gentiles. He also thought that these two
documents upon which he offers commentary in this volume well represented the two great leaders of early Christianity. After presenting some of
Lightfoot's necessary prologomena to 2 Corinthians, we set forth his commentary itself. We follow the same protocol with the materials on 1 Peter.

The commentary on 1 Peter takes us up to 1 Peter 3:21. It is in many ways
richer and fuller throughout than the 2 Corinthians commentary. This is
the case for at least two reasons: (1) Lightfoot basically eschews detailed
attention to text criticism, except where needed, and focuses instead on
verse-by-verse exegesis of the text, and (2) he forgoes the interesting paraphrases we find at points in the 2 Corinthians manuscript and deals more
deeply with theological and ethical matters raised by 1 Peter. Nevertheless,
Lightfoot is interested in showing that Peter knew and drew on the work of
St. Paul, including his Romans and Ephesians letters, as well as using a great
deal of material from the LXX to make his points about suffering, atonement
and Christology. He sees the two apostles as in essential harmony when it
come to matters of theology and ethics, and there can be little doubt that
he has one eye on the offspring of the Tübingen school in some of his
pointed remarks and refutations on this score.

In the appendixes there are two essays of relevance to the commentary
on 2 Corinthians and a third that is a protracted theological reflection that
shows how the lessons of the early church, the suffering church of which
Peter and Paul both speak, and the lessons from the history of Judaism may
still instruct us today. This large, long essay was beautifully handwritten and
is page after page of closely packed argument. On the back of the last page

---

[9]C. K. Barrett, "J. B. Lightfoot as Biblical Commentator," *Durham University Journal* (1992): 53-70,
here p. 69.

Lightfoot apologizes that due to the time constraints it ended somewhat abruptly. In other words, this is surely the original form of Lightfoot's prize-winning essay (wrongly identified by some during Lightfoot's day as perhaps on the Stephen speech). He was given a certain amount of time during a few days to do it, and he did not finish it on time.

Picture a youngish Lightfoot, already a brilliant scholar, sitting at a big wooden table with books stacked all around him, his ink pen and his notebook in hand. And in an amazingly short span of time he writes a detailed essay with full references that goes on for about fifty of our pages! Lightfoot was a churchman through and through, and he always did his scholarship in the service of both his Lord and the Christian church, believing that historical knowledge and vital piety belonged together, not hermetically sealed off from each other. This volume demonstrates both the character of the man and the quality of his scholarship time and again.

Full marks must go to G. R. Treloar and B. N. Kaye for finding this early essay in more than one form and publishing the more polished later form of it,[10] which is in part a response to D. F. Strauss and indeed focuses on early Jewish literature and early Jewish messianic hopes. I (BW3) have had now extensive exchanges during the summer of 2014 with Professor Treloar about the source history of this important essay, and he agrees we are publishing the earliest form of this prize-winning essay.

The source history of this material as I would reconstruct it is as follows: (1) Treloar and Kaye found both the earlier and later forms of Lightfoot's prize-winning essay in the 1980s and published in the 1987 article cited below the *later* form of the essay, which actually has a proper ending. But they also stated clearly on page 166 of the article that "an earlier and in some places fuller draft" had been found by them as well. It is this latter that is published for the first time in an appendix to this volume.

(2) Treloar and Kaye deserve the credit for figuring out that the Strauss and Philo essay was the one he originally wrote for the Cambridge prize. It is important to remember, however, as the abrupt end of the original form of the essay indicates, that this was *a timed essay*. There was no time originally for Lightfoot to revise this manuscript during the contest, and in the

---

[10]G. R. Treloar and B. N. Kaye, "J. B. Lightfoot on Strauss and Christian Origins: An Unpublished Manuscript," *Durham University Journal* 79 (1987): 165-200.

unrevised form, he refused to put it out. Only later did he return to the essay, polishing up the ending and editing out some materials. We do not know for sure how much later the revision was done.

(3) The later *revision* of the original essay *may* have been in response to those that Martin Hengel calls the "Essayists." If so, Lightfoot did this revision long after the original 1850s essay and under some provocation. He did not really want to publish his early essay, but he felt it necessary to do a little light editing, produce a proper ending and contemplate putting it out without fuller research. We need to remember that the book *Supernatural Religion*, as well as the attacks on his friend Hort, put Lightfoot in something of a bind as an English Christian gentleman. He felt a response was required, and certainly his essays on *Supernatural Religion* are his most polemical essays ever. It seems, however, he did not think that this was enough. The earlier Strauss and early Judaism essay suited the purpose of answering others who kept touting the Tübingers and their take on the Gospels and other Scripture. Hence we have two somewhat different versions of the earliest publishable essay Lightfoot ever wrote. It says something about Lightfoot's meticulousness and care, however, that even after revising the essay, and *intending* to put it out, in the end he demurred, and even the revised essay did not see the light of day until thankfully Kaye and Treloar saw to it.

Finally, we are very honored to be able to reprint two key essays on Lightfoot by C. K. Barrett and J. D. G. Dunn that were given at the centennial celebration of the passing of Lightfoot in 1989. These essays first appeared in a special issue of the *Durham University Journal* that came out in the early 1990s but have long since gone out of print. We reprint these essays with minor editing with the blessing and encouragement of Professor Dunn, and the permission of Durham University itself. I am certain as well that C. K. Barrett, my *Doktorvater* of blessed memory, would be glad that his essay was given a further life by its being republished here.

To close this introduction we would like to express our sincere and abiding appreciation to Jeanette M. Hagen for her assistance in coordinating, transcribing and editing the three volumes that constitute the Lightfoot Legacy. Thanks are also due to Andrew Stubblefield and Gehard Stübben for their help in editing and compiling the abbreviations and indexes in this volume.

Finally, we would convey our profound gratitude to Benjamin Snyder for offering readers an expansive bibliography on works by and about the inimitable Joseph Barber Lightfoot.

Ben Witherington III
Asbury Theological Seminary

Todd D. Still
Baylor University, Truett Theological Seminary
Lent 2016

ABBREVIATIONS

BIBLICAL VERSIONS

A/al.	Codex Alexandrinus
A.V.	Authorized Version
arm	Armenian
B	Codex Vaticanus
B.M.T.	Byzantine Majority Text
C	Codex Ephraemi Syri Rescriptus
cop	Coptic
D	Codex Claromontanus
E	Codex Basilensis
Ethiop.	Ethiopian
E.V.	English version
F	Codex Augiensis
G	Codex Seidelianus I/Codex Harleianus
it	Old Latin
Harcl.	Harclean Syriac
K	Codex Cyprius
L	Codex Regius
Lat.	Latin
P	Papyrus manuscripts
Peshit.	Peshitta
S	Codex Sinaiticus
Syr.	Syriac
T.R.	Textus Receptus
Vulg.	Vulgate
Ψ	Codex Athous Laurae

ANCIENT AUTHORS AND WORKS

Act. Perpet. et Felic.	*The Acts of Perpetua and Felicitas*
Aeschylus	
Agam.	*Agamemnon*
Prom.	*Prometheus Bound*
Theb.	*Seven Against Thebes*
Apostl. Constitut.	*Apostolic Constitutions*
Athan.	Athanasius
Apol. c. Arian.	*Apologia secunda (Apologia contra Arianos)*

Augustine

   Quaest. Vet. et Novi Test.   *Quaestiones Veteris et Novi Testamenti*

   Retract.   *Retractationum Libri II*

B.T.   Babylonian Talmud

Barnab.   *Barnabas*

Chr.   Chrysostom

   Hom.   *Homilies*

Cicero

   ad Atticus   *Epistulae ad Atticum*

   de. offic.   *De Officiis*

   pro Balb.   *Pro Balbo*

   Ver./Verr.   *In Verrem*

Clem. Alex.   Clement of Alexandria

   Paed.   *Paedagogus*

   Quis div. salv.   *Quis dives salvetur*

   Strom.   *Stromata*

Clem. Hom.   *Clementine Homilies*

Clem. of Rom.   Clement of Rome (1 Clement)

Clement. Recogn.   *Clementine Recognitions*

Cyprian

   De Unit. Eccl.   *De catholicae ecclesiae unitate*

Cyr. of Alex.   Cyril of Alexandria

Demosth.   Demosthenes

   Timocr.   *In Timocratem*

Denys   Pseudo-Dionysus the Areopagite

   Cor.   *Corpus Areopagiticum*

Ep. Petr.   *The Epistle of Peter to James*

Epiphanius

   ad Haeres.   *Adversus haereses*

Epistle Clem. Ad Jac.   *The Epistle of Clement to James*

Eur.   Euripides

   Rhes.   *Rhesus*

Eusebius

   H.E.   *Historia ecclesiastica*

   Prop. Ev.   *Praeparatio evangelica*

Eutych.   Eutychius of Alexandria

   Ann.   *Eutychii Annales*

Evang. Thomas   *Gospel of Thomas*

Hippol.   Hippolytus

   Haer./adv. Haers.   *Refutatio omnium haeresium*

Hist. Man.	Petrus Siculus, *Historia Manichaeorum qui Pauliciani dicuntur*
Horace	
Sat.	*Satirae*
Ignatius	
Ephes.	*Epistle to the Ephesians*
Magn./Magnes.	*Epistle to the Magnesians*
Phil./Philad./Philadel.	*Epistle to the Philadelphians*
Polyc.	*Epistle to Polycarp*
Rom.	*Epistle to the Romans*
Smyrn.	*Epistle to the Smyrnaeans*
Trall.	*Epistle to the Trallians*
Il.	*Iliad*
Jerome	
Vir. Ill.	*De viris illustribus*
Josephus	
Ant.	*Antiquitates judaicae*
Bell. Jud.	*Bellum judaicum*
Vit. Jos.	*Vita*
Justin	
Apol.	*Apology*
Lact.	Lactantius
Inst. Div.	*Divinarum institutionum*
M. Fragm.	*Commentariorum in Matthaeum*
Martyr. Ignat. Ant.	*Martyrdom of Ignatius of Antioch*
Martyr. Polyc.	*Martyrdom of Polycarp*
Offic.	Cicero, *De Officiis*
Origen	
Comm. Matt.	*Commentarium in evangelium Matthae*
de Orat.	*De oratione*
Hom. in Lev.	*Homiliae in Leviticum*
In Joan	*Commentarii in evangelium Joannis*
Philo	
Cherub.	*De cherubim*
de Agric.	*De agricultura*
de confus. Ling.	*De confusione linguarum*
de Migrat. Abr.	*De migratione Abrahami*
de Mund Opif.	*De opificio mundi*
de Post.	*De posteritate Caini*
de Prob./Quod Omn. Prob. Lib.	*Quod omnis probus liber sit*
de somn.	*De somnis*

de Vita Mos.	*De vita Mosis*
Leg. Alleg.	*Legum allegoriae*
Plato	
Axioch.	*Axiochus*
Tim.	*Timaeus*
Pliny	
Nat. Hist.	*Naturalis historia*
Plutarch	
Cim.	*Cimon*
Polycarp	
Phil.	*Epistle to the Philippians*
Seneca	
Dialog.	*Dialogi*
Shepherd of Hermas	
Mand.	*Mandates*
Sim.	*Similitudes*
Vis.	*Visions*
Soph. *Phil.*	Sophocles, *Philoctetes*
Sym.	Symmachus
Tacitus	
Annal.	*Annales*
Tertullian	
ad omnes. haers.	Pseudo-Tertullian, *Adversus Omnes Haereses*
ad Uxor.	*Ad uxorem*
adv. Jud.	*Adversus Judaeos*
adv. Marc.	*Adversus Marcionem*
de Cult. Fem.	*de cultu feminarum*
de Exh. Cast.	*De exhortation castitatis*
de Monog.	*De monogamia*
de Pall.	*De pallio*
de Praesc./Prescrip.	*De praescriptione haeriticorum*
de Pudic.	*De pudicitia*
de Spectac.	*De spectaculis*
de Virg. Vel.	*De virginibus velandis*
Test. XII Patr.	*Testament of the Twelve Patriarchs*
Theod.	Theodotion
Theoph./Theophyl.	Theophylact
Thuc./Thucy.	Thucydides
Vopiscus	
Vit. Saturn.	*Vita Saturnini*
Xenophon	
Mem.	*Memorabilia*

MODERN SOURCES AND PERSONS

Alford	Henry Alford, *The New Testament for English Readers*, 4 vols. (London: Rivingtons, 1866)
Baumgarten, *Acts*	Michael Baumgarten, *The Acts of the Apostles*, trans. A. J. W. Morrison, 3 vols. (Edinburgh: T&T Clark, 1854)
Baur, *Ursprung des Episcopats*	Ferdinand Christian Baur, *Ueber den Ursprung des Episcopats in der christlichen Kirche* (Tübingen: Fues, 1838)
Bengel	Johannes Bengel
Bingham, *Antiq.*	Joseph Bingham, *Origines ecclesiasticæ. The antiquities of the Christian church* (London: William Straker, 1834)
Blass	Friedrich Blass
Blunt, *First Three Centuries*	John James Blunt, *A History of the Christian Church During the First Three Centuries* (London: J. Murray, 1856)
Böhner, *Diss. Jur. Eccl.*	Henning Böhner, *Dissertationes juris ecclesiastici antiqui ad Plinium secundum et Tertullianum*
Bunsen, *Hippolyt.*	C. J. Bunsen, *Hippolytus and His Age* (1852)
Casar Morgan, *Tim. of Plato*	Caesar Morgan, *An investigation of the Trinity of* Plato *and of* Philo Judaeus, *and of the effects which an attachment to their writings had upon the principles and reasonings of the Fathers of the Christian Church* (Cambridge: Cambridge University Press, 1853)
Clinton	Henry Fynes Clinton
Conybeare and Howson	W. J. Conybeare and J. S. Howson, *The Life and Epistles of St. Paul*, 2nd ed., 2 vols. (London: Longman, Brown, Green, Longmans, & Roberts, 1856)
Davidson, *Intro.*	Samuel Davidson, *Introduction to the Study of the New Testament* (London: Longman, Green, and Co., 1868)
de Rossi, *Sotterr.*	Giovanni Battista de Rossi, *La Roma sotterranea cristiana* (Rome: Litographia Pontificia, 1864)
De Wette	W. M. L. de Wette, *Einleitung in das Neue Testament* (1826)
Dorner, *Lehre*	Isaak Dorner, *Entwicklungsgeschichte der Lehre von der Person Christi von den ältesten Zeiten bis auf die neuesten* (Stuttgart: S. G. Leisching, 1839; revised and expanded, 1845–1856)
Dupin, *Optat. Milev.*	Louis Ellies Dupin, ed., *Sancti Optati Afri Milevitani episcopi De schismate donatistarum libri septem : ad manuscriptos codices et veteres editiones collati et innumeris in locis emendati; quibus accessere historia Donatistarum una cum monumentis veteribus ad eam spectandibus* (Paris: G. Gallet, 1702)
Ewald, *Gesch. des V.*	Heinrich Ewald, *Geschichte des Volkes Israel bis Christus* (Göttingen: Dieterich'schen Buchhandlung, 1843)
Fields, *Hex.*	Frederick Field, *Prolegomena to Origenis Hexaplorum Quae Supersunt, Sive Veterum Interpretum Graecorum in Totum Vetus Testamentum Fragmenta* (Oxford: Clarendon, 1875)
Giesler	J. C. I. Giesler, *Text-Book of Ecclesiastical History* (Philadelphia: Carey, Lea, and Blanchard, 1836)
Gesenius	W. Gesenius, *Hebräisches und Chaldäisches Handwörterbuch* (1812)

Gfrörer, *Das Jahrhundert des Heils*	August Friedrich Gfrörer, *Das Jahrhundert des Heils* (Stuttgart: Schweizerbart, 1838)
Gildemeister, *Sextus Sententiae*	Johann Gildemeister, *Sexti Sententiarum: Recensiones* (Bonn: Adolphus Marcus, 1873)
Gött. Gel. Anz.	*Göttingische gelehrte Anzeigen*
Greek Anthol.	*The Greek Anthology*
Greenwood, *Cathedra Petri*	Thomas Greenwood, *Cathedra Petri: A Political History of the Great Latin Patriarchate* (London: William Macintosh, 1865)
Gregorovius, *Kaiser Hadrian*	Ferdinand Gregorovius, *Der Kaiser Hadrian: Gemälde der römisch-hellenischen Welt zu seiner Zeit* (1884)
Hefele, *Consiliengesch.*	Karl Joseph von Hefele, *Conciliengeschichte* (Freiburg im Breisgau: Herder, 1869)
Hilgenfeld, *Zeitschrift*	A. Hilgenfeld, *Zeitschrift für wissenschaftliche Theologie* (Leipzig: Fues's Verlag, 1878)
Hort	F. J. A. Hort
Hug	Johann Leonhard Hug
Kaye, *Clement of Alexandria*	John Kaye, *Some Account of the Writings and Opinions of Clement of Alexandria* (London: J. G. & F. Rivington, 1835)
Lachmann	Karl Lachmann
Lange, *Apost. Zeit.*	Johann Peter Lange, *Das apostolische Zeitalter* (Braunschweig: C. A. Schwetschke, 1853)
Le Quien, *Oriens Christianus*	Michel Le Quien, *Oriens christianus in quatuor patriarchatus digestus, in quo exhibentur Ecclesiae patriarchae caeterique praesules totius Orientis* (Paris: Typographia Regia, 1740)
Lipsius, *Chronologie*	Richard Adelbert Lipsius, *Chronologie der römischen Bischöfe bis zur Mitte des vierten Jahrhunderts* (Kiel: Schwers'sche Buchhandlung, 1869)
Lobeck, on Phys.	Christian August Lobeck, *Phrynichi eclogae nominum et verborum Atticorum* (Lipsiae, 1820)
Maurice, *Kingdom of Christ*	Frederick Denison Maurice, *The Kingdom of Christ* (London: Darton and Clark, 1838)
Maurice, *Moral and Metaphysical Phil.*	Frederick Denison Maurice, *Moral and Metaphysical Philosophy* (London: R. Griffin, 1854)
Meyer	H. A. W. Meyer
Migne, *Patrolog. Graec.*	*Patrologia Cursus Completus: Series Graeca.* Edited by Jacques-Paul Migne. 162 vols. (Paris: 1857–1886)
Mommsen	Theodor Mommsen
Mosheim, *de Reb. Christ.*	Johann Lorenz von Mosheim, *De rebus christianorum ante Constantinum commentarii* (Helmstad: Christianum Fredericum Weygand, 1853)
Munter, *Primord. Eccl. Afric.*	Frederich Christian Carl Henrick Münter, *Primordia Ecclesiae Africanae* (Copenhagen: Prostant in Libraria Schubothania, 1829)
Neander, *Ch. Hist.*	Johann August Wilhelm Neander, *General History of the Christian Religion and Church* (London: Henry G. Bohn, 1851)

Neander, *Hist. of Pla.*	Johann August Wilhelm Neander, *History of the Planting and Training of the Christian Church by the Apostles* (London: G. Bell & Sons, 1889-1898)
Neander, *Life of Christ*	Johann August Wilhelm Neander, *Life of Jesus Christ in Its Historical Connexion and Historical Development* (London: H.G. Bohn, 1852).
Neander, *Plant.*	Johann August Wilhelm Neander, *History of the Planting and Training of the Christian Church by the Apostles* (London: G. Bell & Sons, 1889-1898)
Paley, *Hora. Paul.*	William Paley, *Horae Paulina*
Redepenning, *Origenes*	Ernst Rudolph Redepenning, *Origenes de Principiis* (Lipsiae: In Bibliopolio Dykiano, 1836)
Renan, *Les Apotres*	Ernest Renan, *Les apôtres* (Paris: Calmann-Lévy, 1880)
Ritschl	Albrecht Ritschl
Ritter and Preller, *Hist. Phil. Graeco-Rom*	Heinrich Ludwig Ritter and Preller, *Historia Philosophiae Graecae et Romanae* (Gothae: F. A. Perthes, 1838)
Rothe, *Anfange*	Richard Rothe, *Die Anfänge der christlichen Kirche und ihrer Verfassung* (Wittenberg : Zimmermann, 1837)
Routh, *Rel. Sacr.*	Martin Routh, *Reliquiæ sacræ sive auctorum fere jam perditorum secundi tertiique seculi post Christum natum quæ supersunt* (Oxford: Oxford University Press, 1846)
Ruinart, *Victor Vitensis*	Thierry Ruinart, translation of *Historia persecutionis Africanae provinciae* by Victor Vitensis (Paris 1699)
Sänger, *Judische Zeitschrift*	Max Sänger, *Maleachi. Eine exegetische Studie über die Eigenthümlichkeiten seiner Redweise* (Jena: W. Ratz, 1867)
Schaff, *Hist. of Apost.*	Philip Schaff, *History of the Apostolic Church* (New York: Schribner, Armstrong, & Co., 1874)
Schliemann, *Die Clement.*	Adolph Schliemann, *Die Clementinen* (Hamburg: Friedrich Berthes, 1844)
Smith's *Dictionary*	William Smith, *Dictionary of the Bible*
Steph. *Thes.*	Henri Estienne (Henricus Stephanus), *Thesaurus Graecae Linguae* (1854)
Strauss, *Life of Jesus*	David Friedrich Strauss, *Das Leben Jesu, kritisch bearbeitet* (Tübingen: C. F. Osiander, 1835)
Thiersch, *Gesch. der Apost. Kirche*	Heinrich W. J. Thiersch, *Die Geschichte der christlichen Kirche im Alterthum: Die Kirche im apostolischen Zeitalter und die Entstehung der neutestamentlichen Schriften* (Frankfurt and Erlangen: Heyder and Zimmer, 1852)
Thiersch, *Versuch*	Heinrich W. J. Thiersch, *Versuch zur Herstellung des historischen Standpuncts für die Kritik der neutestamentlichen Schriften* (Erlangen: Carl Heyder, 1845)
Tillemont, *Hist, des Emp.*	Louis-Sébastien Le Nain de Tillemont, *Histoire des empereurs* (Paris: Charles Robustel, 1690)
Tillemont	Louis-Sébastien Le Nain de Tillemont, *Mémoires pour servir à l'histoire ecclésiastique des six premiers siècles* (Paris: C. Robustel, 1701)

Tisch./Tischendorf	Constantin von Tischendorf
Tregelles	S. P. Tregelles, *Account of the Printed Text of the Greek New Testament* (1854)
Trench, *Epistles to the Seven Churches*	Richard Chenevix Trench, *Epistles to the Seven Churches in Asia* (London: Parker, Son, & Bourn, 1861).
Trench, *Study of Words*	Richard Chenevix Trench, *On the Study of Words* (London: John W. Parker and Son, 1853).
Trench's *Synon./Synonyms*	R. C. Trench, *Synonyms of the New Testament*, 9th ed. (London: Macmillan, 1880)
Vitringa, *de Synag.*	Campeius Vitringa the Elder, *De Synagoga Vetere Libri Tres* (Franeker, 1685)
W+H	Westcott and Hort
Wahl, Classical	C. Abraham Wahl, *Clavis Novi Testamenti Philologica usibis Scholarum et Juvenum Theologiae studiosorum accommadata*
Westcott, *Canon*	B. F. Westcott, *A General Survey of the History of the Canon of the New Testament* (1855; revised 1875)
Wettstein	J. J. Wettstein, *Novum Testamentum Graecum editionis receptae cum lectionibus variantibus codicum manuscript* (1751)
Wieseler, *Chron. Der ap. Zeitalt.*	Karl Georg Wieseler, *Chronologie des apostolischen Zeitalters bis zum Tode der Apostel Paulus und Petrus: Ein Versuch über die Chronologie und Abfassungszeit der Apostelgeschichte und der paulinischen Briefe* (Göttingen: Vandenhoeck and Ruprecht, 1848)
Wilson, *New Testament*	William Wilson, *An Illustration of the Method of Explaining the New Testament by the Early Opinions of Jews and Christians Concerning Christ* (Cambridge: J. W. Parker, 1838)
Winer	Georg Benedict Winer, *Grammatik des neutestamentlichen Sprachidioms*, 7th ed. (Leipzig: F. C. W. Vogel, 1867)
Winer, *Real.*	Georg Benedict Winer, *Biblisches Realwörterbuch zum Handgebrauch für Studirende, Kandidaten, Gymnasiallehrer und Prediger*, 2 vols. (Leipzig: C. H. Reclam, 1833)
Wordsworth, *Theop. Angl.*	Christopher Wordsworth, *Theophilus Anglicanus* (London: F. & J. Rivington, 1850)
Zahn, *Hermas*	Theodor Zahn, *Der Hirt des Hermas untersucht* (Gotha: Friedrich Andreas Berthes, 1868)
Zeller, *Philos. der Griechen*	Eduard Gottlob Zeller, *Die Philosophie der Griechen in ihrer geschichtlichen Entwicklung dargestellt von Eduard Zeller die nacharistotelische Philosophie zweite Halfte* (Leipzig: Fues's Verlag, 1868)

MISCELLANEOUS

act.	active
l.c.	loco citato
LXX	Septuagint
med.	medium (middle)
sq./sqq.	the following one(s)
v.l.	varias lectiones

Editors' Introduction

J. B. Lightfoot as
Biblical Commentator

No one could match Lightfoot for "exactness of scholarship, width of erudition,
scientific method, sobriety of judgment and lucidity of style."[1]

WILLIAM SANDAY

No one ever loitered so late in the Great Court that he did not see Lightfoot's
lamp burning in his study window, though not many either was so
regularly present in morning Chapel at seven o'clock that he
did not find Lightfoot always there with him.[2]

BISHOP HANDLEY C. G. MOULE

JOSEPH BARBER LIGHTFOOT (1828–1889) was in many ways ideally suited to be a commentator on the New Testament. He had mastery of at least seven ancient and modern languages (German, French, Spanish, Italian, Latin, Classical Greek, Koine Greek, and the Greek of the church fathers)

---

[1]William Sanday, "Bishop Lightfoot," *The Expositor* 4 (1886): 13-29 (on 13). Sanday was also a Durhamite, most well known for producing the International Critical Commentary on Romans with Arthur Headlam.
[2]Lightfoot's successor (with one in between) as bishop of Durham.

and a good working knowledge of many others, including Hebrew, Aramaic, Syriac, Armenian, Ethiopic and Coptic. Some of these languages he taught himself. It was clear enough from early on that Lightfoot had a gift for languages. He once asked a friend whether he did not find it to be the case that *one forgets what language one is reading* when one becomes absorbed in a text![3] There have been precious few biblical scholars over time that could have candidly made such a remark about so many different languages.

Lightfoot also had a keen interest in history and understood its importance for the study of a historical religion like Christianity. He was a critical and perspicuous thinker and writer with few peers in any age of Christian history. Furthermore, Lightfoot was able to devote himself to the study of the New Testament in ways and to a degree that few scholars before or since his time have been able to do, not least because he never married and had no family for whom to care.[4] Yet when we look at the list of his publications, we may be somewhat surprised that there are not more works of biblical exegesis. Here is a list of his works that were first published in the nineteenth century.

- *Saint Paul's Epistle to the Galatians* (London: Macmillan, 1865)

- *Saint Paul's Epistle to the Philippians* (London: Macmillan, 1868)

- *S. Clement of Rome* (London: Macmillan, 1869)

- *Fresh Revision of the English New Testament* (London: Macmillan, 1871)

---

[3]He made this remark to J. R. Harmer. See G. R. Eden and F. C. Macdonald, *Lightfoot of Durham: Memorials and Appreciations* (Cambridge: Cambridge University Press, 1932), 118-19. Apparently, Lightfoot also knew Arabic. It is a great pity that no proper biography has ever been written on Lightfoot. What we have in *Lightfoot of Durham* is some fond remembrances of the man by a few of the people who knew him. Only a portion of the volume discusses his academic work, and even then only very cursorily. Do see, however, pp. 105-22 and the brief discussions by H. E. Savage and Bishop J. R. Harmer (Lightfoot's chaplain, secretary and proofreader for some years, before becoming a bishop himself). Note also the essays by the dean of Wells and the bishop of Gloucester (pp. 123–41). Notice that there are *no scholars* writing essays in this volume. This speaks volumes about Lightfoot's work for and impact on the church. There is a nice anecdote in appendix D below about how as a boy at school, when someone asked how he was coming along with his German, the reply given from the school was: "Oh he's mastered German, he's moved on to Anglo-Saxon!" (BW3)

[4]If one wonders why someone like Lightfoot agreed to take a post like the episcopal seat in Durham after a thriving academic life in Cambridge and after having turned down becoming bishop of Litchfield, the answer in part is family connections. He had a great love for the "north" of England, as his mother was from Newcastle and his family on his father's side was from Yorkshire. He saw it, in one sense, as returning to his ancestral home. (BW3)

- *Saint Paul's Epistles to the Colossians and Philemon* (London: Macmillan, 1875)
- *Primary Charge* (London: Macmillan, 1882)
- *The Apostolic Fathers, Part 2, S. Ignatius, S. Polycarp*, 3 vols. (London: Macmillan, 1885–1889)
- *Essays on Supernatural Religion* (London: Macmillan, 1889)
- *The Apostolic Fathers, Part 1, S. Clement of Rome*, 2 vols. (London: Macmillan, 1890)
- *Cambridge Sermons* (London: Macmillan, 1890)
- *Leaders in the Northern Church* (London: Macmillan, 1890)
- *Ordination Addresses* (London: Macmillan, 1890)
- *Apostolic Fathers Abridged* (London: Macmillan, 1891)
- *Sermons Preached in St. Paul's* (London: Macmillan 1891)
- *Special Sermons* (London: Macmillan, 1891)
- *The Contemporary Pulpit Library: Sermons by Bishop Lightfoot* (London: Swan Sonnenschein, 1892)
- *Dissertations on the Apostolic Age* (London: Macmillan, 1892)
- *Biblical Essays* (London: Macmillan, 1893)
- *Historical Essays* (London: Macmillan, 1895)
- *Notes on the Epistles of St. Paul from Unpublished Commentaries* (London: Macmillan, 1895)

Compare this to the inventory created by B. N. Kaye after inspecting everything the Durham Cathedral Library had in handwritten script by Lightfoot:

- Lecture notes on Acts
- Lecture notes on Ephesians
- Script on the destination of Ephesians (published in *Biblical Essays*)
- Lecture notes on 1 Corinthians 1:1–15:54
- Lecture notes on 1 Peter
- Internal evidence for the authencity and genuineness of St. John's Gospel (printed in *Biblical Essays*)

- External evidence for the authenticity and genuineness of St. John's Gospel (printed in *Biblical Essays*)

- External testimony for St. John's Gospel (rough notes worked up in *Biblical Essays*)

- Second set of notes on internal evidence (printed in *The Expositor* [1890])

- Notes on introduction to John and John 1:1–12:2

- Notes on introduction to Romans and Romans 1:1–9:6 and a separate set of incomplete notes briefly covering Romans 4–13

- Notes on Thessalonians

- Preliminary text for William Smith's *Dictionary of the Bible* article

- Chronology of St. Paul's life and epistles

- The text of St. Paul's epistles

- St. Paul's preparation for the ministry

- Chronology of St. Paul's life and epistles (printed in *Biblical Essays*)

- The churches of Madedonia (printed in *Biblical Essays*)

- The church of Thessalonica (printed in *Biblical Essays*)

- Notes on the genuineness of 1 and 2 Thessalonians

- Unlabeled notes on the text of 1 and 2 Thessalonians

From even a cursory comparison of these two lists, several things become apparent: (1) There is a good deal of material on Acts, John, Paul and 1 Peter that never saw the light of day; and (2) Lightfoot wrote as much, and as often, for the sake of the church and its ministry and about the church and its ministry as he did on subjects of historical or exegetical interest. But where had Lightfoot gained all his knowledge and erudition? What sort of education and what teachers produced such a scholar and churchman?

THE GROOMING OF A SCHOLAR

C. K. Barrett reminds us that Lightfoot in the first instance gained his skills as a commentator on the Bible from studying at King Edward's School in Birmingham under James Lee Prince. Such study gave him a thoroughgoing training in both Greek and Latin, with wide reading in classical literature and history. When Lightfoot went to study at Trinity College, Cambridge, he worked with B. F. Westcott, who was three years his senior. In 1851 he took the Classical Tripos and came out as a Senior Classic.[5] Barrett relates the well-known story that Lightfoot wrote his tripos exam without a single mistake, which Barrett thinks refers to his work on the language parts of the exam. Afterward, Lightfoot was elected to a fellowship at Trinity and went on to teach languages to other students at Trinity. In his "spare" time he was learning theology and reading the apostolic fathers.[6]

At the tender age of thirty-three, Lightfoot was named Hulsean Professor of Divinity and was the mainstay of the faculty there, even with the addition of Westcott and Hort. Of his lectures in Cambridge, F. J. A. Hort reports,

> They consisted chiefly, if not wholly, of expositions of parts of books of the New Testament, and especially of St. Paul's Epistles, with discussions and leading topics usually included in "Introductions" to these books. Their value and interest were soon widely recognized in the university, and before long no lecture-room then available sufficed to contain the hearers, both candidates for holy orders and older residents; so that leave had to be obtained for the use of the hall of Trinity.[7]

His commentaries on what we now call the later Pauline letters (Philippians, Colossians and Philemon) as well as on Galatians began to come out in the 1860s, but it is clear that already in the 1850s, based on his Cambridge lecture notes, which we can now inspect, Lightfoot had already sorted out his view of Acts and its relationship to the Pauline corpus as well as Pauline chronology. He had also done extensive work on the Gospel of John and 1 Peter. Indeed, we find some of his Galatians commentary in the same notebook as his lecture notes on Acts. In other words, Lightfoot's previously unpublished work on Acts, John, 1 Peter and some of Paul's letters was produced when he was at the height of his powers and commentary-writing ability. *These heretofore unpublished notes are often as detailed as the published commentaries and are from the same period of Lightfoot's life.*

---

[5]A tripos is an exam taken for the BA degree with honors at Cambridge University. (TDS)
[6]C. K. Barrett, "J. B. Lightfoot as Biblical Commentator," *Durham University Journal* (1992): 53-70 (on 54).
[7]F. J. A. Hort, "Lightfoot, Joseph Barber," *Dictionary of National Biography, 1885-1900* (London: Smith, Elder), 33:232-40, on p. 233.

If we ask why some of this material was not published during Light-foot's lifetime, the answer is ready to hand—it is incomplete. None of these unpublished manuscripts were full commentaries on the books in question. But there are further reasons why Lightfoot did not publish his voluminous materials on Acts and John. As Barrett notes, Lightfoot, Westcott and Hort had agreed to divide up the New Testament among them and to write commentaries on each book.[8] Lightfoot was tasked with treating the Pauline corpus, not the Gospels, Acts or 1 Peter.[9] Fur-thermore, the last of his published commentaries (on Colossians and Phi-lemon) came out less than four years before Lightfoot became bishop of Durham in 1879, a work in which he became almost totally absorbed for the rest of his life, which proved to be ten years.[10] Regarding Lightfoot's commentary work, Hort remarks:

> Technical language is as far as possible avoided and exposition, essentially scientific, is clothed in simple and transparent language. The natural meaning of each verse is set forth without polemical matter. The prevailing character-istic is . . . good sense unaccompanied by either the insight or delusion of subtlety. Introductions, which precede the commentaries, handle the subject-matter with freshness and reality, almost every section being in effect a bright little historical essay. To each commentary is appended a dissertation, which includes some of Lightfoot's most careful and thorough work.[11]

---

[8]At an earlier point in time, Lightfoot, Westcott and Hort were meant to write commentaries for the Smith's Commentary series. Although this plan did not pan out, it is of present import to note that Lightfoot was supposed to have commented on Acts for this series. (TDS)

[9]It was Alexander Macmillan who suggested to Westcott the possibility of a Cambridge com-mentary on the entire New Testament. Westcott in turn enlisted Lightfoot and Hort for the project, to be based on the Westcott and Hort Greek text.

Until beginning this work on Lightfoot, I had not realized that the original attempt to have a Cambridge Bible Commentary on the whole New Testament had begun with this agreement, although it never came to full fruition. In the 1960s and '70s, C. F. D. Moule, the relative of the successor of Lightfoot in the Durham episcopacy (H. G. C. Moule), revived the attempt to have a Cambridge Bible Commentary on the Greek New Testament, but it too was destined not to be completed. Indeed, it produced only a couple of notable volumes, C. E. B. Cranfield's volume on Mark and Moule's on Colossians and Philemon. This brings us to the turn of the twenty-first century when I, another Durham man, was named editor of the New Cambridge Bible Com-mentary series, along with my Asbury colleague Bill Arnold, who is the Old Testament editor. This third attempt has now produced volumes on both Old and New Testament books, but there is still much to be done, and more volumes are forthcoming. (BW3)

[10]For example, he became absorbed in training ordinands for the Anglican ministry, in setting up the diocese of Newcastle and in paying for churches to be built.

[11]Hort, "Lightfoot," pp. 237-38.

St. Peter.

<u>His father's name</u>

Jonas
    Matt. xvi. 17. Βαρ Ἰωνᾶ

John.
    John. i. 43, xxi. 15, 16, 17 (pp. 382, 485 Naples)
    The correct reading.
    Common text Ἰωνα

The name
    see Renan p. 159 sq.
    The significance of Matt. xvi. 17,

<u>His own name.</u>

Symeon. Acts xv. 14, 2 Pet. i. 1. שמעון
Simon a Grecized form
    a not uncommon Greek name.

    Jason Jesus
    Alcimus. Eliakim

Jos. Ant. xii. 5. 1. ὁ μὲν οὖν Ἰησοῦς Ἰάσονα
ἑαυτὸν μετωνόμασεν, ὁ δὲ Ὀνίας ἐκλήθη
Μενέλαος.

In this particular case there will be
ready analogy.
Jason in the LXX e.g. from Maccabees

Lightfoot's notes on Peter's martyrdom

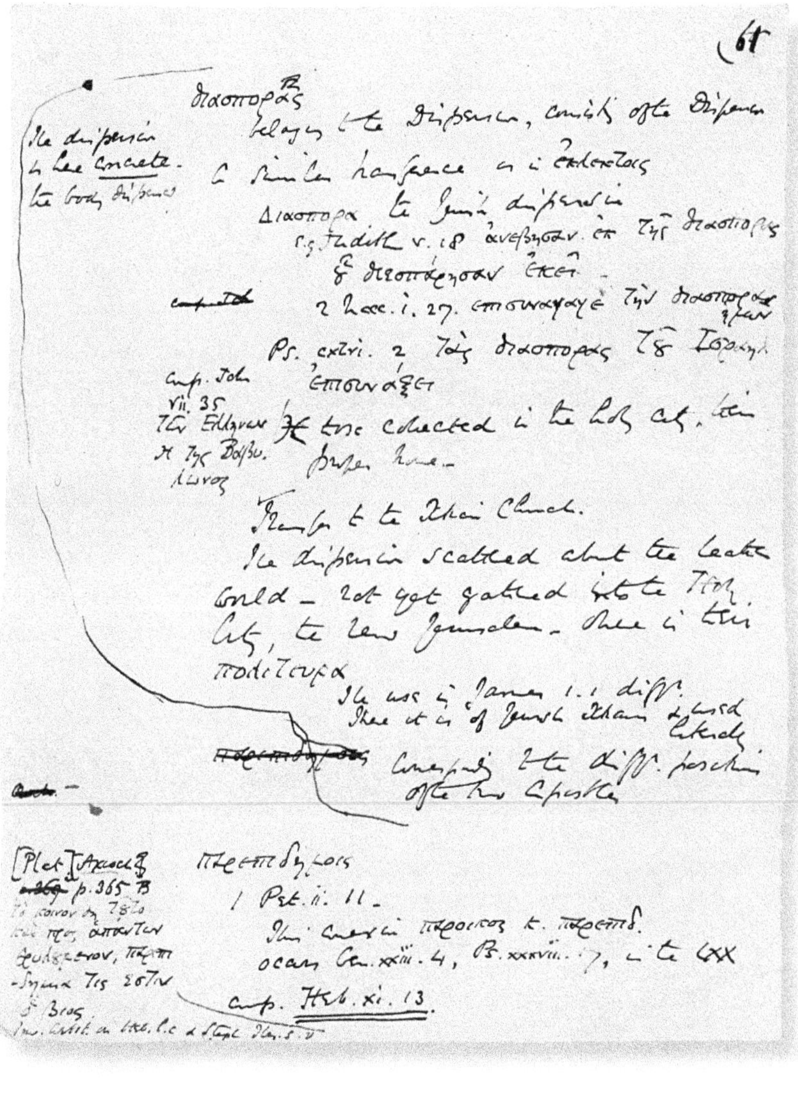

διασπορᾶς

διασπορὰ ...

1 Pet. i. 11 —

cp. Heb. xi. 13.

Lightfoot's remarks regarding the "Dispersion" spoken of in 1 Peter 1:1

αὐξηθῆτε metaphor continued

εἰς οἰκοδομήν to standard of nature growth
as e.g. Ephes. iv. 13, 15

εἰ ἐγεύσασθε
Now ye accepted the fact of it.

from ~~Ps. cxviii (cxvii). 22~~
Ps. xxxiv (xxxiii). 9 γεύσασθε καὶ ἴδετε
ὅτι Χρηστὸς ὁ κύριος .

Χρηστός
ref. to Χριστός imperceptible.

Observe the κύριος (Jehovah), of the O. T.,
applied by St. Peter here, as freq. by St. Paul,
to our Lord .

4 sq.
Ps. cxviii (cxvii). 22
λίθον ὃν ἀπεδοκίμασαν οἱ οἰκοδομοῦντες, οὗτος
ἐγενήθη εἰς κεφαλὴν γωνίας . παρὰ κυρίου
ἐγένετο αὕτη καὶ ἔστιν θαυμαστὴ ἐν
ὀφθαλμοῖς ἡμῶν

Is. xxviii. 16 ἰδοὺ ἐγὼ ἐμβάλλω εἰς τὰ θεμέλια
Σιὼν λίθον πολυτελῆ ἐκλεκτὸν, εἰς τὰ θεμέλια
(ἐκλεκτὸν, ἀκρογωνιαῖον) αὐτῆς καὶ ὁ πιστεύων
ἐπ᾽ αὐτῷ οὐ μὴ
καταισχυνθῇ .

Comments on 1 Peter 2:6-7

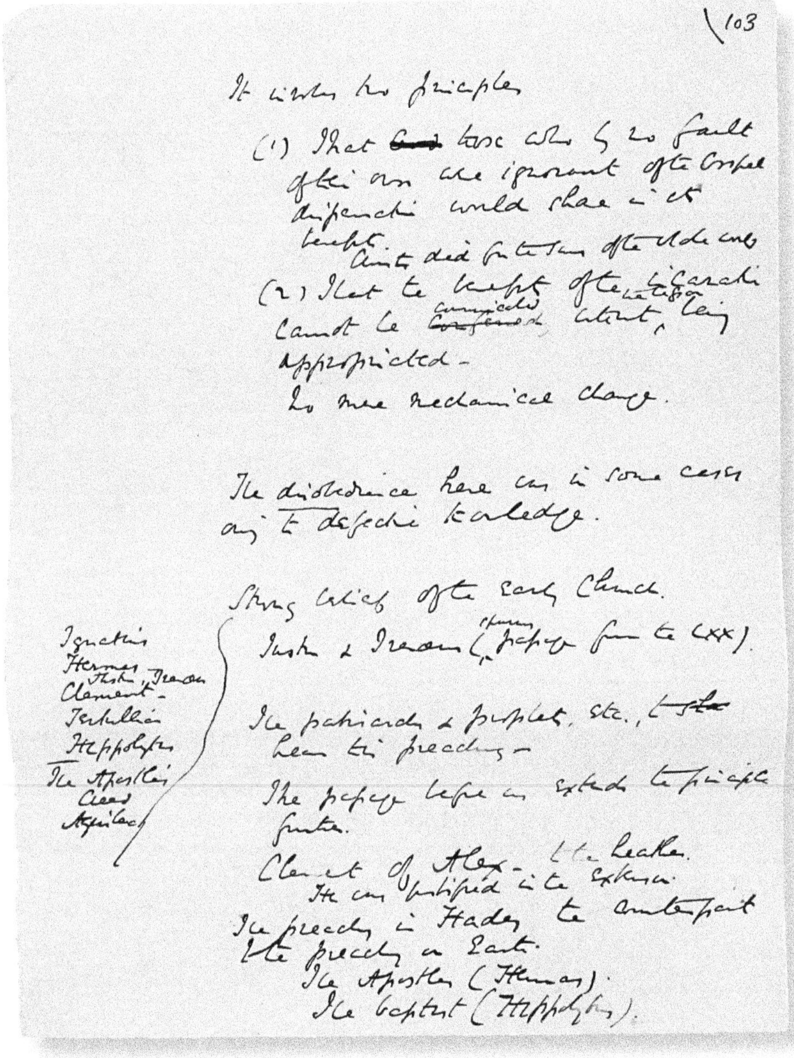
\103

It involves two principles

(1) That those who by no fault of their own are ignorant of the Gospel dispensation would share in its benefit.
Christ died for the sins of the whole world

(2) That the benefit of the Incarnation cannot be communicated without being appropriated —
No mere mechanical change.

The disobedience here was in some cases owing to defective knowledge.

Strong belief of the early Church.

Ignatius
Hermas
Justin, Irenaeus
Clement
Tertullian
Hippolytus
The Apostles' Creed
[Aquileia]

Justin & Irenaeus (spurious passage from the LXX).

The patriarchs & prophets, etc., to hear this preaching —

The passage before us extends the principle further.

Clement of Alex. — the heathen.
He was justified in the extension.

The preaching in Hades the counterpart of the preaching on Earth.
The Apostles (Hermas).
The baptist (Hippolytus).

Lightfoot's notes on 1 Peter conclude with his reflections on the "disobedient" referred to in 1 Peter 3:20

§. 1. Introduction

Let knowledge grow from more to more,
But more of reverence in us dwell;
That mind and soul, according well,
May make one music as before.

B..cester.   Tennyson.

There are periods in the history of the church
when powerful and well-directed attacks from without
aided by errors and discussions within, seem to threaten
her strongholds with well-nigh with total destruction;
and the Christian, turning away from this sickening
scene of desolation, clings only more firmly to his
Lord's promises, though perhaps in the signs of the
times, as he reads them, he sees nothing to justify
his hope.

It is well at seasons like this that the study
of past history should come to the rescue of a
wavering faith; It would show the Christian that
the crisis, which he, in his immediate terror, is
disposed to represent to himself as unparalleled
in the previous history of the church has been equalled
or even surpassed by the dangers of former times;
It would point out to him how the attacks have
been once and again renewed from the same quarters
and triumphantly repelled; It would teach him
to distinguish between the real & substantial knowledge, which accumulates from age to age, and
the illusive phantoms, and one-sided sentiments,
which characterise his own time. Still more;
he would be warned not to fight for the bulwarks and outposts, which have been raised by
human hands, when by so doing he is endangering

§. 3. The Messiah.

Ύμεῖς, δὲ πάντα σαρκικῶς νενοήκατε. Justin.

In the present section it will be our task to ascertain how *partly* the relation between the Law and the Gospel, and the Person and office of the Messiah were justly apprehended by the Jewish mind at the time of the Christian era.

The Law was in its nature temporary and imperfect. It was its mission to develope the moral consciousness of the separation between God and man, and to teach the creature to look forward anxiously to the time when he should enjoy a closer communion with the Creator. In other words it created a want which it did not supply, and raised hopes and aspirations which it could not fulfil.

Hence there necessity of a second Dispensation which must be at once the fulfilment and the abrogation of the former — a fulfilment because it supplied the wants, and realized the hopes created by its predecessor, an abrogation because it substituted the reality for the expectation, the substance for the shadow, the thing typified for the type —

The Jew was not unaware that a higher destiny awaited his nation; he looked forward hopefully even against hope for the day of deliverance from his present bondage, of triumph over his enemies. But he did not see that it was a spiritual freedom, a moral victory, which the prophets had foretold, — Hence the fulfilment was unappreciated by him, the abrogation ignored. "There is no difference," says one of their writers "between the days of Messiah and these times, except that Israel shall no more serve the Kings of the Gentiles but shall be lord over them." [*]

In consequence of this carnal view they made a distinction between Messiah's earthly and heavenly kingdom

The beginning of Lightfoot's treatment of "The Messiah" in his essay that was granted the Norrisian Prize

The writer regrets that the time limit has expired; he has been obliged therefore to finish abruptly

The abrupt conclusion of Lightfoot's award-winning essay

There was one gargantuan academic project Lightfoot continued to work on even after he became bishop—his monumental and groundbreaking studies on the apostolic fathers, though he mostly only found time to work on this project during holidays and while traveling.

> There are vivid descriptions of Lightfoot being found in a boat or railway carriage with an Armenian or Coptic grammar in hand or calmly correcting proofs while being driven down precipitous paths in Norway. . . . But above all the secret lay in his ability to switch off, giving himself totally to what was before him. As his chaplain [J. R. Harmer] put it . . . "His power of detachment and concentration was extraordinary. I have seen him break off from an incomplete sentence for a momentous interview with one of his clergy, give him his undivided and sympathetic attention followed by the wisest counsel and final decision, and almost before the door was closed upon his visitor become once more absorbed in his literary work."[12]

Lest we worry that in later life Lightfoot went off the boil as he labored away on the apostolic fathers, Stephen Neill assuages such concern. "If I had my way," Neill maintains, "at least five hundred pages of Lightfoot's *Apostolic Fathers* would be required reading for every theological student in his first year. I cannot imagine any better introduction to critical method, or a better preparation for facing some of the difficult problems of New Testament interpretation that yet remain unsolved."[13]

There was probably, however, another reason why Lightfoot never published his work on John and Acts. His friend, colleague and original Cambridge mentor B. F. Westcott *was* producing a commentary on John. Lightfoot would likely have regarded it as bad form to publish something that competed with his colleague's work, especially when they had already agreed regarding the division of labor when it came to the New Testament. Furthermore, his other colleague F. J. A. Hort was scheduled to do Acts.

Turning to another academic matter, we learn early on what kind of man Lightfoot was when it came to collegiality. Having become Hulsean Professor of Divinity at Cambridge at the remarkably young age of thirty-three, when

---

[12]John A. T. Robinson, "Joseph Barber Lightfoot" (Durham Cathedral Lecture, 1981), p. 13.
[13]Stephen C. Neill, *The Interpretation of the New Testament 1861–1961* (Oxford: Oxford University Press, 1966), p. 57.

the Regius Professorship of Divinity became open in 1870, it was assumed that he would take it. But when Lightfoot learned that Westcott would be returning to Cambridge after fulfilling an ecclesiastical assignment, he turned down the post so that it might be given to Westcott.

> Lightfoot used all his influence to induce his friend Westcott to become a candidate and resolutely declined to stand himself. After Lightfoot's death, Dr. Westcott wrote, "He called me to Cambridge to occupy a place which was his own by right; and having done this he spared no pains to secure for his colleague favorable opportunities for action, while he himself withdrew from the position which he had so long virtually occupied."[14]

This speaks volumes about the character of the man.

Instead of becoming Regius Professor, five years later Lightfoot accepted the Lady Margaret's chair. As such, Lightfoot focused on his exegetical work, work that went into his lectures. These labors remained largely unknown after he died, since they were mostly unpublished. In fact, Lightfoot never fully revised any non-Pauline materials into commentary form since there was neither time nor opportunity to do so once he became bishop of Durham. Then, he died prematurely.

So it was that these invaluable Cambridge New Testament notes of Lightfoot remained unpublished. They were presumably first moved to Bishop Auckland Palace (the residence of the bishop of Durham) when Lightfoot moved to Durham. Following his death, they were transported to the Durham Cathedral Library.[15] There, they have barely seen the light of day since 1889, with only a handful of scholars and clerics even reading a small part of these materials over the last 150 years.[16] We trust that these Lightfoot volumes will remedy this regrettable neglect.

---

[14]Hort, "Lightfoot," p. 234.

[15]Hort ("Lightfoot," p. 237) says that Lightfoot's library was divided between the divinity school at Cambridge and the University of Durham. What he does not tell us is what happened to his papers, letters and unpublished manuscripts. We now know that they stayed in Durham in a cupboard in the Monk's Dormitory in the cathedral close.

[16]Barrett ("Lightfoot as Biblical Commentator," p. 55) observes, "Three commentaries [i.e. Galatians, Philippians, Colossians and Philemon] were published in Lightfoot's lifetime. He left lecture notes, and other notes, on other epistles which doubtless he would have used in published work had he lived, and had his interest not become absorbed in what must be regarded as his greatest work, that on the text of 1 Clement and the Epistles of Ignatius (with 2 Clement and Polycarp thrown in for full measure)—not to mention his conscientious, time-consuming work as bishop of Durham."

LIGHTFOOT'S METHOD

Lightfoot learned early on about the value of writing out one's thoughts about the Scriptures. He once advised: "Begin to write as soon as you possibly can. That was what Prince Lee [his headmaster at King Edward's, Birmingham] always said to us. This is the way to learn. Almost all I have learnt has come from writing books. If you write a book on a subject, you have to read everything that has been written about it."[17]

As John A. T. Robinson stresses, "One turns back with relief to his patient, inductive method after so many of the pre-judgments and unexamined assumptions of form- and redaction-criticism. . . . Lightfoot would have been horrified to think that serious scholarship could by-pass the historical questions or suppose they could be settled *a priori* by the theological."[18] *This is because Lightfoot believed wholeheartedly that nothing could be theologically true that was historically false when it comes to matters involving a historical religion like Christianity.*

If we ask about Lightfoot's particular modus operandi with respect to commentary writing, his approach is basically the same inductive method: (1) Establish the text by dealing with the text-critical issues, including the textual variants. (2) Offer necessary grammatical and syntactical notes and discussions. (3) Proceed with exegesis proper. For Lightfoot, this sometimes entailed long excursuses on special topics and more exegetically problematic matters as well as translations of key phrases into English. (4) Deal with theological issues and larger topics that might involve several New Testament documents.

Lightfoot assumed that his audience would know enough Greek and scholia to be able to figure out his elliptical references to parallels in other Greek texts and the like as well as his brief (and sometimes infrequent) footnotes referencing the work of other scholars. "The permanent value of Lightfoot's historical work depends on his sagacity in dealing with the materials out of which history has to be constructed. He was invariably faithful to a rigorous philological discipline, and was preserved by native candor from distorting influences."[19]

---

[17]Robinson, "Lightfoot," p. 13.
[18]Ibid., p. 16.
[19]Hort, "Lightfoot," p. 239.

It may be asked at this juncture, What is the value of this material today, since many good commentaries on Acts, John, 2 Corinthians and 1 Peter have been written since the time of Lightfoot? The answer to this question is twofold. First, there is Lightfoot's encyclopedic knowledge of early Greek literature, a knowledge that is probably unequaled to this day by any subsequent commentator on the New Testament.[20] As Barrett points out, Lightfoot did not have, nor did he need, a lexicon to find parallels to New Testament Greek usage. As a close look at his Galatians commentary shows: "He knows Origen, Ephraem Syrus, Eusebius of Emesa, Chrysostom, Severianus, Theodore of Mopsuestia, Theodoret, Euthalius, Gennadius, Photius, Victorinus, Hilary, Jerome, Augustine, Pelagius, Cassiodorus, John of Damascus," not to mention all the pagan Greek literature and later catenae of Greek and Latin sources.[21] Lightfoot was a walking lexicon of Greek literature of all sorts, and not infrequently he was able to cite definitive parallels to New Testament usage that decided the issue of the meaning of a word or a phrase.

Second, as Dunn notes, time and again Lightfoot "*clearly demonstrates the importance of reading a historical text within its historical context, that the meaning of a text does not arise out of the text alone, but out of the text read in context and that the original context and intention of the author is a determinative and controlling factor in what may be read or heard from such a text. . . . Lightfoot would certainly have approved a referential theory of meaning: that that to which the language of the text refers determines and controls the meaning of the text.*"[22]

This approach is sorely needed today as commentators increasingly dismiss or ignore the importance of original-language study and of the original historical context of a document, or who try to do "theological in-

---

[20]The only New Testament scholar I have ever met, studied with or talked to who was even close to Lightfoot in these skills was Bruce Metzger, with whom I studied the apostolic fathers in a summer course at Princeton. He too had a vast panoply of languages at his command as well as an encyclopedic knowledge of Greek and early Christian literature. It appears he had a photographic memory, and one wonders whether Lightfoot did as well. Savage (*Lightfoot of Durham*, p. 110) seems to confirm this conjecture when he speaks of Lightfoot's "remarkable accuracy of memory which enabled him to apply it readily. Page after page was written *currente calamo* with few or no books of reference at hand, and with only a 'ver.' here and there in the margin, where future verification was required." (BW3)

[21]Barrett, "Lightfoot as Biblical Commentator," p. 57.

[22]James D. G. Dunn, "Lightfoot in Retrospect," *Durham University Journal* (1992): 71-94 (here 75-76), italics added for emphasis.

terpretation" of the text without first having done their historical homework to determine the original contextual meaning of the text, whether theological in character or not. It may be hoped that this series of volumes will revive an interest in the full gamut of subjects relevant to the study of the New Testament, not least ancient history, including social history; the classics; a precise knowledge of Greek, including its grammar and syntax and rhetoric; and, of course, the theology and ethics of the material itself. Doubtless Lightfoot himself would be pleased if this were one outcome of the publication of his long-lost exegetical studies on the New Testament.[23]

Finally, these commentaries show exactly the way Lightfoot approached his study of the New Testament—carefully, prayerfully and, in his own words, with "the highest reason and the fullest faith." Not one or the other, but both. Time and again Lightfoot's intellect and his piety shine through in these lost manuscripts. He shows us repeatedly that faith and reason need not be at odds with one another, especially if it is *fides quaerens intellectum* ("faith seeking understanding"). Honesty about early Christianity and its Lord need not be feared by a person of Christian faith, whether then or now. Taken for what they are, Lightfoot's notes will not merely "tease the mind into active thought" (a phrase made famous by C. H. Dodd, a Cambridge man like Lightfoot)[24] but also nourish the soul.

---

[23]It is possible that he might be a bit miffed to see all this material published since it is incomplete. Lightfoot was nothing if not a perfectionist when it came to fully completing tasks to the best of his ability. The numerous little parenthetical notes to himself to verify a reference or the check marks in the manuscript indicating a reference verified testify to this scholarly habit. Nevertheless, this material, even though incomplete, is extremely valuable, as even a casual reading of what follows should demonstrate. (BW3)

[24]C. H. Dodd, *The Parables of the Kingdom*, rev. ed. (New York: Scribner's, 1961), p. 5.

Part One

PAULINE PROLEGOMENA

Of Chronology and Context

CHRONOLOGY OF PAUL'S CHRISTIAN LIFE

Surprisingly enough, there are in fact only two fixed points in the history of the Acts, and indeed only two that have a bearing on Pauline chronology: 1) the death of Herod Agrippa in A.D. 44; 2) the removal of Felix and the installing of Festus as procurator of Judaea. Even this is not directly related but can be made out with tolerable accuracy, searching for a *terminus ad quem*. In fact we will find that the *terminus ad quem* and the *terminus a quo* [the latest and earliest dates that something could have happened], in this case coincide. Felix was brother of Claudius' favorite, Pellas, and after he had been removed to make room for Festus, he was only saved from a lawsuit with the Jews by the intercession of his brother. Now Pellas was poisoned in A.D. 62 (cf. Tacitus, *Annals* xiv.65). And in any case these events must have transpired before the removal of Pellas from power in A.D. 55 (Tacitus, *Annals* xiii.14).[1] Thus the removal and the intercession must have been before this last event. 3) Again, Paul preaches for two whole years unmolested in Rome (Acts 28:30, 31). Rome was burnt and the persecution of the Christians broke out in July 64 A.D., in fact after July 19th 64 A.D. The apostle Paul then

---

[1]Wieseler [?], *Chronologie*, p. 72sq. [Bracketed question marks that appear in the text are editorial. They indicate uncertainty arising from the difficulty in deciphering Lightfoot's handwriting.]

must have been in Rome by the Spring of the year A.D. 62. Therefore, Felix must have been recalled in the summer of 61 at the latest. This is confirmed by another consideration. 4) The Jews who preferred the charges against Felix are said by Josephus to have obtained certain privileges from the Syrian inhabitants of Caesarea by means of Burrus. Now Burrus died in February A.D. 62 at the latest, perhaps even in January. Therefore, Felix was recalled in A.D. 61 at the latest (see *Ant.* 20.8.9). In Acts 28:16 Paul's fellow prisoners are given up παρέδωκεν τοὺς δεσμίους τῷ στρατοπεδάρχῃ, i.e. by the *prefectus praetorio.* Now Burrus was the sole *prefectus praetorio,* but after his death, the office was shared by two persons, as it had been before. The singular then points to only one *prefectus,* hence Burrus was still living.

But Paul cannot have arrived in Rome so early in the year as February. The νηστεία had already passed when he was at the harbor in Crete. He is shipwrecked off of Malta after a voyage of fourteen days from Crete. He stays at Malta for three months and then he proceeds. The νηστεία was on the tenth day of Tishri, (sometime in October), so that Paul could not have arrived in Rome before March. It must have been not later than in year 61 when he arrived, but not earlier than 60 when Felix was recalled. Thus much on the *terminus ad quem,* what of the *terminus a quo*?

Paul was imprisoned after Pentecost and remained two years in prison before Festus' arrival. Therefore Festus arrived after Pentecost. At the νηστεία (Acts 24:27) Paul was as far as Crete on his way to Rome, between Pentecost then and October. Festus must have entered into his procuratorship, probably in the summer. What is the earliest possible year? 1) Josephus mentions several acts of Felix after the accession of Nero in October A.D. 54. Therefore, he was still procurator in A.D. 55; 2) in Acts 21:38 there is an allusion to the rebellion headed by the Egyptian as having happened πρὸ τούτων τῶν ἡμερῶν. We know that this rebellion took place in Nero's reign, allowing sufficient time for the events themselves, and taking πρὸ τούτων τῶν ἡμερῶν into account. Perhaps then the earliest for Paul's two year imprisonment in Caesarea is Pentecost A.D. 58 and therefore 60 for the arrival of Festus.

Again, St. Paul says (Acts 24:10) that Felix Ἐκ πολλῶν ἐτῶν ὄντα σε κριτὴν τῷ ἔθνει. Felix entered into his procuratorship in A.D. 52-53. We cannot well allow less than five years for πολλῶν ἐτῶν, and this will be sufficient when we remember how frequently the office changed hands. Further, the events which happened during Felix's procuratorship took time. Five years would be πολλῶν ἐτῶν, compared to the time it was generally held by one man. Therefore, the *terminus a quo* for Festus' arrival is the summer of A.D. 60, and this was also found to be the *terminus ad quem*.

We have thus two dates given. There are other events which may be employed to verify the chronology, but only to confirm results, as being uncertain in themselves, e.g. the edict of Claudius and the ethnarchy of Aretas in Damascus and the proconsulship of Gallio in Corinth. The chronology has to be determined for these events by *relative* chronology given in the Acts and in Galatians. The most convenient way is to work backwards from the arrival of Festus in Judaea in A.D. 60. By this means (see Davidson *Intro.* Vol. ii. p. 110) we arrive at these results:

PAUL'S CONVERSION—A.D. 38? (Gal 2:1—Paul went up to Jerusalem fourteen years after his conversion). Probably however, Meyer is right in insisting that διὰ δεκατεσσάρων ἐτῶν must denote 'after an interval of fourteen years' from the visit narrated in Gal 1. In this case the date would be

PAUL'S CONVERSION—A.D. 35 with the first visit to Jerusalem in A.D. 38?[2]

FIRST VISIT TO JERUSALEM—A.D. 41 (Gal 1:18, three years after the conversion).

TARSUS, ANTIOCH

SECOND VISIT TO JERUSALEM—44 or 45?[3] The same years as the death of Herod Agrippa. His death seems to have transpired between Paul's arrival in Jerusalem and his departure (Acts 11:30–12:25).

> I.) FIRST MISSIONARY JOURNEY—After the death of Herod and before A.D. 51.
>
> THIRD VISIT TO JERUSALEM
>
> II.) SECOND MISSIONARY JOURNEY—A.D. 51 (this date and those hereafter are determined by the date of Festus' procuratorship and from notices of their relative chronology)

---

[2]The penciled notes in the facing page are where the comment from Meyer comes in, and clearly Lightfoot is entertaining this earlier chronology, but the full page of chronological reflections continues with the assumption that the conversion was in 38. (BW3)

[3]44 is underlined twice in pencil here. So, this must be his final verdict. (BW3)

ARRIVAL AT CORINTH—A.D. 52

FOURTH VISIT TO JERUSALEM—A.D. 53

III.) THIRD MISSIONARY JOURNEY—A.D. 54

RESIDENCE IN EPHESUS—A.D. 54–57

IMPRISONMENT—A.D. 58

DEPARTURE FROM CAESAREA TO ROME—A.D. 60

ARRIVAL IN ROME—A.D. 61

CLOSE OF THE NARRATIVE IN ACTS—A.D. 63.

CHRONOLOGY OF PAUL'S EPISTLES

The letters may be divided into two classes: 1) those written before the Apostle's arrival in Rome—Romans, 1, 2 Corinthians, Galatians, 1, 2 Thessalonians and; 2) those written after his arrival in Rome—Colossians, Ephesians, Philippians, 1, 2 Timothy and Titus (though several critics remove one or more of these and place them in the first division e.g. Torischer [?] places 1 Timothy and Titus before Paul's last imprisonment). We are only concerned here with the letters in this first division, and none of the letters included in this division present any difficulty except perhaps Galatians. The order seems to be this:

SECOND MISSIONARY JOURNEY—1 Thessalonians soon after his visit to Thessalonike. Written from Corinth A.D. 52. 2 Thessalonians, also from Corinth (not long after the first letter), towards the end of his stay there so—53–54.

THIRD MISSIONARY JOURNEY—Galatians perhaps written from Ephesus perhaps in 55 at the beginning of Paul's stay there (though perhaps in 57–58).

1 Corinthians at Ephesus in A.D. 57 toward the close of Paul's Ephesian stay.

2 Corinthians in Macedonia A.D. 57–58 on his way to Greece.

Romans during his last (2nd or 3rd) stay at Corinth, before the journey to Jerusalem and Rome. This is seen from the allusion to Priscilla and Aquila and from the information with regard to the collection of alms in Macedonia and Achaia and from the names mentioned in the salutations (see Paley's *Hora. Paul.*).

How many epistles did St. Paul write to the Corinthians? In other words, had he written one before the one that bears the name of First Corinthians

(N.B. with the speculations of critics who have a faculty for multiplying things, we have no concern)? 1) 1 Cor 5:8 says—Ἔγραψα ὑμῖν ἐν τῇ ἐπιστολῇ μὴ συναναμίγνυσθαι πόρνοις. Ἔγραψα is an aorist. It is said that if it refers to the present letter then γράφω or γέγραφα would be required. This is certainly not true. Cf. Rom 15:15; Heb 13:22; 1 Cor 9:15; Gal 6:11; Philem 19, 21; 1 John 2:14, 21, 26; 1 Cor 5:13.

On the other hand, in 2 Cor 2:3, 4, 9, and 2 Cor 7:12 ἔγραψα refers to the previous letter (i.e. 1 Corinthians), similarly 3 John 9. These references cannot, as Stanley supposes (p. 87), refer to what immediately precedes. Bunsen (*Hippolytus* i. p. 24) finds it necessary to refer the words of 1 Pet 5:12 to an earlier epistle [on similar grounds].

The argument that Ἔγραψα in 1 Cor 5:9 refers to a previous letter is also based on the argument that: 1) there is a definite article before ἐπιστολῇ and 2) the supposed contrast between Ἔγραψα in vs. 9 and the νυνὶ δὲ[4] at the beginning of 1 Cor 5:11 as for instance rendered in the A.V. 'I wrote to you in an Epistle. . . . But now I have written . . .'. And it is said perhaps the aorist might stand at the end of a letter but it cannot at the beginning (see Davidson *Intro.* ii, p. 140). This is equally untrue. Not to mention 1 John 2:14 where the meaning there attached to ἔγραψα may be doubtful (cf. *Martyrdom of Poly.* Chap. 1, where immediately after the salutation before anything more is said we find ἔγραψαν ὑμιν . . .). This epistolary aorist is not infrequent! The writer transfers himself to the time when the letter would be read by the receiver, and uses his tenses accordingly. This is also frequent in Latin (cf. Cicero, *ad Atticus.* vi.2.3). The Latin usage is more constant than the Greek.

That the phrase τῇ ἐπιστολῇ may refer grammatically to the Epistle itself is not doubted (cf. Rom 16:22; Col 4:16; 1 Thess 5:27; 2 Thess 3:14). But on the other hand, can we deny that the phrase 'Ἔγραψα ὑμιν . . .' *may* be used of a former letter (2 Cor 7:8)? No. But there is no grammatical difficulty in applying the words to the epistle in which they occur, and in fact the Greek commentators on 1 Cor 5:9, Chrysostom, Theophylact., Theodoret do so refer it, evidently feeling that they were not doing violence to the Greek.

[The question may be asked] To what can we refer it in this First Epistle? I can think to nothing which has gone before, but that this epistolary aorist

---

[4]He is following Tischendorf here with νυνὶ instead of νῦν.

may well refer to the immediate words themselves—as we should say in English 'I *write* to you not to . . .'. The νυνὶ δὲ ἔγραψα in 1 Cor 5:11 seems to point to this, although νυνὶ is certainly not an adverb of time, but = 'as it is' or 'under the circumstances' or 'things being what they are' and is explained by ἐπεὶ ὠφείλετε ἄρα ἐκ τοῦ κόσμου ἐξελθεῖν (1 Cor 5:10).

There is a textual issue in 1 Cor 5:11: 1) νῦν is read by A, B, Aleph, F, G, 17, L, P but 2) νυνὶ Aleph*, C, D, and others. For the sense of νῦν/νυνί, see 1 Cor 7:14; 12:18 where νῦν is probably the right reading though the Textus Receptus has νυνί (so also in 1 Cor 5:2). See 1 Cor 15:20 where it is opposed not to some other (past or future) time but to another (hypothetical) state of things. See also Rom 7:17. Stanley resorts to the theory of a marginal note (p. 88) on the grounds of the interruption of sequence. But in fact the passage here is not more disrupted than in lots of passages in St. Paul's Epistles. Though disrupted in form, it is connected in the passage in content in the text to explain what follows. St. Paul deals: 1) with the sin of licentiousness (1 Cor 5:1-13) and he passes on to 2) the sin of cocksureness or over-reaching (1 Cor 6:1-8), the lack of connection being because of the accidental thought in 1 Cor 5:12—τί γάρ μοι. . . . Then the two are connected together in 1 Cor 6:9. Thus the two lapses of sin are condemned.

In fact, each thought supports the following one. The sexual offense is denounced; they are ἐκκαθάρατε τὴν παλαιὰν ζύμην (1 Cor 5:7). Then St. Paul refers to a former charge he had given to them, and explains the force of it. It refers to judging within the church. He has no wish to judge outside the church. But they must cast out him from them to the Evil One. 1 Cor 5:13 then is connected with 1 Cor 5:6-7. No one from without should judge them. And yet the Corinthians actually go to law, brother against brother, before heathen judges. It would be better to suffer wrong, to suffer fraud. Yet they commit wrong, commit fraud. The unjust shall not inherit the Kingdom of God. Thus the first part of 1 Cor 5:9 is directly suggested by what goes before. And the second part is directly suggested by the first. 'The Kingdom of heaven, nay be not deceived, the Kingdom of heaven is not for such as some among you are, not for whoremongers, adulterers etc. These ye are!'

The reference to other passages and their 'abruptness' also fail. In 2 Cor 6:14–7:1, which is the strongest case of a subject abruptly introduced and abruptly dismissed. The Apostle then returns to the former subject. This must be explained by some sudden thought that passes through the Apostle's mind. The very fact that it has no obvious connection with the context shows that it is not a marginal note, because a marginal note must be a note on something in the text.

All these arguments therefore must be dismissed. Only one remains—ἐν τῇ ἐπιστολῇ is irrelevant and unnecessary on the supposition that it refers to itself. This is true, and for this reason, and this reason only, does it seem necessary to suppose that a previous letter had been written. Otherwise, we should be disposed to refer the passage to the First Epistle itself.[5]

AN INTERACTION WITH MR. WIESELER'S CHRONOLOGY

Did the Apostle leave Ephesus at Pentecost as he intended? One view is that there is no reason to suppose that St. Paul's departure was hastened by the tumult, as he does not appear to have been in any personal danger. Mr. Wieseler has some good remarks on this tumult, and he considers it probable that the Apostle may have left Ephesus *some short time* before he had intended (see Wieseler *Chron. Der ap. Zeitalt.* p. 54sqq.).

> An account must be given of the succession of events, seeking to determine the chronology shortly before the writing of 1 Corinthians. Timothy and others had departed for Macedonia (cf. Acts xix.22), and St. Paul expected to be in Corinth (cf. iv.17, xvi.1) soon after his letter (ταχέως ([iv.19]—cf. 1 Cor. xvi.10, 11). After the departure of Timothy and Erastus, he stayed some time (χρόνος) in Asia i.e. Ephesus (xix.26). It is clear from these considerations also that the Apostle cannot have left Ephesus before Pentecost. Note that the others have returned before the second letter has begun (cf. 2 Cor. i.1). Now it is *possible* that Paul did not meet Timothy again until he arrived in Macedonia, and that Timothy had not yet gone to Corinth; but it is *improbable* that Timothy should have stayed so long in Macedonia, not at all consistent with the commission entrusted to him.

To this I respond—*why improbable? Perhaps his business in Macedonia was more important even than the business in Achaia and if his place was supplied by Titus, surely there is nothing improbable in his lengthening his stay in Macedonia.*

---

[5]On the spurious Armenian Epistle, see Stanley p. 609.

Wieseler goes on 'he was ordered to hurry his journey to Corinth, in order that he might rejoin the Apostle in Ephesus before Pentecost.' I rejoin: *Where is any mention of Ephesus? It is much more probable that some other place of meeting was agreed upon. According to my view, it was Troas.*

Wieseler goes on—'the use of the plural in 2 Cor 1:3-11 makes it probable that Timothy was a participator in the sufferings there described.' I respond— *Probably so, but it is by no means certain that St. Paul there refers to the tumult at Ephesus, nay it is almost certain that he does not refer to that alone. In 1 Corinthians he speaks of fighting with beasts, of his 'many opponents,' and this was while Timothy was with him, so that Timothy had thus far participated in his suffering at Ephesus, that he could be spoken of in comparison with St. Paul in connection with this, without any impropriety.*

Wieseler goes on '2 Cor. i.12–ii.11 is written with reference to the impression of the opposition which the First Epistle had occasioned (2 Corinthians ii.3-4).' To which I say *or 'would probably occasion,' for St. Paul's language here betrays no actual knowledge of what actually has taken place.* Wieseler adds, 'The Apostle had already received the bad news of the state of affairs at Corinth before he arrived at Troas for in 2 Cor. ii.12 he speaks of the restlessness of his spirit which he felt there.' To which I respond—*There is still no indication of news actually received. He felt that a letter which he had written in much tribulation and anguish was only too likely to provoke opposition, and therefore he was afraid of the results. When the information did come through Titus, it was more favorable than he expected.*

Wieseler then argues—'From 1 Cor. xvi.11 we may conclude with great probability that Timothy was the bringer of the news.' *But if there was no news, there would be no bringer.* Wieseler presses, 'But suppose he [Timothy] was not, it does not alter our chronology result inasmuch as St. Paul must have waited at Ephesus until the letter would have been conveyed to Corinth and a message had returned.' *But no news seems to have reached him for at least thirty days.*

He adds, 'But however there are other reasons for supposing that St. Paul's stay was even more protracted. Titus was sent off after the penning of the First Epistle and so there is no mention of him there.' I respond—*According to our theory he was one of the ἀδελφοί there alluded to, and the circumstances that he is not mentioned by name is explained by supposing that he was personally unknown to the Corinthian Church. His case is parallel to the other brothers who accompanied him on his second mission tour.* And yet the Apostle hopes to find him arrived in Troas.

Wieseler's next observation is worthy of attention. This proves, he says, that the tumult in Ephesus cannot have altered Paul's purpose to any considerable extent. 'For if he had left Ephesus much earlier than he had intended, he would scarcely expect to find Titus already at Troas.' *Yet this is not conclusive. St. Paul may have delayed on the way to Troas (cf. 2 Cor 2:12), or again he may have expected Titus to return to him at Ephesus, and having been obliged to hurry his departure, he thought to meet Titus at Troas.*

Wieseler's assumptions on p. 359 and elsewhere are twofold: 1) that St. Paul received some information when he commenced writing the Second Epistle; 2) that Titus did not join him until after the former part of 2 Corinthians had been written. Hence, he is obliged to infer that Paul had received the information from someone else. From whom then more probably than from Timothy? Therefore, he rejects the two opinions: 1) that Timothy never arrived at Corinth at all; and 2) whether he arrived there or not, he did not join the Apostle again until he reached Macedonia.

However, if my view is right, Titus was the bearer of the letter, and as he returned by land, it is not improbable that he went by land as well. He seems to have stayed some considerable time at Corinth, as indeed the purposes of his mission demanded. Cf. 2 Cor 12:17, 18 (where ἐπλεονέκτησα, judging from the context, evidently refers to his maintenance and has no connection with the contributions, as Conybeare hastily assumes). It should be asked—Did Titus go and come by land on account of the season of the year?

Wieseler offers further reflections (pp. 325ff.). Here is a thought worth considering—if Chloe (1 Cor 1:16) was a Corinthian, then Stephanus, Fortunatus, and Achaius (1 Cor 16:17) may have been her sons—those 'of Chloe' (ὑπὸ τῶν Χλόης) and so the household of Chloe may be the same as the household of Stephanus (1 Cor 16:15).

On the issue of the dating of 1 Corinthians, Wieseler maintains 'Paul intended to remain at Ephesus until Pentecost (1 Cor xvi.8). From Acts xix.21-22, it appears that the dispatching of Timothy did not long precede the Apostle's departure, and accordingly in 1 Cor. iv.19, St. Paul says that he will come speedily.' I respond—*Wieseler evidently infers that the mission of Timothy related in the Acts is identical to that to Macedonia and Corinth. Does he do so*

elsewhere, yes he does also on p. 358. But the language of St. Luke evidently leads to the understanding that Timothy had not advanced beyond Macedonia when he was joined by St. Paul. This seems to be much more consistent with those who regard this as a second mission subsequently to his return from Corinth.
Wieseler goes on,

> at most therefore the letter was written a few months before Pentecost. Again Paul expected that the letter would arrive before Timothy. The direct journey to Athens from Ephesus occupied fourteen days. Allowing fourteen days for going and fourteen days for returning, and eight for staying there, we get thirty-six days plus a bit, say four days which elapsed between the arrival of the letter and that of Timothy at Corinth i.e. about 40 days in all. Then we have to take into account that Titus was despatched *after* the sending of the Epistle.

(I ask—*why after?*). *And yet Paul hoped to meet him at Troas so that we must extend the time to 40-50 days?* On this reckoning then the letter must be written at Easter, and this accounts for the allusion in 1 Cor 5:6-8 though too much stress may not be laid on this. [Lightfoot stops at this point, having established that he thinks his view more probable than Wieseler's.]

HOW MANY TIMES DID ST. PAUL VISIT CORINTH?

There are two visits recorded in Acts: 1) Acts 18:1-18 where a tolerably detailed account is given of his preaching there. This is on his second missionary journey (A.D. 52); 2) Acts 20:2-3: ἦλθεν εἰς τὴν Ἑλλάδα, ποιήσας τε μῆνας τρεῖς (A.D. 57-58). The last of these can be proved to be subsequent to the writing of the two Epistles (the one in fact where he is meditating, when the Second Epistle is written). Therefore, there is only one previous to this date recorded in Acts. But there are intimations in the Epistles (especially in 2 Corinthians), that he had already visited them twice: 1) e.g. 2 Cor 2:1—τὸ μὴ πάλιν ἐν λύπῃ πρὸς ὑμᾶς ἐλθεῖν (this is the right reading). The uncials vary in word order (ἐλθεῖν before the prepositional phrase or after, but πάλιν ἐν λύπῃ go together in all the best authorities). The Textus Receptus ἐλθεῖν ἐν λύπῃ is unsupported except by [?] manuscripts. We naturally then take πάλιν ἐν λύπῃ together. Now the first visit (Acts 18) cannot be termed ἐν λύπῃ. Therefore, we must look for a second visit and 2 Cor 12:21 points to the same conclusion, though perhaps that verse might be differently taken; 2) 2 Cor 12:4. Paley's argument. The words Τρίτον τοῦτο ἔρχομαι πρὸς ὑμᾶς (2 Cor 13:1) do not in themselves require three actual visits, but three *intended* visits, but the context practically requires that St. Paul should have been in Corinth twice previously. The mere purpose of paying them a visit would not have been 'burdensome.' The mention of an intention of a visit would be quite out of place in such a connection. The time which Stanley (p. 571) gives to the phrase Τρίτον τοῦτο ἔρχομαι πρὸς ὑμᾶς finds no justification in the context. Some of the copyists have felt that Τρίτον τοῦτο ἔρχομαι must be altered if only an intended visit was meant. And so A, Syr. Peshit., Coptic versions, Memphis change the number or alter the phrase in some way. 1 Cor 5:3 however could lead to a completely different interpretation if the phrase here is taken to mean 'if I were with you a second time, even though absent,' leaving out of sight his first visit to Corinth, inasmuch as the evil had not yet broken out, and he had not then had occasion to censure them.

But consider 2 Cor 13:1, 2. This seems to be decisive. προείρηκα καὶ προλέγω in vs. 2 is answered by ὡς παρὼν τὸ δεύτερον καὶ ἀπὼν νῦν, i.e. when I paid you my second visit so (for καί see Phil 1:20), again τοῖς προημαρτηκόσιν can scarcely apply to anything which had happened during the first visit of all. Τρίτον τοῦτο ἔρχομαι most naturally means 'this will be my third visit to you' and if this is the more natural meaning, it is also the more probable meaning. And again it is that which is imperatively demanded by the context. Why should St. Paul lay such stress on an intended visit? The actual visit might be regarded as a stressor, but not a proposed visit. The idea is his being confronted with a face to face, a third time.

Consider 1 Cor 16:7. This has been thought to show that St. Paul had already paid one short visit to Corinth (and therefore two in all, the first one being a long one—Acts 18). This appears to be a mistake. ἄρτι means 'at present' not 'now.' It is not opposed to any former occasion. The sentence in that case would read 'I do not want to see you at the present moment, when my visit would necessarily only be a brief one.' Meyer rightly rejects the inference from taking ἄρτι to mean now, but on the wrong grounds. He merely notes the position of ἄρτι, and says that if the meaning had been intended, it would have been ἄρτι γὰρ and θέλω. De Wette repeats Meyer's argument—'dem ἄρτι gehört zu ἰδεῖν nicht zu θέλω.' Alford's note on this is obscure. Wieseler (p. 240) thinks the inference probable, and indeed Meyer only

shows that it is not necessary. At all events the natural antithesis to ἄρτι
would be the future and not the past, natural though perhaps not necessary.
See Gal 1:9, 10 though it is difficult to say exactly what ἄρτι means there. In
Gal 4:20 ἄρτι is now, i.e. without deferring my visit, and not as Meyer (ἄρτι
is used with the present and past tenses but never with the future). See
Lobeck, on Phys. p. 20.

There seems to be sufficient reason for believing that St. Paul had already
paid two visits to Corinth (i.e. one not recorded in Acts). The opposition
view is taken by Davidson (*Intro.* ii. p. 213) and by Paley (*Hora Paul.*) and by
Stanley. But it is thought that 2 Cor 1:15-16 are a severe obstacle to this view.
But this evidently means 'My intention was to have paid you two visits, instead of one' the word πρότερον leading us to the solution of the meaning
of the words ἵνα δευτέραν χάριν σχῆτε. Compare 1 Corinthians 16:5, 6
written after his first intention has been abandoned and if this be the case,
there is no allusion at all to a previous visit.

On the other interpretation, ἵνα δευτέραν χάριν σχῆτε is rendered meaningless. Why specify the χάρις they would receive on that occasion rather
than on a subsequent projected visit? 'I was desirous of visiting you before
(before this visit which is now impending) so that I might be enabled to see
you twice, instead of once.'

When then did this visit take place, which is unrecorded in the Acts?
Some suppose that on the occasion of his first visit to Greece, when he is
said to have remained at Corinth a year and a half (Acts 18), he made an
excursion into the neighborhood and returned to Corinth and thus may be
said to have paid two visits. This is improbable. The more probable supposition is that he came over during his three year stay at Ephesus (54-57). This
view we shall adopt (other views enumerated in Davidson, *Intro.* ii, p. 219).

Paul's Communication with the Corinthians and His Social Network

What communication did St. Paul have with the Corinthian Church either:
1) personally, or 2) through the medium of letters? The former investigation
may be considered preliminary to this one. In the year A.D. 52 in the course of
his second missionary tour in which he crossed over to Europe for the first
time, he passed from Athens to Corinth. This was his *first visit.* And on this

occasion he laid the foundation of the Christian Church there. A detailed account is given in the Acts 18. We are there told that he was joined by Sylvanus and Timothy whom he had left behind in Macedonia (Acts 18:5). Accordingly, in 2 Cor 1:19 he speaks of the Gospel having been preached to them by himself and Sylvanus and Timothy. On this first occasion he meets with Aquila and Priscilla at Corinth. In 1 Cor 16:19 they salute the Church of Corinth.

While he is on his *third missionary tour*, Apollos having been instructed by Aquila and Priscilla at Ephesus, goes to Corinth and preaches the Gospel there (A.D. 54). Meanwhile, Paul arrives at Ephesus (Acts 18:27, 28; 19:1).

From Ephesus he probably crossed the Aegean to Corinth. This is his *second visit*. It is passed over in silence in the Acts. It was probably of no long duration and as the facilities of intercourse between the two cities were great, the transit could not occupy much time. Of the occasion of this visit we know nothing. He calls it a visit of sorrow (2 Cor 2:1). Probably, signs of impurity and profligacy had manifested themselves in the Corinthian Church (A.D. 55).

Paul seems not to have been satisfied with this visit. He felt it necessary to deepen the impression made on the Church of Corinth by addressing a *letter* to the Christians there. This letter is not preserved to us. Probably it was merely of temporary interest. We know that in it he warned the Corinthian Christians to separate themselves from the profligate of their own body (1 Cor 5:9). It is probable too that he expressed in it his intention of paying them a double visit, taking Corinth both on his way to Macedonia and on his return, a design which afterwards he had to abandon, and the abandonment of which exposed him unjustly to a charge of fickleness (2 Cor 1:16), against which he subsequently defends himself. It was probably also in this letter that he mentioned the projected visit of the brethren (1 Cor 16:11, 12) for we find him speaking on it in the First Epistle in a manner which shows that the Corinthians were not unacquainted with this proposed mission.

Subsequently, he heard from the household of Chloe (1 Cor 1:11) of the disastrous state of the Christian Church in Corinth, and the divisions that rent the community. On the former, 'it was commonly reported' that some of its members had been guilty of the most shameless and revolting profligacy. On whose authority this was reported the Apostle does not say (1 Cor 5:1) but we cannot doubt that Stephanus and other members of his household (Fortunatus, Achaius) must have given St. Paul information. There was an obvious reason why St. Paul should not mention them by name as the authors of the report. He did not want to place them in an unfavorable position with regard to their fellow Corinthians. Meyer suggests Apollos might have brought information. If then Fortunatus was a son of Stephanus and was a young man at this time, it is not improbable he is the same person mentioned by St. Clement in his Epistle to the Corinthians.

If we were to enumerate St. Paul's sources of information it might look like this: 1) subsequent to his first visit, St. Paul obtains information about the state of the church in Corinth from various sources including—a letter from the Corinthian Church itself (see 1 Cor 7:1); 2) members of the household of Chloe (1 Cor 1:11); 3) Stephanus, Fortunatus and Achaius (1 Cor 16:15-17). Perhaps to these he added the information referred to in 1 Cor 5:1 ἀκούεται ἐν ὑμῖν πορνεία and also that of 1 Cor 11:18 ἀκούω σχίσματα ἐν ὑμῖν ὑπάρχειν, καὶ μέρος τι πιστεύω though this too might have been reported by the household of Chloe (1 Cor 1:11). Indeed, 1 Cor 16:15-18 seems framed as if intended to shield the household of Stephanus from some suspected odium which they might incur; 4) possibly Apollos if he was in Corinth after St. Paul's departure, which however may not be very likely.

And so, St. Paul addressed to them a second letter, our First Epistle to the Corinthians (A.D. 51) to correct these abuses. He had by this time given up his previous intention of visiting them on his way to Macedonia. He now declares he shall go to Macedonia first (1 Cor 16:5). Apollos was at this time in Ephesus or its neighborhood, or at least St. Paul seems to have had personal communication with him (1 Cor 16:12). He may probably have returned from Corinth before Paul's second visit.

Now either before this letter or at about the same time St. Paul sent off Timothy[6] to Corinth (1 Cor 4:17; 16:10), but I think that it is certain that Timothy did not visit Corinth, for: 1) the Apostle expresses a doubt whether he would (1 Cor 16:10—Ἐὰν δὲ ἔλθῃ Τιμόθεος), contemplating the possibility that he might have some business detaining him in Macedonia; 2) in the Acts, this mission of Timothy (for there is no reason for supposing it is another) is seen as a mission to Macedonia (Acts 19:22), seeming to imply that this was the limit of his journey before he was overtaken by St. Paul; 3) there

---

[6]Probably before the letter, but evidently expressing at least the probability that the letter would arrive before or without Timothy—see Paley, *Hora. Paul.*

is no mention in 2 Corinthians of Timothy's visit to Corinth, but Titus seems to take his place. This is scarcely credible if Timothy had actually been there. It is not only that there is no mention of a visit by Timothy, but also that there is no mention of any information received from the Corinthian Church prior to the arrival of Titus (though indeed Giesler [?] p. 58 sees it otherwise), a circumstance which is very remarkable if there was a visit of Timothy which surely would have brought very definite news. The language of the Apostle is of one who entertains vague fears.

Nearly at the same time, perhaps even as the bearers of the letter, Paul dispatches οἱ ἀδελφοί (1 Cor 16:11, 12). Who then are οἱ ἀδελφοί mentioned in 1 Cor 16? Erastus accompanied him, but he probably did not proceed further than Macedonia (Acts 19:22), until St. Paul overtook them and he accompanied him to Corinth, the city of which he was a native and his name is found in the salutation for Romans (Rom 16:23).

I think that Titus was one of those that St. Paul had requested Apollos form a company with (Titus was known to Apollos—Titus 3:13), but Apollos declined doing so, thinking it was not a fit season (εὐκαιρία). He probably thought his visit would be ill-timed while his name was being made a handle for strife and division. In default of Apollos, it was not unnatural that St. Paul should select Titus, more especially as he felt there was some uncertainty of Timothy being able to extend his journey to Corinth during the other engagements. There was another brother with Titus (2 Cor 12:18). It would almost seem as if they were two strangers who arrived there on their missions—Titus and ὁ ἀδελφός.

Though the name Sosthenes is common, it is at least unlikely that two of the same name should both be so intimately connected to the fortunes of the Church in Corinth.[7] Besides, the mention of the name of the ἀρχισυνάγωγος seems to show that afterwards he was a man of some note among the Christians (though it may have been simply to distinguish him from Gaius). It cannot be concluded from the absence of this name in Acts 18:18 that he did not accompany St. Paul as others of Paul's previous companions are not mentioned. Aquila and Priscilla may only be alluded to in the account for their meeting with Apollos and the consequences of the meeting.

---

[7]The view here taken of Sosthenes I find is the same as that of Paley, *Hora. Paul.* c. iii, v. viii, note.

The name of Sosthenes is found with that of Paul in the superscription of
1 Corinthians. It is not improbable that this Sosthenes is the ἀρχισυνάγωγος
of Acts 18:17. According to the Textus Receptus this is scarcely possible. The
words οἱ Ἕλληνες (Acts 18:17) are to be rejected as unsupported, and the word
πάντες refers naturally to αὐτοί i.e. the Jews. If so, Sosthenes may have excited
the anger of the Jews by favoring the preaching of St. Paul and then subsequently have become a Christian and have been withdrawn from the anger
of his fellow countrymen (Jews) at Corinth, as we find one Sosthenes here
with Paul in Ephesus joining in the salutation to the Corinthians. The gloss,
οἱ Ἰουδαῖοι, which is found in some manuscripts, seems to be the correct one.
Alford's objections to this view are invalid. I see no real probability in the
party driven to the tribunal having been one of their antagonists before the
tribunal. The words καὶ οὐδὲν τούτων τῷ Γαλλίωνι ἔμελεν (Acts 18:17) seem
to explain any irregularity of this kind, and Alford's question 'why did they
not beat Paul himself' admits of a very simple answer: Sosthenes had become
a renegade and therefore would be a particular object of their dislike.

Stephanus, Fortunatus, and Achaius may have formed part of a company,
or they may have travelled separately. At all events, they would probably not
return [to Macedonia] as they were all natives of Corinth. St. Paul tells the
Corinthians that they should wait for the return of Timothy with the
brethren (ἐκδέχομαι γὰρ αὐτὸν μετὰ τῶν ἀδελφῶν—1 Cor 16:11). Now
something occurred which prevented Timothy from accomplishing his
mission; but we find St. Paul later on at Troas, evidently expecting Titus (οὐκ
ἔσχηκα ἄνεσιν τῷ πνεύματί μου τῷ μὴ εὑρεῖν με Τίτον τὸν ἀδελφόν μου—
2 Cor 2:13). It is probable therefore that this was the place of meeting agreed
upon. Whether St. Paul expected anyone else with Titus and whether Titus
had any companions on his return or whether on the other hand the
company styled οἱ ἀδελφοί (in 1 Cor) had by this time dwindled down to
Titus alone, we are not told. But I should certainly connect the mission of
Titus with that of the οἱ ἀδελφοί of 1 Cor 16.[8]

St. Paul, soon after writing the letter leaves Ephesus for Troas, perhaps
earlier than he had intended. He is there distressed at not finding Titus, from
whom he expected to hear tidings of the Corinthian Church. He passes on

---

[8]See my [i.e., Lightfoot's] paper in the *Journal of Philology*, ii, p. 194. [See now appendix A. (BW3)]

into Macedonia and there Titus joins him (2 Cor 2:12) bearing a very fa-vorable report (2 Cor 7:6). On receiving this, Paul writes his third letter, our Second Epistle to the Corinthians. He is now on his way to Corinth, but not satisfied with this, he at once dispatches Titus with the other brethren, who are described but whose names are not given (2 Cor 8:6, 16-18) to reassure the Corinthians and at the same time to collect their contributions (2 Cor 8:3).

Timothy, who had not advanced beyond Macedonia, had by this time joined St. Paul (his name is found in the superscription) and perhaps Erastus too. They seem to have accompanied him on his *third and last visit to Corinth,* at least they were both with him when he wrote the letter to the church at Rome (Rom 16:21, 23). Paul remained in Greece this time for three months (see Acts 20:3), wrote the Epistle to the Galatians from here probably, and the Epistle to the Romans certainly. The next notice we have about the state of the church in Corinth is in the Epistle of St. Clement (see Conybeare and Howson, ii, p.155). But after his release in Rome St. Paul again visited Corinth (2 Tim 4:20).

THE STATE OF THE PARTIES IN THE CORINTHIAN CHURCH

We are not led by the language of St. Paul to look for well-defined parties.[9] Indeed, from the very nature of the case this is unlikely. We must rather regard 1 Cor 1:10 as describing symptoms which threatened to develop into definite sects. St. Paul's words are ἔριδες ἐν ὑμῖν εἰσιν 'there are strifes among you' and later on (1 Cor 11:18) he says I hear that there are always divisions among you (σχίσματα ἐν ὑμῖν ὑπάρχειν, καὶ μέρος τι πιστεύω), and thus he says he is ready to believe as occurring in the natural order of things, 'for there must be even sects among you' (δεῖ γὰρ καὶ αἱρέσεις); these σχίσματα must develop into αἱρέσεις so that those who are approved may be made manifest. And St. Paul's words—Ταῦτα δέ, ἀδελφοί, μετεσχημάτισα εἰς ἐμαυτὸν καὶ Ἀπολλῶν (1 Cor 4:6) lead to the same conclusion. He has employed his own name and that of Apollos in a figure by way of giving a vividness to his representation, not that there were actually Paulines, Apollonians, and Petrines.

At the same time, the whole language of the Epistle requires us to believe, that the four names given (1 Cor 1:10) as the watchwords of different members do correspond in some degree to four shades of opinions held by

---

[9]The best account of the parties is found in Schaff, *History of the Apostolic Church* I, p. 334.

members of the community, and threatening to develop into four distinct parties or sects. What opinions then do they represent?

The truth though one, has many sides. It may be regarded from many different points of view. One mind may dwell on one phase or another without however regarding that phase exclusively. Thus there is nothing derogatory to St. Peter or St. Paul or Apollos in supposing that the aspect in which they viewed Christianity was different, so far different that is, as not to distort the relation of its parts. And we cannot doubt that they had each their part amplified to them in building up the church because they each were calculated to serve the cause of truth in a different way. *Heresy is the exaggeration of some part of the truth and the tendency to heresy is the tendency to this exaggeration. Sheer undiluted error could not stand for a moment.* Man's natural conscience would revolt against it. Heresy therefore must have some handle in truth. When undue prominence is given to one point, then there is danger of heresy.

Bearing this in mind, we shall have no difficulty in explaining the position of these half-developed parties described by the words Ἐγὼ μέν εἰμι Παύλου, Ἐγὼ δὲ Ἀπολλῶ, Ἐγὼ δὲ Κηφᾶ, though the favorite Ἐγὼ δὲ Χριστοῦ will present some difficulty (1 Cor 1:12). Does not St. Paul's language here and elsewhere in dealing with these divisions in Corinth show the true gentleman? Observe the ascending scale—Paul, Apollos, Peter, Christ. He places himself in the lowest grade next to the teacher who is associated with him, and highest of human instructors of him who was placed by his 'enemies' in direct antagonism with him. Again, when he wants to enforce the opposition between the servant and the master, between the human agent and the divine head, he selects his own name as the meanest of all μεμέρισται ὁ Χριστός; μὴ Παῦλος ἐσταυρώθη ὑπὲρ ὑμῶν; and again in 1 Cor 3:5 τί οὖν ἐστιν Ἀπολλῶς; τί δέ ἐστιν Παῦλος; There is no mention of Cephas here. His well-known friendly relations with Apollos allowed him to mention his name here and again at 1 Cor 4:6. The very fact that his relation with St. Peter had been so misrepresented makes him abstain, with true gentlemanly feeling, from any expression that might seem to depreciate his supposed adversary. In the Epistle to the Galatians where he found it necessary to defend his apostleship, the case is different.

St. Paul preached the liberty of the Gospel and its spirituality. The Pauline faction degraded liberty into license and found in the spiritual

character of Christianity an excuse for disregarding all outward observances—even decent forms. Theirs was an antinomian tendency. They
viewed their γνῶσις with self-complacency. The directions about meat offered to idols (1 Cor 8) have reference to them. To such St. Paul says
Ἐλεύθερος γὰρ ὢν ἐκ πάντων πᾶσιν ἐμαυτὸν ἐδούλωσα, ἵνα τοὺς πλείονας
κερδήσω (1 Cor 9:19) and again Πάντα ἔξεστιν, ἀλλ᾿ οὐ πάντα συμφέρει.
πάντα ἔξεστιν, ἀλλ᾿ οὐ πάντα οἰκοδομεῖ (1 Cor 10:23).

Apollos was an Alexandrian Jew. He would dwell on all that is mystical in
Christianity. He would enforce his teaching with great eloquence and with
frequent application of allegorical interpretation. This style would possess a
charm for the Corinthians, which they could not find in the simple teaching
of St. Paul. Paul's rebuke to the Apollonians can be found in 1 Cor 1:18 sq.
and 1 Cor 2:1 sq.

St. Peter would dwell on the connection of Christianity with the older
dispensation. The Petrines would represent the Judaizing tendencies in the
Corinthian Church i.e. the express leaning toward outward observances—
the direct antithesis to the Paulines, though doubtless the Judaism of Corinth
would be less decided in its character than that found elsewhere, the social
influence of the place being opposed to strict formalism. There is no reason
for supposing that St. Peter had ever been to Corinth. Indeed the silence
regarding him in 1 Cor 3:6 seems to show that he had not been there. His
recognized position as the Apostle to the circumcision would mark him out
to the Judaizers, as the proper antagonist of St. Paul.

But who were the Christ party? The words Ἐγὼ δὲ Χριστοῦ would naturally
lead to the view that they were those who discarded all apostolic authority.
They rejected Paul, Apollos, and Cephas alike together with their views that
were *supposed* to be characteristic of each. Their distinctive views were entirely
negative. And thus while professing the greatest Catholicity, as often happens
with such negative tendencies, they degenerated into the narrowest sectari-
anism. Schaff gives a good parallel in the sect of 'Christians' in the United
States of America (Vol. I, p. 339 note).[10] The natural character of these self-
styled "we are of Christ" persons would be arrogance and self-complacency.

---

[10]Here, Lightfoot gives a further illustration that he later marked out in pencil, thinking better of
it. He said, "So far as their negativism is concerned we may compare the Quakers with their
absence of creed, but beyond this the comparison to the modern sect of Quakers would be unfair."

They would depreciate the labors and authority of the Apostles, of St. Paul chiefly as the most active and influential. We can scarcely doubt that the reference is to them in 2 Corinthians 10:7. Clement in Epistle to the Corinthians Chapter 47 mentions only the three former parties—ἐπ᾽ ἀληθείας πνευματικῶς ἐπέστειλεν ὑμῖν περὶ αὑτοῦ τε καὶ τε Κηφᾷ καὶ Ἀπολλώ, διὰ τὸ καὶ τότε προσκλίσεις ὑμᾶς πεποιῆσθαι· Schaff (Vol. I, p 337) rightly explains his silence about the fourth party by supposing that when Clement wrote, it had ceased to exist "which" he says "is the more probable if it consisted of personal disciples of Jesus." The latter supposition is in itself very improbable. But the disappearance of the sect is easily explained if it had that negative character which we have assigned to it. A negative bond can only be temporary. It has no element of continuance in it.[11]

While the First Epistle was directed chiefly against the former two parties—the Paulines and Apollonians, the Second Epistle has in view almost entirely the Petrines, and the self-style 'Christians.' But with the same delicacy that has been noticed before, St. Paul avoids mentioning the name of Cephas. The rebukes which the former letter contain seem to have been successful with those who acknowledged the authority of St. Paul himself and his fellow teacher, Apollos. The report of Titus was most cheering.

THE OUTLINE OF 2 CORINTHIANS

The treatment in this Epistle is historical. The idea of 'suffering for Christ' and the παράκλησις that attends it, with which the Epistle opens, runs throughout the letter. The common division of the letter is as exact as any which can be made:

1) 2 Cor 1–7
2) 2 Cor 8–9
3) 2 Cor 10–13

These we may characterize as thus comprising:

1) Explanations (regarding the past)

---

[11]He adds the illustration—"Thus we see that the Society of Friends is fast dying away, its ranks being deserted on the one hand to Unitarianism and on the other for orthodox Christianity. And it is only the positive moral excellence of the sect which has kept it alive so long and rescued it from the consequences of its negative doctrinal views."

2) Directions for their present conduct (especially in regard to the Collection)

3) Warnings with respect to the future (explanations resumed)

Of course in a letter we cannot expect that the subjects will be kept entirely distinct and must require a well-defined line of demarcation.

Part Two

THE COMMENTARY ON 2 CORINTHIANS

The Salutation and the Supplication
(2 Corinthians 1:1-14)

Paul an Apostle of Jesus Christ, by the will of God, and Timothy the brother, to the Church of God which is in Corinth with all the saints that are in the whole (throughout) Achaia, grace be to you and peace from God our Father and the Lord Jesus Christ.

Blessed is God, the Father of our Lord Jesus Christ, the compassionate Father (the Father who bestows mercies) of all comfort, He that comforts us in all our tribulation to the end that we may be able to comfort you who *are involved* in every tribulation and the comfort wherewith we are comforted ourselves of God; for as the sufferings of Christ befall us abundantly, so through Christ's agency does our consolation also abound. So *on the one hand* whether we undergo tribulation it is for your comfort and salvation who works in *your* patient enduring the same sufferings which we also suffer (and our hope of *you that will so steadfastly endure*, is unshaken) or whether *on the other hand* we are consoled *here again* it is for your comfort and salvation, for you know that as you share our sufferings *with us*, so *you will also share* our comfort. *I speak of our sufferings* for we would not have you ignorant, neither about the tribulation which befell us in Asia, how that beyond measure and beyond our powers (of endurance) we were oppressed, so that we utterly despaired even of life, but (*this was not without a good purpose for*) we have had the answer of death in ourselves (*in our own hearts*) that we may not place our confidence in ourselves, but in God who raises the dead; who delivered us from so great a death and is delivering us (ῥύσεται) on whom we have rested our hopes that he will still deliver us, while you too deliver your joint aid on our behalf in your supplication that so for the gift *bestowed* on us by *the intercession* of many, thanks may be given by many persons on our behalf.

For our boasting is thus, the testimony of our conscience that in godly singleness (*of heart*) and sincerity, not in fleshly wisdom but in the grace of God, we walked (in our conversation) in the world, and especially *in our dealings* with you.

For we write none other things, but only those which you read, or even acknowledge *without their being written*, and I hope you will acknowledge them to the end, as also you did acknowledge us in part, how that we are your boast, even as you also are ours, in the day of our Lord Jesus.[1]

TEXTUAL ISSUES

The Title—is πρός Κορίνθιας B with A, B, C [?], K, l.

Vs. 6—the Textus Receptus has no authority. It differs from the correct reading (B, D, E, F, K etc) by placing ἡ ἐλπὶς ἡμῶν βεβαία ὑπὲρ ὑμῶν after the second παρακλήσεως καὶ σωτηρίας. It ought to come after πάσχομεν. A third reading (supported by A, C, syr. Eth. etc.) leaves out καὶ σωτηρίας in the second clause, and transfers the whole clause τῆς ἐνεργουμένης ἐν ὑπομονῇ τῶν αὐτῶν παθημάτων thither.

Vs. 8—ὑπέρ, so Tischendorf, B, K, Theoph. etc. Lachmann

περί—with A, C, D, E, F, etc.

Omit ἡμῖν—A, B, C, D, F, Jerome. Tischendorf previously retained it.

ὑπὲρ δύναμιν after ἐβαρήθημεν with Tischendorf rather than before it as Lachmann.

Vs. 10—καὶ ῥύεται—D, S, K, l, syr. Peshit.

καὶ ῥύσεται—B, C, G, arm, cop, etc.

Omit—A, D*, d, e.

Order of renderings as ranked above. The second reading was corrupted by the following ῥύσεται, though it is the more difficult reading. The omission happened to simplify the text. I believe on the whole that Meyer is right in retaining ῥύεται for the reason which he gives, ῥύσεται would naturally be written by a careless scribe, after ἐρρύσατο ἡμᾶς without regard to what follows.

---

[1] All the italicized words are underlined in the handwritten original of Lightfoot.

Vs. 12—ἁπλότητι—D, E, F, G, L vulgate, so Tischendorf. ἁγιότητι—A, B, C, K, cop, arm, Clem., Or., Lact. In favor of this last rendering is that it is found nowhere else in St. Paul. ἁπλότητι is found at Eph 6:5; Col 3:22. ἁπλότητι seems not to have satisfied the copyists who substituted ἁγιότητι.

Vs. 16—Lachmann's reading ἀπελθεῖν seems plausible, though not so well supported.

COMMENTARY

Vs. 1—Achaia—the church at Cenchreae (Rom 16). At an early date there were large and flourishing churches in Greece as may be inferred from Melito, cf. Denys, *Cor.* p. 118.

Vs. 8—ὑπὲρ τῆς θλίψεως . . . τῆς γενομένης ἐν τῇ Ἀσίᾳ. This is not sufficiently explained by the tumult in Ephesus (Acts 19). It is quite possible indeed that St. Paul may have incurred some personal danger, though this does not appear in the narrative. But this will not account for the language here. Besides the plural ἡμᾶς would include Timothy, and Timothy was absent at the time of the outbreak. It cannot refer, as some think, to a severe illness, for that would scarcely come under the category of τὰ παθήματα τοῦ Χριστοῦ. In the absence of any direct evidence the historian can only approximate a solution.

The language here seems to refer not to some *momentary* danger, as that at Ephesus must have been, if there was any danger at all. We are not led to believe by St. Luke's narrative that St. Paul was in any personal danger, though with a sudden outbreak of popular feeling this is possible. Rather this seems to refer to some *continuing* suffering whether from external persecution, from bodily sickness, or from mental suffering. Consider the language here—θλίψεως, ὑπὲρ δύναμιν ἐβαρήθημεν, ἐξαπορηθῆναι. Meyer's remark is very pertinent—namely that it must come under the category of τὰ παθήματα τοῦ Χριστοῦ, else it would not be a case in point, and therefore cannot be a severe illness as some think.

Compare 1 Cor 16:9—καὶ ἀντικείμενοι πολλοί, and again 1 Cor 15:32—εἰ κατὰ ἄνθρωπον ἐθηριομάχησα ἐν Ἐφέσῳ. He seems therefore to have been exposed to some steady, continuous persecution. And the persecution had not ceased, as we can infer from 2 Cor 1:10. The solution offered in vs. 10 seems probable and if so it is strengthened by Acts 20:3 where we read that on the occasion of the visit to Corinth which he was now projecting, he had to alter the plan of departure, owing to a conspiracy of the Jews.

ὑπὲρ δύναμιν—beyond our (unassisted) power (of endurance).

ἐξαπορηθῆναι—'we were utterly at a loss.'

Vs. 9—ἀλλὰ—Meyer translates 'im.' It is rather 'but *it was all working for our good, for . . .*'

ἐσχήκαμεν—'we have had' and so the effect remains. This circumstance has taught us where to place our confidence.

ἀπόκριμα—is a hapax in the New Testament and the LXX. The reading can never have been κατακριμα which is 'the answer' i.e. 'When we inquired of ourselves what was the fate which awaited us, our hearts gave answer that we should die.'

τῷ ἐγείροντι τοὺς νεκρούς—'Denn der Todtenerwecker muss auch der Retter sein können aus Todesgefahr'—Meyer. One who can raise the dead can *a fortiori* deliver from the fear of death.

Vs. 10—ἐκ τηλικούτου θανάτου—'so fearful a death.' The death here would not be death actually, but a long course of suffering. 1 Cor 15:31—καθ' ἡμέραν ἀποθνήσκω. 2 Cor 4:10—πάντοτε τὴν νέκρωσιν τοῦ Ἰησοῦ ἐν τῷ σώματι περιφέροντες.

ῥύεται—ῥύσεται—This seems to show that the danger was still threatening. Perhaps from the words ἐν τῇ Ἀσίᾳ (note it is not 'in Ephesus'), we may conclude that it was not confined to one place; and from this passage it seems to have followed St. Paul into Macedonia. We are reminded by this of a persecution from his own countrymen, the Jews, who drove him from town to town on a former occasions (Acts 13–14). It is not unlikely that this θλίψις may have been of a similar kind.

ἠλπίκαμεν—perfect tense, 'have rested our hopes,' 'on whom our hopes are set.'

Vs. 11—συνυπουργούντων—i.e. with the other churches. Meyer—'Daher καὶ ὑμῶν, auch ihn.' Perhaps 'aiding me.'

ἵνα ἐκ πολλῶν προσώπων τὸ εἰς ἡμᾶς χάρισμα διὰ πολλῶν εὐχαριστηθῇ ὑπὲρ ἡμῶν. I have no doubt that Meyer's order is right, taking διὰ πολλῶν with ἐν τῇ ἡμέρᾳ τοῦ Κυρίου ἡμῶν Ἰησοῦ (2 Cor 1:14) and comparing Thucy. i.18. διὰ πολλῶν = τὸ διὰ πολλῶν, the article being often omitted in St. Paul's letters. Cf. notes on 1 Thess 1:1, p. 4.

χάρισμα—i.e. his deliverance.

εὐχαριστηθῇ—See notes on 1 Thess 1:2 (p. 6) for the meaning.

προσώπων—'persons,' not as Stanley has it. On what Προσώπα cannot mean 'Antlitze' (countenance)—Munch, Black, Misener. On Προσώπων see Meyer, Wettstein.

Observe the antithetical character of the sentence—

ἐκ πολλῶν προσώπων answered by διὰ πολλῶν

εἰς ἡμᾶς answered by ὑπὲρ ἡμῶν

χάρισμα answered by εὐχαριστηθῇ.

δέησις (supplication—especial) προσευχή (prayer—general).

Vs. 12—γὰρ. The Apostle goes on to justify it. So Meyer (rejected in his second edition?).

καύχησις—(not καύχησα). 'Our boasting' (noting the subject of our boasting). The boasting is nothing more or less than the witness of our conscience. Contrast the καύχησις here with the καύχησα below. 'For our boasting, our confidence, is this. Our assurance, and so our vaunt, that you will aid us, arises from a consciousness that we acted in all sincerity towards you' (συνειδήσεως).

ἁγιότητι only occurs elsewhere at Heb 12:10. See notes on 1 Thess 3:13 (p. 56).

σαρκικῇ—i.e. human wisdom. On σαρκικῇ/σαρκινος see notes on 1 Cor 3:1 p. 48.

ἐν τῷ κόσμῳ opposed to πρὸς ὑμᾶς.

εἰλικρινείᾳ τοῦ Θεοῦ—sincerity which comes from God.

Vs. 13—οὐ γὰρ ἄλλα . . . ἀλλ' ἤ. ἀλλ' ἤ only elsewhere in the New Testament in Luke 12:51, and 1 Cor 3:5 (and in the latter passage it is possibly not genuine, though grammatically quite legitimate). After ἄλλα, it is very unusual cf. Pl. Phod. P. 97 and Self [?] ii. par. 773,5.

οὐ γὰρ ἄλλα γράφομεν ὑμῖν ἀλλ' ἢ ἃ ἀναγινώσκετε—'What I wrote is not equivocal.' I write nothing else besides what the obvious sense of the words convey to you on reading it.

ἢ καὶ ἐπιγινώσκετε—or even recognize (as true), even without their being stated in writing.

On the sort of play on words ἀναγινώσκετε . . . ἐπιγινώσκετε see Giesler.

ἐπιγίνωσις in St. Paul has a special sense, but this does not apply to this present passage.

Vs. 14—It is better to connect ὅτι καύχημα ὑμῶν etc. (vs. 14) with καθὼς καὶ ἐπέγνωτε etc. rather than with Meyer, who takes the latter clause as parenthetical. ὅτι—'that' not 'for.' With Lette [?] and others.

ἀπὸ μέρους—There seems to be no reference here to the Apostle's opponents. The rebuke is out of place. You have recognized it partially, but not as hereafter you will recognize it. Like the ἐκ μέρους in 1 Cor 13:9.

ἐν τῇ ἡμέρᾳ τοῦ Κυρίου ἡμῶν Ἰησοῦ. In the expression ἕως τέλους and to some extent with ἐν τῇ ἡμέρᾳ τοῦ Κυρίου ἡμῶν Ἰησοῦ we see the Apostle's anticipation of the near approach of the Lord's Day, yet the anticipation is vague and undefined. ἐν τῇ ἡμέρᾳ τοῦ Κυρίου ἡμῶν Ἰησοῦ refers to both clauses equally in vs. 14 and ἐσμεν does not militate against this. It is anticipatory i.e. in the day when all things are revealed in their true light.

Vs. 15—πρότερον ἐλθεῖν πρὸς ὑμᾶς (the correct word order) and πρότερον to be taken with this clause, not with ἐβουλόμην, 'before (visiting Macedonia, the now impending visit), that you might receive the benefit of a second visit (a visit on my return as well).'

πρότερον is explained by the δευτέραν.

χάρις—i.e. the conferring of spiritual gifts (χαρίσματα) by the presence of the Apostle (cf. Rom 1:11). χάρις is not to be taken as χαρὰν, a mistake that is charged unjustly to Chrysostom. What Chrysostom says is that the benefit here mentioned is the *joy* that his presence would afford.

Vs. 16—δι' ὑμῶν διελθεῖν v.l. ἀπελθεῖν. On the former verb used—Rom 15:28, on the latter 1 Cor 16:5.

ὑφ' ὑμῶν προπεμφθῆναι εἰς τὴν Ἰουδαίαν is the latter part of the intention. He was frustrated by a plot of the Jews (cf. Acts 20:2) so that ultimately Macedonia got the double visit instead of Corinth.

Vs. 17—μήτι ἄρα—μή looks for a negative answer, ἄρα expresses a degree of uncertainty in the speaker as to the answer he will receive.

κατὰ σάρκα—'from mere human motives,' like κατὰ ἄνθρωπον in 1 Cor 15:32.

ἵνα ᾖ παρ' ἐμοὶ . . . that strong affirmation and strong negation should have place with me i.e. that I shall strongly affirm a thing and then afterwards as strongly deny it, so that there be no fixity in my plans. The context seems imperatively to demand this sense. Otherwise we should be disposed (if only on account of the repetition of the article τό) to accede to the interpretation of the Greek commentators adopted by Winer and others 'that my yes should be yes, and that my no should be no' i.e. 'That I should stick to what I said through thick and thin' (cf. James 5:12). This literal interpretation however is certainly more in accordance with the Greek and is adopted by all the Greek commentators.

For the doubling of the ναὶ see Mt 5:37 and Wettstein and Midrash Tehillim viii.3 (and cf. the nickname of Richard I—*oui et non*).

τῇ ἐλαφρίᾳ—the lightness with which I am charged. The sense 'Leichtsinn as solcher überhaupt, in abstracto' (Winer, Meyer) can have no place here, where he is speaking of a concrete act. Cf 1 Cor 16:1.

Vs. 18—'But God is true, for . . .' 'Getreu erweist sich Gott dadurch dass etc.'—Meyer. It is often taken as an adjuration (so E.V.) and Rom 14:11 is compared. But the use of πιστὸς ὁ Θεὸς in the other passages in 1 Cor 1:9; 5:13; 1 Thess 5:24 is against this interpretation. Cf. a similar expression in 2 Cor 11:10—ἔστιν ἀλήθεια Χριστοῦ ἐν ἐμοὶ (cf. Rom 4:1). This does not seem to be the correct way of stating the argument. The truthfulness of God is confirmed in the trustworthiness of our preaching to you: 1) the truthfulness of God is concerned in this matter, for (2 Cor 1:21-22) we are under the guidance of God's Spirit; and 2) this truthfulness is established (2 Cor 1:18) for we preached Jesus Christ, and He is the confirmation of all God's promises and therefore he established the truth of all of them. Therefore, our preaching is true. The whole stress of the argument here depends on the assumed connection between the life of the preacher, and the subject of his preaching. The doctrine which he taught must mold his character. If there is fickleness in the one, there is fickleness in the other.

Vss. 19-22—Meyer who takes ὁ λόγος (2 Cor 1:18) not of 'our preaching' but of 'our professions' and promises. He consequently states the syllogism thus: 1) Seeing that God has bound us fast with Christ and consecrated us and given us the Spirit, God would stand in contradiction to Himself, if we did not also bear the character of Christ (vss. 21-22); 2) but the character of Christ is not uncertainty, but certainty has been found in Him (vs. 19, 20); 3) Therefore, that which is affirmed (in 2 Cor 1:18) cannot be questioned.

Vs. 19—ὁ τοῦ Θεοῦ γὰρ Υἱὸς Χριστὸς Ἰησοῦς—τοῦ Θεοῦ is very emphatic. δι' ἐμοῦ καὶ Σιλουανοῦ καὶ Τιμοθέου—to mark the first preaching of the

Gospel at Corinth. Meyer therefore does not mention the others, who are mentioned to avoid any appearance of self-assertion.

Σιλουανοῦ—This form of the name always in St. Paul and St. Peter (1 Pet 5:12). Silas is a connection link between the two apostles. He appears to have parted with St. Paul at the end of the second missionary tour, perhaps at Jerusalem and then to have joined St. Peter. See notes on 1 Thess 1:1 p. 2.

Σιλουανοῦ καὶ Τιμοθέου—Silas mentioned before Timothy as in the Thessalonian Epistles as being associated with Paul in his work before Timothy (cf. Acts 15).

οὐκ ἐγένετο Ναί καὶ Οὔ—was not found to be involved in uncertainty. Ναί must be taken to be the nominative with γέγονεν. For to say nothing of the harshness of the construction Χριστὸς γέγονεν Ναί ἐν αὐτῷ, (i.e. ἐν Χριστῷ for ἐν αὐτῷ), the following verse requires it—ἐν αὐτῷ τὸ Ναί.

ἀλλὰ Ναί ἐν αὐτῷ γέγονεν—'but verification has been found in Him' fulfillment of all that was foretold. Observe the changes in tense from ἐγένετο to γέγονεν.

Vs. 20—In the previous verse we had ναί without the article. Here it is added. There it was confirmation 'indefinitely.' Here it is 'the confirmation of the special promises' ὅσαι γὰρ ἐπαγγελίαι. The verification (i.e. fulfillment of all the promises).

διὸ καὶ δι' αὐτοῦ—The correct reading. Meyer has an admirable note on τὸ Ναί and τὸ Ἀμήν. τὸ Ναί is the objective truthfulness. τὸ Ἀμὴν is the subjective confidence. [A long quotation from Meyer follows here; it is now too difficult to decipher.] Cf. 1 Cor 14:16.

τῷ Θεῷ πρὸς δόξαν—'to the glory of God'

δι' ἡμῶν—through our preaching.

Vs. 21—ὁ δὲ βεβαιῶν ἡμᾶς 'who makes us steadfast,' 'confirms,' 'holds us fast' with accusative of a person as in 1 Cor 1:8; Col 2:17; Heb 13:9

ἡμᾶς σὺν ὑμῖν—'us and you alike'

εἰς Χριστὸν—towards Christ.

Χριστὸν, χρίσας. Of the latter term, cf. 1 John 2:20, χρῖσμα, where it is said that the χρῖσμα τῆς ἀληθείς ἔστι, by which unction the Christian is made prophet and king and priest.

Vs. 22—ὁ καὶ σφραγισάμενος—σφραγισάμενος is a middle, 'to set one's own seal on,' cf. Eph 1:13 where the sealing and the earnest are once again joined together (also Eph 4:30). cf. 2 Cor 3:2-3.

τὸν ἀρραβῶνα τοῦ Πνεύματος—'Der Genit. 1st G. Apposition. wie 1. Kor. 5,8: das Angeld, welches in dem Geiste besteht.'

Meyer. And this seems to be correct, cf. Eph 1:13 (though Meyer afterwards explains it incorrectly). Otherwise we might compare Rom 8:23—τὴν ἀπαρχὴν τοῦ Πνεύματος.

ἀρραβῶνα shortened into ἀρραβα Plautus nc[?] 3.20; cf. Aulus Gellius xvii.2.21—*arrabo* and especially *arrba* are condemned by Gellius. Stanley blunders. See Trench, *Study of Words*, p. 125.

Why a Further Visit Failed to Happen
(2 Corinthians 1:23–2:17)

1:23—Ἐγὼ δὲ 'But for my own part'

ἐπὶ τὴν ἐμὴν ψυχήν—'nach meiner Seele hin.' But there is some objection to the common reading—'against my soul.' On Meyer's objection see Josh 24:22. For the strength of the objection cf. Rom 9:3.

The expression φειδόμενος ὑμῶν was dictated not by tyranny but by sympathy.

Vs. 24—He corrects any false impression which his use of the word φειδόμενος might create. 'By speaking of sparing you, I do not mean to imply that we are lords over your faith.'

Συνεργοί—fellow workers.

τῇ γὰρ πίστει ἑστήκατε—'For it is by your faith that you stand' and therefore your faith must be allowed free action, it must not be lorded over by anyone. It is a matter between yourself and God. Cf. Rom 11:20. Meyer is wrong about this.

2:1—Read πάλιν ἐν λύπῃ with all the best authorities.

Read πρὸς ὑμᾶς ἐλθεῖν with Lachmann, and not as Tischendorf. The versions are of no authority in determining such a point and discarding these the weight of the testimony is with Lachmann.

Vs. 3—The words ἐπὶ λύπην inserted in many authorities seem to be genuine unless they be imported in from Phil 2:27.

Vs. 7—omit μᾶλλον with Lactanius?

Vs. 9—εἰ—See Lachmann—ἦ with the absolut.

Vs. 10—Read ἐγὼ ὃ κεχάρισμαι, εἴ τι κεχάρισμαι with Tischendorf (and A, B, C, D, F, G, it) not as the Textus Receptus—εἴ τι κεχάρισμαι, ᾧ κεχάρισμαι.

Vs. 16—Insert ἐκ before θανάτου and ζωῆς with Tischendorf.

Vs. 17—Read οἱ λοιποί and not οἱ πολλοί. οἱ λοιποί is well supported and οἱ πολλοί is evidently a correction of a transcriber who could not allow such a sweeping condemnation of the other teachers understood in part as contained in οἱ λοιποί. He seems to have considered that it implied all the other teachers except Paul and Silas and Timothy were included under this charge. To get out of such an imaginary implication, the text was altered.

COMMENTARY

2:1—ἔκρινα δὲ ἐμαυτῷ—the latter word means not 'in myself' but 'for myself' ('im Bezeichnung an mich selbst'—Meyer). 'I came to this verdict in regards my conduct.' He decided upon this course [of action] for himself.

μὴ πάλιν ἐν λύπῃ—Not to pay you a second visit of sorrow. λύπῃ here is natural grief. Cf. 2 Cor 2:2, 5.

Vs. 2—For it would be unnatural that I should grieve you, since I should be grieving those who are the source of my own gratification.

καὶ τίς does not in itself signify inconsequence or inconsistency—it simply binds the two propositions together, and by thus placing them in juxtaposition shows how irreconcilable they are. Cf. Winer, p. 514. τίς here is not the offender, but the Corinthian Church generally.

Vs. 3—ἔγραψα τοῦτο αὐτὸ

Questions—1) Does ἔγραψα refer to the present or the previous letter? Is it 'I write' (epistolary aorist), or 'I wrote'? 2) Does τοῦτο αὐτὸ refer to the contents or the object of the letter? Is it 'this very thing' or 'this very account'?

With regard to 1) the ἐκ γὰρ πολλῆς θλίψεως καὶ συνοχῆς καρδίας can hardly describe the Apostle's state of mind when he wrote the Second Epistle. Cf. 2 Cor 7:6 sq., 2 Cor 7:13. Below, when he is speaking of the Second Epistle, he uses different language—in 2 Cor 2:9-10. With regard to 2), 1) being settled, if ἔγραψα τοῦτο αὐτὸ means 'I wrote this very thing,' then τοῦτο αὐτὸ must refer either a) to the continuation of the irregularities in the Corinthian Church, but there is no sufficient distinct reference to that in the immediate context of the phrase τοῦτο αὐτὸ or b) it refers to the change of intention, but obviously from the next verse it refers to something far more important and more likely to grieve the Corinthians. Therefore, I take τοῦτο αὐτὸ to mean 'this very account' cf. 2 Peter 1:5.

τοῦτο αὐτὸ in the sense of 'for this very purpose' is foreign to St. Paul's usage (Meyer), and besides that it is quite inconsistent with the order of the words καὶ ἔγραψα τοῦτο αὐτὸ (though authorities differ on this). Again to translate it 'I put in writing the same thing' seems to me unnatural, especially as there is nothing to which τοῦτο αὐτὸ can be referred. On the whole, perhaps it is better with Chrysostom, Oc., Theophyl., Erasmus, Grot. to refer τοῦτο αὐτὸ to this present Epistle, which agrees well with ἐκ γὰρ πολλῆς θλίψεως καὶ συνοχῆς καρδίας ἔγραψα ὑμῖν (2 Cor 2:4). In this case οὐχ ἵνα λυπηθῆτε will be not to grieve you, not to rebuke you. τὴν ἀγάπην ἵνα γνῶτε ἣν ἔχω περισσοτέρως εἰς ὑμᾶς refers much more suitably to this Epistle.

πεποιθὼς ἐπὶ πάντας

For the reading sorrow upon sorrow (λύπη ἐπὶ λύπη) see Philostratus.

Vs. 5—On τις as the offender, see the comments of Tertullian, *de Prescrip.* c. 13.

ἀλλὰ ἀπὸ μέρους, ἵνα μὴ ἐπιβαρῶ, πάντας ὑμᾶς—But all of you, to a certain extent (that I may not be too hard on the offender). The opposition is between οὐκ ἐμὲ and ἀλλὰ . . . πάντας ὑμᾶς (as Meyer, truly) for the position of οὐκ ἐμὲ requires this opposition.

Vs. 6—ἡ ἐπιτιμία—E.V. is wrong. Not in the classical sense where ἡ ἀτιμία = to the Classical ἐπιτιμίον.

ἡ ὑπὸ τῶν πλειόνων seems to denote merely the legitimate way of punishing the offender.

Vs. 8—To stamp and ratify—i.e. by an outward act for the restoration of the offender.

Vs. 9—ἔγραψα here seems evidently to refer to our present Epistle—'for this was my object in writing this letter, that I may know the proof of you, whether you are obedient in all things' (i.e. in forgiving now as you were condemning before). And whether εἰς τοῦτο refers to what precedes or what follows, the reference to the Second Epistle seems required. From the connecting particle γὰρ it is evident that εἰς τοῦτο refers to what follows.

Vs. 10—ἐν προσώπῳ Χριστοῦ 'in the sight of Christ' (cf. 2 Cor 4:6 where the same phrase occurs however without leading to a solution), or does it mean 'in the person of Christ' (cf. 1 Cor 5:4)? Yes certainly so, cf. however Prov 8:30 which supports the former. The forgiveness now, as the punishment before was rendered in the name and person of Christ. For the connection between God's presence and the deliberations, see Acts 15.

Κεχάρισμαι—Must be transitive for the sense so obviously requires it. The instances of the aorist in the intransitive do not affect the perfects.

δι' ὑμᾶς—He loses sight of the subordinate reasons. One of these would be the redeeming of the offender but this is for the moment neglected, in the consideration of the general weal of the Corinthian Church. Cf. 2 Cor 2:5 and 2 Cor 7:12.

Vs. 11—ὑπὸ τοῦ Σατανᾶ. Compare the expression used of the offender in 1 Cor 5:5.

Vs. 12—δὲ—returning to the main subject after the digression from 2 Cor 2:5-11.

See *Journal of Philology*, iii, p. 97.

θύρας μοι ἀνεῳγμένης ἐν κυρίῳ—cf. 1 Cor 16:9. The expression shows how far the metaphor had retained from the background.

τὴν Τρῳάδα—See Stanley.

εἰς τὸ εὐαγγέλιον τοῦ Χριστοῦ—subjective not objective genitive (Meyer).

Vs. 13—ἔσχηκα cf. Rev 5:7 and 2 Cor 1:9. We cannot however suppose that it is equivalent to an aorist.

ἄνεσιν τῷ πνεύματί cf. on 2 Thess 1:7 (notes p. 6).

ἀποταξάμενος—See Sween [?] *Lex. Nov. Test.* s.v.

On ἐξῆλθον see Stanley.

Vs. 14—St. Paul here loses himself in a thanksgiving, the thanksgiving leads to a review of his position as a minister of the Church, and his relationship to the Corinthians. He works around to the old topic in 2 Cor 7:5.

θριαμβεύοντι—cf. Wettstein and Meyer. See Col 2:15 and cf. 1 Cor 4:9. The E.V. not unaccountably wrong inasmuch as verbs ending in ευω can have both a transitive and an intransitive sense.

τὴν ὀσμὴν—fragrance, which consists in the knowledge of Christ.

αὐτοῦ i.e. Χριστῷ. The ὀσμὴν will refer more naturally to the incense being used during the Triumph (see Thucy. Tacit. Ad. iv.2.50) rather than to the sacrifice, though the sacrifice is the metaphor in Eph 5:2.

Vs. 15—Here the application of the metaphor is changed. The Apostles are no longer the captives led in the Triumph, but the incense offered up.

For instances of St. Paul turning about a metaphor see e.g. 1 Thess 2:7 (and notes p. 25).

τοῖς σωζομένοις καὶ ἐν τοῖς ἀπολλυμένοις—Cf. notes on 1 Cor 1:18 (p. 18).

Vs. 16—Apparently using language common with Jewish teachers. Thus the law was called 'odoramentus vito Israelites' 'odoramentus mortis Gentiles.' Is the image of the Triumph lost sight of here or not? No! cf. especially Josephus, *Bell. Jud.* vii.5.6; Cicero, *Ver.* ii.5.30.

Vs. 17—καπηλεύοντες—see Aeschylus Thet. 541. Blass seems to be right with regard to Aeschylus, but the καπηλεύοντες of Apostle here is more allied to the *cauponari* of Eunius. See Eun. *Ap.* Cicero *de. Offic.* 1.38—'. . . nec cauponantes bellum, sed belligerantes. Ferro, non auro vitam cernamus utrique.' The ideas involved here in this word then are 'making gain' and 'adulterating.'

EXCURSUS: ON THE USE OF THE FIRST PERSON PLURAL IN ST. PAUL'S EPISTLES

It is maintained by Mr. Conybeare (vol. i, p. 419 note 3, and vol. ii, p. 95 note 1) that St. Paul uses 'we' 'according to the idiom of many ancient writers' where a modern writer would use 'I' (see his former reference), or as he expresses it elsewhere (second reference), 'He uses ἐγώ frequently, interchangeably with ἡμεῖς and when he includes others in the ἡμεῖς, he specifies it.' In regard to 2 Corinthians in particular, Mr. Conybeare asserts (vol. ii, p. 95) 'that Timothy was not with him during the danger in Asia.' But this of course is presuming that the danger in question is the tumult in Asia (Acts 19). Mr. Conybeare then appears to entirely disconnect the use of the plural in 2 Corinthians from the plurality of persons in whose name the letter is written. Mr. Alford has a slovenly note (2 Cor 1:4) in which he seems to adopt the same view.

Accordingly, Mr. Conybeare professes to act upon this view. I shall not inquire here into what inconsistencies he is led and how far he is obliged to forsake his theory. Nor yet shall I lay much stress on the idiom of the epistolary 'we' which is much more common in Latin than in Greek. But I will offer two or three facts for consideration:

1.) The Epistles which are written in St. Paul's name alone are Romans, Galatians, Ephesians, 1, 2 Timothy, and Titus. In all of these, the singular is used when the writer is speaking in his own name. The plural is never so used. It is only employed where he speaks of himself as a member of a class, whether as a part of the class of ministers or Christ, or of the whole body of Christians generally. He also uses 'we' to refer to himself and the audience together.

2.) Of the other Epistles, those to the Philippians and to Philemon (after the opening salutation), adhere to the singular throughout. Phil 3:17 is only an apparent exception where there is a personal matter between Paul and his readers. The other letters use the plural (and in 1 Corinthians it occurs every now and then). The plural is very common in 2 Corinthians. In 1 and 2 Thessalonians the plural is very seldom departed from. As a general rule we may say that wherever the communication is more directly personal, there the singular is used, where it is more general, the plural is preferred. The plural is common as Paul identifies those whose names are added in the opening salutation with himself and with the ministry work.

Conclusions

We may conclude: 1) that the plural 'we' is not merely an epistolary 'we' but it is connected with the plurality of persons in whose name the Epistle is written; 2) that so far from being correct to translate it 'I' ordinarily, it is only to be so translated where the context shows that it clearly refers to the Apostle *alone*. 3) In every instance where the plural is used, we find that it will apply to those who are associated with the Apostle, as well as the Apostle himself (except perhaps in 1 Thess 3:1, 2 where however he distinctly states he is speaking of himself only—1 Thess 3:5); 4) There are passages where it is quite impossible to refer the plural to St. Paul alone, and where Mr. Conybeare has violated all rules of language in attempting so to restrict it e.g. 1 Thess 2:4—ἀλλὰ Θεῷ τῷ δοκιμάζοντι τὰς καρδίας ἡμῶν, where Mr. Conybeare translates 'as one who strives to please God, whose search tries *my heart*, although I might have been burdensome to you as being Christ's apostle.' And again 2 Cor 7:3—προείρηκα γὰρ ὅτι ἐν ταῖς καρδίαις ἡμῶν ἐστε εἰς τὸ συναποθανεῖν καὶ συνζῆν, which Mr. Conybeare renders 'I have said before that I have you in my heart, and live and die with "you"—(and in a third passage, 2 Cor 3:2 the error is stereotyped).' Now no one will deny that a King or an editor may employ the plural 'we' with propriety, but it may be questioned whether one could balk at 'our crowns' or 'our pens,' when only one person was meant. And thus, though the Apostle might say 'we' *he would not call himself apostles or speak of his hearts*; 5) But in very fact, Paul's own language shows that by the use of the plural he does generally include more than himself, for in particular cases he is careful to substitute the singular for the plural when he refers to himself personally, or in some other way to qualify the expression. Thus, in 1 Thess 2:18 St. Paul is careful to distinguish himself from the others who are included in the plural. Mr. Conybeare has avoided the inference by a loose and incorrect translation (cf. τὸ εὐαγγέλιον ἡμῶν with 'my Gospel,' and passages collected in the Notes on 1 Thess 1:5). See again διότι ἠθελήσαμεν ἐλθεῖν πρὸς ὑμᾶς, ἐγὼ μὲν Παῦλος καὶ ἅπαξ καὶ δίς (1 Thess 2:18), 'we were desirous of visiting you, (for my part, I have entertained the desire more than once), but' etc. Mr. Conybeare translates it 'wherefore I Paul (for my own part) would have returned to visit you.' [This will not do].[1]

[Here is a list Lightfoot drew up to make his point]

Romans 15:15—critical use of 'I' when he means 'I.'

1 Thess 2:18—ἐγὼ μὲν Παῦλος

1 Thess 3:5—διὰ τοῦτο κἀγώ, ἔπεμψα, . . . ὁ κόπος ἡμῶν.

1 Thess 5:27—Ἐνορκίζω ὑμᾶς τὸν κύριον.

2 Thess 2:5—ταῦτα ἔλεγον ὑμῖν.

2 Thess 3:17—Ὁ ἀσπασμὸς τῇ ἐμῇ χειρὶ Παύλου, ὅ ἐστιν σημεῖον ἐν πάσῃ ἐπιστολῇ· οὕτως γράφω.

ELSEWHERE IN 1 AND 2 THESSALONIANS WE HAVE THE PLURAL

Philippians always has the singular, and accordingly he speaks of Timothy in the third person (Phil 2:19).

Apparent exceptions Phil 3:17—καθὼς ἔχετε τύπον ἡμᾶς.

Phil 3:20—He uses the plural when speaking of himself with those he addresses, and the faithful generally.

Philemon—Philem 2—τῷ συστρατιώτῃ ἡμῶν, where ἡμῶν may include Philemon.

---

[1]Since this is the clear thrust and implication of what Lightfoot says throughout about careless exegesis, I have concluded the excursus this way so one will feel the full force of his complaint against those who are sloppy or inexact (Conybeare et al.). (BW3)

Philem 7—ἔσχον or ἔχομεν.

Elsewhere in Philemon the singular.

Romans, singular always, with the apparent exception of Rom 16:9—τὸν συνεργὸν ἡμῶν, which is entirely explicable as in 1 Corinthians.

1 Corinthians—singular throughout where the writer speaks of himself. Exceptions: 1) where he speaks of believers generally, as in 1 Cor 8:8; 2) when together with certain other persons e.g. Apollos and other preachers (e.g. 1 Cor 1:23; 2:6; 4:1, 9).

THE MINISTRY OF DEATH, AND
THE MINISTRY OF LIFE
(2 CORINTHIANS 3)

A PARAPHRASE

Will it be thought that in thus contrasting ourselves with false teachers that we are beginning again to recommend ourselves (as we have been obliged necessarily to do)? Surely, no one will suppose that like certain other persons we require letters of recommendation from others to you, or from you to others. You are yourselves our letter written in our hearts (which we bear about with us not as material documents but inscribed upon our inward conscience which bears witness that our working and preaching among you is a sufficient recommendation)—a letter too which is recognized, and so is read by all men, for it is manifest that you are a letter in the hand-writing of Christ to all (his finger has traced the characters in your souls, his sign-name is set upon you)—a letter which is borne about by us as ministers, from place to place, the characters whereof are traced not in ink but in the Spirit of the living God on no tablets of stone, but on tablets of flesh, I mean on men's hearts.[2]

But if this language betokens confidence, it must be remembered that we owe this confidence in regard to God (i.e. in our relations to Him, to Christ). It is not that we are competent before any judgment by our own unaided efforts, as if it depended only on our own resources, but our competence has God for its source for he has ever made us competent as ministers of a new

---

[2]There is no necessity for referring the καρδίαις here to anything different from the καρδίαις in vs. 2.

covenant, a spiritual and not a formal covenant, for the external form kills, but the inward Spirit gives life. Now if the dispensation of which death was a consequence, a dispensation of outward form written on stones was ushered in with glory, so that the sons of Israel would not look with steadfast gaze on the face of Moses, owing to the glory of his face, a glory which after all was fleeting and transitory, must we not a fortiori believe that the dispensation of the Spirit shall continue to be in glory, since if the dispensation which brings condemnation is glorious, a fortiori does the dispensation which brings righteousness (by our justification through Christ) abound in glory, nay the glory of the former covenant is no glory at all in this respect (comparatively) on account of the superior glory of the latter. For if the transitory was attended with glory, much more shall the enduring abide in glory [and this thought inspires us with hope].

Therefore, having such a hope (the expectation of this future glory), we use much plainness of speech and here as we just enforced the contrast between the two dispensations themselves by reference to the Old Testament history, may we carry the contrast further and apply it not only to the Christian dispensation itself, but also to the teachers and professors of Christianity.

Moses placed a veil over his face when he left off speaking to the people, and thus the brightness of his face faded away unperceived. By this was foreshadowed the future history of the race, it was a token that something would interfere with their spiritual vision, that they would not see to what the transitory ordinances of the Mosaic dispensation led; they would not discern how they were annulled in Christ. Nay we may apply this type of Moses in another way, a veil is over the face of the people of Israel, as there was a veil over the face of Moses. When they turn to the Lord, this veil will be removed, in the same manner as his was; and by turning to the Lord is meant communing with the Spirit, looking beneath the outward form of the Mosaic law, and discerning its inward meaning, and so of a necessity accepting the Christian dispensation as that to which the Mosaic pointed. And this communing with the Spirit will bring freedom. They will be relieved from the bondage of the law. For where the Spirit is, there is freedom. Now we all of us (we Christians) enjoy this freedom, for we all look with our face unveiled on the glory of the Lord, though at present only in a mirror and not as we shall see it hereafter, yet uninterruptedly, and not by snatches as Moses, and doing so we catch this reflection, a light is shone upon us; a gradual change is being wrought in us; we are advancing from glory to glory. Christ, the image of the invisible God, is being formed in us. And this is the result we rightly looked for, seeing that the Lord, whose glory we behold is the Spirit. Therefore, we have freedom to speak with much boldness.

Textual Issues

3:1—ἢ μὴ. Considerable authority for Εἰ μὴ.

The second συστατικῶν to be omitted.

Vs. 3—The best supported reading is καρδίαις.

Vs. 4—τοιαύτην as is implied in 2 Cor 2:16-17.

Vs. 5—Position of ἀφ᾽ ἑαυτῶν varies.

Vs. 7—ἐν γράμματι—correct reading, so Lachmann.

Vs. 9—τῇ διακονία to be read (with W+H).

Vs. 10—οὐ not οὐδὲ.

Vs. 13—αὐτοῦ not ἑαυτοῦ.

Vs. 15—Peshit. has ἂν ἀναγιγνώσκηται.

Vs. 17—Omit ἐκεῖ.

Commentary

Vs. 1—πάλιν See Stanley.

Εἰ μὴ—ironical.

ὥς τινες—probably the Judaizing teachers.

Vs. 3—διακονηθεῖσα ὑφ᾽ ἡμῶν probably does not refer to the amanuensis but rather to the bearer of the letter.

ἐν πλαξὶν καρδίαις σαρκίναις. See Aeschyl. *Prom.* 789.

Observe in this verse two circumstances that confuse the metaphor: 1) he confuses two different kinds of writing, on parchment and on tablets of stone; 2) he . . . s [?] about the metaphor. The ἐν ταῖς καρδίαις ἡμῶν (2 Cor 3:2) being understood in a somewhat different sense than the ἐν πλαξὶν καρδίαις σαρκίναις.

γινωσκομένη καὶ ἀναγινωσκομένη—This seems at first sight to contradict ἐν ταῖς καρδίαις ἡμῶν, for if the writing was traced in the mind and consciousness of Paul and Timothy, how could it be outwardly manifested? Meyer has a very good note on this—'So far as Paul and Timothy have the consciousness in their hearts, that they are recommended by the Corinthians themselves, these (i.e. the Corinthians) are a letter of recommendation written in their hearts, and still inasmuch as everyone is acquainted with the fact and the manner in which the Corinthians have served to recommend Paul and Timothy, this letter is recognized and read by all men. Thus, the letter has both the properties that would be contradictory in an actual letter, and the figure is not confused with the proper thing, but adapted to it.'

Here Christ is the penman and the Spirit the ink.

Vs. 5—Explaining the reason why God ἱκανοί ἐσμεν λογίσασθαί. The stages of the argument are then: 1) the superiority of the new covenant to the old is in its results; 2) the greater glory which consequently attaches to it (of which the present glory is an earnest); 3) the hope which Christians possess.

Vs. 6—καινῆς διαθήκης, not as the E.V. but with Alford. See Jer 31:31 quoted in Heb 8:8. What is described in Jeremiah is not of the letter but of the Spirit.

τὸ γὰρ γράμμα ἀποκτείνει—cf. 1 Cor 15:56 so that he goes on to 'the ministry of death.'

Vs. 7—ἡ διακονία τοῦ θανάτου. There is a double impact of the law—the obvious one is given in Rom 6:12, ἐν γράμμασιν.

On ἐν δόξῃ see the δεδόξασται in Exodus. See also Rom 4:4; Luke 2:32; 1 Cor 15:41.

Vs. 9—τῇ διακονίᾳ brings out the contrast better than ἡ διακονία.

Vs. 10—ἐν τούτῳ τῷ μέρει cf. 2 Cor 4:3 and 1 Pet 4:16.

Vs. 11—διὰ δόξης surpasses what was given ἐν δόξῃ.

Vss. 12-17—In Exodus 34:29 we are told that when Moses came down from the Mount, his face shone, so that at first the people were afraid to come near, that he called them to him, and he spoke to them, that having spoken, he draws the veil over his face. The veil remained there and was only withdrawn when Moses went in to speak to the Lord. He came out from the tent with his face uncovered after speaking with the Lord and he spoke to the people, each time drawing the veil over his face when he had finished speaking. In the E.V. of Exodus 34:33 for 'til' read 'when.' The translation there of the E.V. seems to have arisen from misconception of St. Paul's application here and the error has carried over to this passage and entirely confused the understanding of it.

Vs. 13—καὶ οὐ καθάπερ—See the introduction of comparison in Gal 3:6. πρὸς τὸ μὴ ἀτενίσαι—i.e. the divine Purpose is implied in the πρὸς as De Wette rightly says.

Vs. 14—ἀλλὰ ἐπωρώθη is attached to the μὴ ἀτενίσαι (not as Alford has it). St. Paul here passes from the type to the thing typified almost unconsciously. This is very common in Scripture and not uncommon elsewhere. See especially Aeschylus, *Agam.* 121sqq (in the prophecy) where type and antitype are mixed up in the same way. See Stanley.

μὴ ἀνακαλυπτόμενον—An accusative absolute, 'it not being revealed' not as the E.V. has it.

On the παλαιᾶς διαθήκης and the αὐτὸ κάλυμμα see Stanley.

Now from the end of vs. 14, the application is simple—We employ παρρησία openness, plainness of speech, we withdraw nothing, we conceal nothing. Herein the preaching of the new covenant differs widely from the promulgation of the old. There, there was something hidden, something unrevealed. This is symbolized by what we read of Moses. When the reflected glory of God (betokening the majesty of the covenant), shone upon his face at the giving of the law, he came out and spoke to the people, but when he had done speaking he covered his face. He would not let them see that glory fade away, thus symbolizing their future history, for their minds were hardened, and so to this day, when Moses speaks to them in the reading of the Old Testament, their same veil interferes with their seeing, they cannot see how it fades away, how it is annulled and abrogated in Christ.

Vs. 15—With vs. 15 the application of this passage in the Mosaic history is somewhat changed. Just as we saw in 2 Cor 2:14-17, where St. Paul employed the metaphor of the Roman triumphal procession, he was not careful to preserve the same application throughout. His exuberance of thought leads him to see a new analogy, but first he compares the Apostles and preachers of the Gospel to the captives led in the victor's train, and then again to the incense, which is scattered in the path. So here Moses with his face veiled is at first taken to symbolize the obscurity which hung over the Old Dispensation, hiding its meaning from the Jews, and afterwards the image denotes the faithful Jew who accepts the Gospel, for there is a veil hanging over his heart, as there was over the face of Moses, and the veil is only removed, like that of Moses, when he turns unto the Lord i.e. accepts the Gospel truth. Paul explains what is symbolized and meant by turning to the Lord—'the Lord is the Spirit' i.e. by turning to the Lord is meant, the abandonment of the weak and beggarly elements, the reading of the types and ordinances of the Mosaic Dispensation in a spiritual light, and so seeing that they lead to the Gospel as their proper end, and the consequent acceptance of Christianity. And where the Spirit of the Lord is, there is freedom. Hence the παρρησία (2 Cor 3:12) of those who commune with the Spirit. In the verse by verse he applies it to Christians. 'This freedom pertains to us, for we all . . . etc.'

'Now we all (not just the Apostles and teachers only but the whole body of Christians) have our face unveiled, whereas Moses veiled his face from time to time, the veil is never drawn over ours. And we see the glory of the Lord. We do not yet see the Lord as he is, but we still see His glory as in a mirror, but it is a mirror of perfect clarity in which His attributes are reflected, working in the church is the reflection, the image of the invisible God himself (εἰκὼν τοῦ Θεοῦ τοῦ ἀοράτου—Col 1:15; ἀπαύγασμα τῆς δόξης, Heb 1:3).' It is still however only in a mirror, as St. Paul says elsewhere (1 Cor 13:12), 'but hereafter, we shall see face to face.'

'But not only do we see this glory, we are transformed thereby. The radiance from the divine image is reflected back from the mirror on our own countenances, and like that of Moses, our faces are lit up by its brilliancy. But the glory which is then shed on us is more permanent and effective than that which shone on Moses.'

Vs. 16—cf. the words of the LXX here.

Vs. 17—ὁ Κύριος is the subject, τὸ πνεῦμα the predicate.

Vs. 18—κατοπτριζόμενοι cf. Philo *Leg. Alleg.* iii.33 (and Alford). See the passages in the *Schol. Hell.* here and on 2 Cor 4:4. Cf. Clement of Rome, i.36. 'No one has seen God at any time. The only begotten Son who is in the bosom of the Father, he has declared Him' (John 1:18). cf. 2 Cor 4:4 which carries out the idea here.

Μεταμορφούμεθα—distinguish μορφή (the essential form) from σχῆμα (the outward fashion). St. Paul's use of μορφή = the Greek philosophers' use of εἶδος. Cf. Rom 12:2—συνσχηματίζεσθε τῷ αἰῶνι τούτῳ, ἀλλὰ μεταμορφοῦσθε τῇ ἀνακαινώσει τοῦ νοός, (E.V. wrong here), cf. 1 Pet 1:14. Cf. also Phil 2:5-7—ὃς ἐν μορφῇ Θεοῦ ὑπάρχων οὐχ ἁρπαγμὸν ἡγήσατο τὸ εἶναι ἴσα Θεῷ, ἀλλὰ ἑαυτὸν ἐκένωσεν μορφὴν δούλου λαβών, ἐν ὁμοιώματι ἀνθρώπων γενόμενος· καὶ σχήματι εὑρεθεὶς ὡς ἄνθρωπος. And cf. 1 Cor 7:31—παράγει γὰρ τὸ σχῆμα τοῦ κόσμου τούτου. Cf. *Journal of Philology*, p. 114, 121.

'We then are transformed (undergo an essential change), and the new form we assume is τὴν αὐτὴν εἰκόνα, the same image which is reflected in the mirror.' This transformation is what is called elsewhere 'putting on Christ' (Rom 13:14) what is spoken of in Gal 4:19 as Christ being formed in us, οὗ μορφωθῇ Χριστὸς ἐν ὑμῖν. But this transformation is not sudden, the change is gradual. We advance from one grade of glory to a higher one. The glory on Moses' face faded away each time as he left the presence of the Lord and had to be renewed again; but with us it is different. We are constantly in His sight, and so instead of the reflected brightness which is coming and going, it is ever becoming more and more bright, i.e. more and more like the image from which it is reflected—Christ himself.

ἀπὸ Κυρίου πνεύματος—'as is natural since it comes from the Lord i.e. the Spirit.' Not as the E.V. has it. 'As then we have this close communication with the Spirit, and as there is freedom where the Spirit is present (see 2 Cor 3:17), we therefore are free and so πολλῇ παρρησίᾳ χρώμεθα, we use much plainness of speech.' Thus the assertion of 2 Cor 3:12 is justified and explained.

Eternal Treasures in Earthen Vessels (2 Corinthians 4)

Textual Issues

Vs. 1—ἐγκακοῦμεν. Textus Receptus—ἐκκακοῦμεν—C, D*, E, J, K etc. and the same v.l. in 2 Cor 4:16. Cf. 2 Thess 3:13 (p. 45 in my notes). ἐγκακοῦμεν is the Classical word, ἐκκακοῦμεν is found only in the New Testament and the Greek Fathers. It is probably therefore the reading here and the alteration has been made in order to substitute the more Classical word. 'Wahrscheinliche was ἐκκακοῦμεν damals nur in mündlichen Schanck [?] und ist erst durch Paulus und Lukas in die kirchliche Schriftsprache gekommen.'—Meyer.

Vs. 4—αὐτοῖς τὸν with D, E, J, K, Chr., others. Tischendorf omits with A, B, C, F, G, arm, it, Lat. αὐτοῖς seems to be inserted to make the construction plain.

Vs. 6—λάμψει—Best supported? Lachmann has this reading with A, B, D* and a few others.

τοῦ Θεοῦ—Others αὐτω which apparently is a correction to get rid of the repetition of the word Θεος.

Ἰησοῦ Χριστοῦ as the Textus Receptus has it is probably correct?

Vs. 14—σὺν Ἰησοῦ should be read for διὰ Ἰησοῦ (Textus Receptus).

Vs. 16—ὁ ἔξω ἡμῶν (latter word added in B, C, D, F, G sy. et al), read with Lachmann. ὁ ἔσωθεν is apparently a correction. And yet Meyer is perhaps right that ὁ ἔξω ἡμῶν has been read to balance the former clause of the sentence.

Vs. 17—ἐλαφρὸν. v.l.—πρός καιρὸν καὶ ἐλαφρὸν, a gloss of παραυτίκα.

COMMENTARY

Vs. 1—Διὰ τοῦτο which is further explained by ἔχοντες τὴν διακονίαν ταύτην, 'since we have this ministry' 'since this ministry with which we are entrusted is so glorious . . .'

καθὼς ἠλεήθημεν—The thought is that we owe all these privileges to the mercy of God, is calculated to stir us up to greater activity. See the 'Misericordia Dei' quote in Bengel.

i.e. not of ourselves cf. Rom 9:16.

ἐκκακοῦμεν, See Jerome here and my note on 2 Thess 3:13.

Vs. 2—ἀπειπάμεθα—'renounced,' 'warned off.'

τὰ κρυπτὰ τῆς αἰσχύνης—No limit should be placed to these words. St. Paul opposes with the openness of the Gospel the secrecy that conceals actions from shame. Put another way, Paul contrasts the openness and universality of the Gospel with the mysterious, esoteric character of other systems. The words τῆς αἰσχύνης have little to do with the context here, but is suggested by some definite system that is beyond our view.

δολοῦντες τὸν λόγον τοῦ Θεοῦ cf. 2 Cor 2:17—καπηλεύοντες τὸν λόγον τοῦ Θεοῦ and 2 Cor 3:1—συνιστάνειν. So St. Paul returns to the subject with which he closed 2 Cor 2.

πρὸς πᾶσαν συνείδησιν ἀνθρώπων—not exactly the 'everyman's' conscience, but rather every kind of conscience. Christianity is a response to the wants of man which addresses itself to the conscience.

Vs. 3—A sort of qualification of the statement at 2 Cor 3:13 sq.

τὸ εὐαγγέλιον ἡμῶν.

ἐν τοῖς ἀπολλυμένοις—'in the case of' rather than 'among.' Cf. 2 Cor 2:15.

Vs. 4—ἐν οἷς ὁ θεὸς τοῦ αἰῶνος τούτου ἐτύφλωσεν τὰ νοήματα τῶν ἀπίστων. The work of the Devil is to blind the minds of the unbelieving, and he has done his work in the case of these. The Church Fathers, Origen, Tertullian, Chrysostom, Augustine, Theophylact. etc. take τῶν ἀπίστων together with τοῦ αἰῶνος τούτου to get rid of the argument in favor of dualism—the Marcionites and the Manicheans (not as Stanley?).

On the phrase ὁ θεὸς τοῦ αἰῶνος cf. John 12:31—νῦν κρίσις ἐστὶν τοῦ κόσμου τούτου· νῦν ὁ ἄρχων τοῦ κόσμου τούτου ἐκβληθήσεται ἔξω and again John 16:30, and Eph 2:2; 6:12.

εἰς τὸ μὴ αὐγάσαι—αὐγάσειν seems in the Greek of this time to mean 'to shine' as always in the LXX. Meyer says that the sense 'to see' is rare and confined to a few poetical passages (act., Soph. *Phil.* 217; med., Il. Ψ 458; Eur. 554). Ought he not to have said that in earlier and purer Greek it is entirely a poetical word? His list is certainly not exhaustive cf. Eur. *Rhes.* 793 and yet he says 'im activo nur Soph. Phil. 217.'

φωτισμόν—'the illumination' not 'light' as in the E.V. φώτισμα, φωτισμὸς was the ecclesiastical term for baptism. See Sauer [?].

τοῦ εὐαγγελίου τῆς δόξης τοῦ Χριστοῦ—he here gives the subject of the Gospel.

Observe that the same idea is conveyed in αὐγάσαι, φωτισμόν, δόξης, εἰκὼν.

Vs. 5—The Gospel which we preach is the Gospel of the glory of Christ for . . . etc.

Χριστὸν Ἰησοῦν Κύριον—Jesus Christ, as Lord.

Vs. 6—Your servants for Jesus Christ's sake, since/for we have the commands of God and the commands of God we cannot resist. He gave this illumination so that it might 'shine before men.'

ὅτι ὁ Θεὸς ὁ εἰπών—'For it is God who bade the light to shine out of darkness (that shone in our hearts).'

ὁ εἰπὼν ἐκ σκότους φῶς λάμψει—An allusion to Gen 1:3. The same God who rules the physical world, rules the moral world also. In both he is the source of all light.

ἔλαμψεν—not transitive, for which sense the authority of the earlier Greek poets is not sufficient.

φωτισμὸν τῆς γνώσεως—subjective genitive—the illumination which proceeds from the knowledge.

προσώπῳ Χριστοῦ—to be attached to φωτισμόν with Meyer and not as Alford. 'In the face of Christ' cf. 2 Cor 3:7 to which there is a manifest allusion, but the sense of face and person cannot be separated here.

Vs. 7—In spite of Meyer's and Alford's notes, we can scarcely suppose that the reproach of his enemies was absent from his mind when he wrote this. It may not be written with any direct polemical aim, but it can scarcely have been written without any thought of the reproach uttered against him.

τὸν θησαυρὸν τοῦτον—i.e. the φῶς of which he has been speaking.

ὀστρακίνοις σκεύεσιν—in its literal sense 2 Tim 2:20, not only made of clay, but fragile, frail.

ὀστρακίνοις—a potsherd, a sort of disparaging vulgar term which in the later language has replaced the Classical κεράμοιν cf. caballus = ψωμίζειν.

ἵνα ἡ ὑπερβολὴ τῆς δυνάμεως ᾖ τοῦ θεοῦ καὶ μὴ ἐξ ἡμῶν· that the surpassing power (that is exhibited in our lives) may be due to God, and not proceed from any physical advantages which we possess (though even those must be ultimately assigned to Him alone). 2 Cor 4:8-11 are in fact an explanation of this phrase, showing how the power of God, is to be manifested.

Vs. 8—The participles are to be construed with Ἔχομεν in 2 Cor 4:7, but logically they depend on ἵνα ἡ ὑπερβολὴ τῆς δυνάμεως etc.

ἐν παντὶ—cf. 2 Cor 7:5, 11, 16; 8:7; 9:8, 11; 11:6, 9; 1 Cor 1:5; Eph 5:24; Phil 4:12. ἐν παντὶ cannot = πάντοτε, merely of time, for it is coupled with πάντοτε (cf. 2 Cor 9:8). In Phil 4:12 and 2 Cor 11:6 it is distinguished from ἐν πᾶσι. ἐν παντὶ would regard the character of things, ἐν πᾶσι simply the number of things. 'Under every circumstance,' 'in every respect.'

θλιβόμενοι (present) and ἀπορούμενοι (impending) = internal distress of mind

διωκόμενοι (impending persecution) and καταβαλλόμενοι (present persecution) = external distress of body. There is a climax here—distress of mind on account of present afflictions, perplexity about the future, superadded to present distress and actual persecution imminent, actual persecution raging and victorious. There is evidently a connection too, as Meyer says, between διωκόμενοι and καταβαλλόμενοι, but he does not extend the climax between these two chiasms.

In addition, ἐγκαταλειπόμενοι (*derelinguere*) means left in the lurch, left to fall into enemy hands. καταβαλλόμενοι means struck down, as by a dart.

Vs. 10—τὴν νέκρωσιν—a continuous process, not 'a state' of mortifying and killing and not a state of 'deadness.' Νέκρωσιν is elsewhere expressed by St. Paul in 1 Cor 15:31—καθ' ἡμέραν ἀποθνήσκω. On τὴν νέκρωσιν τοῦ Ἰησοῦ cf. 2 Cor 1:5 τὰ παθήματα τοῦ Χριστοῦ—i.e. we are in ' . . . ly' [?] or 'inherently' [?] [in] danger of death as Jesus was.

ἡ ζωὴ—Meyer seems to interpret this rightly, as our sufferings resemble the death of Jesus, so our deliverances resemble his resurrection.

Vs. 11—οἱ ζῶντες as naturally antagonistic to εἰς θάνατον παραδιδόμεθα obscures the words

οἱ ζῶντες . . . εἰς θάνατον παραδιδόμεθα

ἡ ζωὴ . . . ἐν τῇ θνητῇ σαρκὶ ἡμῶν which Alford has remarked on. This verse does not express any new thought beyond 2 Cor 4:10, but heightens the contrast between life and death.

Vs. 12—'And thus, death is active in us, but life in you' i.e. we are in constant peril of death, but each time we are delivered, our deliverance (our raising, as it were, to life), is a token to you of the power of Christ and his Gospel which also is active in you.

On ἐνεργεῖται cf. 1 Thess 2:13.

Vs. 13—ἔχοντες δὲ. Meyer takes this to be an explanation of ἐνεργεῖται, ἡ δὲ ζωὴ ἐν ὑμῖν. It works in you because the spirit of faith leads us to preach. It is better however to take it in opposition to the other clause ὁ θάνατος ἐν ἡμῖν. 'Though death is active in us . . . though having the same spirit . . .'

τὸ αὐτὸ πνεῦμα τῆς πίστεως—'the same spirit which is described in the language of the following verses.'

Ἐπίστευσα, διὸ ἐλάλησα LXX (so Vulgate), Ps 116:10. The Hebrew is הֶאֱמַנְתִּי כִּי אֲדַבֵּר which is thought to mean 'I believed, although I said "I am sore troubled."' But כִּי seems to have the meaning 'so, then' at the beginning of the apodosis, or turn of the sentence. See the note of Gesenius himself, though he translates it 'although.'

Vs. 14—Knowing that whatever may be the result of 'these deaths' (θάνατοι) that we die daily, whether we shall be delivered from them or not, still, from the actual and final death, when it comes, we shall be raised. And therefore the importance of 'these deaths' vanishes in comparison. Meyer's objection to taking this to refer to actual death is worthless, and is well answered by Alford.

Vs. 15—'And will present us with you . . .' with *you*, I say for everything is for your sake both our θλίψις and our παράκλησις cf. 2 Cor 1:6, 7.

Both of the words πλεονάσειν and περισσεύειν are apparently used transitively in 1 Thess 3:12. But this is the only instance in the New Testament (πλεονάσειν is found more than once in the LXX). Therefore it is better to take the intransitive?

περισσεύσῃ εἰς τὴν δόξαν τοῦ Θεοῦ. The construction is favored by comparison with 2 Cor 8:3.

ἡ χάρις—Grace as manifested in the salvation of men.

Πλεονάσασα—being multiplied, extended to a great number.

περισσεύσῃ εἰς τὴν δόξαν τοῦ Θεοῦ may redound to the glory of God.
διὰ τῶν πλειόνων τὴν εὐχαριστίαν—owing to the thanksgiving. The idea
is of the thanksgiving of the church and the honor paid to God thereby, as
the end of the Christian ministration, seems to have been present to the
mind of the Apostle while writing this Epistle. Cf. 2 Cor 1:11 and again 2 Cor
9:11, 12 where it is περισσεύουσα διὰ πολλῶν εὐχαριστιῶν τῷ Θεῷ.

Perhaps the most probable construction is ἵνα ἡ χάρις πλεονάσασα . . .
[?] διὰ τῶν πλειόνων.

Vs. 16—Returning to the subject of 2 Cor 4:1. ἐκκακοῦμεν, see 2 Cor 5:1.

εἰ καὶ—a concession—'granting that.'

Διαφθείρεται . . . ἀνακαινοῦται.

ἡμέρᾳ καὶ ἡμέρᾳ—יוֹם וָיוֹם

Vs. 17—Explaining the manner of this ἀνακαίνωσις.

τὸ γὰρ παραυτίκα—cf. Bengel—notates praesens here. 'Als "*terminus ad
quem*" ist die nahe Parusie gedacht' (Meyer).

καθ᾽ ὑπερβολὴν εἰς ὑπερβολὴν—καθ᾽ ὑπερβολὴν occurs six times in St. Paul
elsewhere, but εἰς ὑπερβολὴν never. Lit. 'in excess to excess' i.e. 'from one
degree of excess to a higher one.'

βάρος (and ἐλαφρόν), no notion of burdensomeness, but simply of
weight. It is viewed as a compensation weighed out. The αἰώνιον βάρος
δόξης is composed of τὰ μὴ βλεπόμενα which we strive to attain to.

Vs. 18—μὴ σκοπούντων—the condition. Do not look to, as our own. For
if we looked to τὰ βλεπόμενα and regarded them as our object, the compensation would not satisfy us. And therefore it is an αἰώνιον βάρος.

τὰ μὴ βλεπόμενα—indefinite. τὰ μὴ βλεπόμενα would be certain definite
things hidden from sight, which would not be so appropriate. 'Things not
seen' are almost of necessity indefinite. Alford's note is absurd.

OF TEMPORARY TENTS
AND ETERNAL HOUSES
(2 CORINTHIANS 5)

TEXTUAL ISSUES—VSS. 1-16

Vs. 3—εἴπερ—B, D, E, F, G τίνες ap. Chrysostom.
ἐνδυσάμενοι—2 Cor 5:1. ἐκδυσάμενοι which Tischendorf has, but with much inferior authorities.

Vs. 4—Omit τούτω, though there is considerable support for it.

Vs. 5—ὁ δούς—omit καὶ vs. the B.M.T.[1]

Vs. 10—κακόν (B.M.T.)—An overwhelming support for φαῦλον.

Vs. 12—Omit γὰρ on overwhelming testimony.
Lachmann—καὶ μὴ ἐν, probably it should be retained and ἐν read.

Vs. 15—Omit δέ.

Vs. 16—εἰ δὲ καὶ (B.M.T.) Omit the δὲ.

Vs. 17—Omit τὰ πάντα (B.M.T).

Vs. 21—Omit γάρ.
Read γενώμεθα for γινώμεθα (T.R.).

COMMENTARY

5:1—οἴδαμεν γάρ—We are assured that our present affliction is working out our future glory, for we know (i.e. we feel a conviction) . . .

---

[1]B.M.T. is the Byzantine Majority Text, and as is the case with the Textus Receptus, Lightfoot is convinced it often has the wrong readings, with an especial tendency to add words to make sentences smoother or more complete. (BW3)

ὅτι ἐὰν—'that if,' showing that in the Apostle's mind, that this was quite as supposable a case, as that they should remain until the coming of Christ.

ἡ ἐπίγειος ἡμῶν οἰκία τοῦ σκήνους—'this transitory abode.' The ὀστρακινον σκήνους, ἐπίγειος σκήνους both denoting its temporary character.

ἡμῶν οἰκία—'our house' which consists in this tent.

καταλυθῇ—taken to pieces as a tent, broken up, not as Alford has it.

ἔχομεν—present

οἰκοδομὴν—a permanent dwelling not a σκῆνος, i.e. the spiritual body of which St. Paul speaks (1 Cor 15:44).

Vs. 2—καὶ γὰρ—our restlessness in our present abode is an evidence that some more glorious dwelling awaits us.

'We have a conviction . . . for in our present tabernacle we groan.'

Στενάζομεν—is of one who feels himself pent up or confined, who seeks to be delivered from his prior house that he may enjoy his natural freedom and may have room to develop according to the law of his being—who groans and sighs for release. St. Paul elsewhere adduces this feeling as an evidence that the subject of it is destined to attain the higher state hereafter. See Rom 8:22-23— οἴδαμεν γὰρ ὅτι πᾶσα ἡ κτίσις συνστενάζει καὶ συνωδίνει ἄχρι τοῦ νῦν οὐ μόνον δέ, ἀλλὰ καὶ αὐτοὶ τὴν ἀπαρχὴν τοῦ Πνεύματος ἔχοντες ἡμεῖς καὶ αὐτοὶ ἐν ἑαυτοῖς στενάζομεν, υἱοθεσίαν ἀπεκδεχόμενοι, τὴν ἀπολύτρωσιν τοῦ σώματος ἡμῶν. The connection of ideas of groaning and confinement is well illustrated by 'As You Like It' ii.2.—'The wretched animal heav'd forth such groans / That their discharge did stretch his leather coat almost to bursting.'

Bengel—oikía est quiddam majus absolutem.

οἰκητήριον—domicilium respicit incolum [?].

τὸ ἐξ οὐρανοῦ—the *from* heaven (dwelling).

ἐπιποθοῦντες. Of the expectations of the Apostle, see 1 Cor 15:52, 53; 1 Thess 4:15.

Vs. 3—The εἴπερ of Lachmann is well supported.

ἐκδυσάμενοι must be rejected.

Whatever may be the exact meaning of εἴ γε καὶ Alford's and Meyer's interpretation can scarcely stand, for these particles cannot certainly affirm positively = ἐπει. In regard to εἴ γε all that can be said is that this phrase assumes that the balance of probabilities is rather in favor of the event occurring. Cf. Col 1:23. The addition of the καί removes the probability of the event's happening one degree further, for it shows that there are some difficulties in the supposition. Cf. Gal 3:4 where Chrysostom is right in considering that εἴ γε καὶ εἰκῇ, supposing it to be really in vain, implies a charitable hope that it was not.

Vs. 4—This verse is in justification of 2 Cor 5:2, being parenthetical and an explanation of the word ἐπενδύσασθαι.

ἐφ᾽ ᾧ οὐ θέλομεν ἐκδύσασθαι ἀλλ᾽ ἐπενδύσασθαι. The sense requires us to give this clause a slightly different translation from that which Alford has given it. Observe that it is ἐφ᾽ ᾧ not ἐπείδη, and the θέλομεν = 'we are not willing' *not* 'we are unwilling.' ἐφ᾽ ᾧ means 'under the circumstances that . . .' But the common interpretation seems to destroy the force of στενάζομεν and to ignore the connection καὶ γὰρ, while the objection to death it imparts to the Apostle is quite unworthy and contradictory to Phil 1:23. ἐφ᾽ ᾧ is much more general than ἐπείδη. It equals 'wherein' cf. Phil 3:12; 4:10. Consequently, it is = to either 'therefore' or 'because.'

The passage given by Alford from Xenophon, *Mem.* ii.1.17 is not a parallel to this for two reasons: 1) first, there is no καὶ, and this materially affects the sense; 2) and secondly the future tense there is of a quite different kind from that here. It expresses there a *destination*, whereas here it simply refers to future time.

The sense of εἴ γε καὶ in 2 Cor 5:3 depends on the word ἐπενδύσασθαι, for this word ἐπενδύσασθαι is only appropriate in case of the Lord's coming. We are still found ενδύσασθαι, that is 'in the body' and not 'out of the body' (γυμνοὶ). The ἐπενδύσασθαι is explained by 1 Cor 15:53—δεῖ γὰρ τὸ φθαρτὸν τοῦτο ἐνδύσασθαι ἀφθαρσίαν. And cf. 2 Cor 5:4.

οὐ θέλομεν—'it is not that we wish.' The common understanding says 'we groan and are afflicted because we are unwilling to die, and desire rather to be alive at the Lord's coming.' Meyer expresses it strongly—'weil im eine Antipathie davor haben.' On this see Bengel.

Vs. 5—τὸν ἀρραβῶνα τοῦ πνεύματος. Cf. 2 Cor 1:22.

ὁ δὲ κατεργασάμενος . . . εἰς αὐτὸ τοῦτο.

Vs. 6—Θαρροῦντες οὖν—'Since God has wrought us for this purpose, and since he has given us assurance thereof in the earnest of the Spirit . . .'

ἐνδημοῦντες ἐν τῷ σώματι ἐκδημοῦμεν ἀπὸ τοῦ Κυρίου—'while the present body is our home, we are absent from our eternal home with Christ.' This is the third image he uses to discuss this—οἰκία, ἔνδυμα, δῆμος.

εἰδότες ὅτι ... διὰ πίστεως γὰρ 'we know this for faith is the rule of our life. We don't confine our view to what we see.'

Vs. 7—διὰ πίστεως γὰρ—explaining the reason of εἰδότες. Yet it is generally referred to the ἀπὸ τοῦ Κυρίου—so that διὰ πίστεως γὰρ περιπατοῦμεν, οὐ διὰ εἴδους would mean 'we are absent from the Lord, we do not *see* Him now, we *believe* that we shall see him hereafter.' I think that the θαρροῦμεν δὲ is rather in favor of my way of reading it.

Vs. 8—θαρροῦμεν δὲ. Alford's note, (which however as usual, is borrowed from Meyer), on this change of construction is very good.

Vs. 9—διὸ—Therefore, since we wish to be present with the Lord.

Φιλοτιμούμεθα—our ambition is.

εἴτε ἐνδημοῦντες εἴτε ἐκδημοῦντες—This seems to be explained by Phil 1:20—καὶ νῦν μεγαλυνθήσεται Χριστὸς ἐν τῷ σώματί μου, εἴτε διὰ ζωῆς εἴτε διὰ θανάτου. We wish to please God whether it is his pleasure that we remain in this life or no.

'almost as'—De Wette.

Vs. 10—τὰ διὰ τοῦ σώματος (Vulg. al. has ἰδία).

πρὸς ἃ ἔπραξεν, εἴτε ἀγαθὸν εἴτε φαῦλον is an explanation of τὰ διὰ τοῦ σώματος i.e. κομίσηται ... πρὸς ἃ ἔπραξεν.

Vs. 11—Εἰδότες οὖν τὸν φόβον τοῦ Κυρίου ἀνθρώπους πείθομεν. φόβον is subjective and therefore not quite as Stanley has it. τοῦ Κυρίου is an objective not the subjective genitive.

ἀνθρώπους πείθομεν Θεῷ δὲ πεφανερώμεθα—The second clause is the emphasized clause, the first is the subordinate clause. 'Knowing then the fear of the Lord, though we persuade men, it is to God we are made manifest' (cf. Gal 1:10 ἀνθρώπους πείθω). 'Our office is to influence men, but it is not to them that we are responsible.'

Πεφανερώμεθα—One would think that in Alford's note the words beginning 'here however' contained his own view, but see the whole note in Meyer. 'Thus I hope we are made manifest also.'

Vs. 12—οὐ πάλιν ἑαυτοὺς 'As we shall be accused of doing.'

ἀφορμὴν διδόντες ὑμῖν καυχήματος ὑπὲρ ἡμῶν—For both our extravagance and our prudence are a matter for boasting.

ἐν προσώπῳ καυχωμένους καὶ μὴ ἐν καρδίᾳ—As those who laud style or eloquence of speech (2 Cor 5:9), or a personal presence (2 Cor 5:10), or a direct connection with the Lord, but especially the last (cf. 2 Cor 5:7) for it is obviously to the Christian 'parties' to whom he is especially alluding, who seem from the passage just cited to have objected to him on all these accounts.

ἐν καρδίᾳ—Bengel says Paul is appealing to the conscience here.

Vs. 13—ἐξέστημεν . . . σωφρονοῦμεν See Stanley who seems to have exactly hit the mark.

εὐδοκοῦμεν μᾶλλον ἐκδημῆσαι ἐκ τοῦ σώματος καὶ ἐνδημῆσαι πρὸς τὸν Κύριον . . . cf. Phil 1:23—εἰς τὸ ἀναλῦσαι καὶ σὺν Χριστῷ εἶναι, πολλῷ γὰρ μᾶλλον κρεῖσσον.

Vs. 14—ἡ γὰρ ἀγάπη τοῦ Χριστοῦ . . . τοῦ Χριστοῦ is a subjective genitive. The love of Christ as specially exhibited in his dying for sinners.

κρίναντας not κρίνοντας

Omit εἰ—This passage more forcible without it. Stanley's reasons for the inclusion are all wrong.

ἄρα οἱ πάντες.

ἀπέθανον—"then all died" i.e. with Christ, died to sin, died to the pleasures, and temptations of the world. Cf. especially Rom 6:1-11 and Col 3:3, not as the E.V. for: 1) ἀπέθανον cannot be = to νεκροὶ ἦσαν and 2) it does not suit this phrase.

ἐγερθέντι—See the references to ζῶσιν in Stanley.

Vs. 16—ἡμεῖς—"We the servants of Christ." Cf. *Journal of Philology* iii, p. 120. "Even if we have known Christ, as some of us with Judaizing tendencies have known . . . " cf. 2 Cor 4:1. See Stanley's remark on the feelings which Paul here describes.

ἐγνώκαμεν, οἴδαμεν cf. 1 Cor 2:8, 11. Cf. Acts 19:15—Τὸν Ἰησοῦν γινώσκω καὶ τὸν Παῦλον ἐπίσταμαι· ὑμεῖς δὲ τίνες ἐστέ and John 21:17—πάντα σὺ οἶδας, σὺ γινώσκεις ὅτι φιλῶ σε.

Verbs of Knowing:

A state—εἰδέναι—'to know'—referring to external proofs (see Stanley p. 138)

A state—ἐπίσταμαι—'to know well'—by accuracy of knowledge

A condition—γινώσκειν—'to recognize' referring to the internal standard, some connection (ἐπιγινώσκω). This latter is employed of knowing Jesus as the Christ (cf. John 6:69 and John 3:24). See the *Journal of Philology* iii, p. 116.

Vs. 17—'If anyone is in Christ, as these Judaizing teachers say they are . . .'

καινὴ κτίσις—St. Paul applies a common rabbinical expression (see Wettstein) of the earlier days but gives it a spiritual significance.

ἰδοὺ γέγονεν καινά—New things have come into being—cf. Is 48:18 (see Stanley).

Vs. 18—τὰ δὲ πάντα

ἡμᾶς—here the preachers of the Gospel especially.

Vs. 19—ὡς ὅτι Stanley all wrong, see my note on 2 Thess 2:2. E.V. is correct.

Vs. 20—Ὑπὲρ Χριστοῦ οὖν πρεσβεύομεν ὡς τοῦ Θεοῦ—the appropriate words. Ὑπὲρ Χριστοῦ—in the person of, as the representative of.

καταλλάγητε—cf. the passive σώθητε—Acts 2:40.

Vs. 21—ἁμαρτίαν ἐποίησεν cf. Gal 3:13—γενόμενος ὑπὲρ ἡμῶν κατάρα.

The Ministry of Suffering and Reconciliation (2 Corinthians 6)

Vs. 1—Συνεργοῦντες δὲ. See Stanley and my notes on 1 Thess 3:2; 1 Cor 3:9.

Vs. 4ff.—ἐν ὑπομονῇ πολλῇ—Bengel has a good note on this passage. As it is not to be supposed that the Apostle balanced the words in his mind, so it is inconceivable on the other hand that the order of the words should be a disorder. We may then expect to find some general principle of arrangement, though we may fail on a particular point in establishing the system. Bengel is evidently right in his first 'ternarius' but do not the words thereafter go in pairs?

    I.) Part One

        A. In Physical Endurance

            ἐν ὑπομονῇ πολλῇ

                a) sub-divided, ascend.—θλίψεσιν . . . ἀνάγκαις . . . στενοχωρίαις

                by amount of pressure (θλίψεσιν is not as severe as στενοχωρίαις)

                Cf. especially 2 Cor 4:8 also Rom 2:9 (Rom 8:35) ἀνάγκαις also less severe than στενοχωρίαις. Cf. 2 Cor 12:10 where the four terms of ἀσθενείαι are ὕβρεσιν, ἀνάγκαις, διωγμοῖς, στενοχωρίαις. Note that the superlative of ὕβρεσιν is διωγμοῖς, the superlative of ἀνάγκαις is στενοχωρίαις; as ὕβρεσιν is to διωγμοῖς, so ἀνάγκαις is to στενοχωρίαις.

b) subdivided and enumerated according to their character (so Bengel)

> 1) suffering personal violence—ἐν πληγαῖς, ἐν φυλακαῖς
>
> 2) overtaxing bodily strength—ἐν ἀκαταστασίαις, ἐν κόποις
>
> 3) denying bodily cravings—ἐν ἀγρυπνίαις, ἐν νηστείαις
>
> (the first three in the list reflect external persecution, the next three are self-imposed cf. 2 Cor 11:27). ἀκατάστατος almost as Chrysostom 'hurrying from place to place' but this word always has the sense of 'tumult' in the New Testament. ἐν νηστείαις—voluntary abstinence (cf. 2 Cor 11:27). Also, πληγαῖς, φυλακαῖς, ἀκαταστασίαις are in a descending scale.

B. In the display of inward virtues (self)

 Moral—ἐν ἁγνότητι

 Intellectual—ἐν γνώσει

In the display of outward excellences (fellow-men)

 Passive forbearance (μακροθυμίᾳ)

 Active kindness (χρηστότητι) (cf. 1 Cor 13:4; Gal 5:22)

II.) Part II. In the Specifically Christian Character

 In the inward spirit—ἐν πνεύματι ἁγίῳ

 In the outward manifestation—ἐν ἀγάπῃ ἀνυποκρίτῳ (cf. Gal 5:22).

 In the Apostolic (Ministerial) Character

 In Preaching—ἐν λόγῳ ἀληθείας

 In Working Wonders—ἐν δυνάμει Θεοῦ

THEN, διὰ τῶν ὅπλων τῆς δικαιοσύνης τῶν δεξιῶν καὶ ἀριστερῶν seems to sum it all up, δικαιοσύνη in its credit sense.

Vs. 7—τῶν δεξιῶν καὶ ἀριστερῶν Alford argues from the *absence* of the article before ἀριστερῶν that there is no reference to arms, offensive and defensive. It might much more plausibly be argued from the *presence* of the article before δεξιῶν that there is such a reference. On only defensive armor— see 1 Thess 5:8, on both offensive and defensive see Eph 6:14 sqq.

Vs. 8—ὡς πλάνοι καὶ ἀληθεῖς. Alford is right in rejecting the 'putative' meaning of ὡς. The Apostle argues that they are recommended by the contrast between a superficial view of them and their real position, as being deceivers (in the eyes of the world), and (in reality) true men. πλάνοι so the Jews and Judaizers regarded him. It is the very term applied to our Lord in Mt 27:63.

Vs. 9—This entire passage speaks to the strange and paradoxical character of the social phenomena. There was the superficial and the true view of their state. Note the paradoxical character of this very sentence. It seems to break down with the clause ὡς παιδευόμενοι καὶ μὴ θανατούμενοι. This is owing to the humility of the Apostle. In παιδευόμενοι as chastened by God, the accusations of his enemies, the [????] . . . his humility will not let him affirm. See Meyer.

ὡς ἀποθνήσκοντες καὶ ἰδοὺ ζῶμεν cf. the rhetoric of the Greek orator.

Vs. 10—ὡς πτωχοὶ cf. Trench's *Synon.* p. 141. See Ar. Plaut. 549.

Frank Speech and Fresh Hope
(2 Corinthians 6:11–7:16)

Textual Issues

2 Cor 6:14—ἢ τίς for τίς δὲ of the Textus Receptus.

Vs. 15—Βελιάρ not Βελιάλ with the Textus Receptus.

Vs. 16—Perhaps ἡμεῖς . . . ἐσμεν with Lachmann instead of Ὑμεῖς . . . ἐστε of the B.M.T.

Vs. 17—ἐξέλθατε—the right reading over against T.R. and B.M.T.

2 Cor 7:8—Perhaps read as Tischendorf and the T.R. but then arises the question of particulars.

Vs. 10—ἐργάζεται not κατεργάζεται of the T.R. in the first case.

Vs. 11—Omit ὑμᾶς (T.R.), omit ἐν at end of verse (T.R.).

Vs. 12—T.R. has ἡμῶν . . . ὑμῶν end of verse. Should be the reverse.

Vs. 13—Should be Ἐπὶ δὲ, not with δέ after περισσοτέρως.

Vs. 14—Retain ὑμῶν in spite of Lachmann.

Commentary

2 Cor 6:11—'We speak our minds freely to you, our hearts are open to receive you.'

Κορίνθιοι—This personal address bespeaks deep feeling, whether of anxiety, as here, or of love (as in Phil 4:15) or of anger (Gal 3:1).

Vs. 12—'If there is any want of sympathy, it is not due to ourselves, but you.'

Vs. 13—'I am asking for a return of affection (σπλάγχνοις), as a father would ask it from a child.'

Vs. 14—The link of connection not obvious—see Stanley p. 465. 2 Cor 6:14–7:1 is to be regarded as parenthetical. In 2 Cor 7:2 he returns to the theme of their constant sympathy. This looks to be something in the uppermost thoughts in the Apostle's mind. But what was that? 'Your heart is too narrow in my direction, and only too large in another. Your sympathies are too closed against us, and all too open to the enemies of Christ. You have adopted a spurious liberality instead of the true liberality.' What is he alluding to? 1) the sin of profligacy—δικαιοσύνῃ καὶ ἀνομίᾳ, . . . φωτὶ πρὸς σκότος; . . . Χριστοῦ πρὸς Βελιάρ, and 2) the sin of idolatry—πιστῷ μετὰ ἀπίστου; . . . ναῷ Θεοῦ μετὰ εἰδώλων, *and these are the two offenses which appear in the First Epistle.* Though doubtless the two were not unconnected especially in the case of Aphrodite at Corinth, hence the outburst that is 2 Cor 6:14ff.

ἑτεροζυγοῦντες—This word is used either of a balance (cf. Plutarch, *Cim.* xvi. p. 489 and Pseudo-Phylact.) or of cattle unevenly yoked (cf. Lev 19:19). The explanation of Plotinus (see Steph. *Thes*[?] as if ἑτεροζυγοῦντες is common as illustrating the procreation[?]).

δικαιοσύνῃ covers the whole field of moral right and wrong.

Vs. 15—Βελιάρ—The Hebrew form is Βελίαλ. Βελιάρ is by far the most textually supported here. For the change of words cf. Βεελζεβούλ—Mark 3:22. Of the meaning of the word see Smith's Dictionary on 'Devil' s.v. This is not a proper name in the OT (or LXX—referring to someone haughty), though it seems to have become one afterwards and occurs in Theodotion Judges 19:22.

Vs. 16—συνκατάθεσις. Stanley is all wrong here. It is to cast one's vote in the same way. Cf. Plutarch, *Sng* [?] 501C.

ναῷ Θεοῦ cf. 1 Corinthians.

Vs. 18—θυγατέρας. Not in 2 Sam 7:14. See Stanley.

2 Corinthians 7

Vs. 1—καθαρίσωμεν—Since the promises are conditional on our doing so, and are combined with threats . . . the person as a Temple.

σαρκὸς καὶ πνεύματος

ἐπιτελοῦντες—completing ἀπὸ παντός.

Vs. 2—ἠδικήσαμεν, οὐδένα ἐφθείραμεν, οὐδένα ἐπλεονεκτήσαμεν. Cf. 7:16; 1 Thess 2:3 (and my note 22).

The confusion between ἀκαθαρσία and πλεονεξία in the commentaries is inexcusable. See *Journal of Philology* iii. p. 97.

Vs. 3—'If I seem to imply a rebuke, my object in saying this is not taking an opportunity for condemning you.'

On προείρηκα cf. especially 2 Cor 3:2 and 2 Cor 6:11.

On εἰς τὸ συναποθανεῖν καὶ συνζῆν, see Meyer.

Vs. 5—Returning to the subject left off at 2 Cor 2:14.

ἔσωθεν φόβοι—Not from something coming from outside the church, for then the phrase ἡ σὰρξ ἡμῶν, would have no reference.

Θλιβόμενοι—See Rom 12:9 and 2 Cor 1:7.

Vs. 8—There is an issue here with the punctuation.

Vs. 10—μετάνοια There is a sort of opposite in ἐξ ἡμῶν to κατὰ Θεόν.

Vs. 11—τῷ πράγματι See 1 Thess 4:5 (p. 65 of my notes).

Vs. 12—ἔγραψα οὐχ ἕνεκεν—overlooking the main reason cf. 2 Cor 2:10.

τὴν σπουδὴν ὑμῶν τὴν ὑπὲρ ἡμῶν—if this reading be taken then the πρὸς ὑμᾶς must go with φανερωθῆναι i.e. to convince you of the large interest you have in us. But I do not see how the πρὸς ὑμᾶς if the other reading be taken is tautological as Stanley asserts.

Vs. 13—Ἐπὶ δὲ τῇ παρακλήσει ἡμῶν is the right reading. 'Over and above our consolation.'

Vs. 14—As *to* you, so *of* you. cf. 2 Cor 7:4.

ἡ καύχησις ἡμῶν—Must mean our boasting of you. The reading is correct.

περισσοτέρως εἰς ὑμᾶς—cf. my notes on 1 Thess 1:5—p. 11.

About the Collection
(2 Corinthians 8)

Textual Issues

Vs. 3—παρὰ δύναμιν not ὑπὲρ δύναμιν (T.R., B.M.T.).

Vs. 4—T.R. has δέξασθαι ἡμᾶς after ἁγίους which should be struck out.

Vs. 12—Omit τις (T.R.) after ἔχῃ.

Vs. 19—ἐν τῇ χάριτι is the right reading not σὺν.

Vs. 21—προνοοῦμεν γὰρ not προνοούμενοι (T.R., B.M.T.)

Vs. 24—ἐνδεικνύμενοι not ἐνδείξασθε.

Commentary

Vs. 1—τὴν χάριν—Showing the range of meaning. Cf. εὐλογίαν 2 Cor 9:5, and κοινωνία.

ἐν ταῖς ἐκκλησίαις—See Paley *Hora. Paul.* p. 121.

δεδομένην ἐν cf. 2 Cor 8:16 and 2 Cor 1:22; Acts 4:12.

Vs. 2—At a time when they were surely burdend by afflictions.

ἡ περισσεία—is certainly further amplified by ἐπερίσσευσεν.

τὸ πλοῦτος—the right reading, cf. Winer.

ἁπλότητος—liberality, cf. Rom 12:8.

Vs. 4—δέξασθαι ἡμᾶς of the T.R. is to be omitted. Meyer has taken χάριν after δεόμενοι but it is better taken with ἔδωκαν.

Vs. 5—πρῶτον, not as E.V. but refers to καὶ οὐ . . . and in the second place . . .

Vs. 6—εἰς τὸ παρακαλέσαι ἡμᾶς—so that we.

Vs. 8—By way of command, as if I would command you. cf. 1 Cor 7:6.

τῆς ἑτέρων—the Macedonian Churches.

Vs. 9—Parenthetical.

Vs. 10—γνώμην—advice, judgment. τοῦτο γὰρ ὑμῖν συμφέρει This is due to our friendship that I would advise rather than command. καὶ τὸ θέλειν προενήρξασθε ἀπὸ πέρυσι, not only the execution, but the design, intention.

προενήρξασθε—before whom? It is generally said 'before the Macedonians' but perhaps Wordsworth is right that it is 'before we suggested it to you.'

Vs. 12—πρόκειται is there to begin with. Omit τις (cf. 2 Cor 3:16).

Vs. 13—ἐξ ἰσότητος according to a principle of equality. To equalize things.

Vs. 15—Exodus 16:18—Here used as an illustration, not an authority.

πλεονεξία—where the one yields as little and the other gets as much as he needs.

Vs. 17—σπουδαιότερος, ὑπάρχων. I do not say he received no exhortation, but that it was not needed.

Vs. 19—ἐν τῇ χάριτι in the mention of the bounty.

Vs. 20—στελλόμενοι cf. 2 Thess 3:6 (my notes p. 41).

Vs. 22—Who are the two brethren? See Stanley.

2 Corinthians 9

Vs. 4—τῆς καυχήσεως (T.R. B.M.T.) after ταύτῃ to be struck out.

Vs. 15—Χάρις δὲ omit δὲ (T.R., B.M.T.)

Commentary

Vs. 1—'For while it is unnecessary to give you any special instructions, I sent the brethren . . .' The second clause here being the important one.

Vs. 4—ὑποστάσις—1) a foundation or substratum—Heb 3:14; 2) confidence, as the thing on which a foundation rests. See Heb 11:1—Ἔστιν δὲ πίστις ἐλπιζομένων ὑπόστασις, πραγμάτων ἔλεγχος οὐ βλεπομένων; 3) elsewhere 'substance' that on which the qualities rest as a substratum—Heb 1:3—ὃς ὢν ἀπαύγασμα τῆς δόξης καὶ χαρακτὴρ τῆς ὑποστάσεως αὐτοῦ.

Vs. 6—Τοῦτο δέ—but herein . . . as Meyer.

ἐπ᾽ εὐλογίαις—as a bounty was called ἐλεημοσύνη for the feelings which prompted it; so was it styled εὐλογία for the blessing which was pronounced in conferring it.

2 CORINTHIANS 10

TEXTUAL ISSUES

Vs. 7—Omit Χριστοῦ (T.R.) after ἡμεῖς.

Vs. 8—τε is omitted by B, F, etc. but probably should be included.

καὶ before περισσότερόν to be omitted.

Vs. 10—φησίν, Lachmann has φασίν.

Vss. 12-13—Probably the T.R. is correct here, others omit οὐ συνιᾶσιν ἡμεῖς δὲ.

καυχησόμεθα omitted by some and καυχησόμενοι read by others.

Vs. 14—οὐ γὰρ ὡς μὴ—Lachmann read ὡς γὰρ μὴ with B but on insufficient authorities.

COMMENTARY

Vs. 1—Αὐτὸς δὲ ἐγὼ Παῦλος—Some have thought that this, the third part of the Epistle was written by St. Paul's own hand; this is not improbable. But there can be no allusion to this in the words Αὐτὸς δὲ ἐγὼ Παῦλος as then we should have γράφω τῇ ἐμῇ χειρὶ Παύλου or at least γράφω in place of the παρακαλῶ. See Meyer. 'I myself, I that very Paul who has been so decried, whose bodily presence has been called weak, and his speech contemptible . . .'

διὰ τῆς πραΰτητος καὶ ἐπιεικείας—These two words distinguished see Trench, *Synonyms*, p. 170sqq. 'By the mildness and gentleness of Christ,' a fit mode of entreaty where his object is to avoid having to inflict severe punishment.

ὃς κατὰ πρόσωπον μὲν ταπεινὸς ἐν ὑμῖν—as represented by my enemies. 'I who am such a time-server, and destitute of moral courage . . .'

Vs. 2—δέομαι δὲ, resuming the sense of παρακαλῶ. The δὲ gives the same turn to the sentence as the ἐάν . . . in 2 Cor 10:8. 'Though accused of being courageous in my absence, yet I . . .'

ἢ λογίζομαι τολμῆσαι—'I reckon, am minded to be bold'

ὡς κατὰ σάρκα περιπατοῦντας—referring to the charges alluded to in vs. 2, the accusation of time-serving and moral cowardice. He is accused of being one of the ὑποκριταὶ and an ἀλαζώνα etc.

Vs. 3—Ἐν σαρκὶ γὰρ—The former verse had implied 'Let my enemies lay aside their unworthy view of me, let them not impute to me such motives, for . . .'

Vs. 4—Parenthetical. δυνατὰ τῷ Θεῷ cf. Acts 7:20.

λογισμοὺς

Vs. 5—πᾶν ὕψωμα—Every building, fortified wall, barrier raised against. . . . Meyer says about πᾶν νόημα 'die νοήματα gehören doch zur Kategorie der διαλογισμοί und diese hatte er vorher nicht als Feinde, die *gefangen geführt werden*, sondern als feindliche Werke, die *destruirt* werden (καθαιροῦντες), sich vorgestellt.' But there is surely a difference between a νόημα and a διαλογισμός, a difference corresponding to that between 'reason' and 'understanding.' Destroying the argumentations and Christianzing the conceptions . . .

εἰς τὴν ὑπακοὴν—'eine österlichen Bereich'—Meyer

ὅταν πληρωθῇ ὑμῶν ἡ ὑπακοή is attached by Lachmann to what follows. In this clause he applies especially to the Corinthian Church what he had hitherto stated generally. 'When your obedience (i.e. that of the Corinthian Church as a body) is fulfilled, vengeance will overtake the offender.'

Vs. 7—Τὰ κατὰ πρόσωπον βλέπετε—Read it interrogatively. 'Do you judge by outward appearances?' Believe in the superiority of those who call themselves 'followers of Christ' (Ἐγὼ δὲ Χριστοῦ) merely on account of their professions?

Vs. 8—τε γὰρ. The τε has no particle answering it. 'I use this language fearlessly, for if I boast . . .'

περισσότερόν τι—'than I have done hitherto' in 2 Cor 10:3-6.

ἧς ἔδωκεν ὁ κύριος εἰς οἰκοδομὴν καὶ οὐκ εἰς καθαίρεσιν ὑμῶν, οὐκ αἰσχυνθήσομαι—'mit einem doppelten Seitenblicke auf die falschen Apostel, deren Gewalt weder von Christo war, noch zur Erbauung sondern zur Zerstörung der Gemeinde gerichte.'—Meyer

οἰκοδομὴν as the Temple of God.

οὐκ αἰσχυνθήσομαι—i.e. my words will be verified.

Vs. 9—Chrysostom and others make vs. 9 the protasis, of which 2 Cor 10:11 is the apodosis, with 2 Cor 10:10 as parenthetical.

ἵνα μὴ δόξω—'I say this that I may not seem to be attempting to terrify you by my letters, but you should not think my letters contain mere empty threats.'

ὡς ἂν ἐκφοβεῖν ὑμᾶς—To make a show of terrifying you. cf. Winer, p. 319. This phrase is not found elsewhere in the New Testament.

Vs. 10—Αἱ ἐπιστολαί. This seems to imply more than one letter.

Vs. 12—συνιοῦσιν = συνιᾶσιν

Vs. 17—Ὁ δὲ καυχώμενος. See 1 Corinthians 1:31—(p. 32).

2 CORINTHIANS 11

TEXTUAL ISSUES

Vs. 1—ἠνείχεσθέ Perhaps ἀνείχεσθέ is the right reading with D, E, F, G etc. B, K also have this.

μικρόν τι ἀφροσύνης is the right reading, not μικρὸν τῇ ἀφροσύνῃ (B.M.T., T.R.).

Vs. 3—Omit οὕτω (T.R., B.M.T.)

Vs. 4—ἀνείχεσθέ as before

Vs. 6—φανερώσαντες (B.M.T., T.R.). Perhaps read φανερώσαντες with Lachmann, Tischendorf after B, F.

Vs. 14—θαῦμα. Θαυμαστόν (B.M.T., T.R.) is an interpretation.

Vs. 27—ἐν before κόπῳ (B.M.T., T.R.) is to be omitted.

Vs. 28—ἐπισύστασίς (T.R., B.M.T.). But ἐπίστασίς is the correct reading.

Vs. 32—θέλων (T.R., B.M.T.) should be omitted.

[The manuscript breaks off at this juncture, which likely indicates that when Lightfoot taught this material at Cambridge, he never quite got through the epistle. Otherwise we would have at least a few further notes on the last chapters. (BW3)]

Part Three

INTRODUCTION TO THE
COMMENTARY ON 1 PETER

The Name

His father's name—Jonas (Mt 16:17—Βαριωνᾶ), or John (John 1:43; 21:15-17)—
the correct reading see Tregelles, pp. 382, 485. See the article in the *Contemporary Review*, p. 159ff. on the name. The significance of Mt 16:17 should be stressed.

Συμεών, שִׁמְעוֹן The above form is the proper name in 1 Chron 4:20 which the LXX renders Σεμεών or Σεμών, the Hebrew form of the name. James naturally uses the strict Jewish form of Peter's name in Acts 15:14, Συμεών and elsewhere in the New Testament only at 2 Pet 1:1, and even there the use is doubtful (B and several others have Σιμών). Peter's Greek autograph would probably have been Συμεών (cf. Simon in the LXX, e.g. Simon Maccabee) that would easily be changed into more common Greek form, remembering the practice of substituting a Greek name that nearly resembles in sounds the Hebrew one. Σιμών a Grecized form of the name—Simon, Simonides from the Greek σιμός. In this particular case there would be hardly any change. See Josephus, *Ant.* xii.5.1. Note the naturalness of its occurrence at the Jerusalem council in Acts 15. On the meaning of the Hebrew word see Gen 29:33 Peter is nowhere else called simply Simon or Simeon except in the Gospels. Of his other name, Πέτρος, hereafter.

According to John 1:45 he is a native of Bethsaida, and his fellow townsmen are Andrew, John, James, and Philip. In regard to the house of St. Peter we have Mt 8:14; Mk 1:30; Luke 4:38. It was not necessarily at Capernaum, though without the narrative of St. John, it might be thought so. Still, there is no difficulty in supposing that he lived at Capernaum. St. John does not say more than that Bethsaida is the city (i.e. the native place), of Andrew and Peter.

Peter was a married man—so 1 Cor 9:5. On the later tradition, see Clement of Alexandria, *Strom.* iii.6, p. 535; *Strom.* vii.11, p. 869, Eusebius, *H.E.* iii.30 (Schwegler [?], p. 105). For other traditions of possible relevance see *Clement. Homilies* xiii.1,11; *Clement. Recogn.* vii.25, 36; ix. 28. On his daughter Petronilla, see Tillemont I, p. 189.

What of his possible education? The Galileans were bilingual: 1) Aramaic, a corrupt dialect thereof (cf. Mt 26:69-73; Acts 2:7)[1] and 2) Greek. On the general spread of the Greek language, see Josephus, *Ant.* xii.12.5 on Tyre, xiv.10.2 on Sidon, and xiv.10.3 on Askelon (cf. Hug, II, p. 35). On Caesarea see Josephus, *Bell. Jud.* iii.9.1; ii.13.7; ii.14.4, especially in the neighborhood of Galilee. On Galilee of the Gentiles see Isaiah 9:1. But what must be taken into account is the Greek cities set up after the time of Alexander in the region. We have the catalogue of the Greek cities defeated by the Jews at Caesarea in Josephus, *Bell. Jud.* ii.18.1 (see Hug, II, pp. 40sqq. pp. 259sq). Gadara and Hippos were especially Greek cities (*Ant.* xvi.11.2— Hug, p. 38). On Tiberias as a Greek city see Josephus, *Vit. Jos.* xii (Hug, p. 39); see *Bell. Jud.* iii.3.2. As for Jewish encounters with Roman governors notice that the pleadings with Titus by the Jewish Zealots were in Greek— *Bell. Jud.* vi.6.2 (cf. v.9.2; vi.2.1; vi.6.2). As for the Apostles speaking Greek, see Acts 2:14 for St. Peter, Acts 7:1 sq. for St. Stephen, and for St. Paul Acts 21:40 and Acts 22:1, whose Greek was of exceptional character. For an important statement that speaks to the linguistic state of the times, Josephus, *Ant.* xx.12.1 after talking about his own skill in Greek adds 'For our people do not favor those persons who have mastered the speech of many nations, or who adorn their style with smoothness of diction, *because they consider that such skill is common to ordinary freemen but that even slaves who so*

---

[1]See Lightfoot, *Galatians*, p. 194; and John Lightfoot, I, p. 78.

choose may acquire it.'[2] Josephus is reliable for a general testimony about the linguistic state of things.

The impression left is that the priests in Jerusalem did not highly value linguistic or literary culture, but rather 'rabbinical' culture.[3] It was the trade classes that had a larger knowledge and use of Greek, not the learned classes, so Acts 4:13. They may have in other respects been much better educated practically than the Jewish leaders, but they had not the learning from the schools which qualified them to teach. They were not disciples of the schools. Comp. John 7:15. They were the *'am ha'aretz.*

The Galileans were more free from the influence of the priests and scribes, and therefore more likely to learn the Greek language and adopt the customs of their Greek neighbors. According to John Lightfoot (Vol. II, p. 78) there were no priests there—see Bab. Erubhim 5.5—'The Galileans hear one Master in one language and another in another and the distinctions of language and pronunciation confounded them so that they forgot.'

On the trade of Galileans see Kern I, p. 312. The bearing this has on the genuineness of 1 Peter. The 'gift of tongues' was apparently not available for the general preaching of the Gospel (Acts 14:11). Peter had interpreters—Mark (so Papias in Eusebius, *H.E.* iii.39—for Greek) and Glaucus (so Clement of Alexandria, *Strom.* vii.17 p. 898—i.e. for Latin). Thus we must concur with the possibility that Peter had aid in composing 1 Peter—see 1 Pet 5:12-13. On Sylvanus see Acts 15:22, obviously from the part that he bears here, he is able to speak Greek. So also he is a companion and fellow-preacher of St. Paul's in Greece. But in Paul's case an interpreter was not necessary.

The Galileans however seem to have been bilingual or in some cases of old trilingual, but it is difficult to state the level of interest or knowledge of Greek at this time (see Robert's discussion on the Gospels). We do have Greek

---

[2]By way of editorial comment, the attempt to make Galilee a linguistic or cultural backwater where Greek was not prevalent was utterly rejected by Lightfoot, and on good grounds. See for example the statement of Rabbi Simeon, the son of Rabbi Gamaliel (B.T. Sotah 49b) that his father at the very beginning of the second century had a thousand students, five hundred of whom studied Torah, and five hundred of whom studied Greek wisdom. This might help account for the some fifteen hundred Greek loan words in the Talmud, and the prevalence of Greek inscriptions on Jewish tombs in Galilee and Judea, not to mention references like Mishnah, Shek. 5.1, which tells us Rabbi Mordecai knew seventy languages. Even allowing for classic hyperbole in these examples, they make clear the multilingual nature of the region. (BW3)

[3]By "rabbinical" Lightfoot seems to mean early Jewish Torah-centric culture, not the later rabbinical culture. (BW3)

names at Bethsaida—Philip, and Andrew. The general impression about the character of the Galileans is that they were hearty, handy, honest, courageous, Peter being a typical Galilean of the higher type (see Kern I, p. 315).

As for St. Peter's position in life, note that his house was a large one— Mt 8:4; Mark 1:30; Luke 4:38. On his property see Mt 19:27—what he left behind to follow Jesus. On his call see John 1:22 (and Notes on St. John's Gospel, p. 11).[4] Note that the incident in Mt 4:18; Mark 1:16; Luke 5:1 sqq. *is later.*

ON THE CONFESSION, CONVERSION, AND PRIMACY OF ST. PETER[5]

On the familiar confession and conversion see Mt 16:18. Jesus is the Son of God, but Simon Βαριωνᾶ—the son of God's grace (remembering the story of Jonah), as is evident from the words ὅτι σὰρξ καὶ αἷμα οὐκ ἀπεκάλυψέν σοι. Comp. 1 Pet 1:3—ὁ κατὰ τὸ πολὺ αὐτοῦ ἔλεος ἀναγεννήσας ἡμᾶς εἰς ἐλπίδα ζῶσαν (and 1 Pet 1:23).

Jesus says, 'Thou art Peter and upon this πέτρα.' The πέτρα is clearly Peter. The original would be Cephas (Aramaic) which includes both πέτρα and Πέτρος. The former is a rock, the latter a place of rock, stone, or the substance rock, stone. In this case it must be Peter himself or something connected with St. Peter—his faith, his constancy, the foundation of the Apostles and Prophets.

There are two ways of regarding the relationship of our Lord to the edifice (built upon it): 1) He is the foundation—see 1 Cor 2:12; 2) He is the chief cornerstone, Eph 2:20. This last concept appears in St. Peter's Epistle itself—1 Pet 2:5 sqq. But in this case the Apostles are the foundation stone. Cf. Ephesians l.c. to Revelation 21:14—of the New Jerusalem and the Church of Christ glorified.

The prominent position held by St. Peter in these earliest days of the church leads naturally to the question: What is meant by the primacy of St. Peter, and how far are the Romanists justified in the views which they hold? It seems both futile and dangerous to deny this primacy altogether, for it is clearly enunciated in Holy Scripture and this in two ways. Directly and indirectly—or in other words dogmatically and historically—in the account

---

[4]This material is provided in the second volume in the Lightfoot Legacy series. (BW3)
[5]I have taken the basic template for this section from Lightfoot's Acts notes and then added all the additional material from his 1 Peter notes, where the discussion is more thorough. There are no signs, however, of development or change on this matter from one set of notes to the other. (BW3)

of the promises given to Peter, and in the narrative of his subsequent Acts. Peter is one of the favored three. This however is, of course, inconclusive.

Consider the special prominence given to Peter, and commands addressed to him.

(1) Matthew 16:13-19.

σὺ εἶ Πέτρος. Πέτρα is certainly to be preferred to Πέτρος. The change of gender being easily accounted for (cf. Stanley p. 120), and so not an allusion to a spot or building, in allusion to which Ruskin says, speaking of what he calls the 'accursed architecture, that mighty place where the seven hills slope to the Tiber, that marks by its dome the central spot where Rome has reversed the words of Christ and as he vivified the stone of the apostleship, she petrifies the apostleship into the stumbling stone.' (*Lectures* p. 138)

(2) John 21:15-23.

(3) Luke 5:1-10. Luke 22:31, 32

Allowing then the primacy of St. Peter, we may challenge the Romanist to show that the Bishop of Rome, or the Roman church has a real title to this inheritance.

May we go further?

1.) These promises to Peter are exactly of the same character as those to other apostles. ἐπὶ ταύτῃ τῇ πέτρᾳ. cf. Eph 2:13[6] the church is said to be built ἐπὶ τῷ θεμελίῳ τῶν ἀποστόλων καὶ προφητῶν cf. John 21:22, 3

2.) That these promises are made to depend on the personal character of St. Peter, and therefore may be expected to be the inheritance of those who represent him in this respect (πάντα ὅστις ἂν πετρός) Origen.

3.) That, as history shows us the fulfillment of these promises, so does it show us that as regarding St. Peter personally they were only intended to be temporary. St. Peter disappears from the scene and St. Paul takes his place. St. Paul knows of no such supremacy as the Roman church attaches to St. Peter. And it is St. Peter himself who utters the caution against lording it over God's heritage (κατακυριεύοντες) 1 Pet 5:3.

4.) The Church Fathers remark that the view of this matter should be the same as that Christ himself enunciated. See e.g. Augustine, *Retract.* I.2

---

[6]It is actually Eph 2:20.

(I, p. 32): 'In a passage in this book I said about the Apostle, "On him, as on a rock the Church was built." This idea is also expressed in song by the voice of many in the verses of the most blessed Ambrose, where he says about the crowing of the cock: "he, at this crowing, this rock of the church washed away his guilt." But I know that very frequently at a later time, I so explained what the Lord said, "Thou art Peter and upon this rock I will build my Church" that it be understood as built upon Him whom Peter confessed, "Thou art the Christ, the Son of the Living God," and so Peter called after this rock, represented the person of the Church which is built upon this rock, and has received "the keys of the kingdom of heaven." For "thou art Peter" and not "thou art the rock" was said to him. But "the rock was Christ" in confessing whom, as also the whole Church, Simon was called Peter. But let the reader decide which of these two opinions is the most probable' (cf. Cyr. of Alex. in Isa 3:3). But generally, the Fathers interpret the Matthean saying of Peter, in some sense. In Origen it is of Peter's qualities (see his Comm. Matt. ad loc). *The majority of the Fathers speak of the faith of Peter, or the witness of Peter or the confession of Peter as being 'the rock.'* See for example frequently in Chrysostom (see his comment on the Matthean text). Cyr. of Alex. refers it to the faith of Peter, hence the application of this in Origen, and Origen is largely followed by the later Fathers (Basil, Gregory of Nyssa, etc.).

5.) But whatever the secondary application may be, it must refer to St. Peter himself primarily for the Greek is—σὺ εἶ Πέτρος (Mt 16:18). It must describe some historical manifestation that sprung from Peter, or Peter's faith, or Peter's constancy. Not just any faith or constancy or confession, but 'the faith, the confession, the constancy.' I think this cannot mean Peter himself, because we should expect not ἐπὶ ταύτῃ but rather ἐπὶ σοί. It is this constancy, this firmness of faith that has just evinced itself in this confession. It denotes a certain primacy given to Peter in this. But *his office and work is the same in kind* as the other Apostles. So far Origen is right. It *is* said of Peter here, but it might have been said of others, certainly of the other Apostles. Of them, indeed the same thing is said. Peter is only one of them. They too have the power of the keys, so John 20:22, 23.

6.) But *still*, it is a primacy, a pre-eminence (see Mt 10:2—πρῶτος Σίμων). In what sense? Note the special charge—see Luke 22:32; John 21. Note the fulfillment of this in the Acts—Acts 1:15—completion of the apostolate; Acts 2:14, 37—preaching; Acts 3:1—healing; Acts 4:8; 7:3—confession and suffering; Acts 5:3—the sentence of the Church; the evangelism of Samaria—Acts 8:14; conflict with heresy Acts 8:18; vision of St. Peter and Cornelius Acts 10:1 sqq. *It is just at this point that St. Paul appears on the scene, and Peter's primacy is ended.* Peter (and his primacy) only comes up once more in Acts 15:7. But he does not play the chief part on this occasion. The president is James, the chief agent is Paul.

7.) St. Paul's Epistles assert his independence generally, and his equality with St. Peter and the first of the apostles (2 Cor 11:5; 12:11), with St. Peter especially. On his authority see Gal 2:7 sqq. (and the previous passage, Gal 1:18 as opposed to this). On this occasion, James is mentioned before Peter (Gal 2:9—the correct reading). On his privileges (to act as Peter does), see 1 Cor 9:5. He also assumes a position of superiority at Antioch (Gal 2:11).

8.) On the true and false conceptions of Peter's primacy, see the true and false readings in Cyprian. See *De unitate Ecclesiae* 4 (p. 212 Hartsel).

If we ask the question what happened to St. Peter and his work after the last mention in Acts while Acts 12:17 (ἐπορεύθη εἰς ἕτερον τόπον) has been interpreted to mean that Peter went to Rome, this is most unlikely. Such an important fact would not be slurred over in this way. The simple interpretation is the correct one—he got out of the way of Herod. When we meet him again he is not in the West, he is still in the East. Acts 15:15 (about 51 A.D.) he is in Jerusalem, and shortly after Gal 2:11 he is in Antioch. He could probably remain in Palestine and in the neighboring countries where Jews and Judaic Christians most abounded, thus fulfilling his special function as Apostle of the Circumcision (Gal 2:7).

Was he at Corinth? There is mention of him in 1 Cor 1:12 and 3:22, but this does not imply his *presence*. His name would naturally be adopted as a party standard. While 1 Cor 9:5 speaks of his journeys, *it does not say where*. On the other hand, the silence of St. Paul is important, but where we should expect him to mention St. Peter's labors, if he had labors in the same sphere (cf. 1 Cor 2:6; 2 Cor 1:19; 10:12 sq.). This points to an entire distinctness of sphere (in accordance with Gal 2:19). This language seems altogether inconceivable if St. Peter labored at Corinth, and indeed not natural if he had been at Corinth at all. Furthermore, the silence of St. Paul conforms with the silence of Acts, more especially as regards Corinth. The *inference* is that up to the close of the period comprised in Acts or thereabouts, St. Peter had confined his labors to the East.

What of what Dionysius says (in Eusebius, *H.E.* ii.25; Schwegler, p. 72)?[7] But Dionysius or his authorities may have inferred this from St. Paul's of St. Peter, and it may not rest on any independent tradition. Or it may refer to a later date than St. Paul's visits recorded in the Acts. It will therefore be at a time subsequent to the Acts that St. Peter turned his steps westwards, *if at all*. Did he actually visit the West? More especially did he visit Rome? He writes to the churches in Asia Minor. But there is no mention of any personal intercourse thoroughout, indeed nothing suggests it. In 2 Pet 3:2 the correct reading is ὑμῶν, but even if ἡμῶν (T.R.) is the correct reading it does not imply *personal* intercourse. But Rome?

It is one thing to accept the visit to Rome, and another to accept the Papal legends and pretensions built thereupon. The visit to Rome and martyrdom there, seem to be sufficiently authenticated. Notices combine to this end: 1) 1 Pet 5:13—The interpretation—a church is meant. Note the opening of the letter's ἐκλεκτοῖς the closing συνεκλεκτή (1 Pet 5:13). 2) the personification, compare 2 John—the opening ἐκλεκτῇ κυρίᾳ (2 John 1:1) and the closing τῆς ἐκλεκτῆς (2 John 1:13). Obviously a church is meant throughout the Epistle (cf. 2 John 1:4—the children, 2 John 1:6; 2 John 1:7—the antichrist, going out from us; 2 John 1:10). On the personification of the church cf. the Apocalypse and the Shepherd of Hermas. 2) But what church? Not Babylon in Egypt, though St. Mark's connection with the Egyptian Church might suggest this. But the Egyptian Babylon was a mere fortress (see Strabo, xvii. p. 807). Therefore, it must refer to either the great Babylon, or Rome. There is no a priori necessity as to why St. Peter should not have been at the great Babylon. But Mark at this time is said to be in the West (Col 4:10; Philem 24; 2 Tim 4:11). Thus the earliest traditions point to Rome as to the scene of his first

---

[7]See Lightfoot, *Galatians*, p. 341.

labors with St. Peter (e.g. Papias, Irenaeus, etc.). Probably therefore we must conclude that Rome is locale.

In regard to the Neronian persecution, and the application of the term Babylon to Rome (as a result), see Rev 14:8; 16:19; 17:5; 18:2, 10, 21. It is said that the Apocalypse is prophecy, but such allegorical designations reach far beyond the limitations of prophecy, properly so called (cf. e.g. Edom = Rome, Feubauer [?] Geg [?], p. 425). At this juncture we should consider the Sybilline Oracle v.158 which refers to Βαβυλῶνα Ἰταλίης. This comes from a Hebrew Sibylline writer during the time of the Flavians. The quote here is in accordance with the allegorical expressions elsewhere in the Epistle— 1 Pet 1:1 παρεπιδήμοις Διασπορᾶς, 1 Pet 2:11—παρεπιδήμους; and Μάρκος ὁ υἱός μου (notice 'my son'; figurative not τό τέκνον).

Early Tradition. ἐκκλησία added in Aleph. Syr. Peshit., Arm. Vulg. It is generally interpreted of the Church in Rome in early times. See Hippolytus p. 51 (περί Βαβυλῶνος see Hillenb. *Zeitschrift* xv, p. 355); Origen, *Comm. Matt.* III p. 440; Clement of Alexandria, *Adumbraetiones* p. 1007 (IV, p. 56). When we turn to Papias, Irenaeus etc. we shall see that they interpret it in the same way.

John 21:18, 19. It seems to refer to the place and manner of Peter's death. With it we can supplement the other passages. But it will be said that there is no necessary connection between the two. As a matter of fact, even tradition seems to have separated the two. In no form of tradition do we find the idea that St. Peter was martyred somewhere else other than at Rome. Therefore, the tradition has a value for a purpose.

2 Pet 1:14-15. But the genuineness of this tradition is disputed. But even if the Epistle is not genuine, that perhaps makes the tradition even more valuable for my purpose. The Epistle must be very early, and it expresses the belief of the early Church with respect to St. Peter's death.

Clement of Rome 5 (circa A.D. 95). Martyrdom is here implied. The two Apostles are connected together, and they alone are mentioned. The writer is a Roman. It was surely true of James, Jesus' brother, who died about the same time (cf. Peter of Alexandria, Routh [?] iv, p. 34).

Ignatius of Antioch, *Romans* 4—speaking of his coming martyrdom, he adjures the audience not to try and prevent it from happening and then he says:

I do not enjoin you, as Peter and Paul did. They were Apostles, I am a convict;
they were free, but I am a slave to this very hour. Yet if I shall suffer, then am
I a freed-man of Jesus Christ, and I shall rise free in Him. Now I am learning
in my bonds to put away every desire (4.3).[8]

Note that he is writing to the *Romans,* and he singles out *Peter and Paul,*
therefore there must be some special propriety in his doing so, otherwise,
why not John? He was a guest of a disciple of John at the time. He was so-
journing in the country where John was the prominent name (cf. Polycarp,
Phil. 9—see Helg. Zeitschr. xv, p. 354).

Papias, on the authority of the Presbyter John (Eusebius, *H.E.* iii.39), from
perhaps about A.D. 60–70, but written perhaps A.D. 130–40. Whatever be the
meaning of the passage, therefore, it is carried very far back. Note:
1) ἑρμηνευτής—this is not Greek but Latin for interpreter. 2) this notice
seems to have been connected by Papias with 1 Pet 5:13 because: a) Papias
was acquainted with and quoted the First Epistle of Peter, and b) in the
context of the passage edited by Eusebius he had already said something
about the connection of St. Mark with St. Peter. It is thus natural to connect
the two. And 3) Papias was so understood by writers who followed and had
his book before them (e.g. Irenaeus).

Dionysius of Corinth (in Eusebius, *H.E.* ii.25, Schwegler p. 72)—a letter
in the time of Bishop Soter (A.D. 166(7)–75(6)). See Lipsius, *Chronologie,*
p. 263. On this letter see Eusebius, *H.E.* iv.23, p. 148. *Here there is an
explicit statement.*

Muratorian Fragment from about A.D. 170 (Tregelles p. 39). Where the
author is speaking about Luke who wrote Acts and adds that he only mentions—'the individual events that took place in his presence—(37) as he plainly
shows by omitting the martyrdom of Peter (38) as well as the departure of Paul
from the city [of Rome] (39) when he journeyed to Spain.'

Clement of Alexandria (A.D. 197–217), Frag. p. 1024 (IV, p. 88 in Klotz)
quoted in Eusebius, *H.E.* iv.16 (p. 215) comp. Ad . . . [?] (IV, p. 56 Klotz). The
story is already adorned [?]. Clement's opportunities. Tertullian. *De Prescrip.*
36; Scorpiace 15; *de Baptismo 4, adv. Marc.* Gaius (Hippolytus?) A.D. 199–217.
In Eusebius, *H.E.* ii.25 (p. 72). Origen (in Eusebius, *H.E.* iii.1—p. 74 Schuyler).

---

[8]This is Lightfoot's own translation of the Greek at this point. (BW3)

And Op. II, p 24 (Delare?). Cyprian etc. *The Pseudo-Petrine Writings* [Cypr] *de bapt.* 17. Lactantius, *Inst. Div.* iv.21

Origen, *In Joan* xx no.12; *Epistle Clem. Ad Jac.* 1 On the appointment of Clement as a successor cf. e.g. to the extant Acts of Peter and Paul. *No stress can be laid on such sources of information in themselves. But there are some of them very early and it is more probable that they should be grounded in a nucleus of fact (St. Peter's visit to Rome), than not. At all events, the other testimonies are all quite independent and not to be regarded lightly* (cf. Hilgenfeld, *Zeitschrift* XV, p. 351, and Renan, *Ant.* p. 182sq.). *Caution—in the Romish controversy, it is wise not to adopt principles that render history impossible.*

But was Peter bishop of Rome for twenty-five years, or bishop of Rome at all? St. Peter was martyred in A.D. 67–68. Some would put this a bit earlier, but the data supports the later date. Therefore, on the twenty-five year supposition, the chronology must have begun in A.D. 42. So Jerome, *Vir Ill.* 1 who dates it to the 'secundo Claudii Imperatii anno.' The second year of Claudius was A.D. 42–43, the fourteenth year of Nero, A.D. Oct. 67–June 68. *This would be somewhere before Acts xii.* The death of Herod Agrippa related in Acts 12:21 sqq. took place in A.D. 44. *Whence then the silence of Acts about this most important event in the missionary labors of St. Peter?* He appears again on the scene in Acts 15. He says much about Paul's work amongst the Gentiles. He alludes to the conversion of Cornelius etc. in Acts 15:7. But neither he nor anyone there speaks of his preaching in the metropolis of heathendom. And nothing more is said about him in Acts.

St. Paul goes to Rome in A.D. 60–61, his procedure is all as unlikely as possible, if an earlier Apostle had been living there off and on for some eighteen years. See Acts 28:17 sq. and verse Acts 28:20. St. Peter, it will be remembered, is the special Apostle of the Circumcision. Notice the reference to *two whole years* of dialogue with Jews in Acts 28:30-31. The Acts extends over a period of about twenty years from the time when St. Peter's Roman episcopate began. *Yet there is not a word of it.*

St. Paul's Epistles are not only equally silent, they are more than silent. In Galatians 2:17-18 the division of labor is confirmed. Yet according to the hypothesis in question, St. Peter was the head of the first church in Gentile Christendom. The meeting was held in A.D. 51, with the Galatian letter probably A.D. 57–58. Romans in any case was written about A.D. 58. *And there is no mention of Peter notwithstanding the long list of salutations (Rom 16).* And obviously, St. Paul writes as if the church in Rome had never been visited by an Apostle (see Rom 1:11-14; 16:16, 18, 20 sq.).

Then there are the letters written from Rome by St. Paul—Philippians, Colossians, Ephesians, Philemon in A.D. 61–63. Many salutations, but no mention of Peter, though Mark is mentioned. In 2 Timothy we are up to about A.D. 67 and it exhibits the same phenomenon. *Therefore, St. Peter's visit to Rome must have been brief, and probably during St. Paul's absence, a period which is not represented either by the Acts or his Epistles.* But how came then the story of the twenty-five years? What of the list of Popes and papal succession?

Mommsen pointed out from internal evidence that the earlier part of the list ending A.D. 230 came from a different source. The name of the councils is differently given. But what was this other source for the papal sucession list? Mommsen's answer is the Chronicles of Hippolytus. It is actually anonymous, and chronicles from Adam to 235 A.D. It was originally written in Greek, and there are two extant versions. The papal list agrees in all particular with the Chronicles of Hippolytus (see Salman [?] p. 93sqq.). The first part of the manuscript begins with a reference to the 'episcoporum Roma' but this part is lost. But there can be no doubt it [was] present in the Liberian catalogue. Hort says this list of bishops was no part of the Chronicles of Hippolytus (see the *Academy* Sept. 15th 1871, the article on Lipsius' *Chronologie*). Here is the list (see Lipsius, p. 265, the date of the crucifixion thought to be that of Hippolytus):

Petrus xxv.i.ix	A.D. 30–55
Linus xii.iv.xii	A.D. 56–67
Clemens ix.xi.xii	A.D. 68–76
Cletus vi.x	A.D. 77–83
Anaclitus xii.x.iii	A.D. 84–95
(Eu)Aristus xiii.vii.ii	A.D. 96–108
Alexander vii.ii.i	A.D. 109–116

Now the object of these catalogues were to meet Gnostic errors, by exhibiting the succession as a testimony to the orthodox tradition. Now the earliest known catalogues are those of Hegisippus. Eusebius, *H.E.* iv.22 (p. 145—Schwegler). Irenaeus iii.3.1, perhaps founded on Hegisippus before (iii.1.1) spoke of St. Peter and St. Paul as founding the church of Rome. He says that they passed on the Episcopate to Linus, who is mentioned in 2 Timothy by Paul. Anacletus succeeds Linus, and Clement is said to succeed him, the Clement who wrote the letter to the Corinthians. There is then mention of Euarestus and Alexander. According to all traditions, the letter of Clement is placed during the reign of Domitian, and according to the internal evidence of the letter itself. But Hippolytus has a somewhat different list (see above). There are two changes: 1) Cletus split up into two; and 2) Clemens placed before Cletus and Anaclitus. Now Salman's [?] solution is that Hippolytus had before him the list of bishops in the traditional order with those from Linus on with the numbers of years given, AND he had before him the Clementine forgery that represented Clemens as having been consecrated by St. Peter, and he believed it. It was certainly believed before his time (e.g. Tertullian *de Praesc.* 32 which says Peter ordained Clemens). But when one added together the numbers of the dates, this brought back the accession of Linus to the Episcopate to A.D. 55. Linus was bishop for twelve years (see Eusebius, *H.E.* iii.13). Therefore, his Episcopate was from A.D. 55–67. And St. Peter was known, or generally believed to have been martyred in A.D. 67–68. The common order however puts Cletus next to Linus and therefore left no time for the consecration of Clement by St. Peter. He therefore disposed of the difficulty by transposing the order and placing Clemens next to Linus, so that he would be consecrated by St. Peter to the Episcopal office immediately prior to Peter's martyrdom. Thus we get in the Liberian catalogue Peter A.D. 55, Linus A.D. 67, Clement A.D. 76, Cletus A.D. 83, Anaclitus A.D. 95. In Hort's view this was not Hippolytus' catalogue (source). This does not affect the particular solution. The Roman church has continued and still continues today with the old order of its bishops Linus, Cletus, Clemens. If the list be anonymous, it still very extensively prevailed and exerted an enormous influence.

But what results from this list? The crucifixion takes place A.D. 29, Linus becomes bishop A.D. 55. Neglecting the parts of years, as these are habitually neglected in the list, we still have twenty-five years to account for. Now the object of Hippolytus was to trace the succession back to Christ. He therefore lists Peter as having received his consecration from our Lord, and as having himself consecrated Linus. Is it just as an Anglican having the succession in England and going back after Augustine of Canterbury, would name Gregory the Great and his predecessors, as links in the succession, not meaning that they were archbishops of Canterbury?

But two things he did not intend: 1) he did not intend that Peter was bishop of Rome for twenty-five years; and 2) he did not mean that Peter died in the year A.D. 55. He must have known well enough that Peter died after the Neronian persecution but left it out. He probably accepted the common date of A.D. 67 or 68. Compare this to the Liberian catalogue, altered and supplemented as it obviously is, referring to the death of Jesus in 29, and the blessed Peter's episcopate, and his securing of the succession. Here false consuls are given for the year of Peter's death, but the consuls are probably no part of the original list. At all events, the mention of the simultaneous martyrdom of Paul, suggests that in its first form, it suggested that the original notice referred to a later date. *Thus, the twenty-five years origin is the interval between the Ascension and the accession of Linus, supposed to have taken place in A.D. 55. But Peter's death was known to have been in A.D. 67 or 68, and the twenty-five years was afterwards referred to his Roman episcopate, and counted back from the date of his death.* This really referred to something quite different, and was reckoned from a quite different point.

If this solution is correct, the twenty-five years in the orginal form had reference to a false chronology, which placed the twelve years of Linus during the lifetime of St. Peter. But it was afterwards transferred to a truer chronology which placed these twelve years after Peter's death, hence his episcopate is from A.D. 42-67 or 68. It is thus Eusebius who is the first who makes him go to Rome during the reign of Claudius. Jerome then is the first to date the episcopate from A.D. 42-67.

There are other points in the tradition, for example about the conflict with Simon Magus. Due to the Pseudo-Petrine writers: 1) the conflict in Samaria (Acts 8:9 sqq.); 2) the conflict in Syria and Palestine. The *Clementine Homilies* and *Recognitions*. The *Recognitions* refer to Simon's intended visit to Rome, and Peter's also (*Recognitions* iii.63-64 comp. i.74); 3) the conflict in Rome. About Simon in Rome we have Justin's error (*Apol.* i.26). The idea of flying was based on the incident of one Icarus (see Suetonius, *Nero* 12, the place was the same—the Campus Martius, see Acts of Paul at Phil.). His error was propagated but not reported [?] by Hippolytus (comp. *Recognitions* ii.9). Was this error the origin of the story about Simon's visit to Rome?

Possibly, but perhaps not. He was likely enough to go there like any other religious pretender. Did St. Peter meet him there? That we cannot say. The story about Simon involves his magic, attempt to fly, and St. Peter's prayers. See *Acts of Peter and Paul*, 32sq. (p. 13sq. Tisch.). This is a late link but perhaps founded on an earlier one.

What of the famous *Domine quo vadis* legend? See Origen, *Ioannes*. xx. no. 12 (IV, p. 322). ἄνωθεν μέλλω σταυρωθῆναι is quoted, from the *Acts of Paul*. Pseudo-Linus p. 70 [Martyrium Petri, Lipsius 1:7-8]—'Domine, quo vadis. Respondit ei Christus: Romam venio iterum crucifigi.' The tradition occurs in the present *Acts of Peter and Paul* no. 82, (p. 36, Tisch.). It is also related by Ambrose.

THE MARTYRDOM

First of all, the St. Pietro in Vincoli has nothing to do with Peter's chains in Rome. The Mamertine prison may figure in the discussion. As to the mode of crucifixion see Tacitus, *Annals* xv.44 (on Christ's death by crucifixion, but all the crucifixion of Christians). See also Seneca, *Dialog.* iii.2.2—'Can anyone be found who would prefer wasting away in pain dying limb by limb, or letting out his life drop by drop, rather than expiring once for all? Can any man be found willing to be fastened to the accursed tree, long sickly, already deformed, swelling with ugly wounds on shoulders and chest, and drawing the breath of life amid long drawn-out agony? He would have many excuses for dying even before mounting the cross.' St. Paul of course was beheaded, which is natural for a Roman citizen (Eusebius, *H.E.* v.1). Origen first relates it κατά κεφαλῆς. He probably got it from the Acts of Paul, which he quotes there. Thus it is an early tradition.

The Vatican—its place. This is a very likely place, where the circus of Nero was (see *Acts of Peter and Paul*, 84). See Pseudo-Linus p. 71 [Martyrium beati Petri apostoli a Lino, section 10] ('ad locum qui appellatur iuxta obeliscum Neronis, in monte'). On the circus of Caligula and the obelisk of Nero see Birn's *Rome*, p. 270. It was apparently called the circus of Nero because it was so much visited by him. St. Paul's martyrdom by contrast is placed elsewhere, on the Appian Way. See Eusebius, *H.E.* ii.25—the place where they suffered rather than the place of their graves. There is an old tradition that Peter was buried at the catacombs.

The Time of the Martyrdom—1) either during the interval between St. Paul's first and second visits to Rome, say A.D. 63–66, or 2) after the Second Epistle to Timothy was written. This accords with the provenance of the Epistle which was written after Ephesians in A.D. 62–63, and also after the Neronian persecution had broken out in July of A.D. 64. The legend says that both St. Peter and St. Paul died on the same day—the fourteenth year of Nero, June 29th (i.e. A.D. 68). There are obvious objections to this: 1) Nero was no longer living by June 29th; 2) there are reasons for suspecting that June 29th is not the day of the martyrs but the day of the common depositing of their bones at one of their mausoleums. The 22nd of February is given in one authority (see Tillemont I, p. 533), so this tradition may have been the origin of the simultaneous martyrdom tradition. 3) One early tradition speaks of St. Peter suffering on the same *day* as St. Paul but in the previous year (e.g. the Prudentius passage on Peter and Paul from the latter half of the 4th century). Augustine too refers to it—*Sermon* 381 'de natali Apost. Petr. et Pauli' (V, p. 1481A see more in Tillemont p. 533). This seems obviously to be a device to reconcile two different things: 1) the known fact that they did not perish at the same time; and 2) the fact that this day, supposed to be the day of their death but really the day of their deposition or burial was celebrated together. Certainly, if they had perished on the same day, this form of tradition is inexplicable. The different places of their death point to different times.

St. Peter may have come to Rome after St. Paul left, perhaps while he was in Spain. The Muratorian canon connects it to the westward trip. He may have perished in the spent wave of the Neronian persecution. The place and time of his death points to this, say A.D. 65–68. As for the tradition, it places the death of two Apostles in the twelfth year of Nero (i.e. October 65–October 66 A.D.). So Epiphanius xxvii.6—'in the twelfth year of Nero.' So then perhaps Peter went to Rome in A.D. 64, and was martyred in 65 or 66.

THE EPISTLE ITSELF

To whom is it addressed, Jewish or Gentile Christians? Many critics, guided by the use of the term 'diaspora' suppose the audience is Jewish. But certainly there is internal evidence that Gentiles are addressed—1 Pet 1:14, 18—impossible as spoken by a Jew to a Jew. Then there is 1 Pet 2:10, 25; 4:3—the ἡμῖν of the Received Text disappears, and therefore we understand ὑμῖν based on the preceding ὑμεῖς. What then is the meaning of 'diaspora'? It refers to the Christian 'dispersion.' The 'diaspora' in existence in a lost world. Christians are παρεπίδημοι (1 Pet 1:1), not 'among the Dispersion' but 'belonging to the Dispersion' (comp. 1 Pet 2:11). This is a transference to the Israel after the Spirit from the Israel after the flesh. So too 1 Pet 2:9, 10—ὑμεῖς δὲ γένος ἐκλεκτόν, νῦν δὲ λαὸς Θεοῦ and 1 Pet 3:6—ἧς ἐγενήθητε τέκνα ἀγαθοποιοῦσαι.

The Time—When was it written? A season of persecution, see 1 Pet 1:6 (λυπηθέντες ἐν ποικίλοις πειρασμοῖς), 1 Pet 2:12; 3:13-16; 4:12-16; 5:6, 9. Not desultory persecution, but more or less systematic. The leading purport of the letter is to console and encourage those under the fiery trial. There is no other book in the canon so burdened with the subject of persecution, other than the Apocalypse. Persecution is in the atmosphere. Was it part of the Neronian persecution? Nothing previous answers to this condition. Its focus chiefly at Rome, the dogs let loose by the Imperial master. But it was felt in the provinces, most especially in Asia Minor. See Rev 1:9, of St. John himself, and the churches in Rev 2; 3, especially Rev 2:10-11. Rev 2:13—Ἀντιπᾶς ὁ μάρτυς μου ὁ πιστός μου. Comp. Rev 3:11; 4:11; 20:4 and Renan, *Le Antichrist* p. 183. Therefore, not before July A.D. 64. This agrees with other indications, writings known to the author, for example:

ROMANS (A.D. 58)	Rom 12:1—see 1 Pet 2:5
	Rom 12:2—see 1 Pet 1:14
	Rom 12:3-8—see 1 Pet 4:10, 11
	Rom 12:9, 10—see 1 Pet 1:22; 2:17
	Rom 12:14-19—see 1 Pet 3:8-12
	Rom 13:1-7—see 1 Pet 2:13-14
also	Rom 4:24—see 1 Pet 1:21
	Rom 6:7—see 1 Pet 4:1, 2
	Rom 6:18—see 1 Pet 2:24
	Rom 8:18—see 1 Pet 5:1
	Rom 8:3, 4—see 1 Pet 3:22
	Rom 9:33—see 1 Pet 2:6 sqq.

EPHESIANS (A.D. 62 or thereabouts). The whole should be compared with 1 Peter.

1 Pet 1:1	Eph 1:4
1 Pet 1:3	Eph 1:3; 2:2
1 Pet 1:4, 5	Eph 1:10, 18
1 Pet 1:14	Eph 2:3
1 Pet 1:18	Eph 4:17 sq.
1 Pet 2:5	Eph 2:21, 22
1 Pet 2:18 sqq.	Eph 6:5
1 Pet 3:1 sqq.	Eph 5:22
1 Pet 3:7 sqq.	Eph 5:25
1 Pet 3:22	Eph 1:20, 21
1 Pet 4:3	Eph 2:2; 4:17

Comp. also the Epistle of St. James

Therefore 1 Peter written after about A.D. 62, 63.

St. Paul's Life

(main facts—release from captivity A.D. 63–64, martyrdom 67-68)

Notice the reciprocal silence: a) they are not together at Rome; b) did not clash in Asia Minor. Though he **presumed** *that St. Paul was there in the one place, he was in direct communication with the other. These three lines of investigation point to the same conclusion with regard to date. St. Paul's release was before A.D. 64, and his martyrdom about A.D. 67–68. Meanwhile (in between) there is his visit to Spain. These Epistles therefore must probably be placed either during this (Spanish) visit (when Paul was separated from the East), or after his death. Perhaps on the whole the former is more likely and more in accord with the tradition.*

So what is to be placed earlier? The ordination of Linus by St. Peter? According to the view preferred, St. Peter was martyred before St. Paul. Yet we have 2 Tim 4:21, on this supposition, after Peter's death. Nevertheless, Linus is not singled out, but mentioned after others. It is not probable that he was then bishop, in the modern sense of bishop. The earliest form of the tradition in Irenaeus iii.3.3 says 'The blessed apostles then having founded and built the church, commited the ministry of the episcopate to Linus. Of this Linus, Paul makes mention in his Epistles to Timothy.' Notice it says, 'the Apostles' not St. Peter specially. The later attribution to St. Peter does accord with the general tendency of later legends to accumulate (and focus) everything on St. Peter, as 'the prince of the Apostles.' This ordination of Linus may have been one of the latest acts of St. Paul. *The only result however on which we can safely depend is that after the death of the Apostles, Linus held the chief place in the government of the church in Rome, was (we may say), bishop of Rome, though the bishop cannot be separated from his presbyters by such a direct line of demarcation, as is later true.*

Circumstances then had obscured or obliterated the boundary line between the spheres of the two Apostles, laid down in Gal 2:7-9. St. Paul was occupied in missionary work in the far West (Spain). The Asiatic Christians were sorely tired of persecution. St. Peter was prompted [?] out of his prominence to address these words of exhortation and comfort. Accordingly, he writes. *Their conduct under persecution may be regarded as the main topic of the letter.* Compare 1 Pet 5:12—ἔγραψα, παρακαλῶν καὶ ἐπιμαρτυρῶν ταύτην εἶναι ἀληθῆ χάριν τοῦ Θεοῦ, εἰς ἣν στῆτε. The Gospel that they had received from their teachers, especially St. Paul.

On its Genuineness. It was never once questioned until the present [i.e., nineteenth] century. The Paulicianus (on the authority of Petrus Siculus *Hist. Man.* p. 17—'Binas vero catholicas . . . Petri principiis apostolo . . .'). Alford (p. 114) treats this as an insignificant example. It is not an exception at all. They (the Paulicianii) rejected the Epistles not because they were not by St. Peter, but because they *were his.* They regarded him as no apostle because he had denied Christ.[9] Similarly with Marcion. Citing Theodore of Mopsuetia, is a mistake. The First Epistle of Peter is not mentioned. [Check his commentaries to see whether there is any reference to 1 Peter.][10]

The testimony about the genuineness of this letter is very early and of the most satisfactory kind. See Origen in Eusebius, *H.E.* vi.25 and *H.E.* iii.3 (on the second Epistle of Peter), Clement c.36 (cf. 1 Pet 2:9 and see Zahn, *Hermas,* p. 478); Ignatius, *ad Magnes.* viii.9 is doubtful, but Polycarp, a bishop of Asia Minor, is indisputable; Papias, with his probable reference to Mark, Irenaeus iii.17.4 (see 1 Pet 2:2—elder in Irenaeus?), Letter to Diogenetus, Shepherd of Hermas (the date?—see Zahn, p. 421sq.—on 1 Pet 5:7—see Zahn, p. 438; on 1 Pet 1:6 see Zahn, p. 429; on 1 Pet 3:20—see Zahn, p. 425; on 1 Pet 4:14, see

---

[9]On 'Petrus siculus' see Migne, *Patrolog. Graec.* CIV (Phot. Op.) p. 1256; Herzog, xi, p.228 s.v. Peter.
[10]This is a note from Lightfoot to himself. (BW3)

Zahn, p. 429).[11] Then there is Melito to Antonius Caesar p. 51—'an eternal substance which fadeth not away' (see 1 Pet 1:4), and Theophilus ii.34 citing 1 Pet 1:18. As for the Muratorian Canon, it was probably mutilated. Then there is the Old Latin and the Peshitto. What of the Heretics? There was not very much in 1 Peter which would lend itself to Gnostic speculation. On the Simonians see Hippolytus, *Haer.* vi.10, and Theodotus as well.

Turning to the Internal Evidence, since the External Evidence created the very sharpest presentation in its favor, the objection against the genuineness should be really valid to weigh against it. What are these objections based on the Internal Evidence?

THE PAULINE CHARACTER OF THE DOCUMENT

This objection however rests on a *petitio principii*, namely the attempt of the Tübingen school to reconstruct Christian history on the basis of a few verses—Gal 1:18; 2:6-9 (but here it is a matter of a separation of spheres, not a difference of teaching), Gal 2:11-21. It *assumes* throughout that St. Peter was at one with St. Paul in belief. He is only reproached for inconsistency in his practice. But if there was no such fundamental difference in belief, why should St. Peter not have been influenced by St. Paul's modes of expressing the truths of Christianity? This is much more natural than the contrary.

Consider St. Peter's character: 1) essentially open to impression. The stronger intellect and obvious energy of St. Paul would not fail to make itself felt; 2) his opportunities to be influenced see a) personal intercourse at Jerusalem with Paul—first visit, third visit, and at Antioch; b) Paul's Epistles. For example the Corinthian Epistles mention St. Peter's name and influence at Corinth. It is probable he should have seen these letters which were regarded as weighty and powerful and which produced so much effect. But there were two letters above all which he would be likely to have seen—Peter was staying at Rome so Romans (its circular character), and Ephesians, addressed to these very Asiatic churches which 1 Peter addresses. Likewise consider Ephesians' circular character (copies circulated without any special opening address to the Ephesians). These are the two Epistles of which 1 Peter shows the greatest knowledge. 3) Common Friends—Silas, Mark. Silas had been with

---

[11]Another note of Lightfoot to himself in pencil—"investigate Zahn more carefully." (BW3)

St. Paul at Antioch and Jerusalem on his second missionary journey, was with him for several years during the most active part of his life, he takes part in the superscription of 1-2 Thessalonians. Mark was with Paul on his first missionary journey and again in Rome (Col 4:10; Philem 24), so that he was fresh from dealing with things with St. Paul when he found St. Peter.

But how far is the document Pauline? It is very unlike St. Paul's own Epistles, not Pauline in the sense that Hebrews is Pauline. There are indeed reminiscences of St. Paul's language and his thoughts, but there is nothing distinctly Pauline. Yes 'faith' is mentioned in 1 Pet 1:5, 7, 9, 21; 5:9 but it is in all the Apostolic writings (e.g. the Apocalypse). It is not emphasized in 1 Peter nor connected with works. Here it is as much steadfastness, reliance on God as anything else. In short, it has no special prominence. Grace is frequently mentioned but not contrasted with Law. The most Pauline passage is 1 Pet 2:24. It has coincidence with Rom 6:2, 10, 18, but it may be explained by Gal 2:19, 20 (see Lightfoot, *Gal.* p. 339). The ransom/atonement is as strong in St. Peter as St. Paul. [N.B. The manuscript, sadly, breaks off here. We have not found the additional missing pages of the introduction. We do know, however, there were only two more pages, as this page was numbered by Lightfoot as p. 57, and the commentary proper begins on p. 60. (BW3)]

Part Four

COMMENTARY ON 1 PETER

A Living Hope, a Call to Holy Living
(1 Peter 1)

Vs. 1 Πέτρος—This prescript after the pattern of Paul's who set the pattern of Christian epistolography.

ἐκλεκτοῖς—comp. 1 Pet 5:13, i.e. members of the Church. Israel was ἐκλεκτόν γένος—Is 43:20—ποτίσαι τὸ γένος μου τὸ ἐκλεκτόν. See Ps 104:6—σπέρμα Ἀβραὰμ δοῦλοι αὐτοῦ, υἱοὶ Ἰακὼβ ἐκλεκτοί αὐτοῦ. Hence *the* ἐκλεκτοί. Is 65:8, 15, 23. These terms transferred from the Israel after the flesh to the Israel after the Spirit. The ἐκλεκτοὶ therefore are the members of the Christian Church. One can draw an analogy with the term ἅγιοι for instance in Phil 1:1. There is a difference of usage in the Gospels when compared to the Epistles. In the Gospels we have ἐκλεκτοί and κλητοί but in the Epistles (e.g. in Paul) ἐκλεκτοί = κλητοί (see Col 3:12 and my commentary p. 286).

διασπορᾶς—belonging to the Dispersion, consisting of the Dispersion. The Dispersion is here concrete, the body dispersed. A similar transference is in ἐκλεκτοῖς. διασπορᾶ as the Jewish Dispersion—Judith 5:18; 2 Macc 1:27; Ps 146:2; Comp. John 7:35, those collected in the Holy City, their proper home. Transferred to the Christian Church. The dispersion scattered about the heathen world, not yet gathered into the Holy City, where is their New Jerusalem, their πολίτευμα. But the use in James 1:1 is different. There it is used of Jewish Christians and meant literally.

παρεπιδήμοις (cf. [Plat] *Axioch* p.365—see Steph. *Thes.* s.v)—See 1 Pet 2:11. The connection between παρεπιδήμοις to πάροικος occurs in Gen 23:4; Ps 37:17 in the LXX. Comp. Heb 11:13.

Πόντου etc. These are *Political* subdivisions, the Roman provinces. Not as in the Acts and St. Paul where only Asia is a political name. The whole of Asia Minor except the provinces of Cilicia and Pamphylia, the two similar seaboard provinces. The reason Asia is an exception is not obvious. Perhaps they were superintended by the same disciple of St. Paul, and any interference would be intrusive.

What about inferences as to the position of the writer? Rome = Babylon. Inferences from the order of the names are quite fallacious. There is no continuous order. It suits literal Babylon as little as Rome. There is also no notice of the evangelizing of these districts. Probably they were chiefly evangelized through the instrumentality of St. Paul's delegates during his sojourn in Ephesus. The spread of Christianity in some of these districts, Pontus and Bithynia, was about forty years later. Probably the Christian Church flourished more here than anywhere else in the world.

Comp. Pliny Letter x.96-97—

It is my practice, my lord, to refer to you all matters concerning which I am in doubt. For who can better give guidance to my hesitation or inform my ignorance? I have never participated in trials of Christians. I therefore do not know what offenses it is the practice to punish or investigate, and to what extent. And I have been not a little hesitant as to whether there should be any distinction on account of age or no difference between the very young and the more mature; whether pardon is to be granted for repentance, or, if a man has once been a Christian, it does him no good to have ceased to be one; whether the name itself, even without offenses, or only the offenses associated with the name are to be punished.

Meanwhile, in the case of those who were denounced to me as Christians, I have observed the following procedure: I interrogated these as to whether they were Christians; those who confessed I interrogated a second and a third time, threatening them with punishment; those who persisted I ordered executed. For I had no doubt that, whatever the nature of their creed, stubbornness and inflexible obstinacy surely deserve to be punished. There were others possessed of the same folly; but because they were Roman citizens, I signed an order for them to be transferred to Rome.

Soon accusations spread, as usually happens, because of the proceedings going on, and several incidents occurred. An anonymous document was published containing the names of many persons. Those who denied that they

were or had been Christians, when they invoked the gods in words dictated by
me, offered prayer with incense and wine to your image, which I had ordered
to be brought for this purpose together with statues of the gods, and moreover
cursed Christ—none of which those who are really Christians, it is said, can
be forced to do—these I thought should be discharged. Others named by the
informer declared that they were Christians, but then denied it, asserting that
they had been but had ceased to be, some three years before, others many years,
some as much as twenty-five years. They all worshipped your image and the
statues of the gods, and cursed Christ.

They asserted, however, that the sum and substance of their fault or error
had been that they were accustomed to meet on a fixed day before dawn and
sing responsively a hymn to Christ as to a god, and to bind themselves by
oath, not to some crime, but not to commit fraud, theft, or adultery, not
falsify their trust, nor to refuse to return a trust when called upon to do so.
When this was over, it was their custom to depart and to assemble again to
partake of food—but ordinary and innocent food. Even this, they affirmed,
they had ceased to do after my edict by which, in accordance with your instructions, I had forbidden political associations. Accordingly, I judged it all
the more necessary to find out what the truth was by torturing two female
slaves who were called deaconesses. But I discovered nothing else but de-
praved, excessive superstition.

I therefore postponed the investigation and hastened to consult you. For
the matter seemed to me to warrant consulting you, especially because of the
number involved. For many persons of every age, every rank, and also of both
sexes are and will be endangered. For the contagion of this superstition has
spread not only to the cities but also to the villages and farms. But it seems
possible to check and cure it. It is certainly quite clear that the temples, which
had been almost deserted, have begun to be frequented, that the established
religious rites, long neglected, are being resumed, and that from everywhere
sacrificial animals are coming, for which until now very few purchasers could
be found. Hence it is easy to imagine what a multitude of people can be reformed if an opportunity for repentance is afforded.

Vs. 2—κατὰ πρόγνωσιν Θεοῦ Πατρός, ἐν ἁγιασμῷ Πνεύματος, εἰς
ὑπακοὴν καὶ ῥαντισμὸν αἵματος Ἰησοῦ Χριστοῦ· Connected with ἐκλεκτοῖς.
Notice the three persons of the Trinity here—κατὰ—the source, origin; ἐν the
continuance; εἰς—the goal, end.

ἐν ἁγιασμῷ Πνεύματος—Not 'in sanctification of your spirit.' The Spirit is the effective power, the parallelism of the other clauses requires this. And so also perhaps in 2 Thess 2:13, where the same phrase occurs and where roughly εἵλατο ὑμᾶς = κατὰ πρόγνωσιν here. And ἐν ἁγιασμῷ Πνεύματος καὶ πίστει ἀληθείας (the objective power plus the subjective reception) = ἐν ἁγιασμῷ Πνεύματος here. Also εἰς σωτηρίαν = εἰς ὑπακοὴν here.

ὑπακοήν—obedience, i.e. submission and acceptance through faith—Rom 1:5; 16:25. This is the condition and preliminary of ῥαντισμὸν αἵματος Ἰησοῦ Χριστοῦ. The people's part is the contract or covenant. Ex 24:7—'be obedient' (comp. LXX ἀκουσόμεθα).

ῥαντισμὸν αἵματος—All other sprinklings do not answer to the conditions. See Exodus 24:8—ἰδοὺ τὸ αἷμα τῆς διαθήκης, ἧς διέθετο Κύριος πρὸς ὑμᾶς περὶ πάντων τῶν λόγων τούτων. See Heb 9:19 which is the best comment on this present passage.

The old covenant, and the new. τὸ αἷμα τῆς διαθήκης. The institution of the Eucharist. Comp. Mt 26:28 with Mark 14:24—Τοῦτό ἐστιν τὸ αἷμά μου τῆς διαθήκης τὸ ἐκχυννόμενον ὑπὲρ πολλῶν. The idea here is twofold: 1) the covenant, and admission to it. A promise on God's part and the obligation on the people's part; 2) the purification—see Heb 9:19.

χάρις (the source) and εἰρήνη (the end) of all blessings. Note the coincidence with Pauline language.

Vs. 3—Εὐλογητὸς—As in 2 Cor 1:3; Eph 1:3. Rightly translated here and in Eph 1:3 wrongly in 2 Cor 1:3. On ὁ Θεὸς καὶ Πατὴρ see my notes on Ephesians 1:3.

ἀναγεννήσας ἡμᾶς—Potentially at the moment of his resurrection, actually, when the power of that resurrection was available for us, i.e. when we accepted the faith and were baptized into Him.

εἰς ἐλπίδα ζῶσαν—The transition from death to life is the main idea of the sentence.

δι᾽ ἀναστάσεως Ἰησοῦ Χριστοῦ ἐκ νεκρῶν—as the assurance of our immorality and the consummation of God's grace.

ἀναστάσεως not to be connected with ζῶσαν. ζῶσαν is absolute as in 1 Pet 1:23; 2:4, 5. ἄφθαρτον general, imperishable.

Vs. 4—ἀμίαντον καὶ ἀμάραντον—special. The former means without defilement, the latter means without fading. ἀμάραντον is a hapax in the N.T. Wisdom 6:12.

εἰς κληρονομίαν not like the κληρονομία of the Israel after the flesh. Τετηρημένην—See Bengel. **Vs. 5**—φρουρουμένους, not to prevent this doing harm, but to prevent their receiving harm. Comp. Gal 3:23. The form of the sentence in Galatians is followed here, though the meaning is different. ἐφρουρούμεθα συνκλειόμενοι εἰς τὴν μέλλουσαν πίστιν ἀποκαλυφθῆναι. This points to the true construction here in vs. 5. εἰς σωτηρίαν is not co-ordinated with εἰς ἐλπίδα of 1 Pet 1:3, but depends on φρουρουμένους ('being guarded . . . unto salvation'). Preserved, not withstanding the time of persecution. Comp. Romans 8:18—οὐκ ἄξια τὰ παθήματα τοῦ νῦν καιροῦ πρὸς τὴν μέλλουσαν δόξαν ἀποκαλυφθῆναι εἰς ἡμᾶς.

Vs. 6—ἐν ᾧ refers to the whole preceding sentence as in 1 Pet 4:4. For ἀγαλλιᾶσθε compare Rom 5:3—οὐ μόνον δέ, ἀλλὰ καὶ καυχώμεθα ἐν ταῖς θλίψεσιν, εἰδότες ὅτι ἡ θλῖψις ὑπομονὴν κατεργάζεται. The alternative is to take ἐν ᾧ to refer to ἐν καιρῷ ἐσχάτῳ and this in two ways: 1) at which i.e. at the prospect of which you rejoice. But this is no *gain*. The *object.* 2) in which, 'when'—the time, but this requires a future sense to ἀγαλλιᾶσθε which in such a connection as this seems impossible (in spite of Hather and Alford).

ὀλίγον ἄρτι no objection to the construction of ἐν ᾧ that has been adopted here. The continuity of their rejoicing in their glorious destiny is not interrupted by the momentary pains of their suffering.

πειρασμοῖς (see Tischendorf), i.e. afflictions, persecutions, by which their steadfastness is tried. Taken from James 1:2, 3—ὅταν πειρασμοῖς περιπέσητε ποικίλοις, γινώσκοντες ὅτι τὸ δοκίμιον ὑμῶν τῆς πίστεως κατεργάζεται ὑπομονήν.

Vs. 7—τὸ δοκίμιον, test or testing?: 1) testing in James 1:3; 2) instrument of testing e.g. crucible in the LXX. See Proverbs 27:21; Ps 12:7 (furnace of testing); 3) the thing tested an approved example, compare δοκίμα in 2 Cor 13:3. So here. See Prov 27:21—δοκίμιον ἀργύρῳ καὶ χρυσῷ . . . See also Steph. *Thes.* s.v. for its use in classical contexts. See Gesenius in Wahl, Classical s.v. χρυσίς not χρυσές nor χρυσίτιδος.

εἰς ἔπαινον. See Rom 2:9, 29, especially Col 3:4—φανερωθήσεσθε ἐν δόξῃ, not 'to the praise of God,' God being the object, but rather they themselves are the object of praise, etc.

Vs. 8—ἰδόντες not εἰδότες as in B.M.T. and T.R. Perhaps a reminiscence of our Lord's word—John 20:29.

ἄρτι—Now! You do not have to wait for this joy, this glory.

εἰς ὃν ἄρτι μὴ ὁρῶντες πιστεύοντες, 'on whom, believing, though you see him not,' εἰς ὃν to be connected with πιστεύοντες.

ἀνεκλαλήτῳ compare 2 Cor 9:15—ἀνεκδιηγήτῳ, indescribable.

δεδοξασμένη—in earnest of the future glorification.

Vs. 9—κομιζόμενοι already obtaining, for σωτηρία is a present thing, as well as a future one, an actual moral and spiritual change for 'those being saved.' σωτηρίαν ψυχῶν the salvation of your souls. Meant generally, though referring to their own souls. More especially the inclusion of the Gentiles amongst the saved.

τὸ τέλος—the end, object, aim, see Rom 6:21, 22.

Vs. 10 ἐξεζήτησαν καὶ ἐξηραύνησαν—Two strong verbs, the latter stronger than the former, denoting the persistency of the search.

Here a representation of the position of the prophets and the discipline of this inspection. Neither were they: 1) speaking wholly to their own time (the rationalist view), nor 2) looking wholly into the future (the irrationalist view). But rather the thought struggling for expression, with the future vaguely discerned. This exactly answers to the Messianic prophecies as we find them. They were speaking of the future through their present.

προφῆται. See St. Peter's speech in the Acts—Acts 2:21, 23-36; 3:18-26; 4:11, 24.

οἱ περὶ τῆς εἰς ὑμᾶς χάριτος προφητεύσαντες—the grace which was intended for you. χάρις—the characteristic description of the Gospel. The law was a contract, the Gospel is a boon. See Col 1:6 (my commentary p. 202).

Vs. 11 εἰς τίνα—the date, ἢ ποῖον the characteristics.

εἰς ὑμᾶς—you Gentiles, 1 Pet 1:4, 12, 14, 15, 17 etc. This extension is part of the character of the χάρις. The law was confined to a chosen race, the χάρις is offered free to all.

ἐδήλου τὸ ἐν αὐτοῖς Πνεῦμα Χριστοῦ προμαρτυρόμενον τὰ εἰς Χριστὸν— see Ignatius, *Philadel.* 5:2—'Yes, and we love the prophets also, because they too pointed to the Gospel in their preaching and set their hope on Him and awaited Him; in whom also having faith they were saved in the unity of Jesus Christ, being worthy of all love and admiration as holy men, approved of Jesus Christ and numbered together in the Gospel of our common hope.'[1]

---

[1] This is Lightfoot's own translation. (BW3)

See *Barnab.* 5.6—'Understand. The prophets, receiving grace from Him, prophesied concerning Him.'[2]

Πνεῦμα Χριστοῦ—Comp. Acts 16:7; Rom 8:9. It is the Spirit that comes from Christ and speaks of Christ. The former however is the main idea of the expression, the latter being inferential. Χριστοῦ is the subject not the object of the phrase.

τὰ εἰς Χριστὸν παθήματα—The sufferings that should befall Christ, which were destined for the Christ, which corresponds with τῆς εἰς ὑμᾶς χάριτος. There is no reference here to our sufferings for or with Christ.

τὰς μετὰ ταῦτα δόξας—compare Luke 24:25, 26.

Vs. 12—ἀπεκαλύφθη is not the cause of the ἐξεραυνῶντες but contemporaneous with it. Thus much was revealed to them. The rest they felt and searched after.

ὑμῖν—That comparing them with the fulfillment must be assumed—See Ignatius, *Magnes.* s.v.

διηκόνουν αὐτά—these truths? The initiative of the commentators? (Alford), 'those things which.' This is impossible, we have here αὐτά not ἐκεῖνα so it must refer to the preceding words. Similar mistake in Phil 4:3.

νῦν is the present dispensation, hence an aorist. εὐαγγελισαμένων ὑμᾶς—an accusative either of the thing preceded, or of the person to whom preceded, e.g. Acts 8:12, 25, 35, 40. Hence τινι τι—Acts 8:35, τινα τι—Acts 13:32.

ἀποσταλέντι—referring especially to the day of Pentecost. Notice not ἀπέσταλμενω.

Παρακύπτειν—the literal meaning see Luke 24:12; John 20:5, 11; the metaphorical meaning James 1:25.

ἄγγελοι—Outside the scheme of redemption, but a subject of contemplation for them cf. Eph 3:10.

Vs. 13—Διὸ 'therefore' having these hopes, having these blessings in store. ἀναζωσάμενοι—as in Polycarp, *Phil.* 2 cf. Eph 6:14 expediti, cf. Luke 12:35. ἀναζ—the initial act. ἀνα—plus the aorist. Περιεζ—the resultant state Περί—plus the perfect.

[2]Again, Lightfoot's own translation. (BW3)

τῆς διανοίας ὑμῶν—a strong metaphor, Hebraic, e.g. the color of your lips. νήφοντες—comp. 1 Pet 4:7; 5:8. Wakeful and sober, for he will summon you away unexpectedly in the night. Luke 12:37—γρηγοροῦντας. The world is stuck in a drowsy revel. Cf. 1 Thess 5:6.

τελείως with νήφοντες cf. 1 Cor 15:34—ἐκνήψατε δικαίως.

τὴν φερομένην—The present describes the certainty, if not the imminence of the event. So ἔρχεται.

ἐν ἀποκαλύψει—When Jesus shall reveal himself, interpreted by 1 Pet 1:7, cf. 2 Thess 1:7. Illustrated by Luke 12:37. Thus in the Apocalypse of St. John, a presentation of the last things.

Vs. 14—τέκνα ὑπακοῆς comp. 2 Pet 2:14. comp. Eph 5:6—τοὺς υἱοὺς τῆς ἀπειθείας, comp. Eph 2:3—τέκνα φύσει ὀργῆς. Eph 5:6—ἡ ὀργὴ τοῦ Θεοῦ ἐπὶ τοὺς υἱοὺς τῆς ἀπειθείας.

Συσχηματιζόμενοι See Rom 12:2.

On σχῆμα—fleeting, changing fashion. See Lightfoot, *Philippians*, p. 125sq. ἐν τῇ ἀγνοίᾳ—'in the ignorance of the heathen.' Comp. Acts 17:30; Eph 4:18.

Vs. 15—κατά 'after the pattern of '

Vs. 16—γέγραπται. Lev 11:44; 19:2; 20:7, 26. They are rescued from the spiritual Egypt and brought into relationship with Yahweh, like Israel of old. Comp. Clement of Rome 30.1—'Seeing then that we are the special portion of a Holy God, let us do all things that pertain unto holiness, forsaking evil speakings, abominable and impure embraces, drunkennesses and tumults and hateful lusts, abominable adultery, hateful pride' (comp. 1 Pet 2:1).[3]

Vs. 17—Πατέρα ἐπικαλεῖσθε—corresponding to τέκνα ὑπακοῆς. This should not be translated 'if you invoke as Father' (e.g. in the Lord's Prayer), but rather 'if you bear the name of, as your Father,' or 'if you surnamed yourself after, as your Father.' Comp. Eph 3:14-15—πρὸς τὸν Πατέρα, ἐξ οὗ πᾶσα πατριὰ ἐν οὐρανοῖς καὶ ἐπὶ γῆς ὀνομάζεται (where the T.R. interferes with the sense). See 1 Clement 58.1—'Let us therefore be obedient unto His most holy and glorious Name, thereby escaping the threatenings which were spoken of old.' See James 2:7—τὸ καλὸν ὄνομα τὸ ἐπικληθὲν ἐφ' ὑμᾶς. 'If you bear the name of God as your patronymic.'

For Πατήρ in connection with the new birth—see 1 Pet 1:3, 23. If your Father is also your Judge, it follows that a reverential awe must rule your conduct.

---

[3]The Lightfoot translation of 1 Clement. (BW3)

παροικίας—See my note on Clement of Rome I (p. 31sq.).

Vs. 18—And this feeling will be deepened and extended by a sense of the enormous price which has been paid for you. The same notion implied in a similar way in 1 Cor 6:20; 7:23—τιμῆς ἠγοράσθητε.

ἀργυρίῳ ἢ χρυσίῳ

ἐλυτρώθητε—the ransom, atonement.

A double idea: 1) the teleological—a work done for us, the guilt offering is made; 2) the moral and spiritual—the work done in us, an internal change. There is a tendency in modern theology to separate the two and to lay all the stress on the former. Not so the Apostle. e.g here the moral change is emphasized. We are ransomed from a life of wickedness. The ransom has no value for us, or advantage, unless the one goes with the other. So e.g. Gal 6:14.

ματαίας—Careless, reckless, purposelessness, the sport [?] of circumstances.

Πατροπαραδότου—parents to Gentiles.

Vs. 19—ὡς ἀμνοῦ ἀμώμου καὶ ἀσπίλου Χριστοῦ. The Paschal lamb—Ex 12:5 connected with the prophecy Is 53:7, comp. 1 Pet 2:22.

ἀσπίλος (so in the Anthology but perhaps both).

Vs. 20—ἐπ᾽ ἐσχάτου τῶν χρόνων—The whole of the new dispensation gathered up, as it were.

φανερωθέντος—implying pre-existence.

δι᾽ ὑμᾶς—chiefly Gentiles.

Vs. 21—πιστοὺς εἰς Θεὸν—This was not true of the Jews, who knew God before. But the Gentiles were brought to the knowledge of God through Christ. This is a matter of history.

On πιστός whether active or passive, see Lightfoot, *Galatians*, p. 154sq. Here the active sense predominates as in John 20:27.

On πίστις εἰς—Acts 20:21; 24:24; 26:18. See e.g. Col 2:5

πιστεύειν εἰς frequently. So here πιστός εἰς, comp. below ὥστε τὴν πίστιν ὑμῶν.

τὸν ἐγείραντα—This is the central object of this faith, belief in the resurrection. Rom 10:9.

ὥστε—so your faith and hope might be towards God, not as the heathens. Your faith might also be a hope etc.

Vs. 22—ἐν τῇ ὑπακοῇ τῆς ἀληθείας. This is an objective genitive, obedience to the truth. See 2 Cor 10:5—εἰς τὴν ὑπακοὴν τοῦ Χριστοῦ. But in the case of εἰς ὑπακοὴν πίστεως Rom 1:5; 16:26, the sense is subjective.

εἰς φιλαδελφίαν—love of the brethren as rightly here, the brotherhood into which we are born. Not 'brotherly kindness' as in the A.V. 2 Pet 1:7. The new spiritual fatherhood, under a new spiritual brotherhood. To 2 Pet 1:7 comp. Rom 12:10.

Vs. 23—ἀναγεγεννημένοι—being born again.

ἐκ σπορᾶς—comp. John 1:13.

διὰ λόγου ζῶντος Θεοῦ καὶ μένοντος.

Vss. 24-25—Is 40:6 sqq.—φωνὴ λέγοντος· βόησον· καὶ εἶπα· τί βοήσω; πᾶσα σάρξ χόρτος, καὶ πᾶσα δόξα ἀνθρώπου ὡς ἄνθος χόρτου· ἐξηράνθη ὁ χόρτος, καὶ τὸ ἄνθος ἐξέπεσε, τὸ δὲ ῥῆμα τοῦ Θεοῦ ἡμῶν μένει εἰς τὸν αἰῶνα. ἐπ᾽ὄρος ὑψηλὸν ἀνάβηθι, ὁ εὐαγγελιζόμενος Σιών·

Here we have διότι πᾶσα σάρξ ὡς χόρτος, καὶ πᾶσα δόξα αὐτῆς ὡς ἄνθος χόρτου· ἐξηράνθη ὁ χόρτος, καὶ τὸ ἄνθος ἐξέπεσεν· τὸ δὲ ῥῆμα Κυρίου μένει εἰς τὸν αἰῶνα. τοῦτο δέ ἐστιν τὸ ῥῆμα τὸ εὐαγγελισθὲν εἰς ὑμᾶς.

Differences—the use of ὡς; substitute αὐτῆς for ἀνθρώπου thus returning to the Hebrew.

ἐξέπεσεν—after the same words in both.

Κυρίου substituted for Θεοῦ ἡμῶν (LXX and Hebrew).

The εὐαγγέλιον of Isaiah.

Vs. 25—ῥῆμα—the accomplished result.

λόγος—the active principle. The ῥῆμα is the outcome of the λόγος.

THE LIVING STONE AND THE LIVING STONES
(1 PETER 2)

Vs. 1 Ἀποθέμενοι οὖν—See Ephesians 4:25.

κακία—malice, the desire of doing ill to others.

Vs. 2 ὡς ἀρτιγέννητα—the new birth, a leading idea in 1 Peter. The force of this conception in the case of the Gentile.

γάλα—Not here as in St. Paul and the other Epistles, as opposed to βρῶμα, ἡ στερεὰ τροφή (solid food) (cf. 1 Cor 3:2; Heb 5:12), as the inferior to the superior.

ἄδολον—'unadulterated' *not* 'guileless,' for this would be to restrict the meaning too much.

Connected with the previous πάντα δόλον in 1 Pet 2:1. See 2 Cor 4:2—μηδὲ δολοῦντες τὸν λόγον τοῦ Θεοῦ, ἀλλὰ τῇ φανερώσει τῆς ἀληθείας, and so 2 Cor 2:17—καπηλεύοντες τὸν λόγον τοῦ Θεοῦ, ἀλλ᾽ ὡς ἐξ εἰλικρινίας. A practice of Rome in the first century not less than of London in the 19th. See Irenaeus iii.17.4—'as I have already observed, not only do they hold opinions which are different, but absolutely contrary, and in all points full of blasphemies, by which they destroy those persons who, by reason of the resemblance of the words, imbibe a poison which disagrees with their constitution, just as if one, giving lime mixed with water for milk, should mislead by the similitude of the colour; as a man superior to me has said, concerning all that in any way corrupt the things of God and adulterate the truth, "Lime is wickedly mixed with the milk of God."'

λογικόν—to show that it is a metaphor, not the material milk, but rather the spiritual milk. It is the milk for the λόγος in man, and not for his σάρξ.

See Rom 12:1; *Test. of Twelve Patri.* Lev. 3; Eusebius, *H.E.* iv.23—λογικὴ τροφή. A feast of reason and a food of soul.

αὐξηθῆτε—metaphor continued.

εἰς—introducing the standard of mature growth, as e.g. Eph 4:13, 15.

εἰ ἐγεύσασθε—When you accepted the facts of it. From Psalm 34:9 (Ps 33:9)—γεύσασθε καὶ ἴδετε ὅτι χρηστὸς ὁ Κύριος· μακάριος ἀνήρ, ὃς ἐλπίζει ἐπ᾽αὐτόν.

χρηστὸς as a reference to χριστὸς is improbable. Observe that the Κύριος (Jehovah) of the Old Testament applied by St. Peter here, as frequently with St. Paul is our Lord.

See Ps 118 (Ps 117)—λίθον, ὃν ἀπεδοκίμασαν οἱ οἰκοδομοῦντες, οὗτος ἐγενήθη εἰς κεφαλὴν γωνίας· παρὰ Κυρίου ἐγένετο αὕτη καὶ ἔστιν θαυμαστὴ ἐν ὀφθαλμοῖς ἡμῶν.

See Is 28:16—διὰ τοῦτο οὕτως λέγει Κύριος ἰδοὺ ἐγὼ ἐμβαλῶ εἰς τὰ θεμέλια Σιὼν λίθον πολυτελῆ ἐκλεκτὸν ἀκρογωνιαῖον, ἔντιμον, εἰς τὰ θεμέλια αὐτῆς, καὶ ὁ πιστεύων ἐπ᾽αὐτῷ οὐ μὴ καταισχυνθῇ.

Vs. 5—καὶ αὐτοὶ ὡς λίθοι ζῶντες, partaking of the character of the Living Stone.

εἰς ἱεράτευμα. The correct reading. The Temple is for the priesthood. The Church however is both priesthood and Temple.

Vs. 6—διότι—Alford comments as if it read διότι καὶ.

περιέχει—The right reading, impersonal, as e.g. Josephus, *Ant.* xi.4.7 which reads 'just as in it (i.e. the letter), Περιέχει.'

ἐν γραφῇ—A Scripture. Is 28:16. On γραφῇ, γραφαί See Gal 3:22 and whence the use of the definite article or not. The quote here is from the LXX mostly, but as modified after the Hebrew e.g. ἐν Σιὼν for εἰς τὰ θεμέλια Σιὼν λίθον πολυτελῆ. The LXX here obviously has a double translation.

The οὐ μὴ καταισχυνθῇ is decisive for the text in 1 Peter coming from the LXX, for the Hebrew has לכן כה אמר אדני יהוה הנני יסד בציון אבן אבן בחן פנת יקרת מוסד מוסד המאמין לא יחיש

Vs. 7—ἡ τιμὴ and so οὐ μὴ καταισχυνθῇ but with a reference also to ἔντιμον (1 Pet 2:6). His living becomes their living—he is the living λίθος, they are the living λίθοι.

ἀπιστοῦσιν δὲ—the correct reading, but refers to previous disbelieving. The other reading has come from ἀπειθοῦντες (1 Pet 2:8), below.

λίθος is the right reading. See the LXX of Ps 128 (Ps 127):22. There is reference to this passage in St. Peter's speech in Acts 4:11. It is quoted also in Mt 21:42; Mark 12:10; Luke 20:7. But why to unbelievers? We might rather have expected it to be to believers. His glory, their condemnation—see Rev 1:7. So the quotation is a threat in the Gospels, especially in Luke 20:7.

καί is not part of the quotation.

Notice λίθος is not connected with ἐγενήθη (vs. 7), but with ἀπιστοῦσιν directly.

λίθος προσκόμματος, Is 8:14 here culled from the Hebrew, not the LXX which has καὶ ἐὰν ἐπ᾽ αὐτῷ πεποιθὼς ἧς, ἔσται σοι εἰς ἁγίασμα καὶ οὐχ ὡς λίθου προσκόμματι συναντήσεσθε αὐτῷ, οὐδὲ ὡς πέτρας πτώματι· Note the coincidences with St. Paul—Rom 9:33: 1) combination of passages, the third passage referred to in Eph 2:20; 2) coincidences of language, ἐν Σιών connected with the fact that both are adapted from the LXX and the use of the double phrase λίθος προσκόμματος καὶ πέτρα σκανδάλου. See also the connection of τῷ λόγῳ ἀπειθοῦντες as 1 Pet 3:1 (comp. 1 Pet 4:17). It explains how they stumble. Note the ἀπιστοῦσιν (intellectual), ἀπειθοῦντες (practical) basis of stumbling. *St. Peter therefore can hardly be independent of St. Paul here.* Note that Luke 20:17 points to this second passage of Israel.

Vs. 9—ὑμεῖς δὲ. The Church enlarged by the admission of the Gentiles.

γένος ἐκλεκτόν—Is 43:20. See below on ὅπως τάς ἀρετάς.

βασίλειον ἱεράτευμα, see Ex 19:6—ὑμεῖς δὲ ἔσεσθέ μοι βασίλειον ἱεράτευμα καὶ ἔθνος ἅγιον. ταῦτα τὰ ῥήματα ἐρεῖς τοῖς υἱοῖς Ἰσραήλ. The moment of the giving of the Law. The Hebrew however has 'a kingdom of priests' כהנים ממלכת Cf. Rev 1:6—ἡμᾶς βασιλείαν, ἱερεῖς τῷ Θεῷ and Rev 5:10—ἡμῶν βασιλείαν καὶ ἱερεῖς. St. John has probably followed the Targum Onkelos which has 'kingdom, priests' and so Targum Hemos [?]. The Peshitto has 'a kingdom and priests.' Aquila 'a kingdom of priests.' Sym. Theod. has βασίλεια ἱερεῖς (see Fields, Hex. I, p. 114). This is the right meaning, they are both kings and priests.

The Stoic modes of speech, see Horace, *Sat.* i.3.123 (with Aretus [?] notes II, pp. 63, 66)—'If as the Stoics say the wise man's rich, uniquely handsome, a brilliant cobbler, a king for sure, why do you need to be given what you already have?'

ἅγιον denoting consecration, hence οἱ ἅγιοι.

λαὸς εἰς περιποίησιν see Ex 19:5—ἔσεσθέ μοι λαὸς περιούσιος ἀπό πάντων τῶν ἐθνῶν· ἐμὴ γάρ ἐστι πᾶσα ἡ γῆ·

λαὸς εἰς περιποίησιν is an independent translation = λαὸς περιούσιος. See Trench, *Revisions etc.* p. 236. Symmachus—'You are to me chosen from out of all the peoples.'

εἰς περιποίησιν—The verb e.g. Acts 20:28. The substantive is always in the active sense. Thus when it appears, observe—Eph 1:4—εἰς ἀπολύτρωσιν τῆς περιποιήσεως, see 1 Thess 5:9—ἀλλὰ εἰς περιποίησιν σωτηρίας.

ὅπως τὰς ἀρετὰς—Comp. Is 43:21—λαόν μου, ὃν περιεποιησάμην τὰς ἀρετάς μου διηγεῖσθαι. Thus the λαὸς εἰς περιποίησιν is the connecting link between the two passages in Exodus and Isaiah.

In the LXX τὰς ἀρετὰς it translates הוֹדוֹ in Hab 3:3 and תְּהִלָּתִי in Isaiah 43:21 etc. Here 'the excellences' comp. 2 Pet 1:3. There is an avoidance of this Greek term in St. Paul see my note on Phil 4:8.

τοῦ ἐκ σκότους—comp. Col 1:13.

εἰς τὸ θαυμαστὸν αὐτοῦ φῶς—see Clement of Rome 36.

Vs. 10—Here the reference to Hosea 2:23. See Rom 9:25, 26.

λαός and ἔθνος see Acts 4:27; 26:17, 23. For λαὸς and δῆμος See Acts 10:2, and Acts 12:22.

ἠλεημένοι—μακάριοι οἱ ἐλεήμονες, ὅτι αὐτοὶ ἐλεηθήσονται (Mt 5:7). The perfect here in 1 Peter is accounted for by the quotatation.

νῦν—with the aorist, under the present dispensation.

Vs. 11— ὡς παροίκους—as wayfarers ready for the march, simply tenting in this present world, cf. 1 Pet 1:17; 2:11. See 2 Cor 5:1, 4; 2 Pet 1:13, 14. Marching forward to your land of promise, the new Jerusalem, like the participants in the sojourns of old. See Ex 12:11 (LXX)—οὕτως δὲ φάγεσθε αὐτό· αἱ ὀσφύες ὑμῶν περιεζωσμέναι, καὶ τὰ ὑποδήματα ἐν τοῖς ποσὶν ὑμῶν, καὶ αἱ βακτηρίαι ἐν ταῖς χερσὶν ὑμῶν· καὶ ἔδεσθε αὐτὸ μετὰ σπουδῆς· πάσχα ἐστὶ Κυρίῳ. The very expression used by our Lord in St. Luke.

τῶν σαρκικῶν—the fleshly lusts, because in the flesh you are only sojourners, not citizens.

αἵτινες—'seeing that they . . .' They will rise up against you in anger as unprotected aliens.

Στρατεύονται—campaign. See James 4:1—Πόθεν πόλεμοι καὶ πόθεν μάχαι ἐν ὑμῖν; οὐκ ἐντεῦθεν, ἐκ τῶν ἡδονῶν ὑμῶν τῶν στρατευομένων ἐν τοῖς μέλεσιν ὑμῶν; Comp. Rom 8:23.

Vs. 12 ἐν ᾧ—see Rom 1:1; Heb 2:18—'wherein' or 'while'?

κακοποιῶν—See Suetonius, *Nero* 16; Tacitus, *Annal.* xv.44; Pliny x.44 noting the reference to 'flagitia' for the 'nomini' in the last two references. Note the frequent charge in the Apologists.

ἐποπτεύοντες—comp. 1 Pet 3:2—'being spectators of them' as of some magnificent exhibition.

ἐν ἡμέρᾳ ἐπισκοπῆς—Luke 19:44 i.e. when God appears in some signal visit. The ἐπισκοπῆς may be for punishment (Is 10:3 LXX—καὶ τί ποιήσουσιν ἐν τῇ ἡμέρᾳ τῆς ἐπισκοπῆς; ἡ γὰρ θλῖψις ὑμῖν πόρρωθεν ἥξει· καὶ πρὸς τίνα καταφεύξεσθε τοῦ βοηθηθῆναι;).

Vs. 13—Ὑποτάγητε πάσῃ ἀνθρωπίνῃ κτίσει διὰ τὸν Κύριον· εἴτε βασιλεῖ ὡς ὑπερέχοντι, comp. Rom 13:1

κτίσις—creation = institutions, 'unto every human creature'

εἴτε βασιλεῖ ὡς ὑπερέχοντι—This can hardly be said in Latin 'autokrator' = Emperor.

Vs. 14—ἡγεμόσιν—the provincial governors, procurators (legates), and proconsuls.

εἰς ἐκδίκησιν κακοποιῶν ἔπαινον δὲ ἀγαθοποιῶν, used here of a person punished, but elsewhere of a person avenged, e.g. Luke 18:7-8.

Vs. 15 ἀγνωσίαν—stolid ignorance. See 1 Cor 15:34—it implies moral blame which is absent with ἀγνωσία, cf. Ovid xiii.1. An active ignorance is implied in the form.

Vs. 16—ὡς ἐλεύθεροι see Gal 5:13.

Vs. 18—See the imperatives in Eph 6.

Οἱ οἰκέται ὑποτασσόμενοι—participles and adjectives used as imperatives are found frequently in exhortating passages e.g. Rom 8:9 sq, 16sq.; Eph 4:2, 3; Col 3:16 sq.; Heb 13:5. So above 1 Pet 2:16 and again below. It would produce altogether a forced connection to attach the participle to πάντας τιμήσατε (1 Pet 2:17).

ἀγαθοῖς καὶ ἐπιεικέσιν—Kindly and gentle, reasonable.

σκολιοῖς—crooked, perverse.

χάρις—trustworthy, acceptable i.e. something which exceeds the rigid rule of so much for so much, the law of buying and selling. See Rom 4:4, οὐ λογίζεται κατὰ χάριν ἀλλὰ κατὰ ὀφείλημα. And see Rom 4:16—κατὰ χάριν, as opposed to according to works.

See Luke 6:32—not obtaining grace, but in an act of grace. Comp. Mt 5:47—
τί περισσὸν ποιεῖτε, outside the compact.

διὰ συνείδησιν Θεοῦ—See 1 Cor 8:7—the right reading there is συνηθείᾳ.

Vs. 20—ἁμαρτάνοντες καὶ κολαφιζόμενοι. See John 5:35 for the participles. The second participle describes that which is conditional on the first.

ἀλλ᾽ εἰ ἀγαθοποιοῦντες καὶ πάσχοντες ὑπομενεῖτε, τοῦτο χάρις παρὰ Θεῷ refers back to the κλέος.

Vs. 21—εἰς τοῦτο γὰρ ἐκλήθητε—'for this was involved in your calling, you were summoned to this when you were incorporated into the name of Christ.'

καὶ Χριστός—'and Christ, on his part . . .' He was the first great example of χάρις. See Rom 5:7; 8:32.

ὑπολιμπάνων—leaving behind, when he ascended into heaven.

ὑπογραμμόν—See my note on Clement *Rom.* 5 (p. 51), which text shows dependence on St. Peter here. Clement after quoting Is 53 has 'See beloved men, the model (ὑπογραμμός), which we have given you . . .'

ἐπακολουθήσητε—Follow close in.

Vs. 22—Is 53:9—καὶ δώσω τοὺς πονηροὺς ἀντὶ τῆς ταφῆς αὐτοῦ καὶ τοὺς πλουσίους ἀντὶ τοῦ θανάτου αὐτοῦ· ὅτι ἀνομίαν οὐκ ἐποίησεν, οὐδὲ εὑρέθη δόλος ἐν τῷ στόματι αὐτοῦ. The last sentence in vs. 22 shows that it is quoted solely from the LXX here. See my note on Clement of Rome p. 74.

Vs. 23—λοιδορούμενος οὐκ ἀντελοιδόρει. See the parallel in *Greek Anthol.* vi.30—the use of the word ἀντελοιδόρει. Is 53:7—'he opened not his mouth.'

παρεδίδου—If anything is to be understood here, it would not be either Himself, nor (still less), his enemies, but something as general as possible—τά ἑαυτοῦ. There is a tendency with the compounds (prepositions added up front) with δίδοναι to this abstract sense.

Vs. 24—Is 53:11—ἀπὸ τοῦ πόνου τῆς ψυχῆς αὐτοῦ, δεῖξαι αὐτῷ φῶς καὶ πλάσαι τῇ συνέσει, δικαιῶσαι δίκαιον εὖ δουλεύοντα πολλοῖς, καὶ τὰς ἁμαρτίας αὐτῶν αὐτὸς ἀνοίσει. He, says St. Peter in effect, was the fulfillment of this prophecy. So again Heb 9:28.

See James 2:21—ἀνενέγκας Ἰσαὰκ τὸν υἱὸν αὐτοῦ ἐπὶ τὸ θυσιαστήριον. Here τὸ ξύλον = τὸ θυσιαστήριον. Comp. Heb 13:10. On the terminology here see Gen 8:20; Ex 29:18, 25; Lev 3:11, 16 etc. and very common in the LXX.

The translation here should not be 'endured' here, for whatever may be the meaning of the word in Is 53, the ἐπὶ τὸ ξύλον makes it improbable here. Therefore, here 'carried up' and the sacrificial sense is involved.

ἀπογενόμενοι—The sinful part of our nature was crucified with Him, was slain in his death. See Rom 6:2, 6 (συνεσταυρώθη); Rom 6:8, 9. 2 Cor 5:15; Gal 2:20.

οὗ τῷ μώλωπι ἰάθητε—The right reading. See Is 53:5—αὐτὸς δὲ ἐτραυματίσθη διὰ τὰς ἁμαρτίας ἡμῶν καὶ μεμαλάκισται διὰ τὰς ἀνομίας ἡμῶν· παιδεία εἰρήνης ἡμῶν ἐπ᾽ αὐτόν. τῷ μώλωπι αὐτοῦ ἡμεῖς ἰάθημεν. The reading αὐτοῦ in T.R. and B.M.T. inserted from Isaiah, but it is a quite legitimate reading and may have been dropped due to being seen as superfluous. The coincidence of the best authorities however points to the former reading without αὐτοῦ.

Vs. 25—Isaiah 53:6 quoted—πάντες ὡς πρόβατα ἐπλανήθημεν, ἄνθρωπος τῇ ὁδῷ αὐτοῦ ἐπλανήθη· καὶ Κύριος παρέδωκεν αὐτὸν ταῖς ἁμαρτίαις ἡμῶν (LXX). Noting the ἐπεστράφητε νῦν here in 1 Peter. Comp. Ezek 34:6 (LXX)—καὶ διεσπάρη τὰ πρόβατά μου ἐν παντὶ ὄρει καὶ ἐπὶ πᾶν βουνὸν ὑψηλὸν καὶ ἐπὶ προσώπου πάσης τῆς γῆς διεσπάρη, καὶ οὐκ ἦν ὁ ἐκζητῶν οὐδὲ ὁ ἀποστρέφων. And Ezek 34:11 from that passage—διότι τάδε λέγει Κύριος Κύριος· ἰδοὺ ἐγὼ ἐκζητήσω τὰ πρόβατά μου καὶ ἐπισκέψομαι αὐτά. And further Ezek 34:16—τὸ ἀπολωλὸς ζητήσω καὶ τὸ πλανώμενον ἐπιστρέψω καὶ τὸ συντετριμμένον καταδήσω καὶ τὸ ἐκλεῖπον ἐνισχύσω καὶ τὸ ἰσχυρὸν φυλάξω καὶ βοσκήσω αὐτὰ μετὰ κρίματος.

Still, Christ is probably meant by ποιμένα in our vs. 25. Comp. 1 Pet 5:4.

On ἐπίσκοπον, see Ignatius, *Rom.* 9—'Jesus Christ alone shall be its bishop—He and your love' [JBL translation].

Heirs of Life, Followers of Christ's Example of Suffering

(1 Peter 3)

Vs. 1—τοῖς ἰδίοις ἀνδράσιν and see 1 Pet 3:5. Comp. Eph 5:22, 25, 28.

ἄνευ λόγου

κερδηθήσονται—'they may be won.'

Vs. 4—ὁ κρυπτὸς τῆς καρδίας ἄνθρωπος—See Rom 7:22; 2 Cor 4:16; Eph 3:16. Comp. Polycarp in Eusebius, *H.E.* v.24.

Vs. 6—κύριον, comp. Gen 18:12.

ἐγενήθητε—'were made' when you came to the knowledge of Christ. Comp. Rom 4:16, 17; Gal 3:7 sq. As sons of Abraham, so daughters of Sarah.

ἀγαθοποιοῦσαι—'if you do good . . .'

καὶ μὴ φοβούμεναι μηδεμίαν πτόησιν—a reference to the tumultuous times. The spirit of persecution abroad would make itself felt in households. Comp. Mt 5:35; Luke 12:53—son against father, daughter against mother etc. A man's foes will be those of his own household.

πτόησιν—cogn. accus.

Vs. 7—The connection—συνοικοῦντες . . . τῷ γυναικείῳ

ἀπονέμοντες . . . χάριτος ζωῆς

σκεύει—the body so called, as the receptacle of the Spirit. Comp. 2 Cor 4:7— Ἔχομεν δὲ τὸν θησαυρὸν τοῦτον ἐν ὀστρακίνοις σκεύεσιν.

See also 1 Thess 4:4—εἰδέναι ἕκαστον ὑμῶν τὸ ἑαυτοῦ σκεῦος κτᾶσθαι, to make himself master of his own body. See also Barnabas 7, 11, 21—'the vessel of the spirit,' as 'natural beings' (vs. 21).

ἀπονέμοντες τιμήν—The keynote of Christian structure. They are to be honored not *although* they are weak but rather *because* they are weak.

χάριτος—the grace, free gift.

ἐγκόπτεσθαι—'to be hindered' see Gal 5:7.

τὰς προσευχὰς ὑμῶν—as they would be by any want of honor.

Vs. 8—Τὸ δὲ τέλος πάντες—'last of all'

Vs. 9—ὅτι εἰς τοῦτο ἐκλήθητε ἵνα εὐλογίαν κληρονομήσητε. For God would have you inherit a blessing, and this you cannot if you yourselves bless not.

Vs. 10—Ps 34 (33):13 sq. adapted—The LXX here has τίς ἐστιν ἄνθρωπος ὁ θέλων ζωήν, ἀγαπῶν ἡμέρας ἰδεῖν ἀγαθάς;

But our text must be translated 'desires to be content with life,' but it has no continuity with the Hebrew which has 'what man is he that desireth life, length of days, that he may see (to see) good.'

The Psalm adds παῦσον τὴν γλῶσσάν σου ἀπὸ κακοῦ καὶ χείλη σου τοῦ μὴ λαλῆσαι δόλον. ἔκκλινον ἀπὸ κακοῦ καὶ ποίησον ἀγαθόν, ζήτησον εἰρήνην καὶ δίωξον αὐτήν.

Vs. 14—A reference to the beatitude in Mt 5:10—μακάριοι οἱ δεδιωγμένοι ἕνεκεν δικαιοσύνης, ὅτι αὐτῶν ἐστιν ἡ βασιλεία τῶν οὐρανῶν. So here μακάριοι = you have the Lord's word for it.

τὸν δὲ φόβον αὐτῶν μὴ φοβηθῆτε μηδὲ ταραχθῆτε, Comp. Is 8:13— Κύριον αὐτὸν ἁγιάσατε, καὶ αὐτὸς ἔσται σου φόβος. The original shows that the fear phrase means 'do not share their fears,' αὐτός being subjective not objective genitive.

Vs. 15—Sanctify (elsewhere consecrate) the Christ as Lord. Christ takes the place of Yahweh as in 1 Pet 2:3.

Vs. 16—καὶ φόβου—fear, and yet 'no fear'

Vs. 18—περὶ ἁμαρτιῶν, as you are required to suffer, δίκαιος ὑπὲρ ἀδίκων. μὲν σαρκὶ ζωοποιηθεὶς δὲ πνεύματι·—as regards the flesh . . . as regards the spirit.

Vs. 19—ἐν ᾧ καὶ—For the interpretation Christ preaches in Noah see Pearson [?]. This interpretation is altogether forced: 1) ἐν φυλακῇ the construed sense; 2) πνεύμασιν—They were *bodies;* 3) πορευθείς; 4) there is the same subject, Christ, throughout, and the same sequence—sometime after his death; 5) cf. 1 Pet 4:6. *It must therefore be interpreted of the disembodied spirits. It refers therefore to the descensus ad inferno.*

But when? During the three days when his body lay in the grave? So said the early church generally. The passage in St. Peter says nothing on this point. But why? Not for their condemnation, comp. 1 Pet 4:6, though possibly for the condemnation of some.

τοῖς ἐν φυλακῇ—guarded for the last day. See 2 Pet 2:4, 9—ταρταρώσας.

Vs. 20—ἀπειθήσασίν

διεσώθησαν δι’ ὕδατος

This passage indicates two principles: 1) that those who through no fault of their own were ignorant of the Gospel dispensation would share in its benefits. Christ died for the sins of the whole world; 2) that the benefits of the Incarnation cannot be communicated without the religion being appropriated. There is no mere mechanical change. The disobedience here was in some cases owing to defective knowledge.

Consider the strong belief of the early Church. Justin and Irenaeus (a spurious passage from the LXX), Clement, Hermas, Tertullian, Hippolytus, the Apostles' Creed. The patriarchs and the prophets etc. hear the preaching. The passage before us extends the principle further to the heathen—so Clement of Alexandria. He was justified in this extension. The preaching in Hades is the counterpart to the preaching on earth. The Apostles (Hermas), the Baptist (Hippolytus).

[The manuscript breaks off at this point. (BW3)].

Appendix A

The Mission of Titus to
the Corinthians[1]

The mission of Titus, which occupies so prominent a place in the
Second Epistle to the Corinthians, has been the subject of much discussion with regard to its object and relation to other communications of
St. Paul with the same Church, especially the similar and almost contemporaneous mission of Timothy. The explanation here offered has not, as
far as I have seen, been anticipated; it is certainly not the view maintained
by the most recent critics, English or German. At the same time it seems
so far to recommend itself by its simplicity, and to offer so adequate a
solution of all the difficulties which the problem presents, that it can
scarcely have failed to suggest itself to the minds of others besides myself.
But perhaps it may not be superfluous to say a few words on the previous
communications of St. Paul with the Church of Corinth, not only by way
of introduction to my immediate subject, but also because they offer considerable difficulties in themselves.[2]

---

[1] *The Journal of Sacred and Classical Philology* (a journal Lightfoot helped get started) originally published this piece as an article in 1855, vol. 2, pp. 194-205. It was then reprinted in the posthumous
Biblical Essays (London: Macmillan, 1904), then again as a reprint in the Baker 1979 redo of *Biblical
Essays*, and finally it became available as an item in the public domain on the Project Canterbury
website. We are pleased to offer it here. (BW3)

[2] This paper had been partly written and the substance of the whole collected before Mr. Stanley's
book appeared. It was no slight satisfaction to me that with regard to one main point, the identification of the mission of Titus to Corinth with that of the brethren mentioned in the First Epistle, the

It must have been some time during St. Paul's three years' residence at
Ephesus (from A.D. 54 to 57), that he received information of the critical state
of the Corinthian Church, which he had himself founded a few years earlier.
His presence seemed to be required, and he accordingly crossed the Aegean,
and paid a short visit to the capital of Achaia, returning to Ephesus to complete his missionary work there. This seems to be the most probable account
of St. Paul's second visit to Corinth, of which little more than the fact is recorded. For though the circumstance is not noticed by St. Luke, yet his silence is easily accounted for, supposing it intentional, when we reflect that
his object was not to write a complete biography of St. Paul, but a history of
the Christian Church, and that he has accordingly selected out of his materials such facts only as to throw light upon Christianity in all ages—*representative facts*, as we might call them; while on the other hand, if it be supposed that he was unacquainted with the circumstance, this supposition
again is easily explained from the short duration of St. Paul's stay at Corinth,
and the facility of intercourse between the two coasts of the Aegean.

At all events, there are passages in the epistles (e.g. 2 Cor 12:14; 13:1, 2)
which seem inexplicable under any other hypothesis, except that of a
second visit—the difficulty consisting not so much in the words themselves,
as in their relation to their context.[3] It appears necessary therefore to

---

distinguished editor supports the view here maintained. Though so far anticipated, I have ventured
to send this paper to the press because the results were obtained independently and where they agree
with those of Mr. Stanley, are worked out more fully than his plan admitted. I have alluded several
times to Mr. Stanley's book in my notes, chiefly where I have had occasion to differ from him; but I
would not be thought to disparage so valuable a contribution to the history of the apostolic times. I
would wish the same remark to apply to the mention of other distinguished names.

[3]I cannot think, for instance, that Mr. Stanley's explanation of the context of 2 Cor 12:14 τρίτον
τοῦτο ἑτοίμως ἔχω ἐλθεῖν πρὸς ὑμᾶς on the ground of the *designed* visit, is at all satisfactory. And
yet he calls attention to the opposition between the tenses κατενάρκησα and καταναρκήσω which
leads to the true solution, 'I have not been burdensome to you . . . I am on the eve of paying you
a third visit, and I will not be burdensome,' i.e. I will observe the same practices as on the two
former occasions. But the appeal to his projected visit as a proof of his affection (for this is Mr.
Stanley's explanation) is quite out of place in this connexion, to say nothing of the ambiguity of
expression. His interpretation of 2 Cor 13:1 in relation to its context is scarcely less objectionable.
At all events, admitting Mr. Stanley's explanation as possible, it must seem strange that the Apostle should *twice* have veiled his mention of his designed visit under the language which applies at
least as well (in 2 Cor 13:1 Τρίτον τοῦτο ἔρχομαι πρὸς ὑμᾶς, far better) to an actual visit, and in
both cases have introduced it in a manner which so rudely interrupts the obvious train of thought.
On the other hand 1 Cor 16:7 has been unjustly pressed into the service. The words οὐ θέλω γὰρ
ὑμᾶς ἄρτι ἐν παρόδῳ ἰδεῖν have been interpreted 'I will not now pay you a passing visit'; implying that he had done so before, and, as St Paul on his first visit to Achaia stayed eighteen months

abandon the opposite view, chiefly known to the English student through the advocacy of Paley, who seeks to explain these passages on the ground of a visit designed, but never actually paid. The Apostle's visit seems not to have been effectual in checking the evils that called for his interference. It would appear that the shameless profligacy, for which the city was proverbial, had already found its way into the Christian community. He therefore wrote to the Corinthians, warning them to shun the company of offenders in this kind. This letter, which was probably brief and of no permanent interest to the Christian Church, has not been preserved, and we only know that it was written, from a passing allusion to it in a subsequent epistle[4]—the First to the Corinthians. It was probably in this lost letter that he informed them of the design, which he at this time entertained but was afterwards obliged to abandon, of paying them a double visit, on his way to

---

(Acts 18:11) necessarily alluding to a second and shorter visit. Against this, Meyer alleges the order of the words, and de Wette repeats this argument. So far as I can see, the order would admit this interpretation well enough and Wieseler (*Chronologie* p. 240) has a right to make a use of the passage despite this protest. The real objection seems to be that the natural, if not necessary antithesis to ἄρτι 'just now' (when used of the present time) is the future, and not the past. On this ground I should object to Mr. Stanley's explanation 'now according to my present as distinguished from my late intention.'

[4]1 Cor 5:9—Ἔγραψα ὑμῖν ἐν τῇ ἐπιστολῇ μὴ συναναμίγνυσθαι πόρνοις, but as undue weight has been assigned to these words, as showing that a previous letter had been written, it will be as well to see how far they favor such a view: (1) No such conclusion can be drawn from the aorist Ἔγραψα. That this word is frequently used in reference to the letter in which it occurs, any concordance will show; I must also confess myself unable to discern the latent 'philosophical' objections to its being so employed, even at the commencement of a letter (Davidson, *Introd.* p. 140, ed. l); the grammar, at all events, seems unexceptionable. Cf. *Martyr. Polyc.* c. 1: Ἐγράψαμεν ὑμῖν where the words occur immediately after the salutation. (2) It is unnecessary to accumulate instances to show that τῇ ἐπιστολῇ may refer to the letter itself. (3) It has been found difficult to explain the allusion by anything which has preceded. This difficulty must be allowed: verses 2, 6, 8, do not supply what is wanted: but is it necessary to seek any reference beyond the passage itself? Would it not be quite in accordance with this epistolary usage of the aorist to look for the explanation in the same sentence, so that the corresponding English to the phrase in 1 Cor 5:9 would be 'I write to you not to keep company.' The only substantial argument in favour of a previous letter seems to be contained in the words ἐν τῇ ἐπιστολῇ which are quite superfluous in reference to the First Epistle itself, and the comparison with 2 Cor 7:8 makes the allusion to a previous letter even more evident. This argument appears to be insuperable. I suppose that the Chev. Bunsen's 'Restoration,' of the 'Former Epistle of Peter' will carry conviction to few German and still fewer English minds (Hippol. i. p. 24, ed. 2, in *Anal. Anten.* I. p. 35sq.) but perhaps it is worthwhile observing how completely his argument, founded on 1 Pet 5:12 δι' ὀλίγων ἔγραψα, where he finds it necessary to refer to a former and shorter letter, is met by such passages as Heb 13:22 βραχέων ἐπέστειλα ὑμῖν and Ignatius *ad Polyc.* c. vii (shorter Greek). For not only is the aorist used in both these passages in a way in which M. Bunsen seems to think inadvisable, but the writers have also ventured to characterize their epistles as brief, though they considerably exceeded in length that to which he considers such a term inappropriate.

and return from Macedonia (1 Cor 16:5; 2 Cor 1:15). How long an interval elapsed before St. Paul again communicated with the Corinthian Christians, we cannot ascertain; but it was towards the close of his stay at Ephesus, that he despatched Timothy through Macedonia on his way to Corinth, though apparently with some apprehensions that he might not reach that city, and not long after addressed a second letter to them—the First Epistle of our Canon. This he placed in the hands of certain brethren, whom he expected to arrive at Corinth a little before or at any rate not later than Timothy (1 Cor 16:10-12), so that they might return together, and rejoin the Apostle in company. Have we any means of discovering who these brethren were?

It seems more than probable in the first place, that Timotheus never reached Corinth, but was detained in Macedonia so long, that he had not advanced beyond this point, when he was overtaken by St. Paul on his way from Ephesus to Achaia. At all events he must have been in St. Paul's company when the Second Epistle was written, as his name appears in the salutation, and there are sufficient grounds for concluding that this Epistle was sent from Macedonia. But there are numerous reasons for supposing that this was the limit of Timothy's journey. In the *first* place, St. Paul himself in announcing this projected visit of Timothy to Corinth, has evidently some misgivings as to its fulfilment, and consequently speaks of it as un-certain, Ἐὰν δὲ ἔλθῃ Τιμόθεος (1 Cor 16:10). Probably he foresaw circum-stances that would detain his missionary on the way.

Secondly, Timothy is represented in the Acts (Acts 19:22) as being sent with Erastus into Macedonia, as if the sacred historian were not aware of his journey being continued to Corinth. *Thirdly*, if Timothy had actually visited Corinth, he must have brought back some information as to the state of the Church there; and, if he arrived, as was expected, subsequently to the receipt of the First Epistle, he must also have been able to report on a subject that lay nearest to the Apostle's heart—the manner in which his letter was re-ceived by the Corinthian Christians. But we do not find this to have been the case. For while in the Second Epistle to the Corinthians St. Paul dwells at great length on information derived from another source—the epistle in fact arising entirely out of this—there is not the slightest inkling of any knowledge obtained through Timothy on any subject whatever. And *fourthly*, in one passage where St. Paul is enumerating visits recently paid to the Corinthians by the Apostle himself or by his accredited messengers, the name of Timothy does not occur, though it could scarcely have been passed over in such a connexion (2 Cor 12:17, 18).

For these reasons we may infer with extreme probability, that Timothy, finding it advisable to prolong his stay in Macedonia, was prevented from carrying out his original intention of visiting Achaia, before he joined St. Paul. For, though each of these arguments separately is far from conclusive, they seem when combined to form such a body of circumstantial evidence, as fully to justify this verdict. Again, if this conclusion be admitted, it simplifies the problem, and the subsequent communications of the Apostle with the Church of Corinth become easily explicable. This consideration is of course not without weight. On the other hand attempts have been made to impugn some of these arguments. It will be as well to dispose of these before proceeding.

In answer to the *second* argument, it has been maintained that the journey of Timothy to Macedonia (Acts 19:22) was different from, and subsequent to, his mission to Corinth. If such a method of reconciling the accounts can in any way be avoided, it should not be resorted to. The philosopher's rule with entities should be the historian's with facts. They should not be unnecessarily multiplied. Here so far is there from being any necessity, that it is not easy to account for these repeated journeys, which moreover in some degree perplex the chronology, there being a difficulty in compressing all the events within the given time.

In the statement on which my *third* argument is based, I am at issue with Wieseler (*Chron.* p. 58) in a matter of fact. I can therefore only state the case and leave it for the judgment of others. He argues thus. The language with which the Epistle opens (2 Cor 1:12–2:11) was evidently prompted by St. Paul's distress at the opposition that his former letter had occasioned. Now this language describes his state of mind before the arrival of Titus. Therefore some other messenger must have reached him meanwhile from Corinth. Who can this messenger have been but Timothy? With Wieseler's hypothesis as to the composition of the Second Epistle, built upon the argument here given, I have no concern. The argument itself too is unexceptionable, if the premise be once allowed. But does not his statement arise from an entire misconception? I believe ordinary readers will discern no such traces of tidings received before the arrival of Titus. They will read in the opening of the Second Epistle nothing more than the vague apprehensions and misgivings, which would naturally arise in the Apostle's mind as to the manner in which a condemnatory letter, expressed in such fearless and uncompromising language—written moreover in much affliction and anguish of spirit (2 Cor 2:4)—would be received in a community where the most flagrant irregularities prevailed, and where his own apostolic authority was denied by a considerable number, and perverted to factious purposes by others. Surely the language would have been far different; his fears would have been far more clearly defined, if he had actually received tidings; especially if these tidings had been brought by a messenger as trustworthy as Timothy.

The *fourth* argument has been answered on the supposition that St. Paul in 2 Cor 12:17, 18 is only speaking of those who took part in the collection of alms, and that, as the mission of Timothy was quite independent of any such object, his name is properly omitted. But where does it appear that the list of names is so restricted? The word ἐπλεονέκτησα, judging from the context, seems to refer rather to the abuse of the Corinthians' hospitality, than to the gathering of the contributions. Meyer again accounts for the omission of Timothy's name on the ground that only the most recent visits to Corinth are here alluded to. Yet granting that his view is true, as probably it is, still the visit of Timothy must have preceded that of Titus by a few weeks at most, and could not have been omitted on this account. The same able critic even considers that any mention at all of Timothy in the third person would be quite out of place, when his name is found in the superscription of the letter (on 2 Cor 12:18, cf Einl. § 1); and Mr. Alford urges the same argument, though less strongly (Vol. II. Prol. p. 56). It is a sufficient reply to Meyer to observe that, whether out of place or not, it is what St. Paul has done elsewhere (e.g. 1 Thess 3:3, 6), and what therefore he might be supposed to do here.

On the other hand, the direct arguments that have been employed by those who consider it improbable that Timothy should have abandoned his design, do not seem to have much force. Mr. Alford for instance considers the purpose of his mission as stated in 1 Cor 4:17, to be 'too plain and precise to be lightly given up.' That the mission should have been entirely abandoned is certainly unlikely. That it should have been transferred to other hands, when it was found incompatible with the discharge of Timothy's duties in Macedonia, so far from being an improbable supposition, seems to commend itself by its very probability. Again, it is suggested by Meyer, and here too Mr. Alford endorses the suggestion, that the abandonment of the intended journey of Timothy would have furnished another handle for the charge of fickleness against St. Paul, and that we should have found the charge rebutted in the Second Epistle. This reason will probably not be considered of sufficient weight to counterbalance the amount of evidence on the other side. For if we take into account that the charge would lie primarily at the door of Timothy, and not of the Apostle himself—that St. Paul in announcing the design had expressed some doubts as to the possibility of its fulfilment—that the objects of the mission were not abandoned when it was found impossible for Timothy to carry them out—and lastly, that the messengers sent by St. Paul in his stead had a satisfactory explanation to offer to the Corinthians of this change of purpose—we can hardly suppose that the most captious of St. Paul's enemies would have thought it worth their while to employ such a lame expedient to injure his credit. In short, this case is no parallel at all to the circumstance of which his opponents did avail themselves to bring him into disrepute (2 Cor 1:17).

On the whole then, so far from finding anything conflicting in the evidence with regard to this mission of Timothy, it seems that, combining the hint of the possible abandonment of the design in the First Epistle, the account of the journey to Macedonia in the Acts, and the silence maintained with regard to any visit to Corinth or any definite information received thence through Timothy in the Second Epistle, we discover an 'undesigned coincidence' of a striking kind; and that it is therefore a fair and reasonable conclusion that the visit was never paid.

By whom then was this mission fulfilled? At the close of the First Epistle (1 Cor 16:11, 12) certain 'brethren' are mentioned, who appear to have been the bearers of the letter, and whom St. Paul expected to rejoin him in company with Timothy. The Apostle had urged Apollos to accompany this mission to Corinth (1 Cor 16:12), but he for reasons easily intelligible had declined, considering that his visit would be unseasonable. Now there is no mention of the names of these brethren in the First Epistle, but we find St. Paul subsequently after his departure from Ephesus at Troas awaiting the return of Titus from Corinth with tidings of the reception of his letter there (2 Cor 2:12), and falling in with him at length in Macedonia (2 Cor 7:6). From this we might have supposed that Titus was alone. But from another allusion to this mission in the Second Epistle we find he was accompanied by a 'brother,' whose name is not given (2 Cor 8:18). What more probable than that Titus and 'the brother' accompanying him of the Second Epistle, are 'the brethren' of the First?

But why is Titus not mentioned by name? Might we not rather ask, why he should be so mentioned? His name never occurs in the Acts. His influence on the interests of the Church at large was probably not so great as that of Tychicus or Trophimus, certainly not as that of Apollos or Timothy. He is brought into prominent notice in reference to the Churches of Corinth and Crete in particular; but we should doubtless be wrong in judging of his position in the Christian Church by the special importance with which he is invested in regard to individual communities. The fact that an Epistle of St. Paul bears his name leads us almost unconsciously to assign a rank to him that he probably did not hold in the estimation of his contemporaries. Titus then does not appear to have had a church-wide reputation at this time, and there is no reason to suppose that he was known specially to the Christians at Corinth. If so, the omission of his name presents no difficulty, and it is in accordance with St. Paul's manner to speak thus of his fellow-labourers (2 Cor 8:18, 22).[5]

No doubt Titus' strength of character was well known to the Apostle when he despatched him upon this difficult mission, but it only approved itself to the Corinthians during his stay among them; and his earnestness and devotion, while there, raised him so far above his colleague, that St. Paul in writing to the Corinthians subsequently speaks in such a manner as to show that 'the brother' who accompanied him had sunk by his side into comparative insignificance.

Titus then, we may suppose, had been selected by St. Paul as one of the bearers of the letter, that in the event of Timothy being unable to prosecute his mission to Corinth, it might be fulfilled by one who would act in the same loving and devoted spirit. But there is one link yet to be supplied. How did Titus communicate with Timothy? How was it known that Timothy would be detained in Macedonia? Here we are left to mere conjecture; but it seems not improbable that Titus and his companion took the less direct route to Achaia

---

[5] I am at a loss to discover why Mr. Stanley says, 'This mission was composed of Titus and two other brethren' (on 1 Cor 16:12). The Syriac version indeed in 2 Cor 12:18 reads the plural 'the brethren' (I assume this to be the case on Mr. Stanley's authority, though I have found no confirmation) but this has evidently arisen on the basis of a confusion with the subsequent mission mentioned in 2 Cor 8:16. Mr. Stanley does not give his reasons elsewhere (2 Cor 8:16; 12:18).

by way of Macedonia. They certainly returned that way, and there was, as far as we can see, no more reason for haste in the one case than in the other. And if it was the apprehension of danger which deterred them from crossing the open sea at that early season of the year, they would have much more cause to entertain such fears on their journey thither than on their return, when the season was farther advanced. Probably the greater security of the indirect route was thought to compensate for the advantage, in point of time, gained by sailing straight across the Aegean; while the opportunity of communicating with Timothy would be an additional motive in influencing their choice.[6]

If the view here taken be correct, it will overthrow all Wieseler's chronological results with regard to the interval between the writing of the First and Second Epistles. The facts are few and lead to no satisfactory conclusion; but as far as they go, they do not conflict with anything I have advanced. The data for determining the relative chronology of this period are these: (1) St. Paul stayed at Ephesus 'for a season' after sending Timothy into Macedonia (ἐπέσχεν χρόνον, Acts 19:22). (2) Timothy had left before the First Epistle was written (1 Cor 4:17; 16:10). (3) There is an allusion which makes it not improbable that the First Epistle was written shortly before Easter (1 Cor 5:7, 8). (4) St. Paul here declares his intention of setting out to visit Corinth quickly (1 Cor 4:19). (5) We also learn from the same source that he expected to stay at Ephesus till Pentecost (1 Cor 16:8); and lastly (6) there is reason to suppose that he was subsequently led to hasten his departure. It is not evident indeed that his life was endangered by the tumult at Ephesus but such an outbreak must have interfered with his preaching, and rendered his further stay there useless.[7] At all events the language of St. Luke places his

---

[6]The movements of St Paul in the following spring throw some light on this point. He had intended to sail *direct* from Corinth to Syria. His departure was however hastened by the discovery of a conspiracy against him and he went by way of Macedonia, apparently on account of the early season of the year. He left Philippi μετὰ τὰς ἡμέρας τῶν ἀζύμων (Acts 20:6). Cf. Conybeare and Howson, II p. 206.

[7]Wieseler considers it necessary to bring Timothy back from Macedonia to Ephesus, because the plural in 2 Cor 1:8 seems to show that he shared the danger with St. Paul on the occasion of the outbreak. The question of the use of the plural is beset with difficulties; but, waiving this, the language of St. Paul (ὑπὲρ τῆς θλίψεως ἡμῶν τῆς γενομένης ἐν τῇ Ἀσίᾳ, ὅτι καθ᾽ ὑπερβολὴν ὑπὲρ δύναμιν ἐβαρήθημεν, ὥστε ἐξαπορηθῆναι ἡμᾶς καὶ τοῦ ζῆν—2 Cor 1:8) must refer to something more than the mere momentary danger arising from the uproar. St. Paul seems to have been subjected to a continuous persecution at Ephesus, which must have begun before the departure of Timothy, and may have been shared by him. St. Paul speaks in the First Epistle of his many adversaries (1 Cor 16:9), and compares his struggles at Ephesus to a contest with wild beasts

departure in immediate connexion with this disturbance, in such a manner as scarcely to leave a doubt that it was determined by this circumstance (Acts 19:41; 20:1). It is probable, therefore, that he left before he had intended; and this explains another incident. We find St. Paul, after his hurried departure from Ephesus, expecting to meet Titus at Troas, and when he was disappointed of this hope, advancing into Macedonia, where he was ultimately joined by him.

Wieseler (*Chron.* p. 59) uses this as an argument, that St. Paul's departure cannot have taken place much earlier than he had originally intended; for otherwise he could not have expected to find Titus so soon at the place of meeting determined upon. This seems to be a mistake. There is no reason for supposing that they had agreed to meet at Troas. The true state of the case appears to be this. St. Paul had intended to await the return of Titus and his colleague at Ephesus. Subsequently being obliged to hasten his departure, he calculated they would have advanced as far as Troas before they met. In this calculation he proved to be wrong. If this view be correct, the hurried departure from Ephesus will obviously not affect the chronological question, which thus assumes a very simple form.

We have the period from the writing of the First Epistle, shortly before Easter (if we may lay so much stress on a doubtful allusion), till after the feast of Pentecost, when St. Paul expected to leave Ephesus, for the double journey of Titus, to Corinth and back. I have supposed that he went and returned by way of Macedonia. Even assuming that he travelled from Macedonia to Achaia by land, the interval is sufficiently great. Hug (*Introd.* ii. p. 381) calculates the single journey from Corinth to Ephesus at thirty-one days, but then he allows a wide margin that is quite superfluous. But, if it be thought that in this case more time would be required, we may suppose that Titus took ship at some port of Macedonia (Thessalonica for instance), as St. Paul seems to have done on one occasion on leaving Beroea (Acts 17:14; Wieseler's *Chron.* pp. 42, 43), and returned the same way. This would be a considerable saving of time, and the perils of the open sea would in great measure be avoided. [1855.]

(1 Cor 15:32). It is strange that ἐθηριομάχησα should ever have been understood literally, when the same image is used in 1 Cor 5:9—ὡς ἐπιθανατίους, ὅτι θέατρον ἐγενήθημεν.

Appendix B

St. Paul's Preparation for Ministry[1]

St. Paul dates the commencement of his preparation for the ministry as far back as the day of his birth. He describes himself as set apart for the Gospel of God, set apart from his mother's womb (Rom 1:1; Gal 1:15). In his social position, in his intellectual training, in his religious creed—in all the influences which wrought upon his childhood and youth—there was a schooling which eminently adapted him to fill the part for which he was designed—to gather the Gentiles into the fold of Christ, to preach the universality of the new dispensation. This was especially his work—his Gospel. And, when we come to piece together the notices preserved of his early life, we find that this training was in itself very remarkable, that it did in a way forecast his future destination, furnishing him with a large store of varied experiences, idle and unfruitful in Saul the Persecutor, but quickened suddenly into life in Paul the Apostle of Jesus Christ, the Preacher to the Gentiles, by the lightning flash which struck him on the way to Damascus.

We are accustomed to look to three countries especially as the great teachers of the modern world—Rome, Greece, Judaea. Rome, the foremost of all nations in the science of government, has handed down to us the principles of

[1]This essay was in Lightfoot's lecture notes from 1863 at Cambridge. Posthumously they were put with other essays into a volume titled *Biblical Essays*, published by Macmillan last in 1904. Subsequent to this, Baker Books in 1979 reprinted the original lecture notes in its own edition of *Biblical Essays*. Finally, the whole volume has been made available in the public domain at the Project Canterbury website, which includes many previously published Lightfoot works. The essay now is both out of print and out of copyright. We are happy to offer it again here. (BW3)

law and order. Greece, setting before us her rich treasures of thought and imagination, has been a schoolmistress in art and literature. Above all, from Palestine we have learnt our true relation to God, which gives higher significance to art and literature and an eternal value to the principles of law and order. If Rome supplied the bone and sinew to our colossal man, while Greece clothed him with flesh and gave him grace and beauty, it was Judaea that breathed the breath of life into him. Now all these three influences were combined in the great Apostle of the Gentiles. He was a citizen of Rome. His native place, Tarsus, was the great university of Greece. He was brought up in the Jewish religion in its most rigorous and most typical form.

We are accustomed to dwell solely on the Jewish education of St. Paul when considering his preparation for the ministry, not only as the most important, but also as the most prominent in the notices preserved of his early history. But the other elements in his training must not be neglected. It is not probable that one whose maxim it was to 'become all things to all men,' whose nature was eminently sensitive and impressible, could have failed to be moved by these powerful influences, and the traces of their working are sufficiently distinct in his life and writings.

On the other hand, exaggeration must be avoided. It would be a grave mistake to picture to ourselves the Apostle as an active politician, or an erudite philosopher and man of letters. The sphere of his thought was far different. His life was far otherwise spent. But he must have received from his political status as a Roman citizen and from his residence in the heart of a great Greek University impressions which enlarged his sympathies and his views, and thus, enabling him to enter more deeply into the thoughts and strivings of others, and to contemplate the Gospel from different points of view, rendered him a fitter instrument in the hands of God for the special work for which he was destined.

I. ST. PAUL THE ROMAN CITIZEN

Let us first consider St. Paul as a citizen of Rome.[2] The extension of the franchise was the keystone of the Roman system. By this means a connexion and sympathy was kept up in the remotest parts of the Empire. The blood of the political

---

[2]Cicero, pro Balb. 13; Becker, Handbuch der romischen Alterthumer ii, (1), p. 91.

body thus circulated freely by veins and arteries through the great heart of the republic to its extreme members, and any injury done to one limb was an injury done to the whole. The metaphor which I have employed is not my own, I am only expanding the image used by Cicero to express these relations.[3]

To the Roman his citizenship was his passport in distant lands, his talisman in seasons of difficulty and danger. It shielded him alike from the caprice of municipal law and the injustice of local magistrates. In Syria, in Asia, in Greece—wherever he went—he bore about with him this safeguard of his liberties. How valuable such a protection must have been to St. Paul, how often he must have invoked its aid in a life spent in travel and in the midst of enemies, we can well imagine. He had never known what it was to be without this citizenship, for he had been born a citizen of Rome (Acts 22:28). It procured him an honourable discharge from the prison at Philippi (Acts 16:36 sq.); it loosed his fetters in the tower of Antonia (Acts 22:25 sq.); it rescued him from the lawlessness of a zealot mob, and sped him on his way under escort to Caesarea (Acts 23:27); it transferred him from the hearing of a provincial governor to the court of Caesar himself (Acts 25:12). As he lived, so he died—a citizen of Rome. It is recorded that, while his brother-Apostle St. Peter suffered the punishment of a common malefactor on the cross, St. Paul was allowed to die by the sword, as the last recognition of his civic rights conceded by the law, when everything besides had been forfeited.[4] In this way St. Paul's position as a citizen must have been of essential service in the spread of the Gospel.

But this is not exactly the point on which I wish to dwell. I am anxious rather to point out that, having been so constantly in requisition, it must have impressed itself upon his mind with a corresponding force. And thus he must have been led to appreciate, as far as it was necessary for him to appreciate, the position which Rome occupied as a teacher of the world. I think there are very clear indications of this. It was no vulgar pride or idle self-assertion, but a true political instinct, which led St. Paul to demand a practical apology from the magistrates at Philippi. It is clear from his language on this occasion, as on others, that he valued his position as a citizen of Rome. It was something to be connected with that gigantic Empire, whose presence he had felt everywhere, and which, in the restraints it placed on the

[3]Cicero, *Verr.* v. 67; Becker, II (1), p. 98.
[4]Tertullian, *Scorpiace* no. 15, *de Praescr. Heret.* 36, etc. See Wieseler, *Chron.,* p. 542.

lawless opposition of his adversaries, presented itself to him as a type and manifestation of that letting power which keeps Antichrist in check till the last day (2 Thess 2:7).

Nay, so strong is the impression left in his mind, that he chooses the Roman franchise as the fittest image of the position of the believer in his heavenly kingdom. I have already referred to the language of Cicero in which he compares the connexion of the different parts of the Roman empire by this political tie to the circulation of the blood, language which reminds us of the Apostle's own image of the Church as the body knit together by its joints and ligatures (Col 2:19). Another passage of the same writer suggests still more striking points of comparison. 'I maintain it as a universal principle,' says Cicero (pro Balbo c. 13), 'that there is no nation anywhere so hostile or disaffected to the Roman people, none so united by ties of faith and friendship, that we are debarred from admitting them to the right of citizens.'[5] What wonder then if the Apostle saw a peculiar fitness in this image? In the guarantee it offered to individual freedom, in its independence of circumstances of time and place, in its superiority over inferior obligations, in the sympathy which it established between all the members of the community, in the universality of its application, lying as it did within the reach of all, far or near, friend or foe— in all these points it expressed, as no other earthly institution could do, the eternal relations of the kingdom of Christ. Hence the language of St. Paul, 'our citizenship is in heaven' (Phil 3:20). 'Only perform your duties as citizens in a manner worthy of the Gospel of Christ' (Phil 1:27). And in a third passage, where the image reappears, his language seems to be coloured by the legal distinction of cives and peregrini. 'Ye are no longer strangers and foreigners, but fellow-citizens of the saints,'—οὐκέτι ἐστὲ ξένοι (the recognised Greek equivalent of peregrini)[6] καὶ πάροικοι, ἀλλὰ ἐστὲ συνπολῖται τῶν ἁγίων καὶ οἰκεῖοι τοῦ Θεοῦ (Eph 2:19). They were once peregrini, they have been enrolled in the civitas coelitum. All this shows the deep impression that the Roman institutions had made on St. Paul. And this being so, we cannot be wrong in recognising here a special training for the Apostleship of the Gentiles, opening out this wider view of social life, and suggesting to him the true relation between the ordinances of men and the Gospel of Christ.

---

[5] As Becker ii. (1), p. 93, notes.
[6] Plautus, Rudens, Prol. v.2.

II. St. Paul the Native of Tarsus

But secondly, he was a native of Tarsus, the capital of Cilicia, 'no mean city' (Acts 21:39) as he himself styles it. We have it on the authority of Strabo, a contemporary of St. Paul, that Tarsus surpassed all other universities, such as Alexandria and Athens, in the study of philosophy and educational literature in general.[7] Its great pre-eminence, he adds, 'consists in this, that the men of learning here are all natives.' Accordingly, he and others[8] have made up a long catalogue of distinguished men who flourished at Tarsus in the late autumn of Greek learning: philosophers of the Academy, of the Epicurean and Stoic schools; poets, grammarians, physicians. At Tarsus, one might say, you breathed the atmosphere of learning. How far St. Paul may have availed himself of these opportunities of cultivating a knowledge of Greek literature, how much of his boyhood and youth was spent here and how much at Jerusalem, we cannot say. His Jewish teacher Gamaliel, who was distinguished for his liberality in this respect, would, at least, have encouraged him not to neglect this culture.

It has been the tendency of recent writers to underrate St. Paul's attainments. The extravagant language of older writers has produced a natural reaction. A treatise was even published 'On the stupendous erudition of St. Paul.'[9] Such exaggerations would be ludicrous if they were not painful. The majesty of the Gospel is not glorified by such means. St. Paul's strength lay in a widely-different direction. It was 'not with enticing words of wisdom or philosophy but in the demonstration of the Spirit and of power'—οὐκ ἐν πειθοῖς σοφίας λόγοις, ἀλλ᾽ ἐν ἀποδείξει Πνεύματος καὶ δυνάμεως (1 Cor 2:4), that he won his way. There is no ground for saying that St. Paul was a very erudite or highly-cultivated man. An obvious maxim of practical life from Menander (1 Cor 15:33), a religious sentiment of Cleanthes repeated by Aratus, himself a native of Tarsus (Acts 17:28), a pungent satire of Epimenides (Tit 1:12), with possibly a passage here and there which dimly reflects some classical writer, these are very slender grounds on which to build the supposition of vast learning. His style certainly does not conform to classical models: his logic savours little of the dialectics of the schools. But on the

---

[7]Strabo, xiv, p. 673.
[8]See Pauly, *Real-Encyl. der class. Alterthumer*, s.v. Tarsus.
[9]Stramm, *De Stupenda Eruditione Paul* (1710).

other hand he did get directly or indirectly from contact with Greek thought and learning lessons far wider and far more useful for his work than a perfect style or a familiar acquaintance with the classical writers of antiquity.

Whoever will study carefully the picture of the gradual degradation of the heathen world in the opening chapters to the Romans, or, still better, the address to the philosophical Athenians from the Areopagus, will see how thoroughly St. Paul entered into the moral and religious position of the heathen world, and with what deep insight he traced its relations, whether of contact or of contrast, with the great message of which he was the bearer. These are only samples.[10] If we recognise in such passages the voice of inspiration, in union with that instinctive quickness of moral apprehension which a tender love always inspires, we have still to look to external influences to supply the material on which inspiration might work. And foremost among these must be reckoned the lessons derived from his residence in early life in the centre of a great school—the greatest of its day—of Greek thought and learning.

We are disposed indeed to think lightly of the literary efforts of the Greeks at this late date: but though Greek literature had now lost the freshness and beauty of the spring and early summer of its existence, it had in the decline of its autumn still a glory of its own. We must not forget that the later schools of Greek philosophy exhibited a much greater earnestness of moral purpose, whether for good or evil, and achieved in consequence a much wider influence than the earlier. And if later Greek literature was rather critical and reproductive than original and imaginative, as the earlier had been, this only rendered it a fitter handmaid for the diffusion of the Gospel. It was required that the great Apostle of the Gentiles should be able to understand the bearings of the moral and religious life of Greece as expressed in her literature, and this lesson he could learn more impartially and more fully at Tarsus in the days of her decline, than at Athens in the freshness of her glory. Greece in her old age was now summing up, as it were, the experiences of her past life.

III. ST. PAUL THE JEW

I have dwelt hitherto on the Gentile side of St. Paul's training. The most important feature in his education has still to be considered. He was a Jew

---

[10]See Jowett, *The Epistles of St. Paul*, I, p. 352 sq. (1859).

in the strictest sense of the term. Let us take his account of himself—περιτομῇ ὀκταήμερος, ἐκ γένους Ἰσραήλ, φυλῆς Βενιαμείν, Ἑβραῖος ἐξ Ἑβραίων, κατὰ νόμον Φαρισαῖος (Phil 3:5). 'I was not admitted to the privileges of the covenant late in life, as a proselyte. I was circumcised on the earliest day sanctioned by the law. I was not even the son of proselyte parents, but of the race of Israel—Israel the chosen of God. I was not descended from the rebellious Ephraim, who had played fast and loose with the covenant, as many Jews are, but from the select tribe of Benjamin, always faithful to God. I had no admixture of alien blood in my veins, for my ancestors from first to last were Hebrews.'

Thus in respect of these four points, (1) the covenant, (2) race, (3) tribe, (4) lineage, he was identified most closely and narrowly with the chosen people of God. He includes himself in the inmost circle of Judaism. And not only this, but in sect, education and conduct nothing was wanting to identify him fully with Jewish feeling and Jewish life in its most rigid and trenchant form.[11] He was a Pharisee, the son of a Pharisee. He had been instructed at Jerusalem in the strictest principles of the law by Gamaliel, one of the seven great doctors, 'the Beauty of the Law,' whom all the Jews revered. He had carried out these principles with the utmost zeal and devotion. He was surpassed by none. And the lessons which he learnt in this way, and which he could not have learnt so well in any other way, were two-fold.

First of all, there was the negative lesson of what the law could not effect. He had borne in his own person the burden. He had felt its galling pressure, striving earnestly, with all the intensity of his nature, to meet its exactions. In proportion as he increased his efforts, he had to confess his weakness and inability. Who can read his pathetic description in the Epistle to the Romans of the helplessness and despair of one struggling under the weight of this load, without feeling that the Apostle is drawing from his own personal experiences, that these are the words not of a vague theorizer, but of a painful sufferer. And here too it is important to observe the influence of the sect to which he belonged. Of the three great parties who shared the empire of Jewish thought—the Essenes, the Sadducees, the Pharisees—the last alone could teach him the lesson in its completeness. On the Sadducee the law sat

---

[11]The chief passages relating to St. Paul's Jewish experiences are Gal 1:13, 14; Phil 3:5, 6; Acts 22:3 and Acts 26:4, 5; 2 Cor 11:22.

loosely; he could not entirely divest himself of it, for it was the national badge, but he would wear it as lightly as he could. The Essene indeed was a most strict observer of ordinances, but the law was to him the starting-point of his mystical reveries, the foundation of an ascetic practice by which he hoped to extricate the soul from the defilement of matter. Thus the Essenes could abandon the law where it seemed to interfere with their aspiration after purity, e.g. in sacrifice.

To the Pharisee, on the other hand, the law presented itself in a different light. He regarded it as an end, as an absolute rule of conduct. He respected it in and for itself. 'Fulfil the law and you shall live' was his motto. His vision did not extend beyond the law—the law as laid down by Moses, and as enlarged and interpreted by tradition. It was to him a compact strictly binding on the contracting parties in its minutest details. And thus it became to him, what it could scarcely have been to the Essene, the means of righteousness (δικαιοσύνη from the law). This is just the point that St. Paul seizes upon as the important feature of the law regarded as an instrument of training. It is in contrast to, and in consequence of, it that he develops the doctrine of grace, essentially the cardinal point in the Gospel of the Apostle of the Gentiles.

But secondly, the positive influence which St. Paul's Jewish education exercised upon him was equally great and important. Notwithstanding the opposition he met from his countrymen, in spite of all the liberal and the awakened sympathies that he derived from his work, despite the necessity of contending daily and hourly for the freedom of the Gospel among the Gentiles, he never ceased to be a Jew. From his repeated denunciations against the Judaizers we are apt to forget this feature in the Apostle's character until we are startled to find by some passing allusion how deep-seated is this feeling in his heart. The Apostle's whole nature was made up of contrasts, and this was one. 'The strength of sin is the law' and 'the law is holy and righteous and good' (1 Cor 15:56; Rom 7:12) these two maxims he could hold together and repeat in one breath. The most ardent patriot could not enlarge with greater pride on the glories of the chosen race than he does in the Epistle to the Romans. His care for the poor in Judaea is a touching proof of the strength of this national feeling. His attendance at the great annual festivals in Jerusalem is still more significant. 'I must spend the coming feast at Jerusalem' (Δεῖ με πάντως τὴν ἑορτὴν τὴν ἐρχομένην ποιῆσαι εἰς Ἱεροσόλυμα—Acts 28:21 T.R).[12] This language becomes the more striking when we remember that he was then intending to open out a new field of missionary labour in the far West, and was bidding perhaps his last farewell to the Holy City, the joy of the whole earth.

And here again it is important to remark on his connexion with the Pharisees. Whatever may have been their faults, they, and they alone, entered into the religious feeling of the nation. Hence their influence with the people. They were the true historical link with the past, they represented the growing consciousness of the chosen people, in the two all-essential points in which it prepared the way for the Gospel—in their belief in the immortality of the soul and in the cherished expectation of the Messiah. In more senses than one they sat in Moses' seat. The pure negativism of the Sadducee lent no aid here. Even if he did entertain some faint Messianic hopes, which is more than questionable, he deprived them of all religious value by denying a future state. And so again with the Essenes. Whatever importance we may attach to the reveries of the mystic Essene recluse, as testifying to the reality of a spiritual world, when all around was frozen and stiffened into formalism, still in his isolation from the national life of the Jews he lost that true historical instinct which was the life-blood of the people, and with it the vivid anticipations of the coming of Messiah.

It is not the spirit of the Sadducee, or of the Essene, but of the Pharisee, the son of Pharisees, which breathes in these glorious words, 'And now for the hope of the promise made by God to our fathers I stand at the bar as a criminal, unto which promise our twelve tribes, instantly ministering day and night, hope to attain: for this hope I am accused, king Agrippa—*by Jews*' (Acts 26:6, 7). And whatever shadow of worldly policy may for a moment be supposed to have overclouded the Apostle's conscience, as by his timely appeal he divided the two rival sects on the question of the resurrection of the dead (Acts 23:6), still the appeal in itself was perfectly justifiable, because perfectly true. His cause was the cause of the Pharisees, while between them and the Sadducees a great gulf was fixed.

I have thus traced the three threads that were in-woven into the texture of the Apostle's mind, to strengthen its fabric and so to prepare him for his great

---

[12]Cf. Acts 20:16. If the words quoted above are to be rejected as an interpolation this does not affect the fact of his visit to Jerusalem at this crisis (Acts 18:22).

work. It may be said indeed that when he is first brought before our notice, he bears no traces of any other than Jewish influences. He is a bigoted zealot, a narrow-minded persecutor. There is even a strong contrast between the cautious liberality of Gamaliel the master, and the persecuting rage of Saul the pupil. But is it not a matter of common experience, that the lessons of youth often lie for a time dormant and unnoticed, till they are suddenly kindled into flame by some electric stroke from without? The miraculous appearance on the way to Damascus produced in St. Paul a change far greater indeed but analogous to that which the more striking incidents of life have produced on many another. It flashed a new light on vast stores of experience laid up unconsciously in the past. It quickened into energy influences long forgotten and seemingly dead. The atoms of his nature assumed a fresh combination. The lightning fused the Apostle's character and moulded it in a new shape, and the knife of the torturer was forged into the sword of the Spirit. [1863.]

Appendix C

'The Letter Killeth, but the Spirit Giveth Life'[1]

XV. 'THE SPIRIT AND THE LETTER.' 'The letter killeth, but the spirit giveth life,' 2 CORINTHIANS 3:6. Septuagesima Sunday, 1877.

I SUPPOSE that we do not at all realise the extent to which even in the common things of life we are indebted to the teaching of St. Paul. No idea is more familiar to us than the distinction between the spirit and the letter. We talk of the spirit of a promise, of the letter of the law; we speak in condemnation of one person who observes an engagement in the letter but breaks it in the spirit, and in approval of another who disregards a pledge in the letter only that he may fulfil it in the spirit. But we do not connect this idea especially with St. Paul.

If we chance to think of him, it probably occurs to us that he used this distinction, just as we should use it, because it was natural, because it was familiar, because it was on every one's lips in his day, as it is in ours. Yet, so far as I am aware, it occurs in St. Paul for the first time. No doubt the idea was floating in the air before. But he fixed it; he wedded the thought to the

---

[1]In the 1870s Lightfoot was given the post of preacher in St. Paul's Cathedral (while still at Cambridge). He preached a series of sermons, mostly on the Gospels, Acts and Paul. The following is the only one in the published collection on 2 Corinthians, in this case on 2 Corinthians 3:6, and is labeled the fifteenth sermon. These sermons were published posthumously by Macmillan of London in 1893 under the title *Sermons Preached in St. Paul's*. This sermon helps us better understand Lightfoot's exegesis of that critical passage in 2 Corinthians 3. (BW3)

words; he made it current coin. And from him it has penetrated to 'every province of human life,' for St. Paul's words, as Luther truly said, 'are not words; they are live things, they have hands and feet.' Yes, feet to go everywhere, and hands to grasp everything. I propose therefore this afternoon to enquire, what this distinction means in itself, how St. Paul applies it in the first instance, and of what further application it admits.

Now the idea of a 'letter' is something definite, fixed, immoveable. It implies a hard and fast line. It cannot be modified according to times or places or persons. It is inexorable; it is irreversible. When Pilate says, 'What I have written, I have written' he means that the matter has gone beyond the point when discussion is possible. By the maxim 'Litera scripta manet,' 'the written letter abides,' we mean that the thing cannot be hidden, cannot be questioned, cannot be slurred over, cannot be recalled. It is there, as we say, in black and white. It has taken its place among the permanent things of the world.

On the other hand 'spirit' means the direct opposite to all this. Spirit is properly a synonym for breath, a pulsation of air, a gust of wind. The Divine Influence, the Divine Person, is called the Holy Spirit. The name is given, because no other symbol would so fitly describe the operations of the spirit. These operations are silent and imperceptible; they are seen only by the results. The spirit moves invisibly, as the air moves. And, like the air too, it quickens and sustains; it is the one indispensable condition of life for man. Withdraw the spirit, and the movements of the soul languish, the respiration of the soul ceases, the life of the soul is extinguished. Like the air too, its operations are various. Sometimes it resembles a gentle breeze, fanning the earth, giving health and vigour and joy to all things around; sometimes it is a mighty rushing wind, a fierce hurricane tearing up ancient forests, and hurling down strong cities, deafening with the crash of falling ruins, but itself unseen, intangible, imperceptible, mysterious still. 'The wind bloweth where it listeth, and thou hearest the sound thereof, but canst not tell whence it cometh, and whither it goeth: so is every one that is born of the Spirit.' Measure it you cannot; weigh it you cannot; grasp it you cannot. It plays about you; it buffets you; it makes you reel and stagger; it sweeps you onward. And yet you cannot so much as see it.

But the characteristic in which the spirit especially resembles the stirring air, and with which we are most closely concerned, is its adaptability. However small or however great is the space which it is called to fill, it contracts or it expands accordingly. The spirit, as we should say in the language of natural philosophy, is perfectly elastic. A breath of air will make its way through any crevice, however narrow; it will diffuse itself over any room, however large. It adapts itself to every irregularity; it fills every interstice. It is this elasticity that makes it so fit a symbol of the spirit.

This antithesis of the letter and the spirit occurs three times in St. Paul. In the first passage, in the second chapter of the Epistle to the Romans, the Apostle is contrasting the true Jew with the false. The true Jew is that man of what nation soever he may be who acts up to the light that is given him. He may be no descendant of Abraham; he may not have been initiated into the covenant; he may keep no passovers, observe no sabbaths, offer no sacrifices; he may never have heard of the tables of the law. He is a heathen dog in the eyes of yonder Pharisee. But he is just, he is honest, he is pure, he is merciful and loving, he is reverential. Therefore he is the true Jew; therefore his is the true circumcision; for it is, says the Apostle, 'of the heart, in the spirit, not in the letter; whose praise is not of men, but of God.' No, not of men.

The tendency of men is always to prefer the letter to the spirit. An incident, recorded in the history of the earliest conversion of that country, on which the attention of Europe has of late been fixed, is a painful illustration of this. The Bulgarians, when first brought to a knowledge of the Gospel, put to the then Bishop of Rome, one of the most famous of the Popes, a question relating to the state of their deceased heathen forefathers. He sternly excluded all hope of salvation for them. He pointed to the passage that speaks of a sin unto death, a sin past praying for. Do you wonder, that he drove them to look elsewhere for more humane, more righteous teachers?

And indeed this was not the first, as it has not been the last time, when such cruel language has been held. Christian fathers before him, Protestant missionaries after him, have sinned in the same way. Did they need this fierce thought to stimulate their missionary zeal? Nay, might they not have drawn a truer lesson from that chief of missionaries, who laboured more abundantly than all? Was it not enough, that the love of Christ should constrain them, as it constrained him? Was not the sense of God's infinite gift in the death and passion of His only Son, was not the consciousness that He had called them from death to life, that they owed everything which was noblest, best, truest, in themselves to His Gospel, was not the sight of a world steeped in ignorance and sin, was not the obligation of Christ's express command to teach all nations, were not all these combined a sufficient motive to exertion; that they must forge this terrible weapon to wield in their spiritual warfare? Is not this indeed to make sad hearts that God hath not made sad?

And yet all the while the Apostle's own language is clear and explicit, declaring that the Gentiles, not having the law of Moses, had yet a law in themselves, and that by this law they would be judged. And if there were Jews who were Jews in the spirit, though not in the letter, so also must there be Christians. Many heathen shall come from East and West, Zoroaster and Buddha, it may be, Socrates and Epictetus and Marcus Aurelius; while the children of the kingdom and the ministering priest and the learned apologist and the eloquent preacher and the rigid devotee shall be cast out. By the spirit, not by the letter, shall men be judged.

The second passage, in which this distinction occurs, is likewise in the Epistle to the Romans. In the seventh chapter of that Epistle, the Apostle contrasts the Christian dispensation with the Mosaic, the Gospel with the Law, as the newness of the spirit with the oldness of the letter. In the context he describes the fatal effects of the Law. It wakes up the consciousness of guilt in the man. So sin starts into life, and it kills the man.

The same is the idea in the third passage, from which my text is taken. Here too the contrast is between the Law and the Gospel. The one was written on tables of stone, graven in hard and fast lines. The other is altogether different. Here everything is elastic, mobile, flexible, ready of adaptation, full of life. The material, on which it is written, is not the hard slab of stone, but the fleshy tablet of the human heart. The pen, which traces the characters, is not a pen of iron, but the Spirit of the living God. And, corresponding to this difference, is the contrast in the effects. The one was a ministration of death, a ministration of condemnation; the other, a ministration of righteousness.

'We are ministers,' says the Apostle here, 'of a new covenant, not of the letter, but of the spirit; for the letter killeth, but the spirit giveth life.' This then is the primary meaning of the text. The letter is a synonym for the Law; the spirit for the Gospel. The Law was holy and just and good; but the Law could never make perfect. Law may restrain, may educate, may direct, but it cannot give life. On the contrary its effect is, in the Apostle's language, to kill. By giving edge to the conscience, it intensifies the sense of remorse, it wounds, it prostrates, it slays.

A child will go on doing a certain wrong act thoughtlessly and ignorantly, till it has become a habit, without any sense of inward dissatisfaction; till at length some authoritative voice (of a father or of a mother, it may be), which is a law to that child, says, 'That is a wicked act; you must not do that.' Then everything is changed. From that time forward each recurrence of the evil habit brings misery to the child; each fresh outbreak of temptation costs it a cruel struggle. The child's conscience has been awakened by the commandment. The child has been taught the sinfulness of the sin. The child is far better than it was before; but it is far less happy. It has the sentence of condemnation in itself. To use St. Paul's language, the commandment has slain the child.

So it was with the Mosaic Law. The Mosaic Law was given to educate the conscience of the Jews, and, through the Jews, of the whole human race. It issued prohibitions; it imposed penalties; it prescribed rites. Thus by a system of obligations and restraints it taught effectually the heinousness of sin. Every day and every hour, by some rite enjoined or some commandment contravened, it reminded the Jew of his guilt. But all this in itself could only kill; it could not make alive. The Law said, 'Do not this; for, if thou doest it, thou shalt surely die.' The principle of life, under the old dispensation, was not the Law, but something behind the Law the fact of a merciful and loving Father, realised in the heart and conscience of the faithful.

But this realisation was still only shadowy and incomplete, it was then at length in the Incarnation of the Son of God that this love was perfectly manifested, then at length in the atoning blood of Christ that the pardon for sin was fully assured, then at length in the dispensation of the Spirit that the sympathetic union of man with God was completely established, the filial relation was realised and the pardoned one now no more a slave, but a son had courage to look upward and cry, 'Abba, Father.' This is the primary sense, in which the Apostle speaks of the letter killing and the spirit giving life.

But, like many another maxim of St. Paul, the saying is far too full to be exhausted by its primary meaning. It has application as wide as human life is wide, as human thought is wide. On one such application perhaps the most important of all I shall venture to dwell for a few moments. There is probably no serious Christian, who has not at some time or other felt inwardly pained, to think that he does not fulfil, that he makes no earnest attempt to fulfil, that the circumstances of life will not allow him to fulfil, certain precepts of our Lord to the letter.

If a man should sue him at law and take away his coat, would he let him have his cloak also? If a man should compel him to go one mile with him, would he go with him twain? Were he to fulfil these precepts literally, what injustice, what misery, what confusion might not ensue? The words of Christ are the most sacred of all words. Yet even here, even in the words of the Divine Word Himself, it may be said, in some sense, that the letter killeth, but the spirit giveth life. And this, because human language necessarily confines the expression of the Divine thought.

Human language is limited, and the thought is unlimited. In this particular case the spirit of the precept is the condemnation of a litigious, self-assertion. The spirit cannot be too promptly or too absolutely obeyed. One principle is here laid down in a concrete form, as it were in a parable. Human language cannot compass more than this. This principle is inviolate in itself. But right conduct is a very complex affair. Right conduct consists in taking into account many principles at once. In the case before us, by obeying the precept to the letter we might violate some other principle. We might, for instance, encourage a temper of lawlessness and violence in action; we might lead to the moral deterioration of another.

Or again, take the precept, 'Give to him that asketh thee.' The letter would lead to what is called indiscriminate charity; and indiscriminate charity is productive of the greatest evil. But here again the spirit of the precept is plain, and it is imperative. We cannot be too ready to impart to others the best gifts whatever those gifts may be with which God has endowed us. We cannot be too merciful, too self-denying, too sympathetic. But the form, which almsgiving more especially should take, must vary with the varying ages. In our own time, when there are poor laws, and workhouses and hospitals and dispensaries, when there is organized hypocrisy and professional begging, it is quite clear that we cannot follow in exactly the same lines which were the best in Palestine eighteen centuries ago, when none of these things existed.

The question we have to ask, and answer for ourselves, is not only what Christ did or commanded then, but also what He would do or command us to do in this altered state of society now. In short, we must endeavour to ascertain the mind of Christ through the recorded words and works of Christ to ascertain it, and to follow it absolutely, without any reservation or afterthought. And our teacher here must be the Holy Spirit of God, 'the Spirit which searcheth all things, He is the only safe interpreter of Christ's words and works.' He alone can translate them for us into modern language, and adapt them to modern life. This is the promise vouchsafed in His name. 'He shall take of Mine, and shall show it unto you.'

If we go to any other teacher, then our attempts to evolve the spirit from the letter will be a hopeless failure. 'The natural man receiveth not the things of the Spirit of God, for they are foolishness to him.' But, if we approach Him with a single eye and a single heart, not wishing to spare ourselves, not seeking to excuse ourselves from irksome duties, but desiring only to learn, and prompt, when we have learned, to obey, then He will not fail us. 'If any man will do His will, is ready to do His will,' 'he shall know of the doctrine, whether it be of God.'

Appendix D

LESSONS OF HISTORY FROM THE
CRADLE OF CHRISTIANITY[1]

But that you may not have a pretext for saying that Christ must have been crucified, and that those who transgressed must have been among your nation, and that the matter could not have been otherwise, I said briefly by anticipation, that God, wishing men and angels to follow His will, resolved to create them free to do righteousness; possessing reason, that they may know by whom they are created, and through whom they, not existing formerly, do now exist; and with a law that they should be judged by Him, if they do anything contrary to right reason: and of ourselves we, men and angels, shall be convicted of having acted sinfully, unless we repent beforehand. But if the word of God foretells that some angels and men shall be certainly punished, it did so because it foreknew that they would be unchangeably [wicked], but not because God had created them so.

JUSTIN MARTYR, *DIALOGUE WITH TRYPHO*, CXL

---

[1]The original essay of Lightfoot, and indeed its later revision (see the introduction to this volume for the source history), had no title; so I have given it one based on its content. Again, credit must be given to Treloar and Kaye for finding this interesting essay in two forms, and publishing in the 1980s the *later* revised form in the *Durham University Journal*. This is the original and fuller form of the essay, complete with the original abrupt ending as Lightfoot ran out of time. I am happy to report that Professor Treloar is also convinced that we are presenting here the earlier, more original form of this essay. Here is what he has said to me in correspondence on August 16, 2014: "You are undoubtedly correct. There are clearly significant differences between the two versions, and just as clearly 'mine' is later than 'yours.' You will see that the edition published in the *DUJ* interpolates matter from the earlier version." So it does, but we are presenting the whole original essay here. Treloar thinks Lightfoot revised the essay before he submitted it for the prize. To my mind this does not make sense of the ending of this first draft. If he was not submitting it "as is," there was no need for the final apology at the end of this document. The apology clearly implies an official reader of the document. It is not a note to himself. (BW3)

Introduction

'Let knowledge grow from more to more,
But more of reverence in us dwell,
That mind and soul according will,
May make one music as before,
But vaster'—Tennyson

There are periods in the history of the Church where powerful and well-directed attacks from without, aided by errors and discussions from within, seem to threaten her stronghold, well nigh with total destruction; and the Christian turning away from this sickening scene of desolation clings only more firmly to his Lord's promises, though perhaps in the signs of the times as he reads them, he sees nothing to justify his hope.

It were well at seasons like this that the study of past history should come to the rescue of a wavering faith. It would show the Christian that the crisis which he, in his immediate terror, is disposed to represent to himself as unparalleled, in the previous history of the Church has been equaled or even surpassed by the dangers of former times. It would point out to him how the attacks once and again received from the same quarters were triumphantly repelled. It would teach him to distinguish between the real and substantial knowledge that accumulates from age to age, and the illusive phantoms and one-sided sentiments which characterize his own time. Still more he would be warned not to fight for the bulwarks and outposts which have been raised by human hands, when by so doing he is endangering the divine fortress itself, but if need be, cheerfully to surrender these, and to place his confidence in that which forms his real strength, knowing that 'except the Lord keep the city, the watchman watches in vain.'

It is through one of these fiery trials that the Church has been passing during the last half century. During this period the attacks have been renewed from various quarters but all apparently with equal confidence in their ultimate success. It seems that like some ancient warrior in his tomb, the Christian Church which for ages had preserved its integrity, built in by conventional prejudice and protected by superstitious reverence would, when exposed to the light and air of modern criticism and science, crumbles away instantly and leave but a handful of dust in place of its once imposing form.

If the Christian needed any warrant for disregarding these assumptions, he would find it in the discussions that distract his adversary's camp; for each form of unbelief has received its deathblow from its successor in the contest. The attacks in the last century were conceived in a very different spirit from those which have succeeded them; an opposition ushered in during an irreligious age, by those, who cared neither for God nor man— adversaries, who, when it served their purpose, would scoff with as little concern and as much self-complacency at the discoveries of scientific re- search as the revelations of religious truth—were not likely to find much favor with those who strove to undermine the historical basis of Christi- anity, were ready to allow the pre-eminence of its ethical code, and the importance of the truths it inculcates and whose boast it was, that in their opposition, they were following the guidance of the scientific spirit of the age.[2] *Moreover the objection to the miraculous element in the Christian scheme, represented by the elder opponents, was found on closer examination to be fallacious, while the hypothesis, which they introduced to explain the historical phenomena, involving the paradox of a set of men propagating the highest truths by means of the grossest falsehoods at great personal sacrifice was regarded as no less an outrage upon the experience of mankind, than revolting to the moral sensibilities.* Thus neither the destructive nor the con- structive part of their scheme was cordially received by those who inherited their opposition.

As regards the former, the objection to miracles was abandoned, only however to be reproduced under a different guise, and in a more specious form. It was now urged, that the supernatural element was at variance with the deductions of modern science which negatives the idea of any dealings of God with man, otherwise than by the ordinary medium of natural occur- rences. But surely it is great presumption to build a theory on the suppo- sition that we understand the absolute distinction between the mediate and the immediate in the divine agency—terms which, after all, may be merely relative to finite comprehensions. It presumes such a knowledge of the rela- tions of cause and effect that we cannot in any sense be said to have, when it is decided prior to evidence that there must be a certain succession of

---

[2]See for example, Lyalls, *Principles of Geology*, Vol. I p. 75 of Voltaire.

events *even when* the conditions of the problem are avowedly different. Nor indeed are the analogies, which touch the case most nearly, to be found in those objects with which the conclusions of science have hitherto been conversant, but rather in those mysterious relations of mind to matter of which as of yet we are utterly ignorant. Are we then justified in sacrificing to a theory so premature the universal consciousness of mankind of its immediate relations to a supreme ruler and giving the lie to the no less general belief in the development of these relations by means of a direct revelation from God?

But again a scheme had to be constructed to account for the remarkable phenomenon which the case presents. The supposition of deliberate imposture was relinquished as inadequate and two methods were proposed in its place, for solving this historical problem—the Rationalist on the one hand, believing that there must be some basis of facts in the sacred narrative, exercised much ingenuous subtlety in divesting them of the supernatural element with as little violence as possible to their historical fidelity. The mythicizer, on the other hand, more bold and consistent, declaring all search after history as hopeless, was disposed to find in the Biblical record merely a collection of legends, the spontaneous product of national feelings and expectations.

The defects of the former method were easily exposed, for a flaw in the criticism of individual circumstances is not difficult to detect, hence no one has laid open its absurdities with a more remorseless hand than the champion of the mythical theory, but the difficulties in his own solution, if not so patent, are not fewer. In one important respect the Rationalist has the advantage of his rival, he is not required to use such violent treatment in the disposal of historical records. The mythical theorist is conscious and acknowledges that so long as the documents are allowed to proceed from eye-witnesses or contemporaneous writers his solution will not hold,[3] hence the caricature of criticism which the adherents of this school have drawn in the attempt to invalidate the Apostolic Writings.

But it does not come within the scope of the following pages to discuss the difficulties attending the growth of these 'evangelical myths' under the supposed circumstances, it is only proposed to show how inadequate is the

---

[3]See Strauss, *Leben Jesu*, sec. 9 (Eng. Transl).

cause assigned—for the formation of the collection of facts and doctrines presented to us in the Gospels.

'The mythical and the allegorical view,' it is said, 'equally allow that the historian apparently relates that which is historical, but they suppose him under the influence of a higher inspiration, known or unknown to himself, to have made use of this historical semblance merely as the shell of an *idea—of a religious conception*. The only essential distinction therefore between these modes of explanation is that according to the allegorical view, higher intelligence is the immediate divine agency, but according to the mythical view it is the spirit of a people or community. Thus the allegorical view attributes the narrative to a supernatural source, whilst the mythical view ascribes it to that natural process by which legends are developed.' 'The mythical interpreter,' the writer adds, 'is controlled by regard to conformity with the spirit and modes of thought of the people and the age.'[4]

Accordingly, one writer informs us that with a single exception (which indeed is important—the miraculous conception) 'parallels can be produced to every doctrine, nay almost to every position advanced in the New Testament from the Talmud, the Midrashim, etc.'[5] Others, again, have looked to Philo and the Alexandrian school for a solution, while a third party has used contributions from all the Jewish sects in turn, and sought by the admixture of certain Heathen elements with these to make up the sum of Christian doctrine.[6]

It must not be concealed that there has been some provocation to this treatment of the subject. They had been preceded by a class of apologists who looking back on the struggles of unaided humanity by the light of revelation, and anxious to find in the latter a reflex of natural religion, had strained every point to the utmost to produce parallels to the Christian writers in the anterior religions of the world.[7] The impugners of revelation

---

[4]Strauss, sec. 12.

[5]Gfrörer, *Jahrbuch des Heils*, ii, p. 431, cited by Dorner, *Lehre*, p. 3.

[6]See the catalogue of writers given by Giesler, *Eccl. Hist.* I, p. 56, (Engl. Trans.).

[7]'It could produce immeasurable testimonies to prove that the ancient Jews did believe these great doctrines of Christianity, the Trinity, the Incarnation of the Messiah, or son of God, and the atonement he was to make for our sins, as surely as we do at this time, and that they were instructed in them by traditions.' Stehelin's *Rabbincal Literature*, p. 11, and this sort of exaggerated language was used by many.

saw the advantage offered to them, and were not slack in wielding it against their adversaries, the irons forged on their own anvils.

Yet as extravagant as were these views on both sides, the advocate of revealed religion had the advantage in one important respect. He did assign a cause sufficient to produce the effects, to infuse fresh life into the corrupt mass of superstition and infidelity, to leaven society anew, to gather together the scattered fragments of truth, and weld them into a consistent whole; for in proportion as the number of component parts is multiplied, in the same degree does the difficulty of combining them grow, and, to render their theory plausible, our adversaries have been obliged to look far and wide for the elements of their compound.

It is hoped that in the following pages, these extremes are avoided. The history of former controversy ought to have taught us this lesson—Accepting as true the definition of myth that has been cited above, we shall carry on the investigation in the trust that, imperfectly as it is made in this essay, its result will be to confirm our belief in the divine origin of our religion.

At the same time we shall meet with more indications than ever that there was indeed some basis for that boon that Christianity offers us. We shall catch glimpses from time to time of partial truths, breaking out from under the cloud of error and obscurity which envelops them—'broken light' of the great Sun of Righteousness which was soon to rise over the world. We shall recognize here and there faint foreshadowings of that spiritual kingdom which is to include all nations of the earth. We shall find the philosophers and statesmen alike 'Seeking the Lord if happily they might find him, though he was not far from every one of them.'

Part One: The Jews of Palestine and the Dispersion

ἐποίησέν . . . πᾶν ἔθνος ἀνθρώπων . . . ζητεῖν τὸν Θεόν, εἰ ἄρα γε ψηλαφήσειαν αὐτὸν καὶ εὕροιεν καί γε οὐ μακρὰν ἀπὸ ἑνὸς ἑκάστου ἡμῶν ὑπάρχοντα.—St. Paul (Acts 17:26-27)

The history of a people who persevered for many centuries, a national character unaffected by their intercourse with neighboring races, laws and institutions peculiar to themselves, and a deep consciousness of the unity and attributes of the Deity and their own special connection with Him—who, after so long a period of obscurity and seclusion were destined to give to mankind a religious system, which in arts and sciences, in morals and in politics should produce a marvelous change unparalleled in the history of the world—would be an instructive field of inquiry even to those who recognize in such manifestations only the ordinary workings of human society.

For the Christian, the history of the Jewish race possesses a higher interest. He regards it as the cradle of that religion in which all his hopes and plans center, and to which he looks for the future resurrection of the world, as he has seen a light of promise in the past. If he is not ungrateful for that goodly inheritance of literary treasures which he has drawn from the storehouses of Greece, or those prudent maxims of law and government which he owes to the teaching of Imperial Rome, he feels that he is indebted to Palestine for that knowledge without which all literature is hollow and superficial, and all government unstable and transitory. A brief review of the relations of this nation to the Gentile world will be a fit introduction to the examination of its position with respect to Christianity.[8]

Among our deepest intuitions is the idea of God. Reflections on our own weakness and folly and wickedness does by a law of our own nature suggest to us its Divine correlative, a Being of Infinite Power, and Wisdom, and Holiness. Again the contemplation of external Nature, simple in its very complexity, as varied in its results as it is uniform in its operations, directs us to the Idea of a First Cause. Yet each of these proofs, the one from our innate intuition, the other from the world without, in reality includes and presupposes the other, for on the one hand our intuitions are developed by contact with the world, while on the other, no accumulation of facts can call forth an idea, the germ of which is not already planted in our soul. Nor are we without a natural consciousness of the relationship which exists between God and Man, our heart speaks of this, indeed of our entire dependence on Him, but it likewise tells us of the separation between Finite weakness, and Infinite Power, between human Folly and divine Wisdom, above all between the wickedness of man and the Goodness of God.

Coincident with this sense of his separation from God, there is on the part of man an anxiety to atone for his past sins, a desire for his present

---

[8]See Norden, *Phil.* 4, Series 2, Lecture XV.

reconciliation, and a deep craving for closer communion with Him in the time to come. To this he looks as the fulfillment of his deepest aspirations and the realization of that higher destiny for which he feels he was made. We can assign no other meaning to the priesthood, sacrifices, temples, and oracles which we everywhere meet when traversing the domain of religious history.

Thus we find growing up side by side a consciousness of separation from God, and an earnest craving after union with Him. It is not meant to assert that man could ordinarily read and interpret the working of his own heart, still less to imply that this belief and these aspirations burnt brightly and steadily a beacon light to warn and guide him in his voyage through life. Such a view would be contradicted by every page of history, as it would also supercede the necessity of that mission, which we believe was assigned by Divine Providence to the Jewish people.

It was to restore and preserve the original handwriting traced by the finger of God on the heart of man, which had been blurred and overlaid by irregular characters and legends of human invention, in the race by centuries of disobedience and rebellion and in the individual by natural propensities to evil and contact with a world of sin, that this people had been chosen and set apart. For not only had the original Idea been obscured, but men had sought to satisfy their craving by irregular means, in anticipation of which God in his good Providence was pleased to supply. It had been the province of the Law to fence about our consciousness of the true relations between God and man. It was the mission of the Gospel to point out the fountain from which our thirst could be quenched. If the older dispensation had proclaimed the sovereignty of the 'One God,' the watchword of the new is 'the One Mediator between God and Man, the man Christ Jesus.'

What then were the relations of Judaism to Heathenism in these two respects?

There was a twofold tendency which threatened the purity of these natural intuitions. On the one hand, the unity of the Godhead was assailed and the divine attribute portioned out among many, on the other an unholy attempt was made to bridge over the gulf between the Finite and the Infinite, by absorbing the one in the other. Polytheism was the characteristic religion of the West. Pantheism has ever found a resting place in the East.

The chosen people of God, situated midway between such influences, received a national education at the basis of which lay the recognition of those great truths in their integrity. The messenger of Yahweh prefaces his words 'Hear O Israel, the Lord our God is One God' (Deut 6:4). The historical records of the nation commence by narrating how 'In the beginning God created the heavens and the earth' (Gen 1:1).[9] The admission of these truths was their title to a peculiar position among the nations of the world, the center of their religious and political life.

9.) The yearnings of men after closer communion with God found expression in the endeavors which they made to forge the golden chain which was to bind earth to the footstool of heaven. This attempt developed itself in two separate directions, corresponding to the two great divisions of the Gentile world, either taking man for his starting point, the heathen sought to elevate the human to the divine; or setting out from the divine, he invested god with the garb of humanity.

How little the hero worship of the Western world allayed the cravings which it was intended to satisfy, and how far removed it was from the Christian idea, is at once apparent. The Oriental belief, on the other hand, seems to approach nearer to the Christian standard. It bespeaks a deep consciousness of the difficulty with which it grapples; but it is still far from solving the problem of our wants. The incarnation of the deity in Hindu mythology is imperfect. Vishnu appears on earth in human guise, but he appears also in various forms, his humanity is no part of his nature, and the deliverance which he works is only momentary. He returns to heaven and leaves the human race under the dominion of evil, as it was before he visited it.[10]

It is Christianity which teaches us that God 'was made flesh and dwelt among us' (John 1), in such sense as to apprise us of our reconciliation with Him. Here first do we learn that we have a 'great high priest,' 'the son of God,' who has indeed 'passed into the heavens' but yet can be 'touched with the feelings of our infirmities' (Heb 4:14-15).

---

[9]The pantheistic beliefs of the Cabbalists (if they are justly charged with it), is a plant of later growth. At all events it cannot be identified with the religious beliefs of the people. See Dr. Mill, *On the Pantheistic Theory*, Appendix B.

[10]See Dorner, *Lehre von der Person*, p. 8.

Meanwhile, the chosen people, living under the immediate government of the Most High, and thus in some sense realizing a closer communion with Him, were taught to regard that more perfect union after which mankind was yearning as a matter not of human speculation, but of direct revelation from Heaven. They were prepared by a series of intimations becoming more and more distinct as the great day of their accomplishment drew nigh—at first confirming the promise given to the fathers of their race that 'in this seed all the nations of the earth should be blessed,' and speaking of a second lawgiver like unto him by whom the words of the prophecy were uttered, afterwards depicting in more glowing colors and ever increasing brightness the office and person of the great Redeemer till at length they were told of one 'like the Son of Man who should come with the clouds of Heaven, whose dominion was an everlasting dominion which shall not pass away' (Dan 7:13-14), again, foretelling his human lineage, the place of his birth and the very time when this great deliverance should be wrought. We shall see hereafter how the Christian idea was yet 'a mystery, which was kept secret since the world began' (see Col 1:26).

The natural bent of the Hebrew mind was not speculative. They belonged to that family of the human race which is rather receptive than originative, for the greatest systems of philosophy and speculative theology, whether of the East or the West, have had their rise not in the Semitic but in the Indo-Germanic races. If their characteristic warns us to pause, ere we attribute any highly developed religious system to the unaided efforts of the Jewish mind, it betokens a peculiar fitness in their selection to be appointed guardians of 'the oracles of God.'

Again, their national education had prepared them for the important destiny which awaited them. Fenced off from the heathen, by peculiar[11] laws and institutions, warned and guided by the voice of prophecy, and protected by mighty signs and wonders, wrought on their behalf, the chosen race had nevertheless from time to time turned aside to the idolatry of the heathen, but the Babylonian captivity had purged them like a refiner's fire, a great change had been wrought in them, and henceforward we read no more of any great national declension from the God of their

---

[11]Here as so often with Lightfoot, *peculiar* does not mean "strange" but rather "distinctive." (BW 3)

forefathers. The presence of some tyrannical conqueror might tempt them for a moment to forget their allegiance, but this disobedience was not self-sought. The sufferings which befell them from the vices of their native princes and the oppression of foreign despots only strengthened the bond of union among themselves.

To the glories of the Maccabean period more especially they looked back with an honest pride, and the fond remembrances of a later age (contrast 2 Macc with 1 Macc which was nearly contemporaneous with the events it records), delighted to adorn with wonderous stories of daring and might the history of that 'valiant man who delivered Israel' (1 Macc 9:21). The warning of the prophet had not been heard, and the right arm of the Lord had not been revealed as in old times in signs and wonders, but it was felt that He had been present among them in their hour of need. Thus the feeling of nationality was fostered and cherished and with this were bound up those heaven-sent traditions which were to be the preparation for the Gospel.

Hence there was a peculiar fitness in the time that was selected for the revelation of Messiah to his people. But can we venture a step beyond, and say that we see in the popular mind of the day the germ of a natural development of the Christian scheme?

The voice of prophecy had been silent for four centuries, but it was felt to be as the death-like stillness that precedes the hurricane. Hence, men with busy whisperings were anxiously looking for the coming of that great Terrible Day of the Lord which, amidst many horrors, was yet to bring their deliverance. See for example Josephus, *Bell. Jud.* vi.5.4: Ταῦτά τις ἐννοῶν εὑρήσει τὸν μὲν θεὸν ἀνθρώπων κηδόμενον καὶ παντοίως προσημαίνοντα τῷ σφετέρῳ γένει τὰ σωτήρια, τοὺς δ' ὑπ' ἀνοίας καὶ κακῶν αὐθαιρέτων ἀπολλυμένους, which is repeated by Suetonius and Tacitus. The flattery of the Jewish historian would have attributed it to Vespasian.[12]

The iron despotism of foreign masters had naturally led them to these expectations of a temporal Prince, of the overthrow of the heathen and the triumph of the People of God. The best evidence of this feeling is the character of the claimants of the Messiahship at this period, especially Judas of Galilee, and later Bar-Kokhba. Thus while the hopes of men were never

---

[12]Cf. Giesler, Vol. I, p. 39 (Eng. Trans.).

more generally covered, they did not take the direction in which Christianity held out their fulfillment.

Again, the teaching of those who were regarded by the people as their authorized instructors was no less averse to the spirit of Christianity; it was the narrow adherence to the letter, which saw in the Mosaic ritual nothing more than a collection of ordinances, to be enforced and added to according to the caprice of the interpreter.

As a natural consequence, their teaching reacted upon the morals of the people. The Jewish historian gives a fearful picture of the corruption of the time—'No species of vice,' he says, 'was unpracticed by the nation, none could be so much as imagined which had not found a place among them. One moral plague had infected both public and private life. They strove to outbid each other in impiety towards God and injustice towards their neighbors' (*Bell. Jud.* vii.8.1).[13] Thus, Christianity could find no resting place in the state of national opinion or public morals.

The reverence for the institutions of the Mosaic ritual had never in the course of Jewish history been greater than in the interval between the Maccabean period and the Christian era. But narrow in its spirit, and burdensome in its interpretations, it naturally provoked a reaction that found expression in the school of the Sadducees. We are informed that Antigonus of Sokho, the reputed founder of this sect based his teaching on the following thesis: 'Be ye not,' he said, 'as servants who serve their lord for the sake of gain, but as servants who serve their lord without an eye to receiving a reward' and as if to guard against misinterpretation he added, 'The fear of Heaven be upon you.'[14]

We shall doubtless be right in regarding these maxims as a protest against the carnal and selfish worship of his day, but in the hands of his followers, the teaching of the sect assumed a very different aspect. We find them maintaining a principle destructive of all religion that 'good and evil lie within the power of man, and the Deity does not interfere to inflict or chastise evil' (*Bell. Jud.* ii.8.14).[15] Thus, if they did not absolutely deny the doctrine of a divine Providence, they at least trenched upon it in that full sense, in which

---

[13]See Giesler, *Eccles. Hist.* Vol. I p. 37. This writer inadvertently applies to the nation at large what is said only of their leaders in two other passages which he cites—*Bell. Jud.* v.10.5; v.13.6.
[14]Cited in Ewald, *Geschichte des Volkes Israel*, Vol. iii, Part 2, p. 313.
[15]The conjectural reading 'does not see' for 'does not interfere' is unsupported.

it is recognized in the Old Testament writings. It was one additional step to deny the immortality of the soul,[16] and the ministry of angels. The former would not present much difficulty to those who denied the canonical authority[17] of all the sacred writings except the Pentateuch, and subjected even this to a narrow interpretation that recognized nothing beyond the most positive declarations. The latter indeed appears on almost every page of the Mosaic narrative, but it is not difficult to see how a free use of allegory[18] would enable them to reduce even the most stubborn facts to a conformity with their pre-conceived bias. But by whatever path they arrived at these results, their position of direct antagonism to Christianity is evident. In short, the Sadducees sought to fix an arbitrary limit to the Mosaic dispensation, which it was the mission of the Gospel to develop and extend.

The moral character of the Sadducees accorded with their religious creed; they were cold and skeptical (so *Ant.* xviii.1.4), cruel in their punishments, and uncourteous even to members of their own body (so *Bell Jud.* ii.8). They were devoted to a life of luxury and ease. The sect numbered but few adherents, yet these were all men of rank and wealth (see *Ant.* xviii.1.4; xiii.10.6).

The notices we have of the demeanor of the members of this sect to the early Christians accord with what we know of their peculiar tenets. The Sadducees are only mentioned three times in the Gospels: 1) as coming to the baptism of John (Mt 3:7); 2) as the objects of the Lord's reproof (Mt 16:1-12); 3) as questioning the Lord respecting the resurrection of the dead (Mt 22:23; Mark 12:18; Luke 20:27).

During the lifetime of the Savior when the new teachings turned upon the regeneration of the inward life, the Pharisees were the constant opponents of the Lord and his disciples, but subsequently, when the Apostles preaching centered in the fact of resurrection the bitterest persecution was carried out by the Sadducees.[19] The history of their opposition does not close with the evangelical narrative; we meet with them once again (if an authority may be

---

[16]*Ant.* xviii.1.4; Mt 22:23; *Ant.* xxiii.8.

[17]See Neander, *Ch. Hist.* Vol. I, p. 56 (Eng. Trans.)

[18]See Origen, as cited by Neander, p. 58 on angels etc.

[19]See Acts 4:1; 5:7; 13:7, 8. They probably acted not without the connivance of the Pharisees—see *Ant.* xviii.1.4—προσχωροῦσι δ' οὖν οἷς ὁ Φαρισαῖος λέγει διὰ τὸ μὴ ἄλλως ἀνεκτοὺς γενέσθαι τοῖς πλήθεσιν. The conduct of St. Paul is related. Acts 23:7, 8 has been severely censured, perhaps somewhat hastily, for as regards the Sadducees, his cause was one with the Pharisees. He had much in common with the latter, but Sadduceeanism was directly antagonistic to both.

trusted) as the murderers of St. James, the first bishop of Jerusalem. Josephus puts it this way—ὁ δὲ νεώτερος Ἄνανος, ὃν τὴν ἀρχιερωσύνην ἔφαμεν εἰληφέναι, θρασὺς ἦν τὸν τρόπον καὶ τολμητὴς διαφερόντως, αἵρεσιν δὲ μετῄει τὴν Σαδδουκαίων, οἵπερ εἰσὶ περὶ τὰς κρίσεις ὠμοὶ παρὰ πάντας τοὺς Ἰουδαίους, καθὼς ἤδη δεδηλώκαμεν. ἅτε δὴ οὖν τοιοῦτος ὢν ὁ Ἄνανος, νομίσας ἔχειν καιρὸν ἐπιτήδειον διὰ τὸ τεθνάναι μὲν Φῆστον, Ἀλβῖνον δ᾿ ἔτι κατὰ τὴν ὁδὸν ὑπάρχειν, καθίζει συνέδριον κριτῶν καὶ παραγαγὼν εἰς αὐτὸ [τὸν ἀδελφὸν Ἰησοῦ τοῦ λεγομένου Χριστοῦ, Ἰάκωβος ὄνομα αὐτῷ, καί] τινας [ἑτέρους], ὡς παρανομησάντων κατηγορίαν ποιησάμενος παρέδωκε λευσθησομένους (*Ant.* xx.199-200). The words within brackets are considered spurious by some, but the passage is somewhat awkward without them, and one who has left such testimony of the Baptist might well have written these words. At the same time, this account is directly at variance with that given by Hegisippus in Eusebius (see *Hist. Eccl.* ii.23).[20]

The ethical system of the Sadducees, as discarding a morality of consequences has been alleged to have exerted its influence on the Christian scheme. Had the doctrine, as entertained by Antigonus, been held by his successors at this time, this argument might have carried some weight with it, but we have already seen how entirely its complexion had been changed. Thus, the negative tendencies of the Sadducees present no point of resemblance with Christian teaching. If such influences are to be found, they have to be sought rather in the *positive* developments of religious feeling at this period. We shall here examine their claims to such a connection.

The course of positive teaching among the strict adherents of the Mosaic institutions took two separate directions. The one party was satisfied with a formal obedience to a number of set ordinances, without looking for anything of deeper significance. The other, no less strict in outward observances, added to them an element of fanciful mysticism, which the Eastern mind is peculilarly prone to substituting for a spiritual religion. They are represented by the schools of the Pharisees and the Essenes respectively.

The spread of skeptical opinions, and the consequent laxity in religious observances resulting perhaps from a contact with foreign influences, and finding expression, as we have seen, in the sect of the Sadducees, had produced

---

[20]N.B. Neander adopts the account of Josephus.

a strong reaction. A number of men bound themselves by oath to the closest observance of the Mosaic ordinances and from the strictness of their lives assumed to themselves or won from others the name of 'the Pious' (Hasidim, or Assideans—1 Macc 2:42).[21] They had fought bravely in the War of Independence under Judas Maccabeus and it was long before this page of history would be blotted out of the remembrances of the people. The after-growth of this society was the school of the Pharisees. Thus, they were identified with the cause of national freedom (see *Ant.* xvii.2.4), and their consequent influence, perhaps not undeserved in the first instance, with the mass of the people had no bounds. 'So great was their authority,' we are told, 'that if they brought any charge even against the king or the high-priest, they were at once believed' (*Ant.* xiii.10.5; cf. xviii.1.2; xiii.10.6).

The strictness of their outward demeanor (Josephus laying great stress on the strictness of their morals), their tenacious observance of the minutest points of ceremonial law, the comparative purity of their doctrine, all combined to magnify them in the sight of those who could not penetrate beyond the surface or probe the rottenness which was concealed beneath this fair outside. It was reserved for Him, who knew the thoughts of men, to unveil and denounce their hypocrisy. Yet we must not forget, as we are apt to do, the denunciations of woe ever ringing in our ears that He who condemned them as 'blind leaders of the blind,' also told the people that they did well to harken unto them 'for they sat in Moses' seat' (cf. Mt 15:14 with Mt 13:2).

What then is their position with respect to Christianity? So far as they represented the teaching of the Old Testament, they must have prepared the way for the Gospel, but in proportion as they departed from the ancient Hebrew type, they resigned their claim to be considered as forerunners of the new dispensation. The Christian teachers took up the religious development of the nation where it had been laid down by the latest of the prophets. The Pharisees had retrograded for they had sought to crush that spiritual element which it had been the mission of the ancient teachers to evolve from the ordinances of the Law. The only point of contact between Christianity and the *distinctive* teaching of the Pharisees is the recognition of the immorality of the soul.[22]

---

[21]See Ewald, *Gesch. des Volkes* Vol. iii, Part ii, p. 342.
[22]Strauss no. 43, himself rejects the notion of any connection of Christianity with either the Sadducees or the Pharisees. How he speaks of the Essenes we shall see below.

Far more attractive is the picture that is presented of the Essenes. Living apart from the world, and simple in their habits, they engaged only in husbandry, sleep, tending on such other harmless occupations. Moreover, they are represented as being amiable in their private relations of life, devout worshippers of God, regarding a simple affirmation as equally inviolable with the most stringent oath, severe dispensers of justice, patient under suffering, charitable to the poor, and hospitable to strangers. Like the Pythagoreans, they were strictly a religious brotherhood. They had no wives, no slaves, no private property. They took their meals in common, and as for money it was distributed each according to their needs by those who were entrusted with the common purse, as their wants were but few, they could afford to be liberal in almsgiving. 'Everyday,' we are told, 'their numbers were increased by an influx of new settlers, for they were visited by crowds of men, whom the tide of adversity had driven, weary of the world, to their modes of living' (Pliny, *Nat. Hist.* v.5).[23] The principal passages about the Essenes are Josephus, *Bell. Jud.* ii.8; *Ant.* xviii.1.5; Philo, *Quod Omn. Prob. Lib. Vol. II*, p.456; *M. Fragm.* Vol. II. The account of Philo is scarcely trustworthy, for he does not give the reverse side of their character. Josephus, on the other hand, had some connection with them in his early life (see *Vit.* no. 2).

Were there no other lives in the portrait (and Philo gives us little else besides), we might be disposed to admit that there was some connection between this sect and the first preachers of Christianity, but there are other features, painted by a more trustworthy authority which entirely destroy the illusion.

The *historical* bearing of this question is reserved for a later section. At present it will suffice to single out a few points in which there is a marked contrast between the doctrine and the tendencies of the Essenes, and those exhibited in the New Testament. First, we observe in this sect the strictest adherence to the law of ordinances. They practiced the severest asceticism, their meals were spare and of the plainest food, their garments worn and tattered (see *Bell. Jud.* ii.8.9). They shrunk from anointing themselves in the Oriental manner as a pollution; so great was their abhorrence of this practice that if any oil touched them by chance, they carefully wiped it off (so Josephus).

---

[23]Cited by Neander, *Ch. Hist*, I, p 59 (Eng. Trans).

In their ceremonial observances, they surpassed even Pharisaic strictness. None were more careful than they to purify themselves before sitting down to a meal, none were more strict in the observance of the Sabbath.[24] Not only did they prepare their food the day before, that they might not have to light a fire on that day, but they would not willingly before the most trivial offices of life.

Again, we find an exclusive spirit prevailing among them, which indeed was a necessary consequence of their being a religious order. A new member was clothed in the peculiar dress of his grade, and commenced his year of probation. After that period he was admitted into closer communion and allowed to participate in the higher lustrations. Yet even then his novitiate was not ended. Two years more lapsed during which his disposition was tested and if approved he was at length admitted. The oath of admission was of the most stringent kind, besides promising obedience to all moral ordinances, he also engaged not to conceal anything from the brotherhood, nor to divulge their secrets to others, not to communicate their doctrines to anyone in any different way from that in which he himself had received them. There were four grades among them, according to the time which they had passed in religious exercises (τῆς ἀσκήσεως) and so rigidly was this distinction of caste observed, that if a member of a superior grade chanced to touch an inferior, he immediately washed himself to escape defilement.

But the strong and peculiar development of the mystic element presents the sharpest contrast with the simple teaching of the Gospel. They were careful to abstain from any profane expression before the rising of the sun, to whom they offered up certain traditional prayers. They paid particular attention to the writings of the ancients and were acquainted with the healing qualities of herbs and the properties of minerals. Again, when the novice was admitted into the brotherhood, he engaged to guard the sacred books of the sect, and the names of the angels. 'There were some of them also,' says Josephus, 'who professed to foresee future events (see also *Ant.* xv.10.5),[25] being versed from childhood in sacred books and various purifications and in the utterances of the prophets.' He also speaks of their speculations regarding the

---

[24]Philo's account of their observance of the Sabbath suppresses the disagreeable features (p. 45D M). Of the Essenes' observance of Easter see Wiesner, *Chronologie*.

[25]There are scattered notions in Josephus of the Essenes making predictions e.g., xvii.12.3; xiii.2.2; cf. *Bell. Jud.* i.3.4.

nature of the soul and its state after death. Philo adds that they had a system of symbolism in the interpretation of their sacred books in *Quod. Omin. Prob Lib.* ad loc.

It will be seen from this account how little the characteristic teaching of the Essenes had in common with Christianity. Indeed it is allowed by one whose peculiar bias makes the admission more valuable, that certain features in the sect 'are so foreign, nay so directly opposed to the spirit of Jesus, that the aid with which they contributed to his development must be limited to the uncertain influence which might be exercised over him by occasional intercourse with them.'[26]

At Alexandria, the metropolis of art and literature, and the door of communication between the philosophy of the West and the religions of the East, for some centuries had been established a colony of Jews, inferior in number and importance only to those of the mother-state, with a regular priesthood and temple worship of their own, and employing a version of the Scriptures in the language of their adopted country, they had no bond of union with the land of their fathers except that which was furnished by a common faith and origin and the deep impress of nationality, which their past history had stamped upon them.

Even these bulwarks were in danger of being swept away by the tide of Grecian art and philosophy that set in upon them with all its irresistible charms. There was a temptation to smooth down some of the most rugged discrepancies between their religious beliefs, and that of the nations with whom they were brought in contact, and to recommend their traditions to the Heathen, even at the risk of trenching upon the integrity of their faith.

This course, that was dictated by policy, was recommended also by purer motives. They found much in the speculations of some of the heathen writers, especially Plato, which could only be traced to Him, who had gifted their own prophets with riches and a more abundant measure of inspiration.[27] Desirous of incorporating this into their system, but destitute alike of true principles of criticism, and a clear insight into their position among the

---

[26]Strauss, *Life of Jesus*, no. 43. After a merciless exposure of those who had found in Essenism a key to all the peculiarities of the Gospel, and discussing other supposed influences he sums up by saying 'for the reformation of the world, these elements were all too little, and the leaven necessary for this he must obtain "from the depths of his own mind."'

[27]See *de Cant.* f. 699, cited by Neander, *Ch. Hist.* I, p.72.

nations of the world, they resorted to the most violent method for combining elements adverse and irreconcilable.

At times the spirit of accommodation displayed itself in a harmless manner. Thus we read of one who exhibited 'the Exodus' as a Greek drama, of another who celebrated the Holy City in an epic, while a third, probably a Samaritan, chose Shechem as the subject of his poem.[28] But it was Greek philosophy that made the greatest inroads upon the precincts of their faith. They were tempted to merge the ever-present God of the Old Testament with the Absolute Being of the Greek, and invisibly to abandon the moral standing point of their lawgiver and their prophets in favor of the physical or metaphysical grounds on which the speculations of heathen philosophy were built.

Yet the results of these foreign influences must not be exaggerated. Though indiscriminant in their use of allegorical interpretation, they yet believed in the plenary inspiration of the Old Testament writings, nor did they forget that they had an important part assigned to them in the history of mankind, though, as we shall see hereafter, they did not recognize the manner in which their destiny was to be fulfilled. At the same time, there was the greatest earnestness in all their questionings and even their practical excesses on the side of asceticism are a testimony to the sincerity of their purpose.[29]

On the whole it may be doubted whether they had not lost more than they had gained by their partial allegiance with the heathen. On the one hand, they had escaped from that narrow spirit which looked with jealousy on any attempt to bridge over the gulf that separated Jew and Gentile. Indeed, it had been the great aim of their speculations to affect this union with as little violence as possible to their religious creed. And thus a great stumbling block in the way of their reception of the Gospel had been removed. But on the other hand, they had substituted at least partially a pagan element in place of the ancient Hebrew teaching, and Christianity had to replace the latter, as the only basis on which the fabric of the Gospel could be raised.

We find a type of this class of union in Philo as one who wrote on the nature of God and of the Word, when God the Word had already 'been made flesh and dwelt among us,' as one who has left such marked traces in the

---

[28]Ewald, *Gesch. des. V.*, iii, pt. 2, p. 297.
[29]See Neander, *Ch. Hist.* I p. 82sqq. We are only speaking here of the more earnest-minded of the Alexandrian Jews.

writings of many of the Christian fathers, and to whom modern criticism has not scrupled to attribute the highest truths of evangelical teaching—he has a strong claim to an attentive hearing.

The foundation of Philo's system is the attempt to graft the philosophy of Plato upon the religion of the Old Testament. He starts from the proposition that God cannot be known by man as he is. 'There is but one name which can be rightly assigned to Him, "The Being"' (*de mutatione nomine*, 2, p. 579).[30] Any other term is misapplied and only figurative (*de somn.*, 1.3 sq. p. 655). He is superior to virtue and to knowledge, superior to the absolutely good, and the absolutely beautiful (*de Mund Opif.* 2, p.2). 'Men are either lovers of the body or lovers of the soul; the latter only are competent to hold converse with intelligible and immaterial natures, and they do not compare the (absolute) Being with any idea of created things, but divest it of all quality' (*Quod Deus*, 11, p. 281).

Yet in a certain sense, God does reveal Himself to the world. His master Plato had taught him this lesson, and the manifestation of Yahweh recorded in the Old Testament demanded an explanation. The Word then is this link between the Finite and the Infinite. 'The highest aim of the philosopher,' he says, "is to behold the Absolute Being. If he cannot attain to this, he must contemplate His image, the most Sacred Word, and next to this, the most perfect of all sensible works, the visible world' (*de confus. Ling.* Par. xx, p. 419).[31]

What then is this 'Word'? It is the manifestation of God's reason in the Creation and Government of the universe. Thus it has a twofold energy, which Philo describes in the following figurative language; communing with his spirit, he says, he was informed that in the presence of the One Absolute God there are then two highest powers (δύναμις)—goodness and sovereignty. 'By goodness he has created the world. By sovereignty he rules over His creation. Between these is the Word which connects them together, for by the Word God displays his Dominion and his Goodness. The cherubim are the symbols of these two powers, sovereignty and goodness, the flaming sword represents the 'Word"' (*Cherub.* 9, p.144; I p. 205 Lipsius).

---

[30]For the passages of Philo cited herein I am indebted chiefly to Ritter and Preller, *Hist: Phil. Graeco-Rom*, para. 477sqq.; Keil's *Op.* p. 572sqq.; Casar Morgan on *Tim. of Plato*, but especially Dorner, *Lehre von der Person*, p.21sqq.

[31]R+P [Ritter and Preller], p. 552. I have translated λόγος throughout as 'word' as the ordinary though inadequate translation.

In another passage, he carefully guards against attributing distinct personalities to the divine nature, speaking of the appearance of the three angels to Abraham, he says 'in the threefold representation there is one really existing substance, and two shadows. Just as we often cast two shadows.' The substance is the Father, called in Holy Scripture 'He that Is.' The shadows are the creative and regal powers. The creator is God, for by this he founded and ordered everything. The Regal is Lord for that which has created has a right to rule over the things created. Philo then says that the soul that is initiated in the highest mysteries 'ascends not only above the many, but also above the dyad, which resides nearest to the monad.' When not so initiated, it dwells on the threefold representation for it is unable to apprehend the One except by the medium of its workings, either as creating or as governing (de Abraham, par. 24). The Word therefore is the synthesis of these two powers,[32] and is used for either separately. Let us examine how he characterizes it in these two functions.

I. The Word the Creative Power (not ἐφ' ὅ but δ' ὅ). It is here especially that the Platonic side of Philo's system is exhibited as an architect, he says, who is to build a great city, after reviewing the site, designs in his own mind all the parts thereof, the temple, the market, the docks, the walls, and so forth, and afterwards notes them down, as it were, on the tablets of his soul, and when he commences building refers to these and fashions every part of his work accordingly (de Mund. Op. par. 4 and 5, p. 4).[33] So are we to conceive of God. The Word of God corresponds at one time in Philo's language to designing mind of the builder, at another to the plan itself. In the former sense it is the seat of the ideas, in the latter, the ideal world itself. At the creation God said 'Let us make man after the fashion of our image' (καὶ εἶπεν ὁ θεός Ποιήσωμεν ἄνθρωπον κατ' εἰκόνα ἡμετέραν). The image here, according to Philo, is the Word.

II. The Word the Governing Power. The Word of the Absolute Being is that which binds the universe and keeps its parts together so as to prevent their dissolution (de Prop. para. 20 Vol. I, p. 562; Lipsius ed. pp. 32-33). In one place he compares the Word to the viceroy of a great King (de Agric. para. 12, Vol. I,

---

[32]Elsewhere he makes several subdivisions of the λόγος e.g. the creative, the regal, mercy, legislative etc. (de Prob. Vol. I, p. 560; III, p. 130 Lipsius).
[33]cf. Plato Tim. par. 28, cf. Morgan, p. 71-72.

p. 308), in another, to the helm by which the pilot of the universe guides creation (*de Migrat. Abr.* v.i, p. 437). To the Word are to be referred all those manifestations of God recorded in the Old Testament. The Word comprehends and directs all these powers or words (λόγοι) of the one Existent Being, which are called angels.[34]

Hitherto, we have seen no reason for supposing that Philo attributed a distinct personality to the Word. On the contrary, many of his express cautions exclude such a supposition. Sometimes, indeed, his language seems to indicate this, but as his master Plato had often done, he might well *personify* an attribute or an emanation without intending to assign to it a *personality*.[35] This solution is surely more reasonable than to represent Philo in direct contradiction to himself, in accordance with his allegorizing tendencies.

Nor are these personifications difficult to explain. Thus he speaks of the Word as the First-begotten Son of God (*de Agric.* para. 12), for it is the ideal world, the pattern and archetype of the universe, but if we are tempted on this account to attribute a distinct personality to the Word we are reminded that the sensible world is, in the language of Philo, the second-begotten Son (in Eusebius, *Prop. Ev.* vii.13).[36] If the Word is styled 'the arch-angel' it is only, as we have seen, the bond which connects the ruler to those powers or angels by which God manifests himself. If again it is the high-priest (*de Prob.* para. 20), it is so named as being the medium through which creation ascends to the knowledge of the Absolute Being. If it is 'the Image of God' it is so because the Idea of the universe bears the impress of the divine minds to which it owes its origins.

If at the same time there is a striking similarity between the language of the Alexandrian Jew and the inspired writers of the New Testament, this should present no difficulty. Every revelation of God to man is an accommodation in the matter, for our present faculties are not competent to receive the things of God in all their fullness, and the time is

---

[34]It is said that if you deny the personality of the Logos, then you must of angels as well, for similar language is used of them. The answer is obvious. If the Logos is a distinct person, the angels or inferior powers cannot be so, for the Logos is the synthesis of these. Perhaps Philo considered the angels not as persons but as emanations.

[35]A passage of Pindar (*Pylt.[??] (or Parth.??)* iii.50) will perhaps show how readily language approaches to a personification when nothing even so concrete as an emanation is intended.

[36]There are good remarks on the Logos doctrine and its connection with the Incarnation in Bunsen, *Hippolyt.* I, p. 355sq.

not come when we shall know even as we are known in the language, for language is itself a symbol and therefore implies an accommodation. If this be so, what language could be chosen more suitable for the communication of divine truth than that in which the most thoughtful men of the age had invested the questionings of their uninspired reasonings? New combinations would stamp the words with an infinitely deeper significance than they brought with them from the mint in which they were first coined.

Strange indeed has been the unanimity which which the doctrines of Philo have been misconceived by men of the most opposite tendencies. On the one side by the Christian anxious to show that his Faith was also the belief of natural religion; on the other by the unbeliever striving to undermine the Gospel by connecting its doctrines in a natural chain of events with the speculations of the age. Insofar as the natural reason was striving to supply the wants which Christianity has retrieved. There is a grain of truth in these representations. But these men have looked back upon Alexandrian Judaism from the vantage-ground of Christianity instead of placing themselves with Philo, and endeavoring without any guiding star in the heavens, to trace their path to the Apostolic heights.

It is hoped that enough has been said to show that the Word in Philo was far removed from the Word in St. John, but before discussing the Jewish philosopher we must review some points of contact which his doctrine presents to Christian teaching:

1.) It was remarked that the Alexandrian Jews were tempted to desert the moral basis of the Old Testament writers in favor of the Physical standpoint of heathen philosophy. This is true of Philo. This contrast to the Apostolic Teaching is exhibited not only in the general tenor of his writings, but also in particular passages where his language closely resembles that of the inspired teachers. Thus the Alexandrian philosopher and the author of the Epistle to the Hebrews, in describing the power of the Word, employs the same metaphor of the sharp sword. But to the Jew it is the faculty which discriminates the essential form of things, but to the Christian the power of divine truth, probing the inmost thoughts of the heart. These passages are brought together and contrasted by

Neander.[37] He also compares the functions of the High Priest as depicted by Philo and the inspired writers respectively. It would not be difficult to multiply examples. Thus, we might compare the view taken of the office of the Word as the bond of union by St. Paul and by Philo (1 Cor 12:12; Eph 4:6; Philo, *de Post.* par. 1, p. 502; cf, also of the Tabernacle, *De congressu eruditionis*—see Winer *Real.* s.v. Stiftshütte of Philo). To the one it is the Physical connection which holds together the parts of the universe, to the other the spiritual bond that knits together the members of the Church into one body. We might mark the contrast between the communion with God through the Word as portrayed by St. John and in Philo.[38] We might point out how the contemplation of God through the works of this creation has in the Christian Apostle a moral (Rom 1:20 cf. Philo passim), but in the philosophy of Philo a metaphysical bearing.

2.) But if there was an error in his fundamental position, no less vital was his defect in the interpretation of history. From the records of his race he might have drawn a rich store of valuable truths, but he could not read them aright. The facts to him were meaningless except so far as he could extract from them a series of allegories, indeed sometimes even denying the facts themselves (e.g. in the case of Paradise),[39] but to the proper use of history as illustrating the progressive development of man to his fellow and to his God, he was an entire stranger. Christianity, on the other hand, does not merge either the fact in the Idea or the Idea in the fact. It accepts the fact as enforcing the Idea, but it believes that the Idea cannot be properly understood unless the facts are received as such. When St. Paul does give an allegorical interpretation the contrast with Philo is marked. Contrast Gal 4:21 sqq. with Philo's allegory on the same event in *de Abraham*, par. 20. This is the fundamental antithesis of our Faith, corresponding to that of our physical consciousness. The contrast is most strongly marked in the comparison of Philo's writings

---

[37]Neander, *Hist. of Pla.* Vol. ii, pp. 13-14. Cf. Heb 4:12 with Philo, *Quis rerum divinarum* par. 26.
[38]On which see the detailed discussion of the Logos in volume two of the Lightfoot Legacy series, which contains Lightfoot's John commentary. (BW3)
[39]See Neander, *Ch. Hist.* I, p. 77. This was also the tendency of the Christian Fathers of Alexandria, especially Origen, *Comm. on John* I par. 4, and other passages collected by Strauss *Life of Jesus*, par. 4.

with the Epistle to the Hebrews; for the inspired author, if not an Alexandrian by birth, must have been well versed in the philosophy of that school. These two defects combine to render Philo's teaching barren for

3.) He did nothing towards explaining the relations of civil society: 'What one step has he taken towards solving the problem of Plato's *Republic?* If the "Aristotelian theory" is sufficiently honored in his books, what hint is there which can explain Aristotle's assertion that politics is the architectonical science, or can bring his reverence for human relationships into consent with the commission of his master? If the Roman sense of duty meets with some respect from the Alexandrian, how can he enable the Roman to understand his feeling that a divine power had been "building up his city"? On all these questions, Philo was silent.'[40]

4.) But if he made no advance in clearing up the relations between man and his fellows, still less did he answer the questionings of man with respect to his God. He was not unconscious that the human race needed an atonement. He felt that in some way this must be connected with the chosen people. How then does he supply this want? 'I think,' he says, 'that this nation has been invested with the priesthood and prophetic office on behalf of the whole human race' and elsewhere he speaks of the Jews as 'a people which was to be chosen out of the nations of the earth, and consecrated to offer continually its prayers on behalf of all mankind' (cf. *de Abraham,*par. 19; *de Vita Mos.* par. 27). Thus, he had substituted Israel for the Messiah. His physical point of view had obscured his perception of the depth of the need, and his attempt to satisfy it was correspondingly inadequate. The history here of his nation had been lost to him. Hence the warm hopes of the Messiah which inspired the Jews of Palestine had no place with him. 'he that "was to come"' is seldom mentioned by Philo. He never connects his Word with the Christ, he never dreams of an Incarnation of the Son of God. Thus, the germ of truth which was really hidden beneath his Logos doctrine was blighted and bore no fruit.

Philo strikes us as an earnest and moral man, one who can appreciate all the yearnings of unaided humanity towards God and in a certain sense sees good in everything. Yet after all, how barren are his theosophic speculations.

---

[40]Here and below see Maurice, *Moral and Metaphysical Phil.* p. 236.

How little is there here of deep spiritual consciousness. How little to convince the world of sin, of righteousness, of judgment.

But Philo was not the first who spoke of the Word. There were others before his time who tried to represent definitively to themselves the distinction between God as He is, and God as He manifests Himself to our limited faculties. It is difficult perhaps to discover such a bearing in the language used to describe Wisdom in the Book of Proverbs. But when we turn to the Apocryphal writings there are some traces of this tendency. In the Book of Jesus, the son of Sirach, these are very faint (*Sirach* xxiv-xxv). In the Wisdom of Solomon, which was more directly influenced by Alexandrian gnosis, we find these in greater distinctness. Wisdom 'sits by the throne of God' (*Wis. Sol.* ix.4), and is 'conversant with Him and privy to the mysteries of the knowledge of God' (*Wis. Sol.* viii.3-4). She is the breath of the power of God and a pure influence flowing from the glory of the Almighty, the brightness of the everlasting light, the unspotted mirror of the power of God, and the image of His goodness (*Wis. Sol.* vii.25, 26). To her are attributed the works of God's providence, manifested in the creation and throughout the history of the chosen people. Aristobolus, another Alexandrian Jew, exhibited this view in a more definite form, and we cannot doubt that there were many of this school who were struggling to represent to themselves the doctrine with more or less of the distinctness which it appears in Philo.

But were there any counterparts to this in the teaching in the mother country? In the oldest of the Targums that perhaps may be dated as far back as the Christian era, we find a disposition to explain those passages of the Old Testament which speak of the immediate interposition of God, by a periphrasis (e.g. Gen 32:30; Ex 19:17).[41] This was a necessary reaction against the anthropomorphism, which among a large portion of the nation, had assumed the grossest form. But we are not warranted in going beyond this—a desire to anticipate Christianity in the Jewish forms of theosophy has led to much violent treatments of historical records. A disposition to antedate these records themselves, to see the later developments of a system in its earliest manifestations, above all to extract portions of a whole, and by giving them undue prominence and destroy the relations of the parts, has not yet succeeded in producing a faint

---

[41]See passages in Gfrörer, *Jahrhundert des Heils* xxiv. I, p. 29sq.

semblance of the Christian scheme. Thus we are referred to the 'Memra,'[42] the sensible revelation of God to man, or to the 'Shekinah'[43] the abiding spirit of God which directs the universe, to 'Metatron'[44] the angel of the Lord guiding the Israelites in their wanderings, for the Jewish counterparts of the Divine Persons. Yet the first two never assume a concrete personality, and the last is a created being. If we reflect that the writings to which we are referred are some centuries later than the Christian era, if we consider the influences of the dispersion of the Jews among the nations, the fusion of the Jewish sects, their contact with Christian communities, whether orthodox or heretical, must have excited, we shall be little disposed to accept these documents as representing the state of Jewish belief at the time which we are considering. Indeed, the weakness of this point of attack has been felt by our adversaries, and with but few exceptions, they have laid the stress of their argument on the theosophy of the Alexandrian school.

If in all these questionings, we have not failed to recognize foreshadowings which spoke of a coming substance, we must have been struck with the inadequacy of human speculation to explain to itself the great truth that 'no man has seen the Father at any time; the only begotten Son which is in the bosom of the Father, he hath declared Him.'

PART TWO: THE MESSIAH

ὑμεῖς δὲ πάντα σαρκικῶς νενοήκατε—Justin Martyr

In the present section, it will be our task to ascertain how far the relations between the Law and the Gospel, and the person and office of the Messiah, were firstly apprehended by the Jewish mind at the time of the Christian era.

The Law was in its nature temporary and imperfect. It was its mission to develop the national consciousness of the separation between God and man, and to teach the creature to look forward anxiously to the time when he should enjoy a closer communion with the Creator. *In other words, it created a want which it did not supply, and named hopes and aspirations which it could not fulfill.*

Hence, the necessity of a Second Dispensation which must be at once the fulfillment and the abrogation of the former, a fulfillment because it supplied

---

[42]Gfrörer, ibid., p. 307.
[43]Gfrörer, ibid., p. 304.
[44]Gfrörer, ibid., p. 318.

the wants and realized the hopes created by its predecessor, an abrogation because it substituted the reality for the expectation, the substance for the shadow, the thing typified for the type.

The Jew was not unaware that a high destiny awaited his nation. He looked forward hopefully, even against hope for the day of deliverance from his present bondage, of triumph over his enemies. But he did not see that it was a spiritual freedom, a moral victory, which the prophets had foretold. Hence, the fulfillment was misapprehended by him, the abrogation ignored. 'There is no difference,' says one of the writers between the days of Messiah and these times, 'except that Israel shall no more serve the kings of the Gentiles. He shall be lord over them.'[45]

In consequence of this carnal view, they made no distinction between Messiah's earthly and heavenly kingdom, between his first and second advent. 'There are three seasons of the Lord's appointment argues one of the Apostolic Fathers in combatting Jewish errors, the hope of life, the commencement, the consummation' (*Epist. Barnabas*, para. 1). He spoke of the past world of Judaism, the present world of Christianity, and the future world of Glory. And this is the language which the New Testament writers themselves always employ regarding the Christian era. Note the words of Peter using the phrase ἐν ταῖς ἐσχάταις ἡμέραις to interpret the prophecy of Joel (Acts 2:17).

Another early Apologist too complains that in interpreting the prophecies the Jews had applied to Christ's first coming in humility, what was spoken of his second coming in Glory (Justin, *Dialog. with Trypho*). His reign on earth, as they had painted it in the highest coloring of sensuous enjoyment satisfied all their wants; they would not see beyond these earthly glories 'to the city of the living God, the Heavenly Jerusalem, and to an immeasurable company of angels to the general assembly and the Church of the first born which are written in heaven, and to the spirit of just men made perfect and to Jesus the mediator of the new covenant' (Heb 12:22-23 etc.).

It would indeed be unjust to suppose that there were not others who had drawn from the Scriptures of the Old Testament a deeper and more spiritual meaning, but all records, whether sacred or profane, justify the belief that as a nation they had 'understood everything carnally.' Still, among the many

---

[45]See B. T. Berakoth, in Gfrörer, *Jahrhundert des Heils*, ii, p. 219 where other passages are cited.

shades of opinion, which must have existed on a subject at once so obscure and of such stirring interest, we recognize *two* prominent forms, which the Messianic visions of Jews took at this period, both equally inadequate as expressions of the Christian Idea. These two types we may call the Pharisaic and the Essene.[46]

I. A sense of the impending Fall of the Roman Empire, and an ever increasing impatience to throw off the galling yoke of slavery, combined to give a sensuous turn to the national yearnings after that deliverer, whom for centuries past they had been expecting. The Messiah was to be 'a mighty potentate and ruler over all the earth and all the nations and hosts' (Origen, *Contra Celsus* ii.2sq.).[47] The Holy City was to be the seat of his government. The Roman Empire was waning and the 'star of Judah' was to shine forth in its place with far greater brilliancy. So great was the national belief that the time for Israel's deliverance was at hand as to create in the minds of many the suspicion that Messiah was already on earth, though by reason of their sins he had not yet been revealed to his people (see Justin, *Dial. Trypho* p. 226B).[48]

The glories of Messiah's reign were a rich theme for fancy. They told of the wars and victories of their Christ, of the homage paid, and the gifts presented to him, by the kings of the nations. They dwelt on the luxuriant vegetation and splendid palaces of his kingdom, and even the banqueting and festivities with a minuteness not seldom bordering upon the ridiculous.[49]

There was nothing in Christianty to answer such expectations. The Jew had read in prophecy how the glory of the second temple was to exceed that of the first. He had formed his own carnal idea of its fulfillment. He would consider it a mockery to be told that the presence of the long-expected Messiah had already glorified the later building with a brightness greater than that of the visible Shekinah which illuminated the former, that the light had shone in the darkness and the darkness had not comprehended it, that He had come to His own, and His own had received Him not.

---

[46]Gfrörer, *Jahrh. des Heils*, vol. ii, c. x has the fourfold classification: 1) the common prophetic type; 2) the Danielic type; 3) the Mosaic type; 4) the Mystico-Mosaic type, but these classes do not seem to exclude each other.

[47]See Gfrörer, ii, pp. 219, 220.

[48]Gfrörer, ii, p. 224 sqq.

[49]See Gfrörer. ii. p. 238 sqq. a passage from the Zohar, including reflections on Behemoth and Leviathan.

He had dreamt sensuous dreams of the kings of Thrace and their giving presents, of the Kings of Arabia and Sheba bringing gifts. How little would his visions be realized in the humble fulfillment of the Magi presenting their offering at the manger in Bethlehem, or the more glorious fulfillment of the spiritual homage of the kings of the earth? He had pictured to himself the inhabitants of Messiah's kingdom free from bodily hurt or blemish. He would not be satisfied with the cure of a few sick folk, or the healing of the spiritual wounds and bruises of which this was the earnest and the type (see Mt 8:17). Difficult would it be for him to believe if these things did so happen, but if the kings did not present their gifts, if the cures were not performed, who would care to invent such stories in order to honor the carpenter's son of Nazareth, who possessed so few charms to attract their national prejudices, whose claims belied their fondest hopes?

II. Such were the general expectations, but there was yet another type of the Messiah, which was held by some few of the more mystical and less sensuous turn of mind. The Christ was regarded by them as a spirit, which should again become incarnate as it had before sojourned on earth in some of the patriarchs and prophets of the Old Testament. Thus one tradition said that the soul of Adam left him at the Fall, and was incarnate again in David, it deserted him also when he sinned and was once more to be embodied in the person of the Messiah.[50] Probably the most common form of the mystical view was that which was held by the Gnostic Ebionites, and is found in the Clementines, that the spirit of Adam and of the Messiah was the same.[51] Perhaps St. Paul may allude to this opinion when he distinguishes between the first and the second Adam 'the first Adam was made a living soul, the last Adam a quickening spirit. The first man is of the earth, earthy, the second man is the Lord of heaven' (1 Cor 15:45, 47).

We have no direct notices indeed of this Messianic type except in the later Jewish writings, but from its existence in the doctrines of the Gnostic Ebionites and from the strong mystic tendencies of the Essenes, we may reasonably infer that it found place among the members of this brotherhood. Moreover the

---

[50]They ascertained this from the letters in the name אדם—i.e. Adam, David, Messiah. There is a curious story witnessed in some of the Apocryphal Gospels for the sake of giving importance to the Cabbalistic letters. See Evang. Thomas. c.vi.xiv (and Philo in loc.).

[51]See Schliemann, *Die Clementines* p. 500sqq.

notice of Philo with respect to their use of symbols in their interpretation of the sacred books points to the same conclusion. We are therefore perhaps justified in calling this the Essene type. If this view of Messiah's person was higher and more spiritual than the Pharisees, it was still equally removed from the Christian Idea. Even if it had been otherwise, as the religion of the few, it would not have excited any wide influence on the popular feeling.

Hitherto, we have seen no traces of the Christian doctrine of 'God Manifest in the flesh' of 'the Word dwelling among us' having been anticipated in any of the clearest evidences in the records of the sacred writings, in the language of the Apologists, and in the doctrines of the Judaizing sects that this was the great stumbling block in the way of their acceptance of the truth 'as it is in Christ Jesus.' 'Your statement,' says Trypho, 'that this Christ is God, and existed before the world began, and then endured to be born as a man, appeared to men not only strange (παράδοξον) but absolutely foolish' (*Dial. w. Trypho* p. 267B), 'We *all* of us,' (p. 268B)[52] he adds, 'expect that he will be born a man and of human parentage (ἄνθρωπον ἐξ ἄνθρωπον).' The same language is also held by Origen's opponent.

Hence also, the miraculous conception was repugnant to Jewish feeling. 'Such a fable as the birth of the Messiah from a virgin would have arisen anywhere else than among the Jews. Their doctrine of the divine unity which placed an impassable gulf between God and the world, their high regard for the marriage relation, and above all their persuasion that Messiah was to be an ordinary man all conspired to render such an invention impossible among them.'[53] Accordingly, the Christian Apologist spends much labor in proving to his Jewish opponent that the Septuagint had rightly rendered the original 'a virgin shall conceive' and this referred to none other than the Messiah.[54]

The Christian view was disappointing to the Jew in another not unimportant point. It was expected that Elias [i.e., Elijah] would have appeared as the precursor of the new reign. He was to have anointed the Christ and thus

---

[52]There can be no reasonable doubt that Justin fairly represents his Jewish adversary. It would be suicidal not to do so. Cf. B. L. Kays, on Justin Martyr p. 25sqq.

[53]Neander, *Life of Christ*, p. 15 (Eng. Trans.) and the note. We may add that the fact of the existence of the narrative of the miraculous conception in one recension of the Gospel of the Hebrews proves its genuineness, while its omission in another testifies to its repugnance to Jewish notions.

[54]παρθένος (LXX), the Jewish translators Theodotion and Aquila have νεανίς, so also Symmachus, an Ebionite. See Schliemann p. 477, *Dialogue with Trypho* p. 266C sq., p. 310C sqq., p. 291A sq.

'inaugurated him in his kingly office.' That this was a fundamental article in the Messianic creed of the Jews we collect from the same unsuspicious source, the Christian Apologist arguing with one of that nation. The preaching of the Baptist was too mean a fulfillment to satisfy such expectations.

But the death of the Savior, as recorded by the Evangelical writings, was most repugnant to the conception of those who had looked for every accumulation of earthly glory in the person of their Christ. To a tale of suffering they might have listened, though impatiently, but the ignominy of a death on the cross would excite in them only feelings of abhorrence.[55] They did not see that with the Master, as with the Servant, the way to glory was through the portal of Humility. They could not conceive with St. Paul that 'because he humbled Himself, and became obedient unto death, even the death of the cross, *therefore*, God also highly exalted Him' (Phil 2). They could not join in the heavenly song of praise, 'worthy is the Lamb that was slain to receive power and honor and glory and blessing.' Still, recognizing those prophecies which foretold suffering, and when pressed, acknowledging that they referred to Messiah, they sought to escape from conclusions so unacceptable to their national feelings by supposing two Messiahs—the son of Joseph, Christ suffering, and the son of Judah, Christ triumphant.[56]

With such unworthy views of the person of the Savior, they could not rightly have apprehended those truths which cluster around the fact of the Incarnation. They could know nothing with St. Paul of that atoning sacrifice,[57] which was to him the principle of all the actions, and the center of all his teaching. They could know nothing with St. John of that communion with the Father and the Son on which he dwells so fondly and so earnestly.

But there is yet another point of view from which we must contemplate the Savior's office. Christ is to us the pattern man. It had been said 'be ye holy, even as I also am holy,' but the Christian teacher could enforce this by reference to Him, whose human nature was perfectly sanctified by 'the indwelling of the Godhead bodily.' Is humility recommended? 'Let this mind be in you, which was also in Christ Jesus.' Is endurance? 'For inasmuch as Christ has suffered in

---

[55]See *Dial. with Trypho* p. 226B, cf. Berthold, *Christologie*, no. 15. The language of Justin in combatting the Jew and Gentile respectively is an instructive commentary on St. Paul's words 'to the Jews a stumbling block, to the Gentiles foolishness.'

[56]Berthold, *Christologie*, no. 17.

[57]Berthold no. 32 attempts to show the opposite.

the flesh, arm yourselves also with the same minds.' Is forgiveness of wrong? 'Christ has left you an example, that you should follow in his steps, who when he was reviled, reviled not again' (cf. Phil 2:5; 1 Pet 4:1; 2:23).

But if the Christ of the Gospels had been 'fabulous' [i.e., the stuff of fable], where was the artist who could draw so perfect a picture? It has been allowed indeed that a sinful age cannot depict a perfectly sinless Ideal, yet it is hinted that it may produce an image in which the partial eye, 'even of a later and more clear-sighted age' cannot detect any blemish. Waiving the consideration of the defects alleged to exist in the portrait of our great Exemplar, but not conceding them, we may ask 'could such an age have produced an image so free from blemish?' To give weight to the assertion it should be shown that a picture at all approaching to this standard had ever been drawn. How inadequate, for instance, is the Stoic model, their wise man! It is unfair to produce portraiture of a Christian age as a parallel, for these are but copies (often faulty), of one great archetype. Where then are we to look for the artist? Not surely in the cold and skeptical Sadducee, not in the narrow-minded hypocritical Pharisee, not in the mystic Essene recluse, not in any or all these combined, nor even in those faithful few who were waiting hopefully for the expectation of Israel.[58]

For our Pattern is not a mere outline or a shadowy sketch. He appears to us over the funeral bier and at the marriage feast, in the highways and in secret prayer, among the chosen few and in the mixed crowd, before the judgment seat and in the synagogue, in health and in suffering, in honor and in ignominy. We have hitherto been supposing that our rule of faith, the idea of Christ both God and man, was also implicitly the belief of the infant Church. But our opponents have intercalated a stage of transition between the old era of Judaism and the new era of Christianity. We admit this as a confession, that some stepping stone is needed from the one to the other and must now investigate its claims to truth or historical grounds.

Part Three: The Judaizing Christians

'Dum volunt et Judaei esse et Christiani, nec Judaei sunt nec Christiani'
—Jerome[59]

---

[58]See Strauss, sec. 148.
[59]i.e. 'God wishes both Jews and Christians to be neither Jews nor Christians.'

A bishop of the Christian Church, writing towards the end of the fourth century, stigmatizes a certain sect of heretical Christians with more than historical severity. He compares their founder to the 'many-headed Hydra of fable' and describes him as having 'gathered together in one every monstruous and pernicious doctrine, all the abominations and absurdities which any heresy could contribute' (Epiphanius, *ad Haeres.* i.ii.30). It is allowed on all hands that Epiphanius was acquainted with the tenets of the sect (for one of their strongholds was in the neighborhood of his see), that these tenets were directly at variance with those of the orthodox, and lastly that he is here expressing the opinion of the Church. Now we are told that the Ebionites whom he thus describes held mainly the same doctrines as were taught by St. Peter and St. James and even by St. John.

Doubtless, a great change had taken place meanwhile, the number of laborers in the harvest had been multipled, the truth of the Gospel which before had been felt with more or less distinctness had now been laid down in creeds and formularies, discussion and attack had in a certain sense developed doctrines which hitherto had found their resting place in the consciousness of the Church. Doubtless also, many minor errors had crept into the teaching. But does history warrant that the change of feeling had been so entire, as these critics represent?

The distinctive tenets of the Ebionites, as they are handed down to us, are decisive and invariable—the observance of the Mosaic Law is binding on all Christians and the denial of the divine Sonship of Christ.[60] In the minor details there is some variation. Several of the Fathers speak of two classes of Ebionite,[61] and though they often do not observe this distinction, still the features of the picture which they present are so incongruous when combined and range themselves so naturally under two heads, that we cannot be wrong in accepting this view. We shall see moreover how these two classes correspond to the two schools in which the positive religious teaching of the Jews was developed, and these respective tenets regarding the person and office of Jesus, were the natural outgrowth of the Messianic expectations

---

[60]We may add the denial of the Apostleship of St. Paul. See Epiphanius loc. Cit. and Eusebius, *Hist Eccl.* iii.26.

[61]As Eusebius l.c., and Origen, *contra Celsum* v.61. I must once for all acknowledge my obligation to Schliemann, *Die Clement.* from whom most of my information about the Ebionites is taken.

in their two most prevalent forms. Anticipating these results, we shall speak of *the Pharisaic and Essene Ebionites* respectively.[62]

I. Regarding the new dispensation as a continuance of the old, the Pharisaic Ebionites were scrupulous observers of the Mosaic ritual. Though Jerusalem had been destroyed, they still regarded it as the habitation of God, and the seat of Messiah's government when he should again appear on earth and reign for a thousand years, the chosen people being gathered from all parts of the world to this glorious kingdom. Their views of the person of Jesus were correspondingly inadequate. He was the son of Joseph and Mary, a prophet like Moses or Elias, of his pre-existence, miraculous conception, and Godhead, they knew nothing. His Messiahship commenced with his Baptism. Hence their Gospel (a recension of that to the Hebrews), omitted the account of the Lord's birth, and interpolated the narrative of the Baptism in order to give prominence to it. 'They live after the Jewish customs,' says an early Christian writer, affirming that they are justified by the Law, 'saying that Jesus was justified because he observed the Law.' 'Wherefore Jesus, they say was called the Christ of God, since no one before him fulfilled the Law, for if any other had observed the things commanded in the Law, he would have been the Christ, and they consider it possible for themselves to become Christs if they do likewise' (Hippolytus, *adv. Haers.* p. 257).[63]

Thus having so far overcome their Jewish prejudices as to accept the fact of the humble life and conception of the Savior, they made amends for it by the substitution of a millennial reign on earth. Again not able to divest themselves entirely of the common belief that Elias 'must first come and anoint the Messiah' they wrested the facts of history to obtain a closer parallel to the view in the life of the Savior. In other respects, they are simply Jews of the Pharisaic school.

II. The same scrupulous observance of the ritual marked the Essene Ebionites also. The Ebionites of Epiphanius are of this class. His account is confirmed by the Clementines. But their position with respect to the old dispensation is somewhat altered. Christianity with them is a return to the primitive religion of Judaism. They accept the patriarchs as true prophets, and they reject David,

---

[62]After Neander, Vol. I, p. 493. No historical connection is necessarily implied by the use of these terms.

[63]The reference is taken from Bunsen.

Solomon, Isaiah and the later prophets. They therefore only admit the Pentateuch as canonical, and view the Gospel as a reintroduction of the older religion, divested of the excrescences of a later age. Jesus is the successor of the
true prophets. Christ is higher than the archangels and the first of God's crea-
tures. He was incarnate as he had been in Adam. He is the prince of the world
to come, as the devil is the prince of this world. Their asceticism was strictly
of the Essene type. They abstained from eating flesh and drinking wine. The
virtue that they attributed to bathing in cold water elicted the sneer that 'water
was their God.' Though they were particular in the observance of the Sabbath,
they shunned the sacrifice and the Temple service as unholy. We shall see
hereafter how the Essenes avoided the Temple service.

Such is the picture that is painted of these mystic Ebionites. We observe
here that peculiar view of Gnosis which, as we have seen, characterized the
Essenes. In details there is some difference between the two, but even here
often the one presents a germ that would naturally develop into the other.
We must add also that there are faint traces of an historical connection between the Essenes and the Gnostic Ebionites.

In the history of these sects we have an instructive lesson in every way. It
confirms our opinion, derived from other sources, of the direction that
Jewish speculation would, if unaided, naturally take. It explains where existing prejudices and feelings found vent. In their resemblance to Jewish
theosophy and contrast to Christianity it provides a strong proof of the
divine origin of the latter.

But how are we to answer those who tell us that our Christianity is not the
same with that of the primitive Church, least of all the Church of the circumcision? The historical examination of this question is naturally fourfold. What
were the opinions of the early Gentile Church? What were the opinions of the
Jewish Church and how far were they in accordance with those of the former?
What do we know historically of the relation between the two? What was the
attitude assumed by both or either towards Ebionitism?

I. Of the opinions of the Gentile Church we have the most explicit and
decisive testimony. As the Church planted and watered by the one whom
the Ebionites ever regarded as a heretic and an imposter, its doctrines must
have been antagonistic to this sect. But since some have sought to weaken
this testimony by circumscribing the influence of the great Apostle of the

Gentiles, others by denying the authenticity of the Epistles which bear his name, a reference to the opinions of the writer of the Apostolic age, and the period immediately succeeding will not be out of place.

The language of Clement of Rome is clear and unequivocal. Christ is the Son of God far higher than all the angels (chapter 36), yea he is God himself (c. 2). Though he might have come in power, he condescended to take our nature upon him (c. 16.32). Thus he was the mercy of God for the whole world (c. 7). Clement speaks of Christ as our Lord and our Savior, our High Priest (c. 21, 36) through whom we obtain mercy and peace (c. 1.20). Of our membership with Him (c. 46), of our justification by faith (c. 32), of Christ as the center of our spiritual life.

Not less decisive is the Epistle that bears the name of Barnabas. The writer warns his readers of confusing the Law with the Gospel (c. 4). Christ is the consummation of all prophecy and the fulfillment of every type (c. 6sqq.). The deeds of the Law are not acceptable before God (c. 15). The Temple of Jerusalem is no more but the Christian's heart is a new and living temple. Again, how exalted are his conceptions of the person of Christ? 'He endured to suffer for us, even though he is the Lord of the whole world to whom God said before the creation "let us make man in our own image"' (c. 5). 'Let us believe,' he says, 'that the Son of God could not suffer except for our sake' (c. 7), and often and again he speaks of the remission of our sins through his death.

The Ignatian Epistles and that of Polycarp are so explicit on this subject, that any citation would be superfluous. We pass on to the Shepherd of Hermas.[64] Here though we meet with a different type of Christian teaching. The author's language is for our purposes as distinct as any that we have reviewed hitherto.

'The Son of God existed before all creation and all power has been given to Him by the Father; he was incarnate and dwelt on earth that he might open the way of life for us. He suffered for our sins. Through him alone we have access to God. He is the rock on which the Church is built, the door of Life.'

Here are two extracts from the Epistle to Diognetus (the author of which styles himself a disciple of the Apostles—par. 11). After stating that the Christians do not sacrifice or observe the ceremonial law like the Jews, he adds 'their superstitions with respect to meats and Sabbaths, their vaunting

---

[64]On the doctrines of Hermas as opposed to the Ebionites, see Dorner, *Lehre*, pp. 195sqq. The passages from Hermas in the text are taken directly from Schliemann.

boast of circumcision, and their hypocritical observances of fasts and new moons, I think I need not tell you are ridiculous and unworthy of Christ' (par. 8). He says, 'God did not send him among us as a minister or angel or any of the powers of earth or heaven, but he sent the maker and artificer of the universe, by whom he created the heavens and set bounds to the sea, whom the moon and the stars obey etc.' 'Did he send him,' he adds, 'as one might suppose, with sovereignty and terror and dismay? No, but in meekness and gentleness. He sent him as a king sends his son, himself a king. He sent him as God (ὡς θεόν). He sent him as to men. He sent him as their Savior' (par. 4). And he follows out that doctrine in its bearing on Christian life. The acknowledged teaching of the Gentile Church from Justin Martyr downward, obviates the necessity of continuing the chain of evidence any longer.

II. But was there really that difference between the teaching of the Jewish Church and the Gentile Church that some modern critics have discovered? As the Epistle of St. James has generally been selected as the starting point of this criticism, let us examine whether it bears any traces of this 'Ebionite' tendency. What then is the doctrinal relation between St. James and St. Paul? The one regards the Gospel as the fulfillment, the other as the abrogation of the Law. The one looks to works as the fruit of faith, the other to faith as producing works. St. James had known Christ in the flesh, therefore he dwells specially on his human relations; to St. Paul he appeared in the clouds of heaven, therefore to him the human character is absorbed in the contemplation of the divine. But there is here no contradiction. The views are rather complementary, the one to the other. As on the one hand, that is a narrow view of inspiration which would take offense at the appearance of the subjective element, even when duly regulated by the presence of the divine, so that is a loose criticism which refuses to distinguish between different objects and the same object regarded from different points of view.

What, on the other hand, is the relation of St. James to the Ebionites? He lays such stress indeed upon a law, but the ceremonial is here replaced by the moral, the law of bondage here by the perfect law of liberty (James 1:25). In this new covenant, even the outward service of religion (θρησκεία) consists in works of love and purity, how precious then must be the kernel?[65]

---

[65]See Coleridge, *Aids and Reflections*.

Nor again does this writer share the low Ebionite view of the Savior. He who, according to the flesh, was the Lord's brother,[66] here styles himself his slave (James 1:1). He sees in the Son of Man, the Lord of Glory (James 2:1), who is to come again in judgment (James 2:7-9).

If it be asked why St. James dwells so much on the ethical side of Christian teaching, the aim and scope of the Epistle will furnish us with an answer. Its object was not, we believe, as at first sight his words would seem to imply, to counteract the extravagances which some had grafted on the Pauline teaching of justification by faith. The writer had no connection with the Churches founded by St. Paul. His letter was not likely to reach them. Moreover it is addressed to Jewish hearers, who had indeed arrived at the same result, but could scarcely have done so by the same means.[67] We shall therefore be probably right in considering this Epistle as directed against a Pharisaic spirit, which some converts had brought with them into the Christian Church, claiming to itself all the privileges of churchmanship on the ground of a barren orthodoxy. It is obvious that with such a view the writer must neces- sarily have dwelt upon works as the only test of a lively faith.

After these considerations, perhaps a notice in the Hebrew Christian his- torian Hegesippus will not be thought to have a very important bearing on this controversy. 'James,' he tells us, 'was holy from his mother's womb. He drank no wine nor strong drink, nor did he eat any flesh. A razor never touched his head, nor did he anoint himself with oil or use the bath. He wore no wool but only fine linen.' He then narrates how he was constantly found in the Temple, 'kneeling in prayer to God, and asking remission for the people.' St. James appears from this account to have been a Nazarite, but as the facts bear a strong Ebionite coloring, Hegesippus must have received this tradition through that sect probably unconsciously. That he was himself no Ebionite will be shown hereafter.[68]

What again are the relations of the Synoptic Evangelists to St. John? It is not our task here to recite historical difficulties. Our question is simply concerned

---

[66]There can be little doubt that: 1) James, the bishop of Jerusalem, was the Lord's brother. Eusebius, *Hist. Eccles.* ii.23 in addition to the passages of the New Testament; and 2) that James the writer of this Epistle is the bishop of Jerusalem, for he evidently writes as one in authority. The question of his apostleship and of the meaning of the expression 'brother of the Lord' are ulterior to this.
[67]The view here taken is that of Neander, *Plant.* I, p.358; *Ch. Hist.* I, p. 47; cf. Davidson *Intro.*
[68]Hegesippus in Eusebius, *Hist. Eccles.* ii.23.

with their doctrinal views. If it is allowed that the Synoptists present the *facts* while St. John dwells upon the *Ideas*, this is all that the most perfect harmony requires, for there is here no incongruity as each supports the other. This important truth has been more than once insisted upon with regard to the Incarnation, the Baptism, the Last Supper, and the Ascension.[69] We may perhaps add another instance. The rending of the veil of the Temple is recorded by all the Synoptic Evangelists. On this point St. John alone is silent. Yet none of the sacred writers dwells more earnestly (in his own teaching of the records of the Master's words), on the event thus typified, our communion with the Father through the Son, our access by the death of Christ into the Holy of Holies. The Synoptists give the text, St. John the commentary.

But lest we be led into the error of supposing that silence betrays an ignorance or implies a rejection, passages are not wanting to show that the other Evangelists did acknowledge these truths, which St. John advances so prominently. We prefer taking St. Matthew, who as being especially the Hebrew Evangelist, might be supposed to be more exposed to Ebionite influences. What then are we told of Him whom he introduces as 'God with us' (i.e. Emmanuel, 'through whom we have access to the Father'). All things are delivered to Him by His Father. 'No one knoweth the Son but the Father, neither knoweth any man the Father save the Son and he to whomever the Son will reveal Him' (Mt 11:27).[70] All power is given unto Him in heaven and on earth. His disciples are bidden to teach all nations, baptizing them in the name of the Father, and the Son, and the Holy Ghost, and He promises he will be with them always, even unto the end of the world (Mt 28 end). Again, what is his position with respect to the Law? Where can we find stronger protests against the narrow teaching of the Pharisees (Mt 15:ff.)? Or less weight attached to asceticism or ceremonial observances (Mt 11:19; 9:10; 12:9 sqq.), or larger promises of the Extension of the Church among the Heathen (Mt 13:32-35, 47-48; especially Mt 13:40)?

Nor is it difficult to account for the form of teaching adopted by the Synoptists. If we suppose that these Gospels were drawn up as a basis for

---

[69]So Neander, *Plant.* i. p. 354; Giesler, p. 73; cf. Baumgarten on *Acts*, I, pp. 176-77, and the authorities he cites.

[70]We could not demand a more distinct affirmation of the Logos doctrine of St. John. See also Mt 10:32.

catechetical instruction[71] to be enforced and illustrated by oral teaching, we can understand why these authors should have been led to record facts rather than ideas, history rather than doctrine.

The few notices of the Church in Jerusalem which we meet with after leaving the sacred writings, are all confirmatory of the view advocated above. Thus, Sulpicius Severus says[72] that in the reign of Hadrian, 'almost all the Jewish Christians believed in the divinity of Christ, while they observed the ordinances of the Law.' Still, this writer lived some centuries after the events to which he alludes. But the importance of ascertaining the opinions of Hegesippus as representing the state of belief in the Church of Jerusalem in his own day (about the middle of the second century) has been allowed by all. The testimony of Eusebius is explicit on this point: 'The truth,' he says, 'drew out many champions in her cause who carried out her warfare against the godless heretics not only in debate, but also in writing. Among these, Hegesippus was famous.' In another passage he says, 'At that time flourished in the Church Hegesippus, Dionysius, Melito, and lastly Irenaeus, who have left us in their writings the orthodoxy of a sound faith in accordance with the Apostolic tradition.' And if any doubt should arise of his competency to judge of the opinions of Hegesippus, it is dispelled by the following words 'Hegesippus has left in his five books of memoirs which have come down to us, the fullest record of his own opinions.' And elsewhere, he speaks of these memoirs as containing 'the unerring tradition of the Apostolic preaching' (*Hist. Eccles.* iv.7.8; iv. 21.22). That he should have used the Gospel to the Hebrews, which bore a close resemblance to our St. Matthew, will create no surprise; it was cited by many of the Fathers whose orthodoxy was never questioned.

III. When again we come to review the connection between the Jewish and Gentile Churches, the result will not only confirm us in our previous position, but also remove the only remaining difficulty by disclosing the basis upon which the observance of the Mosaic Law by the former group rested. It seems clear that the early Christian Church did fulfill the requirements of the Law and that this was sanctioned by the usage of the Apostles of the circumcision. But there is no evidence that they made this a requisite or even a prominent point of Christian duty. In the case of St. James, the

---

[71]Thiersch has carried out the idea in *Versuch zur Herstellung.*
[72]See Wilson, *New Testament*, p. 144.

absence of any traces of this nature, both in the Epistle which bears his name, and in the notices of him preserved by Hegesippus are all the more important, because both these sources of information concur in representing him as leaning to the ethical side of Christian life.

If the acquiescence of the Apostles in the usages of their countrymen was designed to win favor for the doctrines which they preached, and thus to remove a stumbling block in the way of reception of the Gospel, we may safely conclude that such a course would meet with full approbation from the Gentile Apostle who, in two recorded instances, displayed his readiness to yield to such motives, and who declares of himself that he had become all things to all men in order that he might save some. Still, there were doubtless many both sincere and nominal Christians who would not disentangle themselves from the spirit of bondage. Their day of trial was postponed, for the season had not yet come when the tares were to be separated from the wheat and the 'false brethren' cast out of the Church. In accordance with this view we find the greatest good-feeling existing between St. Paul and the Apostles of the circumcision. He was regarded indeed with jealousy by many of the Jewish converts as one who would have subverted their Law, but he strove ever more earnestly to remove this impression, and the interest which he took in the Collection among the Gentiles Churches for the relief of the Jewish brethren is a noble testimony to the kind feeling with which he viewed his countrymen. On one occasion he finds it necessary to raise his voice against the dissimulation of the brother Apostles. But the terms in which he records this circumstance bear the most unsuspicious evidence that there was a kindly feeling and mutual recognition of Apostleship between St. Paul and the heads of the Jewish Church, and that the error of St. Peter was only momentary. We may well believe that he who shed bitter tears of remorse when he denied his Master formerly would acknowledge with penitence and gratitude the justice of the reproof of 'his beloved brother Paul.'

About a century later we meet with an interesting record that connects the Church at Jerusalem with other parts of the Christian world. Hegesippus, a member of the mother Church, anxious to learn the state of opinion in other Christian communities, made a journey to Rome, staying on his way at many other places and conversing with the bishops. The result of this tour was a conviction that the same doctrine was held throughout the Christian world which was taught at Jerusalem. 'In every city in which I stayed,' he says, 'everything is ordered as according to the commandment of the Law and the prophets and the Lord.' Eusebius in another place adds his own testimony to the integrity of the faith in the Church of Jerusalem until the siege under Hadrian, derived from written record.[73]

IV. On the other hand, the position of the Fathers is one of direct antagonism towards the Ebionites. Justin Martyr, writing shortly after the sect must have arisen, distinguishes between true Jewish Christians who observe the Law as binding upon themselves, and those who would impose it upon others as necessary for salvation (the Ebionites). Justin refuses to recognize the latter, telling them 'There are some of you who allow Jesus to be the Christ, but declare him to be a mere man. . . . With these I do not agree, and I have the majority on my side' (see *Dialog. Trypho* p. 265).[74] The express testimony of Irenaeus, Tertullian, Hippolytus, Cyprian, Origen and others might be added. Of Hegesippus we will speak presently. Eusebius stigmatizes this heresy in strong terms. It is unnecessary to pursue this subject further.

There is only another look requisite to explain the chain of evidence. We have to give some account of the rise of the sect. We learn from Hegesippus that heresy broke out openly in the Jewish Church at the death of Simeon, when it ceased to be presided over by those who had been eye-witnesses of the Lord's life. The Church was then smitten 'by corrupt teaching against God, and against his Christ.'[75] There were some few indeed even before this who undertook 'to corrupt the sound rule of Apostolic teaching' and the historian Hegesippus mentions the name of one Thebulis who immediately after the martyrdom of James the Just commenced undermining the faith. But it was not until the generation of Apostles and apostolic men had passed away that the false teachers ventured openly to promulgate their doctrines. Up to this time the Church was called a virgin, for it was uncorrupted by false teaching. These notices are not in themselves indeed very explicit, but we cannot be wrong if Hegesippus held the opinions which we have assigned to him, in referring them to the outbreak of the Ebionite heresy.

---

[73]See Hegesippus in Eusebius, *Hist. Eccles.* iv.22, and then Eusebius iv.5 for his own comment.
[74]See Schliemann, p. 553.
[75]Cf. Eusebius, *Hist. Eccles.* iii.32 with Hegesippus in Eusebius iv.22. The statement in the text appears to reconcile the chronological difficulties.

If any other impulse was needed to render the separation between the orthodox and the Judaizing sects more complete, it was furnished in the abandonment of the Mosaic ritual, and the appointment of the first Gentile Bishop of Jerusalem. This took place after the destruction of the old city and the foundation of Aelia Capitolina on its sight under Hadrian.

The course of the foregoing argument will in some measure have reported the opinion that Christianity was an outgrowth of the Essene sect. With strange confidence, some have sought to build an argument on the silence observed in the Gospels with respect to this sect.[76] But an argument of this kind is never of much value unless supported by positive proofs. In the present case, it is not difficult to account for the silence in the sacred writers. The sect indeed was not inconsiderable, as it numbered probably about 4,000 adherents, but they did not stand in the same relation to these people as did the Sadducees and Pharisees. They did not, like the Pharisee, move heaven and earth to make one proselyte, nor like the Sadducees did they seek to leaven society with the spirit of coldness and disbelief. They would not be charged with the hypocrisy of the one or the cruelty of the other. Standing aloof from society they led for the most part a blameless and an amiable life. The voice of reproof and denunciation was reserved for more serious offenders.

Some have sought a connecting link between Christianity and Essenism in the preaching of the Baptist, but besides the scene of his ministry, the only other point of contact between John and this sect is his asceticism, and in this there was a marked difference between the Precursor and the Founder of our Faith. Besides, it is not unimportant to observe that even the practice of the Baptist did not fulfill all the requirements of a superstitious formalism, and a later age had to corrupt the sacred records in order to render them conformable to their own standard of asceticism.[77]

On the other hand, we have seen how marked is the contrast between the distinctive features of the sect, and Christianity; and if any further evidence of disconnection is required, it is found that *historically* the Christians are connected not with the Essenes, but with the orthodox Jews.[78] Yet we cannot

---

[76]E.g., Gfrörer. Strauss sec. 43, on the other hand gives the silence as an argument against the connection.

[77]The Ebionite recension of the Hebrew Gospel read ἐγκρίδος for ἀκρίδος. See Gardner [?] *Beiträge*, Vol. i.

[78]On the relation of the Essenes to the orthodox Jews see Josephus, *Ant.* xviii.1.5.

doubt that the 'new way' would attract some at least of those crowds who otherwise would have flocked to the 'retired' abodes of the Essenes and thus more or less the mystic spirit which marked the sect would grow up in the Church. At the same time, the cessation of the Temple worship would swell the numbers of the Christians from the orthodox party. Thus both this Judaizing element, the spirit of Pharisaism, on the one hand, and the spirit of Essenism, on the other, like tares attempting to choke and kill the growth of the plant in the sacred precincts, were plucked out by a violent hand. In the soil of Ebionitism, they would flourish anew with a ranker growth. But even here there were the seeds of division. These elements, though they had much in common, were in many respects incongruous. Ebionitism itself would be rent asunder, and form the two sects which we have been reviewing.

PART FOUR: CONCLUSIONS

The defense of a cause such as that which has been undertaken in the preceding pages, leaves no room for self-congratulation on the part of the advocate. He feels his utter inadequacy to fulfill worthily the important task that he has undertaken. He is aware that he is endangering his cause by fixing attention on a part of that which cannot be duly estimated except as a whole. Above all, he is conscious that there is a higher evidence which can find no expression in the pages of an apology.

For there is a testimony which it is not in the power of historical criticism to grasp; the testimony of the heart which finds in Christianity its deepest aspirations realized and its fondest hopes fulfilled—the testimony of the conscience smitten and pierced as by a sharp two-edged sword, by the record of His words 'who spake as no man spake,' the testimony of experience which reminds the Christian that in proportion as he has cultivated his best faculties and highest feelings of his nature, the clouds of doubt and difficulty have been dispersed before the 'light of the Spirit which bears witness to his spirit,' and have only gathered again when he has been betrayed into spiritual carelessness or moral ambiguity.

But what explanation are we to give of the phantoms that have crowded our path and perhaps startled us by their resemblance to some well-known truth? Are we to accept the account that satisfied some of the early Christian Apologists that they are merely Christian caricatures held out by evil spirits to seduce men from the path of truth? This might be plausible for men of their age but for us it can be no solution. Yet still less shall we be disposed to accede to the views of those modern critics who cut the knot which we would have untied, who would have us believe that sacrifices, oracles, priesthoods are utterly meaningless, that we are to expect no atonement for sin, no direct revelation of the will of heaven, no mediator between God and man. We have a right to demand an account of these wants.

There is a third course open to us, it may accept these as an evidence of the reality of our wants. We may believe that cravings so deep and so universal were not implanted in our race without a purpose. We may expect that he who created the need, will also supply the means of satisfying it. Then regarding these as foreshadowings of a coming substance, as counterfeits of a genuine reality, we shall find in them no more a stumbling block but a confirmation of our faith.

Again if we are told that some cherished precepts and maxims of the Gospel are to be found in the writings of the rabbis, there should be nothing here to dismay or confound us. We must not forget that the scribe prepared for the kingdom of heaven brings out of his treasure, things old as well as new. It is enough that Christianity practice the purest morality; we have no right to dictate the source in which it is nurtured. If He stamps with his image and superscription the deep seated truths of our nature, or the wise saying and other ages shall we refer to . . .

[The manuscript breaks off at this point. It should be remembered that this is Lightfoot's essay from early in his career, an essay that won a considerable prize, finished or not. At the bottom of the last full page are the letters P.T.O. standing for 'please turn over.' When one does so, one finds an apology from Lightfoot as follows: 'The writer regrets that the time designed expired. He has been obliged therefore to finish abruptly.']

[Some later thought the prize-winning essay was on Stephen; another, apparently Hort, suggested it was on Philo. In fact he was partly right. Here is a clue from the obituary that you can find in the final appendix to volume one of the Lightfoot Legacy series: 'The Norrisian Prize was gained in 1853. It was gained but not claimed for with characteristic modesty Lightfoot was dissatisfied with an essay which the examiners had decided to be first, and he never fulfilled the condition of publishing it.' Hopefully Lightfoot would not be too upset that this essay from his early Cambridge days has now seen the light of day. The man was only twenty-five when he wrote this essay, and it showed what great promise he had. (BW3)]

The Christian Ministry[1]

PREFACE. In response to frequent applications from many quarters the Trustees of the Lightfoot Fund have decided to issue in a separate form the Essay on the *Christian Ministry* as it was left by Bishop Lightfoot. The Essay originally appeared in the *Commentary on the Epistle to the Philippians* and afterwards in the volume of Dissertations on the *Apostolic Age*. The Trustees have appended to it (A) extracts explanatory of the Essay selected for this purpose by the Bishop himself, (B) an extract bearing on the subject from his Preface to the Didache, (C) a passage also by the Bishop explaining his change of opinion respecting the Ignatian question. The readers of the foregoing

---

[1]What began as a modest-sized but helpful essay on the Christian ministry in Lightfoot's commentary on Philippians turned into a major treatise as again and again Lightfoot was asked to explain his views on the ministry, including (1) the episcopacy especially and (2) the priesthood of all believers, with some even accusing him of taking an "un-Anglican" view on such matters. Lightfoot, however, was a meticulously careful historian, honest to a fault about the varied evidences on most any given subject that come to us from "hoary antiquity." Since 2 Corinthians and 1 Peter are documents in which the questions of the apostolic office, of who are "apostles of churches," of what it means to be a true ambassador for Christ, and most especially of what is the priesthood of all believers are raised again and again (though without being given full answers in those sacred texts), it seemed appropriate to reprint here the very final form that the essay on Christian ministry took, including the later qualifications Lightfoot made to it. This essay with additions was published separately in 1901 by Macmillan of London and has since gone out of print and into the public domain. The following is taken from that publication and that edition. It is interesting that the very last scholarly activity B. F. Westcott, Lightfoot's mentor and longtime friend (and fellow bishop of Durham), undertook before he died was to work carefully through this essay, checking, editing and pronouncing it fit for publication. He saw it as one of Lightfoot's most important pieces of work. (BW3)

lines will have a chastened interest in learning that they are among the last which passed under Bishop Westcott's eye; and that among his latest judgments was one of entire approval of the appearance of this Essay in its present form. H. W. W. Durham, July 29, 1901.

THE kingdom of Christ, not being a kingdom of this world, is not limited by the restrictions that fetter other societies, political or religious. It is in the fullest sense free, comprehensive, universal. It displays this character, not only in the acceptance of all comers who seek admission, irrespective of race or caste or sex, but also in the instruction and treatment of those who are already its members. It has no sacred days or seasons, no special sanctuaries, because every time and every place alike are holy. Above all it has no sacerdotal system. It interposes no sacrificial tribe or class between God and man, by whose intervention alone God is reconciled and man forgiven. Each individual member holds personal communion with the Divine Head. To Him immediately he is responsible, and from Him directly he obtains pardon and draws strength.

It is most important that we should keep this Necessary ideal definitely in view, and I have therefore stated it as broadly as possible. Yet the broad statement, if allowed to stand alone, would suggest a false impression, or at least would convey only a half-truth. It must be evident that no society of men could hold together without officers, without rules, without institutions of any kind; and the Church of Christ is not exempt from this universal law. The conception in short is strictly an *ideal*, which we must ever hold before our eyes, which should inspire and interpret ecclesiastical polity, but which nevertheless cannot supersede the necessary wants of human society, and, if crudely and hastily applied, will lead only to signal failure. As appointed days and set places are indispensable to her efficiency, so also the Church could not fulfil the purposes for which she exists, without rulers and teachers, without a ministry of reconciliation, in short, without an order of men who may in some sense be designated a priesthood. In this respect the ethics of Christianity present an analogy to the politics. Here also the ideal conception and the actual realization are incommensurate and in a manner contradictory. The Gospel is contrasted with the Law, as the spirit with the letter. Its ethical principle is not a code of positive ordinances, but conformity to a perfect exemplar, incorporation into a divine life. The distinction is most important and eminently fertile in practical results. Yet no man would dare to live without laying down more or less definite rules for his own guidance, without yielding obedience to law in some sense; and those who discard or attempt to discard all such aids are often farthest from the attainment of Christian perfection.

This qualification is introduced here to deprecate any misunderstanding to which the opening statement, if left without compensation, would fairly be exposed. It will be time to enquire hereafter in what sense the Christian ministry may or may not be called a priesthood. But in attempting to investigate the historical development of this divine institution, no better starting-point suggested itself than the characteristic distinction of Christianity, as declared occasionally by the direct language but more frequently by the eloquent silence of the Apostolic writings.

For in this respect Christianity stands apart from all the older religions of the world. So far at least, the Mosaic dispensation did not differ from the religions of Egypt or Asia or Greece. Yet the sacerdotal system of the Old Testament possessed one important characteristic, which separated it from heathen priesthoods and which deserves especial notice. The priestly tribe held this peculiar relation to God only as the *representatives* of the whole nation. As *delegates* of the people, they offered sacrifice and made atonement. The whole community is regarded as 'a kingdom of priests,' 'a holy nation.' When the sons of Levi are set apart, their consecration is distinctly stated to be due under the divine guidance not to any inherent sanctity or to any caste privilege, but to an act of delegation on the part of the entire people. The Levites are, so to speak, ordained by the whole congregation. 'The children of Israel,' it is said, 'shall put their hands upon the Levites.' The nation thus deputes to a single tribe the priestly functions that belong properly to itself as a whole.

The Christian idea therefore was the restitution of this immediate and direct relation with God, which was partly suspended but not abolished by the appointment of a sacerdotal tribe. The Levitical priesthood, like the Mosaic Law, had served its temporary purpose. The period of childhood had passed, and the Church of God was now arrived at mature age. The covenant people resumed their sacerdotal functions. But the privileges of the covenant were no longer confined to the limits of a single nation. Every member of the human family was potentially a member of the Church, and, as such, a priest of God.

The influence of this idea on the moral and spiritual growth of the individual believer is too plain to require any comment; but its social effects may call for a passing remark. It will hardly be denied, I think, by those who have studied the history of modern civilization with attention, that this conception of the Christian Church has been mainly instrumental in the emancipation of the degraded and oppressed, in the removal of artificial barriers between class and class, and in the diffusion of a general philanthropy untrammelled by the fetters of party or race; in short, that to it mainly must be attributed the most important advantages that constitute the superiority of modern societies over ancient. Consciously or unconsciously, the idea of an universal priesthood, of the religious equality of all men, which, though not untaught before, was first embodied in the Church of Christ, has worked and is working untold blessings in political institutions and in social life. But the careful student will also observe that this idea has hitherto been very imperfectly apprehended; that throughout the history of the Church it has been struggling for recognition, at most times discerned in some of its aspects but at all times wholly ignored in others; and that therefore the actual results are a very inadequate measure of its efficacy, if only it could assume due prominence and were allowed free scope in action. *This then is the Christian ideal; a holy season extending the whole year round—a temple confined only by the limits of the habitable world—a priesthood coextensive with the human race.*

Strict loyalty to this conception was not held incompatible with practical measures of organization. As the Church grew in numbers, as new and heterogeneous elements were added, as the early fervour of devotion cooled and strange forms of disorder sprang up, it became necessary to provide for the emergency by fixed rules and definite officers. The community of goods, by which the infant Church had attempted to give effect to the idea of an universal brotherhood, must very soon have been abandoned under the pressure of circumstances. The celebration of the Fixed days—first day in the week at once, the institution of annual festivals afterwards, were seen to be necessary to stimulate and direct the devotion of the believers. The appointment of definite places of meeting in the earliest days, the erection of special buildings for worship at a later date, were found indispensable to the working of the Church. But the Apostles never lost sight of the idea in their teaching, but they proclaimed loudly that 'God dwelleth not in temples made by hands.'

They indignantly denounced those who 'observed days and months and seasons and years.' This language is not satisfied by supposing that they condemned only the temple-worship in the one case, that they reprobated only Jewish sabbaths and new moons in the other. It was against the false principle that they waged war; the principle which exalted the means into an end, and gave an absolute intrinsic value to subordinate aids and expedients. These aids and expedients, for his own sake and for the good of the society to which he belonged, a Christian could not afford to hold lightly or neglect. But they were no part of the essence of God's message to man in the Gospel: they must not be allowed to obscure the idea of Christian worship.

So it was also with the Christian priesthood. For communicating instruction and for preserving public order, for conducting religious worship and for dispensing social charities, it became necessary to appoint special officers. But the priestly functions and privileges of the Christian people are never regarded as transferred or even delegated to these officers. They are called stewards or messengers of God, servants or ministers of the Church, and the like: but the sacerdotal title is never once conferred upon them. The only priests under the Gospel, designated as such in the New Testament, are the saints, the members of the Christian brotherhood.[2]

As individuals, all Christians are priests alike. As members of a corporation, they have their several and distinct offices. The similitude of the human body, where each limb or organ performs its own functions, and the health and growth of the whole frame are promoted by the harmonious but separate working of every part, was chosen by St. Paul to represent the progress and operation of the Church. In two passages, written at two different stages in his apostolic career, he briefly sums up the offices in the Church with reference to this image. In the earlier (1 Cor 12:28) he enumerates 'first apostles, secondly prophets, thirdly teachers, then powers, then gifts of healing, helps, governments, kinds of tongues.' In the second passage (Eph 4:11) the list is briefer; 'some apostles, and some prophets, and some evangelists, and some pastors and teachers.' The earlier enumeration

---

[2] 1 Pet 2:5, 9; Rev 1:6; 5:10; 20:6. The commentator Hilary has expressed this with much distinctness 'in lege nascebantur sacerdotes et generes Aaron Levitate: nunc autem omnes ex genere sunt sacerdotali, dicente Petro Apostolo, Quia estis genus regale et lege nascebantur sacerdotes ex sacerdotale etc' (Ambrosiaster on Eph 4:12). The whole passage, to which I shall have occasion to refer again, contains a singularly appreciative account of the relation of the ministry to the congregation.

differs chiefly from the later in specifying distinctly certain miraculous powers, this being required by the Apostle's argument which is directed against an exaggerated estimate and abuse of such gifts. Neither list can have been intended to be exhaustive. In both the work of converting unbelievers and founding congregations holds the foremost place, while the permanent government and instruction of the several Churches is kept in the background. This prominence was necessary in the earliest age of the Gospel.

The apostles, prophets, evangelists, all range under the former head. But the permanent ministry, though lightly touched upon, is not forgotten; for under the designation of 'teachers, helps, governments' in the one passage, of 'pastors and teachers' in the other, these officers must be intended. Again in both passages alike it will be seen that great stress is laid on the work of the Spirit. The faculty of governing not less than the utterance of prophecy, the gift of healing not less than the gift of tongues, is an inspiration of the Holy Ghost. But on the other hand in both alike there is an entire silence about priestly functions: for the most exalted office in the Church, the highest gift of the Spirit, conveyed no sacerdotal right which was not enjoyed by the humblest member of the Christian community.

From the subordinate place, which it thus occupies in the notices of St. Paul, the permanent ministry gradually emerged, as the Church assumed a more settled form, and the higher but temporary offices, such as the apostolate, fell away. This progressive growth and development of the ministry, until it arrived at its mature and normal state, it will be the object of the following pages to trace.

But before proceeding further, some definition of terms is necessary. On no subject has more serious error arisen from the confusion of language. The word 'priest' has two different senses. In the one it is a synonym for presbyter or elder, and designates the minister who presides over and instructs a Christian congregation: in the other it is equivalent to the Latin sacerdos, the Greek ἱερεύς or the Hebrew כֹּהֵן, the offerer of sacrifices, who also performs other mediatorial offices between God and man. How the confusion between these two meanings has affected the history and theology of the Church, it will be instructive to consider in the sequel. At present it is sufficient to say that 'Priest' the word will be used throughout this essay, as it has been used hitherto, in the latter sense only, so that priestly will be equivalent to 'sacerdotal' or 'hieratic.' Etymologically indeed the other meaning is alone correct (for the words priest and presbyter are the same); but convenience will justify its restriction to this secondary and imported sense, since the English language supplies no other rendering of sacerdos or ἱερεύς. On the other hand, when the Christian elder is meant, the longer form 'presbyter' will be employed throughout.

History seems to show decisively that before the middle of the second century each church or organized Christian community had its three orders of ministers, its bishop, its presbyters, and its deacons. On this point there cannot reasonably be two opinions. But at what time and under what circumstances this organization was matured, and to what extent our allegiance is due to it as an authoritative ordinance, are more difficult questions. Some have recognized in episcopacy an institution of divine origin, absolute and indispensable; others have represented it as destitute of all apostolic sanction and authority. Some again have sought for the archetype of the threefold ministry in the Aaronic priesthood; others in the arrangements of synagogue worship. In this clamour of antagonistic opinions history is obviously the sole upright, impartial referee; and the historical mode of treatment will therefore be strictly adhered to in the following investigation. The doctrine in this instance at all events is involved in the history.[3]

St. Luke's narrative represents the Twelve Apostles in the earliest days as the sole directors and administrators of the Church. For the financial business of the infant community, not less than for its spiritual guidance, they alone are responsible. This state of things could not last long. By the rapid accession of numbers, and still more by the admission of heterogeneous classes into the Church, the work became too vast and too various for them to discharge unaided. To relieve them from the increasing pressure, the inferior and less important functions passed successively into other hands: and thus each grade of the ministry, beginning from the lowest, was created in order.

1. The establishment of the diaconate came first. Complaints had reached the ears of the Apostles from an outlying portion of the community. The

---

[3]The origin of the Christian ministry is ably investigated in Rothe's *Anfänge der Christlichen Kirche* etc. (1837), and Ritschl's *Entstehung der Alt-katholischen Kirche* (2nd ed. 1857). These are the most important of the more recent works on the subject with which I am acquainted, and to both of them I wish to acknowledge my obligations, though in many respects I have arrived at results different from either.

Hellenist widows had been overlooked in the daily distribution of food and alms. To remedy this neglect a new office was created. Seven men were appointed whose duty it was to superintend the public messes (Acts 6:2— διακονεῖν τραπέζαις), and, as we may suppose, to provide in other ways for the bodily wants of the helpless poor. Thus relieved, the Twelve were enabled to devote themselves without interruption 'to prayer and to the ministry of the word.' The Apostles suggested the creation of this new office, but the persons were chosen by popular election and afterwards ordained by the Twelve with imposition of hands. Though the complaint came from the Hellenists, it must not be supposed that the ministrations of the Seven were confined to this class.[4] The object in creating this new office is stated to be not the partial but the entire relief of the Apostles from the serving of tables. This being the case, the appointment of Hellenists (for such they would appear to have been from their names)[5] is a token of the liberal and loving spirit which prompted the Hebrew members of the Church in the selection of persons to fill the office. I have assumed that the office thus established represents the later diaconate; for though this point has been much disputed, I do not see how the identity of the two can reasonably be called in question.[6] If the word 'deacon' does not occur in the passage, yet the corresponding verb διακονεῖν and substantive διακονία, are repeated more than once. The functions moreover are substantially those which devolved on the deacons of the earliest ages, and which still in theory, though not altogether in practice, form the primary duties of the office. Again, it seems clear from the emphasis with which St. Luke dwells on the new institution, that he looks on the establishment of this office, not as an isolated incident, but as the initiation of a new order of things in the Church. It is, in short, one of those representative facts, of which the earlier part of his narrative is almost wholly made up.

---

[4] So for instance Vitringa de Synag. iii. 2. 5, p. 928 sq., and Mosheim de Reb. Christ, p. 119, followed by many later writers.

[5] This inference is far from certain however, since many Hebrews bore Greek names, e.g. the Apostles Andrews and Philip.

[6] It is maintained by Vitringa, iii.2.5 p. 920sq. that the office of the Seven was different from the later diaconate. He quotes Chrysostom Hom. xiv (ix. p. 115, ed. Montf.) and Can. 10 of the Quinisextine Council (comp. p. 146 note 2) as favoring his view. With strange perversity Böhner (Diss. Jur. Eccl. p. 349 sq.) supposes them to be presbyters, and this account has been adopted even by Ritschl, p. 355sq. According to another view, the office of the Seven branched out into the two later orders of the diaconate and the presebyterate, Lange, Apost. Zeit. II.i, p. 75.

Lastly, the tradition of the identity of the two offices has been unanimous from the earliest times. Irenaeus, the first writer who alludes to the appointment of the Seven, distinctly holds them to have been deacons (i.26.3; iii.12.10; iv.15.1). The Roman Church some centuries later, though the presbytery had largely increased meanwhile, still restricted the number of deacons to seven, thus preserving the memory of the first institution of this office.[7] And in like manner a canon of the Council of Neocaesarea (A.D. 315) enacted that there should be no more than seven deacons in any city, however great, alleging the apostolic model.[8] This rule, it is true, was only partially observed; but the tradition was at all events so far respected, that the creation of an order of subdeacons was found necessary in order to remedy the inconvenience arising from the limitation.[9]

The narrative in the Acts, if I mistake not, implies that the office thus created was entirely new. Some writers however have explained the incident as an extension to the Hellenists of an institution that already existed among the Hebrew Christians and is implied in the 'younger men' mentioned in an earlier part of St. Luke's history.[10] This view seems not only to be groundless in itself, but also to contradict the general tenor of the narrative. It would appear moreover, that the institution was not merely new within the Christian Church, but novel absolutely. There is no reason for connecting it with any prototype existing in the Jewish community. The narrative offers no hint that it was either a continuation of the order of Levites or an adaptation of an office in the synagogue. The philanthropic purpose for which it was established presents no direct point of contact with the known duties of either.

The Levite, whose function it was to keep the beasts for slaughter, to cleanse away the blood and offal of the sacrifices, to serve as porter at the temple gates, and to swell the chorus of sacred psalmody, bears no strong resemblance to the Christian deacon, whose ministrations lay among the

---

[7]In the middle of the third century, when Cornelius writes to Fabius, Rome has 46 presbyters but only seven deacons (Eusebius, *Hist. Eccl.* vi.43). See Routh's *Rel. Sacr.* iii. p. 23 with his note p. 61. Even in the fourth and fifth centuries, the number of Roman deacons remained constant. See Ambrosiaster on 1 Tim 3:13, Sozom. viii.19.

[8]Concil. Neocaes. c. 14 (Routh, *Rel. Sacr.* iv. p. 185). See Bingham, *Antiq.* ii. 20. 19. At the Quinisextine or 2nd Trullan council (A.D. 692) this Neocaesarean canon was refuted and rejected. See Hefele, *Consiliengesch.* III, p. 304 and Vitringa, p. 922.

[9]See Bingham, iii.1.3.

[10]Acts 5:6, 10; Mosheim, *de Reb. Christ.* p. 114.

widows and orphans, and whose time was almost wholly spent in works of charity. And again, the Chazan or attendant in the synagogue, whose duties were confined to the care of the building and the preparation for service, has more in common with the modern parish clerk than with the deacon in the infant Church of Christ.[11] It is therefore a baseless, though a very common, assumption that the Christian diaconate was copied from the arrangements of the synagogue. The Hebrew Chazan is not rendered by 'deacon' in the Greek Testament; but a different word is used instead.[12] We may fairly presume that St. Luke dwells at such length on the establishment of the diaconate, because he regards it as a novel creation.

Thus the work primarily assigned to the deacons was the relief of the poor. Their office was essentially a 'serving of tables,' as distinguished from the higher function of preaching and instruction. But partly from the circumstances of their position, partly from the personal character of those first appointed, the deacons at once assumed a prominence which is not indicated in the original creation of the office. Moving about freely among the poorer brethren and charged with the relief of their material wants, they would find opportunities of influence which were denied to the higher officers of the Church who necessarily kept themselves more aloof. The devout zeal of a Stephen or a Philip would turn these opportunities to the best account; and thus, without ceasing to be dispensers of alms, they became also ministers of the Word. The Apostles themselves had directed that the persons chosen should be not only 'men of honest report,' but also 'full of the Holy Ghost and wisdom': and this careful foresight, to which the extended influence of the diaconate may be ascribed, proved also the security against its abuse. But still the work of teaching must be traced rather to the capacity of the individual officer than to the direct functions of the office. St. Paul, writing thirty years later, and stating the requirements of the diaconate, lays the stress mainly on those qualifications which would be most important in persons moving about from house to house and entrusted with the distribution of alms. While he requires that they shall 'hold the mystery

---

[11]Vitringa (iii. 2. 4, p. 914 sq., iii. 2. 22, p. 1130 sq.) derives the Christian deacon from the Chazan of the synagogue. Among other objections to this view, the fact that as a rule there was only one Chazan to each synagogue must not be overlooked.
[12]ὑπηρέτης—Luke 4:20

of the faith in a pure conscience,' in other words, that they shall be sincere believers, he is not anxious, as in the case of the presbyters, to secure 'aptness to teach,' but demands especially that they shall be free from certain vicious habits, such as a love of gossiping, and a greed of paltry gain, into which they might easily fall from the nature of their duties (1 Tim 3:8 sq.).

From the mother Church of Jerusalem the institution spread to Gentile Christian brotherhoods. By the 'helps' (1 Cor 12:28) in the First Epistle to the Corinthians (A.D. 57), and by the 'ministration' (Rom 7:7) in the Epistle to the Romans (A.D. 58), the diaconate solely or chiefly seems to be intended; but besides these incidental allusions, the latter epistle bears more significant testimony to the general extension of the office. The strict seclusion of the female sex in Greece and in some Oriental countries necessarily debarred them from the ministrations of men: and to meet the want thus felt, it was found necessary at an early date to admit women to the diaconate. A woman-deacon belonging to the Church of Cenchreae is mentioned in the Epistle to the Romans (Rom 16:1). As time advances, the diaconate becomes still more prominent. In the Philippian Church a few years later (about A.D. 62) the deacons take their rank after the presbyters, the two orders together constituting the recognised ministry of the Christian society there (Phil 1:1). Again, passing over another interval of some years, we find St. Paul in the First Epistle to Timothy (about A.D. 66) giving express directions as to the qualifications of men-deacons and women-deacons alike (1 Tim 3:8 sq.). From the tenor of his language it seems clear that in the Christian communities of proconsular Asia at all events the institution was so common that ministerial organization would be considered incomplete without it. On the other hand, we may perhaps infer from the instructions which he sends about the same time to Titus in Crete, that he did not consider it indispensable; for while he mentions having given direct orders to his delegate to appoint presbyters in every city, he is silent about a diaconate (Tit 1:5 sq.).

2. While the diaconate was thus an entirely new creation, called forth by a special emergency (Acts 6:9) and developed by the progress of events, the early history of the presbyterate was different. If the sacred historian dwells at length on the institution of the lower office but is silent about the first beginnings of the higher, the explanation seems to be, that the latter had not the claim of novelty like the former. The Christian Church in its earliest stage

was regarded by the body of the Jewish people as nothing more than a new sect springing up by the side of the old. This was not unnatural: for the first disciples conformed to the religion of their fathers in all essential points, practising circumcision, observing the sabbaths, and attending the temple-worship. The sects in the Jewish commonwealth were not, properly speaking, non-conformists. They only superadded their own special organization to the established religion of their country, which for the most part they were careful to observe. The institution of synagogues was flexible enough to allow free scope for wide divergencies of creed and practice. Different races such as the Cyrenians and Alexandrians, different classes of society such as the freedmen (Acts 6:9), perhaps also different sects as the Sadducees or the Essenes, each had or could have their own special synagogue[13] where they might indulge their peculiarities without hindrance. As soon as the expansion of the Church rendered some organization necessary, it would form a 'synagogue' of its own. The Christian congregations in Palestine long continued to be designated by this name[14] though the term 'ecclesia' took its place from the very first in heathen countries. With the synagogue itself they would naturally, if not necessarily, adopt the normal government of a synagogue, and a body of elders or presbyters would be chosen to direct the religious worship and partly also to watch over the temporal well-being of the society. Hence the silence of St. Luke.

When he first mentions the presbyters, he introduces them without preface, as though the institution were a matter of course. But the moment of their introduction is significant. I have pointed out elsewhere that the two persecutions, of which St. Stephen and St. James were respectively the chief victims, mark two important stages in the diffusion of the Gospel.[15] Their connection with the internal organization of the Church is not less remarkable. The first results directly from the establishment of the lowest order in the ministry, the diaconate. To the second may probably be ascribed the adoption of the next higher grade, the presbytery. This later persecution

---

[13]It is stated that there was not less than 480 synagogues in Jerusalem. The number is doubtless greatly exaggerated but it must have been very considerable. See Vitringa, prol. 4, p. 28 and i.1.14, p. 253.
[14]James 2:2; Epiphanius xxx.18, p. 142; See also Jerome, *Epist.* cxii. 13—'per tota orientis synagogus' speaking of the Nazaraens, though his meaning is not altogether clear. Cf. Test. XII Patr. Benj. 11.
[15]See Lightfoot Legacy volume one on Stephen in Acts 7. (BW3)

was the signal for the dispersion of the Twelve on a wider mission. Since Jerusalem would no longer be their home as hitherto, it became necessary to provide for the permanent direction of the Church there; and for this purpose the usual government of the synagogue would be adopted. Now at all events for the first time we read of 'presbyters' in connection with the Christian brotherhood at Jerusalem (Acts 11:30).[16]

From this time forward all official communications with the mother Church are carried on through their intervention. The presbyters Barnabas and Saul bear the alms contributed by the Gentile Churches (Acts 11:30). The presbyters are persistently associated with the Apostles, in convening the congress, in the superscription of the decree, and in the general settlement of the dispute between the Jewish and Gentile Christians (Acts 15:2, 4, 6, 22, 23; 16:4). By the presbyters St. Paul is received many years later on his last visit to Jerusalem, and to them he gives an account of his missionary labors and triumphs (Acts 11:18).

But the office was not confined to the mother Church alone. Jewish presbyteries existed already in all the principal cities of the dispersion, and Gentile Christian presbyteries would early occupy a not less wide area. On their very first missionary journey the Apostles Paul and Barnabas are described as appointing presbyters in every church (Acts 14:23). The same rule was doubtless carried out in all the brotherhoods founded later; but it is mentioned here and here only, because the mode of procedure on this occasion would suffice as a type of the Apostles' dealings elsewhere under similar circumstances.

The name of the presbyter then presents no difficulty. But what must be said of the term 'bishop'? It has been shown that in the Apostolic writings the two are only different designations of one and the same office.[17] How and where was this second name originated? To the officers of Gentile Churches alone is the term applied, as a synonym for presbyter. At Philippi (Phil 1:1), in Asia Minor (Acts 20:28; 1 Tim 3:1, 2; comp. 1 Pet 2:25; 5:2), in Crete (Tit 1:7), the presbyter is so called. In the next generation the title is employed in a letter written by the Greek Church of Rome to the Greek Church of Corinth (Clement, *Rom.* 42,44). Thus the word would seem to be especially

---

[16]See Lightfoot, *Galatians*, p. 124 on the sequence of events at this time.
[17]See Lightfoot, *Philippians*, p. 96sq.

Hellenic. Beyond this we are left to conjecture. But if we may assume that the directors of religious and social clubs among the heathen were commonly so-called,[18] it would naturally occur, if not to the Gentile themselves then at all events to their heathen associates, as a fit designation for the presiding members of the new society. The infant Church of Christ, which appeared to the Jew as a synagogue, would be regarded by the heathen as a confraternity.[19] But whatever may have been the origin of the term, it did not altogether dispossess the earlier name 'presbyter,' which still held its place as a synonym, even in Gentile congregations (Acts 20:17; 1 Tim 5:17; Tit 1:5; 1 Pet 5:1; Clement, *Rom.* 21, 44). And, when at length the term bishop was appropriated to a higher office in the Church, the latter became again, as it had been at first, the sole designation of the Christian elder.[20]

The duties of the presbyters were twofold. They were both rulers and instructors of the congregation. This double function appears in St. Paul's expression 'pastors and teachers,'[21] where, as the form of the original seems to show, the two words describe the same office under different aspects. Though government was probably the first conception of the office, yet the work of teaching must have fallen to the presbyters from the very first and have assumed greater prominence as time went on. With the growth of the Church, the visits of the apostles and evangelists to any individual community must have become less and less frequent, so that the burden of instruction would be gradually transferred from these missionary preachers to the local officers of the congregation. Hence St. Paul in two passages, where he gives directions relating to bishops or presbyters, insists specially on the faculty of teaching as a qualification for the position (1 Tim 3:2; Tit 1:9). Yet even here this work seems to be regarded rather as incidental to, than as inherent in, the office. In the one epistle, he directs that double honor shall be paid to those presbyters who have ruled well, but *especially* to such as 'labor in word

---

[18]The evidence however is slight; see Lightfoot, *Philippians*, p. 95, note 2. Some light is shown on this subject by the fact that the Roman government seems first to have recognized the Christian brotherhoods in their corporate capacity as burial clubs. See de Rossi, *Sotterr.* I, p. 371.

[19]On these clubs and fraternities see Renan, *Les Apotres*, p. 351sq. comp. *Saint Paul*, p. 239.

[20]Other more general designations in the New Testament are οἱ προϊστάμενοι (1 Thess 5:12; Rom 12:8 com. 1 Tim 5:17); or οἱ ἡγουμένοι (Heb 13:7, 17, 24). For the former comp. Hermas, *Vis.* ii.4, Justin, *Apol.* i.67; for the latter Clement, *Rom.* 1, 21 Hermas, *Vis.* ii.2, iii.9.

[21]Eph 4:11—τοὺς δὲ ποιμένας καὶ διδασκάλους. For the former term applied to the ἐπισκόπος or πρεσβυτέρος see Acts 15:28; 1 Pet 5:2; comp. 1 Pet 2:25.

and doctrine,'[22] as though one holding this office might decline the work of instruction. In the other, he closes the list of qualifications with the requirement that the bishop (or presbyter) hold fast the faithful word in accordance with the Apostolic teaching, 'that he may be able both to exhort in the healthy doctrine and to confute gain-sayers,' alleging as a reason the pernicious activity and growing numbers of the false teachers. Nevertheless there is no ground for supposing that the work of teaching and the work of governing pertained to separate members of the presbyteral college.[23] As each had his special gift, so would he devote himself more or less exclusively to the one or the other of these sacred functions.

3. It is clear then that at the close of the Apostolic age, the two lower orders of the threefold ministry were firmly and widely established; but traces of the third and highest order, the episcopate properly so called, are few and indistinct. For the opinion hazarded by Theodoret and adopted by many later writers[24] that the same officers in the Church who were first called apostles came afterwards to be designated bishops, is baseless. If the two offices had been identical, the substitution of the one name for the other would have required some explanation. But in fact the functions of the Apostle and the bishop differed widely. The Apostle, like the prophet or the evangelist, held no local office. He was essentially, as his name denotes, a missionary, moving about from place to place, founding and confirming new brotherhoods. The only ground on which Theodoret builds his theory is a false interpretation of a passage in St. Paul. At the opening of the Epistle to Philippi the presbyters (here called bishops) and deacons are saluted, while in the body of the letter one Epaphroditus is mentioned as an 'apostle' of the Philippians. If 'apostle'

---

[22] 1 Tim 5:17—μάλιστα οἱ κοπιῶντες ἐν λόγῳ καὶ διδασκαλίᾳ. At a much later date we read of 'presbyteri doctors,' whence it may perhaps be inferred that even then the work of teaching was not absolutely indispensable to the presbyteral office. See *Act. Perpet. et Felic.* 13; Cyprian, *Epistl.* 29. see Ritschl p. 352.

[23] The principle of lay or ruling elders, and ministers proper or teaching elders, was laid down by Calvin and has been adopted as the constitution of several Presbyterian Churches. This interpretation of St Paul's language is refuted by Rothe p. 224, Ritschl p. 352sq., and Schaff, *Hist, of Apost.* Ch. II. p. 312, besides older writers such as Vitringa and Mosheim.

[24] Making the claim based on 1 Tim 3:1, but it says οὖν τὸν ἐπίσκοπον ἀνεπίλημπτον εἶναι, μιᾶς γυναικὸς ἄνδρα, νηφάλιον, σώφρονα, κόσμιον, φιλόξενον, διδακτικόν. See also his note on Phil 1:1. See Wordsworth, *Theop. Angl.* C. x; Blunt, *First Three Centuries*, p. 81; Theodoret, as usual, has borrowed from Theodore of Mopsuestia on 1 Tim 3:1 (Raban Maur. vi. p.604D, ed. Migne). Theodore however makes a distinction between the two offices. Nor does he, like Theodoret misinterpret Phil 2:25. The commentator Hilary, also on Eph 4:11 says 'apostoli episcopi sunt.'

here had the meaning which is thus assigned to it, all the three orders of the ministry would be found at Philippi. But this interpretation will not stand. The true Apostle, like St. Peter or St. John, bears this title as the messenger, the delegate, of Christ Himself: while Epaphroditus is only so styled as the messenger of the Philippian brotherhood; and in the very next clause the expression is explained by the statement that he carried their alms to St. Paul (Phil 2:25).[25] The use of the word here has a parallel in another passage (2 Cor 8:23)[26] where messengers (or apostles) of the churches are mentioned. It is not therefore to the apostle that we must look for the prototype of the bishop. How far indeed and in what sense the bishop may be called a successor of the Apostles, will be a proper subject for consideration, but the succession at least does not consist in an identity of office.

The history of the name itself suggests a different account of the origin of the episcopate. If bishop was at first used as a synonym for presbyter and afterwards came to designate the higher officer under whom the presbyters served, the episcopate properly called would seem to have been developed from the subordinate office. In other words, the episcopate was formed not out of the apostolic order by localization but out of the presbyteral by elevation: and the title, which originally was common to all, came at length to be appropriated to the chief among them.[27]

If this account be true, we might expect to find in the mother Church of Jerusalem, which as the earliest founded would soonest ripen into maturity, the first traces of this developed form of the ministry. Nor is this expectation disappointed. James the Lord's brother alone, within the period compassed by the Apostolic writings, can claim to be regarded as a bishop in the later and more special sense of the term. In the language of St. Paul he takes precedence even of the earliest and greatest preachers of the Gospel, St. Peter and St. John (see my note on Gal 2:9), where the affairs of the Jewish Church specially are concerned. In St. Luke's narrative he appears as the local representative of the

---

[25]See Lightfoot, *Philippians*, p. 123.
[26]See Lightfoot, *Galatians*, p. 95, note 3.
[27]A parallel instance from Athenian institutions will illustrate this usage. The ἐπίστατης was chairman of a body of ten (πρόεδροι, Thuc. vi. 14) who themselves were appointed in turn by lot from a larger body of fifty (πρυτάνις). Yet we find the ἐπίστατης not only designated πρυτανις *par excellence*, (Demosth. *Timocr.* par. 157) but even addressed by this name in the presence of the other πρόεδροι (Thucy. vi.4).

brotherhood in Jerusalem, presiding at the congress, whose decision he suggests and whose decree he appears to have framed,[28] receiving the missionary preachers as they revisit the mother Church (Acts 21:18, comp. Acts 12:17. See also Gal 1:19; 2:12), acting generally as the referee in communications with foreign brotherhoods. The place assigned to him in the spurious Clementines, where he is represented as supreme arbiter over the Church universal in matters of doctrine, must be treated as a gross exaggeration. This kind of authority is nowhere conferred upon him in the Apostolic writings, but his social and ecclesiastical position, as it appears in St. Luke and St. Paul, explains how the exaggeration was possible. And this position is the more remarkable if, as seems to have been the case, he was not one of the Twelve.

On the other hand, though especially prominent, he appears in the Acts as a member of a body. When St. Peter, after his escape from prison, is about to leave Jerusalem, he desires that his deliverance shall be reported to 'James and the brethren' (Acts 12:17). When again St. Paul on his last visit to the Holy City goes to see James, we are told that all the presbyters were present (Acts 21:18). If in some passages St. James is named by himself, in others he is omitted and the presbyters alone are mentioned (Acts 11:30; comp. Acts 15:4, 23; 16:4). From this it may be inferred that though holding a position superior to the rest, he was still considered as a member of the presbytery; that he was in fact the head or president of the college. What power this presidency conferred, how far it was recognised as an independent official position, and to what degree it was due to the ascendancy of his personal gifts, are questions, which in the absence of direct information can only be answered by conjecture. But his close relationship with the Lord, his rare energy of character, and his rigid sanctity of life which won the respect even of the unconverted Jews would react upon his office, and may perhaps have elevated it to a level which was not definitely contemplated in its origin.

But while the episcopal office thus existed in the mother Church of Jerusalem from very early days, at least in a rudimentary form, the New Testament presents no distinct traces of such organization in the Gentile congregations. The government of the Gentile churches, as there represented, exhibits two

---

[28] Acts 15:13 sq. St. James speaks last and apparently with some degree of authority (ἐγὼ κρίνω— Acts 15:19). The decree is clearly framed on his recommendations, and some indecisive coincidences of style with his Epistle have been pointed out.

successive stages of development tending in this direction; but the third stage, in which episcopacy definitely appears, still lies beyond the horizon.

(1) We have first of all the Apostles themselves exercising the superintendence of the churches under their care, sometimes in person and on the spot, sometimes at a distance by letter or by message. The imaginary picture drawn by St. Paul, when he directs the punishment of the Corinthian offender, vividly represents his position in this respect. The members of the church are gathered together, the elders, we may suppose, being seated apart on a dais or tribune; he himself, as president, directs their deliberations, collects their votes, pronounces sentence on the guilty man (1 Cor 5:3 sq.). How the absence of the Apostolic president was actually supplied in this instance, we do not know. But a council was held; he did direct their verdict 'in spirit though not in person'; and 'the majority condemned the offender' (2 Cor 2:6—ἡ ἐπιτιμία αὕτη ἡ ὑπὸ τῶν πλειόνων). In the same way St. Peter, giving directions to the elders, claims a place among them. The title 'fellow-presbyter' (1 Pet 5:1), which he applies to himself, would doubtless recall to the memory of his readers the occasions when he himself had presided with the elders and guided their deliberations.

(2) At the first stage then, the Apostles themselves were the superintendents of each individual church. But the wider spread of the Gospel would diminish the frequency of their visits and impair the efficiency of such supervision. In the second stage, therefore we find them, at critical seasons and in important congregations, delegating some trustworthy disciple who should fix his abode in a given place for a time and direct the affairs of the church there. The Pastoral Epistles present this second stage to our view. It is the conception of a later age which represents Timothy as bishop of Ephesus and Titus as bishop of Crete.[29] St. Paul's own language implies that the position which they held was temporary. In both cases their term of office is drawing to a close, when the Apostle writes (see 1 Tim 1:3; 3:14; 2 Tim 4:9, 21; Tit 1:5; 3:12). But the conception is not altogether without foundation. With less permanence but perhaps greater authority, the position occupied by these Apostolic delegates nevertheless fairly represents the functions of the bishop early in the second century. They were in fact the link between the Apostle

---

[29]*Apostl. Constitut.* vii.46; Eusebius, *Hist. Eccl.* iii.4.

whose superintendence was occasional and general and the bishop who exercised a permanent supervision over an individual congregation.

Beyond this second stage the notices in the Apostolic writings do not carry us [very far]. The angels of the seven churches indeed are frequently alleged as an exception.[30] But neither does the name 'angel' itself suggest such an explanation[31] nor is this view in keeping with the highly figurative style of this wonderful book. Its sublime imagery seems to be seriously impaired by this interpretation. On the other hand St. John's own language gives the true key to the symbolism. 'The seven stars,' so it is explained, 'are the seven angels of the seven churches, and the seven candlesticks are the seven churches' (Rev 1:20). This contrast between the heavenly and the earthly fires—the star shining steadily by its own inherent eternal light, and the lamp flickering and uncertain, requiring to be fed with fuel and tended with care—cannot be devoid of meaning. The Star is the suprasensual counterpart, the heavenly representative; the lamp, the earthly realization, the outward embodiment. Whether the angel is here conceived as an actual person, the celestial guardian, or only as a personification, the idea or spirit of the church, it is unnecessary for my present purpose to consider. But whatever may be the exact conception, he is identified with and made responsible for it to a degree wholly unsuited to any human officer. Nothing is predicated of him, which may not be predicated of it. To him are imputed all its hopes, its fears, its graces, its shortcomings. He is punished with it, and he is rewarded with it. In one passage especially the language applied to the angel seems to exclude the common interpretation. In the message to Thyatira the angel is blamed, because he suffers himself to be led astray by 'his

---

[30]See for instance among recent writers Thiersch, *Gesch. der Apost. Kirche*, p. 278, Trench, *Epistles to the Seven Churches*, p. 47 sq. with others. This explanation is as old as the earliest commentators. Rothe supposes that the word 'angel' anticipates the establishment of episcopacy, being a kind of prophetic symbol, p. 423 sq. Others again take the angel to designate the collective ministry, i.e. the whole body of priests and deacons. For various explanations see Schaff, *Hist. of Apost. Ch.* II. p. 223.

[31]Rothe (p. 426) supposes that Diotrephes (3 John 9) was a bishop. This cannot be pronounced impossible, but the language is far too indefinite to encourage such an inference. It is conceivable indeed that a bishop or chief pastor should be called an angel or messenger of God or of Christ (comp. Hag 1:13; Mal 2:7), but he would hardly be styled an angel of the church over which he presides. See the parallel case of ἀπόστολος above. Vitringa (ii. 9, p. 550), and others after him, explain ἄγγελος in the Apocalypse by the 'shaliach' (שְׁלִחַ), the messenger or deputy of the synagogue. These however were only inferior officers, and could not be compared to stars or made responsible for the well-being of the churches; see Rothe p. 504.

wife Jezebel.'[32] In this image of Ahab's idolatrous queen some dangerous and immoral teaching must be personified; for it does violence alike to the general tenor and to the individual expressions in the passage to suppose that an actual woman is meant. Thus the symbolism of the passage is entirely in keeping. Nor again is this mode of representation new. The 'princes' in the prophecy of Daniel (Dan 10:13, 20, 21) present a very near if not an exact parallel to the angels of the Revelation. Here, as elsewhere, St. John seems to adapt the imagery of this earliest apocalyptic book.

Indeed, if with most recent writers we adopt the early date of the Apocalypse of St. John, it is scarcely possible that the episcopal organization should have been so mature when it was written. In this case probably not more than two or three years have elapsed from the date of the Pastoral Epistles[33] and this interval seems quite insufficient to account for so great a change in the administration of the Asiatic churches.

As late therefore as the year 70 no distinct signs of episcopal government have hitherto appeared in Gentile Christendom. Yet unless we have recourse to a sweeping condemnation of received documents, it seems vain to deny that early in the second century the episcopal office was firmly and widely established. Thus during the last three decades of the first century, and consequently during the lifetime of the latest surviving Apostle, this change must have been brought about. But the circumstances under which it was effected are shrouded in darkness; and various attempts have been made to read the obscure enigma. Of several solutions offered one at least deserves special notice. If Rothe's view cannot be accepted as final, its examination will at least serve to bring out the conditions of the problem: and for this reason I shall state and discuss it as briefly as possible.[34] For the words in which the theory is stated I am myself responsible.

The epoch to which we last adverted marks an important crisis in the history of Christianity. The Church was distracted and dismayed by the

---

[32]Rev 2:20. τὴν γυναῖκά σου Ἰεζάβελ. The word σου should probably be retained or at least, if not a correct reading, it seems to be a correct gloss.

[33]The date of the Pastoral Epistles may be as late as A.D. 66 or 67, while the Apocalypse, on this hypothesis, was written not later than A.D. 70.

[34]See Rothe's *Anfange* etc. pp. 354-392. Rothe's account of the origin of episcopacy is assailed (on grounds in many respects differing from those I have urged) by Baur, *Ursprung des Episcopats* p. 39sq., and Ritschl p. 410 sq.

growing dissensions between the Jewish and Gentile brethren and by the menacing apparition of Gnostic heresy. So long as its three most prominent leaders were living, there had been some security against the extravagance of parties, some guarantee of harmonious combination among diverse churches. But St. Peter, St. Paul, and St. James, were carried away by death almost at the same time and in the face of this great emergency. Another blow too had fallen: the long-delayed judgment of God on the once Holy City was delayed no more. With the overthrow of Jerusalem the visible centre of the Church was removed. The keystone of the fabric was withdrawn, and the whole edifice threatened with ruin. There was a crying need for some organization which should cement together the diverse elements of Christian society and preserve it from disintegration.

Out of this need the Catholic Church arose. Catholic Christendom had hitherto existed as a number of distinct isolated congregations, drawn in the same direction by a common faith and common sympathies, accidentally linked one with another by the personal influence and Apostolic authority of their common teachers, but not bound together in a harmonious whole by any permanent external organization. Now at length this great result was brought about. The magnitude of the change effected during this period may be measured by the difference in the constitution and conception of the Christian Church as presented in the Pastoral Epistles of St. Paul and the letters of St. Ignatius respectively.

By whom then was the new constitution organized? To this question only one answer can be given. This great work must be ascribed to the surviving Apostles. St. John especially, who built up the speculative theology of the Church, was mainly instrumental in completing its external constitution also; for Asia Minor was the centre from which the new movement spread. St. John however was not the only Apostle or early disciple who lived in this province. St. Philip is known to have settled in Hierapolis.[35] St. Andrew also seems to have dwelt in these parts.[36] The silence of history clearly proclaims the fact which the voice of history but faintly suggests. If we hear nothing more of the Apostles' missionary labors, it is because they had organized an united Church, to which they had transferred the work of evangelization.

---

[35]Papias in Euseb. *Hist. Eccles.* iii.39. Polycrates and Caius in *Hist. Eccles.* iii.31.
[36]Muratorian Canon (circ. 170 A.D.), Routh, *Rel. Sacr.* i. p. 394.

Of such a combined effort on the part of the Apostles, resulting in a definite ecclesiastical polity, in an united Catholic Church, no direct account is preserved, but incidental notices are not wanting, and in the general paucity of information respecting the whole period more than this was not to be expected.[37]

(1) Eusebius relates that after the martyr of St. James and the fall of Jerusalem, the remaining Apostles and personal disciples of the Lord, with His surviving relations, met together and after consultation unanimously appointed Symeon the son of Clopas to the vacant see.[38] It can hardly be doubted that Eusebius in this passage quotes from the earlier historian Hegesippus, from whom he has derived the other incidents in the lives of James and Symeon: and we may well believe that this council discussed larger questions than the appointment of a single bishop, and that the constitution and prospects of the Church generally came under deliberation. It may have been on this occasion that the surviving Apostles partitioned out the world among them, and 'Asia was assigned to John.'[39]

(2) A fragment of Irenaeus points in the same direction. Writing of the holy eucharist he says, 'They who have paid attention to the second ordinances of the Apostles know that the Lord appointed a new offering in the new covenant.'[40] By these 'second ordinances' must be understood some later decrees or injunctions than those contained in the Apostolic epistles: and these would naturally be framed and promulgated by such a council as the notice of Eusebius suggests.

(3) To the same effect St. Clement of Rome writes, that the Apostles, having appointed elders in every church and foreseeing the disputes which would arise, 'afterwards added a codicil (supplementary direction) that if they should fall asleep, other approved men should succeed to their office.'[41]

---

[37]Besides the evidence that I have stated and discussed in the text, Rothe also brings forward a fragment of the *Praedicatio Pauli* (preserved in the tract *de Baptismo Haereticorum*, which is included among Cyprian's works, app. p. 30, ed. Fell; see p. 111), where the writer mentions a meeting of St. Peter and St. Paul in Rome. The main question however is so little affected thereby, that I have not thought it necessary to investigate the value and bearing of this fragment.

[38]Euseb. *Hist. Eccles.* iii. 1.

[39]According to the tradition reported by Origen in Eusebius, *Hist. Eccles.* iii.1.

[40]One of the Pfaffian fragments no. 38, p. 854 in Stieren's edition of Irenaeus.

[41]Clement of Rome para. 44. The interpretation of the passage depends on the interpretation of the 'they' in the phrase 'after *they* fall asleep.' See my notes on the passage.

Here the pronouns 'they,' 'their,' must refer, not to the first appointed presbyters, but to the Apostles themselves. Thus interpreted, the passage contains a distinct notice of the institution of bishops as successors of the
Apostles; while in the word 'afterwards' is involved an allusion to the later
council to which the 'second ordinances' of Irenaeus also refer.[42]

These notices seem to justify the conclusion that immediately after the
fall of Jerusalem a council of the Apostles and first teachers of the Gospel
was held to deliberate on the crisis, and to frame measures for the well-being
of the Church. The centre of the system then organized was episcopacy,
which at once secured the compact and harmonious working of each individual congregation, and as the link of communication between separate
brotherhoods formed the whole into one undivided Catholic Church. Recommended by this high authority, the new constitution was immediately
and generally adopted.

This theory, which is maintained with much ability and vigor, attracted
considerable notice, as being a new defence of episcopacy advanced by a
member of a Presbyterian Church. On the other hand, its intrinsic value
seems to have been unduly depreciated; for, if it fails to give a satisfactory
solution, it has at least the merit of stating the conditions of the problem
with great distinctness, and of pointing out the direction to be followed. On
this account it seemed worthy of attention.

It must indeed be confessed that the historical notices will not bear the
weight of the inference built upon them. (1) The account of Hegesippus (for
to Hegesippus the statement in Eusebius may fairly be ascribed) confines the
object of this gathering to the appointment of a successor to St. James. If its
deliberations had exerted that vast and permanent influence on the future of
the Church that Rothe's theory supposes, it is scarcely possible that this early
historian should have been ignorant of the fact or knowing it should have
passed it over in silence. (2) The genuineness of the Pfaffian fragments of
Irenaeus must always remain doubtful.[43] Independently of the mystery which

---

[42]A much more explicit though somewhat later authority may be quoted in favour of his view. The
Ambrosian Hilary on Eph 4:12, speaking of the change from the presbyteral to the episcopal
form of government, says 'immutata est ratio, *prospiciente concilio* ut non ordo etc.' If the read
be correct, I suppose he was thinking of the Apostolic Constitutions. See also the expression of
St. Jerome on Tit 1:5—'in toto orbe decretum est.'

[43]The controversial treatise on either side are printed in Stieren's *Irenaeus* ii. p. 381 sq. the ms. It

hangs over their publication, the very passage quoted throws great suspicion on their authorship; for the expression in question[44] seems naturally to refer to the so-called Apostolic Constitutions, which have been swelled to their present size by the accretions of successive generations, but can hardly have existed even in a rudimentary form in the age of Irenaeus, or if existing have been regarded by him as genuine. If he had been acquainted with such later ordinances issued by the authority of an Apostolic council, is it conceivable that in his great work on heresies he should have omitted to quote a sanction so unquestionable, where his main object is to show that the doctrine of the Catholic Church in his day represented the true teaching of the Apostles, and his main argument the fact that the Catholic bishops of his time derived their office by direct succession from the Apostles? (3) The passage in the epistle Clement, of St. Clement cannot be correctly interpreted by Rothe, for his explanation, though elaborately defended, disregards the purpose of the letter. The Corinthian Church is disturbed by a spirit of insubordination. Presbyters, who have faithfully discharged their duties, have nevertheless been ruthlessly expelled from office. St. Clement writes in the name of the Roman Church to correct these irregularities. He reminds the Corinthians that the presbyteral office was established by the Apostles, who not only themselves appointed elders, but also gave directions that the vacancies caused from time to time by death should be filled up by other men of character, thus providing for a succession in the ministry. Consequently in these unworthy feuds they were setting themselves in opposition to officers of repute either actually nominated by Apostles, or appointed by those so nominated in accordance with the apostolic injunctions. There is no mention of episcopacy, properly so called, throughout the epistle; for in the language of St. Clement, 'bishop' and 'presbyter' are still synonymous terms.[45] Thus the pronouns 'they', 'their', refer naturally to the presbyters first appointed by the Apostles themselves. Whether (supposing the reading to be correct)[46] Rothe

is sufficient here to state that shortly after the transcription by Pfafif, the Turin ms. from which they were taken disappeared; so that there was no means of testing the accuracy of the transcriber or ascertaining the character of the ms.

[44]The expression αἱ δεύτεραι τῶν ἀποστόλων διατάξεις closely resembles the language of these Constitutions. See Hippolytus p. 74, 82 (Laguarde).

[45]See Lightfoot, *Philippians*, pp. 97-98.

[46]The right reading is probably ἐπιμόνην. See the notes on the passage.

has rightly translated ἐπινόμην 'a codicil,' it is unnecessary to enquire, as the rendering does not materially affect the question.

Nor again does it appear that the rise of episcopacy was so sudden and so immediate, that an authoritative order issuing from an Apostolic council alone can explain the phenomenon. In the mysterious period which comprises the last thirty years of the first century, and on which history is almost wholly silent, episcopacy must, it is true, have been mainly developed. But before this period its beginnings may be traced, and after the close it is not yet fully matured. It seems vain to deny with Rothe that the position of St. James in the mother Church furnished the precedent and the pattern of the later episcopate. It appears equally mistaken to maintain, as this theory requires, that at the close of the first and the beginning of the second century the organization of all churches alike had arrived at the same stage of development and exhibited the episcopate in an equally perfect form.

On the other hand, the emergency which consolidated the episcopal form of government is correctly and forcibly stated. It was remarked long ago by Jerome, that 'before factions were introduced into religion by the prompting of the devil, the churches were governed by a council of elders, but as soon as each man began to consider those whom he had baptized to belong to himself and not to Christ, it was decided throughout the world that one elected from among the elders should be placed over the rest, so that the care of the church should devolve on him and the seeds of schism be removed.'[47] And again in another passage he writes to the same effect: 'When afterwards one presbyter was elected that he might be placed over the rest, this was done as a remedy against schism, that each man might not drag to himself and thus break up the Church of Christ.'[48] To the dissensions of Jew and Gentile converts, and to the disputes of Gnostic false teachers, the development of episcopacy may be mainly ascribed.

Nor again is Rothe probably wrong as to the authority mainly instrumental in effecting the change. Asia Minor was the adopted home of more than one Apostle after the fall of Jerusalem. Asia Minor too was the nurse, if not the mother, of episcopacy in the Gentile Churches. So important an institution, developed in a Christian community of which St. John was the

---

[47]On Titus 1:5 (vii, p. 694 ed. Vall.).
[48]Epistl. cxlvi *ad Evang.* (i. p. 1080).

living centre and guide, could hardly have grown up without his sanction, and, as will be seen presently, early tradition very distinctly connects his name with the appointment of bishops in these parts.

But to the question how this change was brought about, a somewhat different answer must be given. We have seen that the needs of the Church and the ascendancy of his personal character placed St. James at the head of the Christian brotherhood in Jerusalem. Though remaining a member of the presbyteral council he was singled out from the rest and placed in a position of superior responsibility. His exact power it would be impossible, and it is unnecessary, to define. When therefore after the fall of the city St. John with other surviving Apostles removed to Asia Minor and found there manifold irregularities and threatening symptoms of disruption, he would not unnaturally encourage an approach in these Gentile Churches to the same organization which had been signally blessed, and proved effectual in holding together the mother Church amid dangers not less serious. The existence of a council or college necessarily supposes a presidency of some kind, whether this presidency be assumed by each member in turn, or lodged in the hands of a single person.[49] It was only necessary therefore for him to give permanence, definiteness, stability, to an office which already existed in germ. There is no reason however for supposing that any direct ordinance was issued to the churches. The evident utility and even pressing need of such an office, sanctioned by the most venerated name in Christendom, would be sufficient to secure its wide though gradual reception. Such a reception, it is true, supposes a substantial harmony and freedom of intercourse among the churches, which remained undisturbed by the troubles of the times; but the silence of history is not at all unfavourable to this supposition. In this way, during the blank which extends over half a

---

[49]The Ambrosian Hilary on Eph 4:12 seems to say that the senior member was president; but this may be mere conjecture. The constitution of the synagogue does not aid materially in settling this question. In the New Testament at all events ἀρχισυνάγωγος is only another name for an elder of the synagogue (Mark 5:22; Acts 13:15, 18:8, 17; comp. Justin Dial. c. Tryph. § 137), and therefore corresponds not to the bishop but to the presbyter of the Christian Church. Sometimes however ἀρχισυνάγωγος appears to denote the president of the council of elders. See Vitringa, II, p. 586sq. III, 1.p. 610 sq. The opinions of Vitringa however must be received with caution, as his tendency to press the resemblance between the government of the Jewish synagogue and the Christian Church is strong. The real likeness consists in the council of presbyters. But the threefold order of the Christian ministry seems to have no counterpart in the synagogue.

century after the fall of Jerusalem, episcopacy was matured and the Catholic Church consolidated.[50]

At all events, when we come to trace the early history of the office in the principal churches of Christendom in succession, we shall find all the churches consistent with the account adopted here, while some of them are hardly reconcileable with any other. In this review it will be convenient to commence with the mother Church, and to take the others in order, as they are connected either by neighbourhood or by political or religious sympathy.

1. *The Church of Jerusalem*, as I have already pointed out, presents the earliest instance of a bishop. A certain official prominence is assigned St. James, to James the Lord's brother, both in the Epistles of St. Paul and in the Acts of the Apostles. And the inference drawn from the notices in the canonical Scriptures is borne out by the tradition of the next ages. As early as the middle of the second century all parties concur in representing him as a bishop in the strict sense of the term.[51] In this respect, Catholic Christians and Ebionite Christians hold the same language: the testimony of Hegesippus on the one hand is matched by the testimony of the Clementine writings on the other. On his death, which is recorded as taking place immediately before the war of Vespasian, Symeon was appointed in his place.[52] Hegesippus, who is our authority for this statement, distinctly regards Symeon as holding the same office with James, and no less distinctly calls him a bishop. The same historian also mentions the circumstance that one Thebuthis (apparently on this occasion), being disappointed of the bishopric, raised a schism and attempted to corrupt the virgin purity of the Church with false doctrine. As Symeon died in the reign of Trajan at an advanced age, it is not improbable that Hegesippus was born during his lifetime. Of the successors of Symeon a complete list is preserved by Eusebius.[53] The fact however that it comprises

[50]The expression 'Catholic Church' is found first in the Ignatian letter to the Smyrneans par. 8. In the Martyrdom of Polycarp it occurs several times par. 8, 16, 19. On its meaning see Westcott, *Canon*, p. 28 note (4th edition).
[51]Hegesipp. in Euseb. *Hist. Eccles.* ii. 23, iv. 22; Clem. *Hom.* xi.35, Ep. Petr. init., and Ep. Clem. init.; Clem. Recogn. i. 43, 68, 73; Clem. Alex, in Euseb. *Hist. Eccles.* ii. 1; *Const. Apost.* v. 8, vi. 14.
[52]Hegesippus in Eusebius, *Hist. Eccles.* iv.22.
[53]*Hist. Eccles.* iv.5. suggests. The episcopate of Justus, the successor of Symeon, commences about A.D. 108: that of Marcus, the first Gentile bishop, A.D. 136. Thus thirteen bishops occupy only about twenty-eight years. Even after the foundation of Aelia Capitolina the succession is very rapid. In the period from Marcus (A.D. 136) to Narcissus (A.D. 190) we count fifteen bishops. The repetition of the same names however suggests that some conflict was going on during this interval.

thirteen names within a period of less than thirty years must throw suspicion
on its accuracy. A succession so rapid is hardly consistent with the known
tenure of life offices in ordinary cases, and if the list be correct, the frequent
changes must be attributed to the troubles and uncertainties of the times.[54] If
Eusebius here also had derived his information from Hegesippus, it must at
least have had some solid foundation in fact; but even then the alternation
between Jerusalem and Pella, and the possible confusion of the bishops with
other prominent members of the presbytery, might introduce much error. It
appears however that in this instance he was indebted to less trustworthy
sources of information.[55] The statement that after the foundation of Aelia
Capitolina (A.D. 136) Marcus presided over the mother Church, as its first
Gentile bishop, need not be questioned; and beyond this point it is unnecessary to carry the investigation.[56]

Of other bishops *in Palestine* and the neighborhood, before the latter half
of the second century, no trustworthy notice is preserved, so far as I know.
During the Roman episcopate of Victor however (about A.D. 190), we find
three bishops, Theophilus of Casarea, Cassius of Tyre, and Clarus of Ptol-
emais, in conjunction with Narcissus of Jerusalem, writing an encyclical
letter in favor of the western view in the Paschal controversy.[57] If indeed any
reliance could be placed on the Clementine writings, the episcopate of Palestine was matured at a very early time for St. Peter is there represented as
appointing bishops in every city which he visits, in Caesarea, Tyre, Sidon,
Berytus, Tripolis, and Laodicea.[58] And though the fictions of this theological romance have no direct historical value, it is hardly probable that the
writer would have indulged in such statements, unless an early development
of the episcopate in these parts had invested his narrative with an air of

---

[54]Parallels nevertheless can be found in the annals of the papacy. Thus from A.D. 882 to A.D. 904
there were thirteen popes, and in other times of trouble the succession has been almost as rapid.
[55]This may be inferred from a comparison of *Hist. Eccles.* iv. 5 to v.12. His information was probably
taken from a list kept at Jerusalem; but the case of the spurious correspondence with Abgarus
preserved in the archives of Edessa (Euseb. *Hist. Eccles.* vi. 11) shows how treacherous such sources
of information were.
[56]Narcissus who became bishop in A.D. 190, might well have preserved the memory of much
earlier times. His successor Alexander, in whose favor he resigned in A.D. 214, speaks of him as
still living as the advanced age of 116 (Eusebius, *Hist. Eccles.* vi.11).
[57]Eusebius, *Hist. Eccles.* v.25.
[58]*Clem. Hom.* iii. 68 sq. (Caesarea) vii. 5 (Tyre), vii. 12 (Berytus), xi. 36 (Tripolis), xx.23 (Laodicea),
comp. *Clem. Recogn.* iii.65, 66, vii. 8 74, vi.15, x.68.

probability. The institution would naturally spread from the Church of Jerusalem to the more important communities in the neighborhood, even without the direct intervention of the Apostles.

2. From the mother Church of the Hebrews we pass naturally to the metropolis of Gentile Christendom. *Antioch* is traditionally reported to have received its first bishop Evodius from St. Peter.[59] The story may perhaps rest on some basis of truth, though no confidence can be placed in this class of statements, unless they are known to have been derived from some early authority. But of Ignatius, who stands second in the traditional catalogue of Antiochene bishops, we can speak with more confidence. He is designated a bishop by very early authors, and he himself speaks as such. He writes to one bishop, Polycarp; and he mentions several others. Again and again he urges the duty of obedience to their bishops on his correspondents. And, lest it should be supposed that he uses the term in its earlier sense as a synonym for presbyter, he names in conjunction the three orders of the ministry, the bishop, the presbyter, and the deacons.[60] Altogether it is plain that he looks upon the episcopal system as the one recognised and authoritative form of government in all those churches with which he is most directly concerned. It may be suggested indeed that he would hardly have enforced the claims of episcopacy, unless it were an object of attack, and its comparatively recent origin might therefore be inferred: but still some years would be required before it could have assumed that mature and definite form which it has in his letters. It seems impossible to decide, and it is needless to investigate, the exact date of the epistles of St. Ignatius: but we cannot do wrong in placing them during the earliest years of the second century. The immediate successor of Ignatius is reported to been Hero,[61] and from his time onward the list of Antiochene bishops is complete.[62] If the authenticity of the list, as a whole, is questionable, two bishops of Antioch at least during the second century, Theophilus and Serapion, are known as historical persons.

If the Clementine writings emanated, as seems probable, from Syria or Palestine, this will be the proper place to state their attitude with regard to

[59]*Const. Apost.* vii.46, Euseb. *Hist. Eccles.* iii.22.
[60]E.g. *Polycarp* 6. I single out this passage from several that might be alleged because it is found in Syriac.
[61]*Hist. Eccles.* iii.36.
[62]*Hist. Eccles.* iv.20.

episcopacy. Whether the opinions there advanced exhibit the recognised tenets of a sect or congregtion, or the private views of the individual writer will probably never be ascertained; but, whatever may be said on this point, these heretical books outstrip the most rigid orthodoxy in their reverence for the episcopal office. Monarchy is represented as necessary to the peace of the Church.[63] The bishop occupies the seat of Christ and must be honoured as the image of God.[64] And hence St. Peter, as he moves from place to place, ordains bishops everywhere, as though this were the crowning act of his missionary labors. The divergence of the Clementine doctrine from the tenets of Catholic Christianity only renders this phenomenon more remarkable, when we remember the very early date of these writings; for the Homilies cannot well be placed later than the end, and should perhaps be placed before the middle of the second century.

3. We have hitherto been concerned only with the Greek Church of Syria. Of the early history of the Syrian Church, strictly so called, no trustworthy account is preserved. The documents which profess to give information respecting it are comparatively late, and while their violent anachronisms discredit them as a whole, it is impossible to separate the fabulous from the historic.[65] It should be remarked however, that they exhibit a high sacerdotal view of the episcopate as prevailing in these churches from the earliest times of which any record is preserved.[66]

4. *Asia Minor* follows next in order, and here we find the widest and most unequivocal traces of episcopacy at an early date. Clement of Alexandria distinctly states that St. John went about from city to city, his purpose being 'in some places to establish bishops, in others to consolidate whole churches, in others again to appoint to the clerical office some one of those who had been signified by the Spirit' (*Quis Div. Salv.* 42 p. 959). 'The sequence of bishops,' writes Tertullian, in like manner of Asia Minor, 'traced back to its origin will

---

[63]*Clem. Hom.* iii.62.

[64]*Clem. Hom.* iii.62, 66, 70.

[65]*Ancient Syriac Documents* (ed. Cureton), *The Doctrine of Addai* has recently been published complete by Dr Phillips, London, 1876. This document at all events must be old for it was found by Eusebius in the archives of Edessa (*Hist. Eccles.* i.13); but it abounds in gross anachronisms and probably is not earlier than the middle of the third century; see Zahn, *Gött. Gel. Anz.* 1877, p. 161sq.

[66]See for instance pp. 13, 16, 18, 21, 23, 24, 26, 29, 30, 33, 35, 42, 71 (Cureton). The succession to the priesthood is conferred by 'the Hand of the Priesthood' through the Apostles who received it from our Lord, and is derived ultimately from Moses and Aaron (p. 24).

be found to rest on the authority of John' (*Adv. Marc.* iv.5). And a writer earlier than either speaks of St. John's 'fellow-disciples and bishops' as gathered about him.[67] The conclusiveness even of such testimony might perhaps be doubted, if it were not supported by other more direct evidence. At the beginning of the second century the letters of Ignatius, even if we accept as genuine only the part contained in the Syriac, mention by name two bishops in these parts, Onesimus of Ephesus and Polycarp of Smyrna.[68] Of the former, nothing more is known; the latter evidently writes as a bishop, for he distinguishes himself from his presbyters[69] and is expressly so called by other writers besides Ignatius. His pupil Irenaeus says of him, that he had 'not only been instructed by Apostles and conversed with many who had seen Christ, but had also been established by Apostles in Asia as bishop in the Church at Smyrna.'[70] Polycrates also, a younger contemporary of Polycarp and himself bishop of Ephesus, designates him by this title[71] and again in the letter written by his own church and giving an account of his martyrdom he is styled 'bishop of the Church in Smyrna.'[72] As Polycarp survived the middle of the second century, dying at a very advanced age (A.D. 155 or 156), the possibility of error on this point seems to be excluded, and indeed all historical evidence must be thrown aside as worthless, if testimony so strong can be disregarded.

It is probable however, that we should receive as genuine not only those portions of the Ignatian letters which are represented in the Syriac, but also the Greek text in its shorter form. Under any circumstances, this text can hardly have been made later than the middle of the second century and its witness would still be highly valuable, even if it were a forgery. The staunch advocacy of the episcopate which distinguishes these writings is well known and will be considered hereafter. At present we are only concerned with the historical testimony that they bear to the wide extension and authoritative claims of the episcopal office. Besides Polycarp and Onesimus, mentioned in the Syriac, the writer names also Damas bishop of Magnesia,[73] and Polybius

---

[67]Muratorian Fragment, Routh, *Rel. Sacr.* i. p. 394. Irenaeus too, whose experience was drawn chiefly from Asia Minor, more than once speaks of bishops appointed by the Apostles, iii.3.1 and v. 20.1.

[68]Polyc. inscr. *Ephes.* 1.

[69]Polyc. *Phil.* init.

[70]Irenaeus, iii.3.4; cf. Tertullian, *de Praescr.* 32.

[71]In Eusebius, *Hist. Eccles.* v.24.

[72]*Martyr. Polyc.* 16. Polycarp is called 'bishop of Smyrna' also in *Martyr. Ignat. Ant.* 3.

[73]*Magnes.* 2.

bishop of Tralles,[74] and he urges on the Philadelphians also the duty of obedience to their bishop,[75] though the name is not given. Under any circumstances it seems probable that these were not fictitious personages, for, even if he were a forger, he would be anxious to give an air of reality to his writings, but whether or not we regard his testimony as indirectly affecting the age of Ignatius, for his own time at least it must be regarded as valid.

But the evidence is not confined to the persons and the churches already mentioned. Papias, who was a friend of Polycarp and had conversed with personal disciples of the Lord, is commonly designated bishop of Hierapolis (*Hist. Eccles.* iii.36) and we learn from a younger contemporary Serapion (*Hist. Eccles.* v.19), that Claudius Apollinaris, known as a writer against the Montanists, also held this see in the reign of M. Aurelius. Again Sagaris the martyr, who seems to have perished in the early years of M. Aurelius, about A.D. 165[76] is designated bishop of Laodicea by an author writing towards the close of the same century, who also alludes to Melito the contemporary of Sagaris as holding the see of Sardis.[77] The authority just quoted, Polycrates of Ephesus, who flourished in the last decade of the century, says moreover that he had had seven relations with bishops before him, himself being the eighth, and that he followed their tradition (in *Hist. Eccles.* v.24). When he wrote, he had been 'sixty-five years in the Lord' so that even if this period dates from the time of his birth and not of his conversion or baptism, he must have been born scarcely a quarter of a century after the death of the last surviving Apostle, whose latest years were spent in the very Church over which Polycrates himself presided. It appears moreover from his language that none of these relations to whom he refers were surviving when he wrote.

Thus the evidence for the early and wide extension of episcopacy throughout proconsular Asia, the scene of St. John's latest labors, may be considered irrefragable. And when we pass to Bishops in other districts of Asia Minor, examples are not wanting though these are neither so early nor so frequent.

---

[74]*Trall.* 1.

[75]*Phil.* 1.

[76]On the authority of his contemporary Melito in Eusebius, *Hist. Eccles.* iv.26; See Lightfoot, *Colossians*, p. 63.

[77]Polycrates in Eusebius *Hist. Eccles.* v.24. Melito's office may be inferred in the contrast implied by Eusebius calling him 'Melito, the Eunuch who lived altogether in the Holy Spirit, and who lies in Sardis, awaiting the episcopate (ἐπίσκοπην) from heaven, when he shall rise from the dead?'

Marcion, a native of Sinope, is related to have been the son of a Christian bishop,[78] and Marcion himself had elaborated his theological system before the middle of the second century. Again, a bishop of Eumenia, Thraseas by name, is stated by Polycrates to have been martyred and buried at Smyrna (*Hist. Eccles.* v.24) and, as he is mentioned in connection with Polycarp, it may fairly be supposed that the two suffered in the same persecution. Dionysius of Corinth moreover, writing to Amastris and the other churches of Pontus (about A.D. 170), mentions Palmas the bishop of this city (*Hist. Eccles.* iv.23), and when the Paschal controversy breaks out afresh under Victor of Rome, we find this same Pahnas putting his signature first to a circular letter, as the senior of the bishops of Pontus (*Hist. Eccles.* v.23). An anonymous writer also, who took part in the Montanist controversy, speaks of two bishops of repute, Zoticus of Comana and Julianus of Apamea, as having resisted the Episcopal impostures of the false prophetesses.[79] But indeed frequent notices of encyclical letters written and synods held towards the close of the second century are a much more powerful testimony to the wide extension of episcopacy throughout the provinces of Asia Minor than the incidental mention of individual names. On one such occasion Polycrates speaks of the 'crowds' of bishops whom he had summoned to confer with him on the Paschal question (*Hist. Eccles.* v.24).

As we turn from Asia Minor to *Macedonia* the evidence becomes fainter and scantier. This circumstance is no doubt due partly to the fact that these churches were much less active and important during the second century than the Christian communities of Asia Minor, but the phenomena cannot perhaps be wholly explained by this consideration. When Tertullian in one of his rhetorical flights challenges the heretical teachers to consult the Apostolic churches, where 'the very sees of the Apostles still preside' adding, 'If Achaia is nearest to you, then you have Corinth; if you are not far from Macedonia, you have Philippi, you have the Thessalonians; if you can reach Asia, you have Ephesus.'[80] His main argument was doubtless just, and even the language would commend itself to its own age, for episcopacy was the only form of government known or remembered in the church when he wrote, but

---

[78][Tertullian] *ad omnes. haers.* 6.
[79]*Hist. Eccles.* v.16. As Apamea on the Meander is mentioned at the end of the chapter, probably this is the place meant.
[80]Tertullian, *de praescens.* 37

a careful investigation scarcely allows, and certainly does not encourage us, to place Corinth and Philippi and Thessalonica in the same category with Ephesus as regards episcopacy. The term 'apostolic see' was appropriate to the latter; but so far as we know, it cannot be strictly applied to the former.

During the early years of the second century, when episcopacy was firmly established in the principal churches of Asia Minor, Polycarp sends a letter to the Philippians. He writes in the name of himself and his presbyters; he gives advice to the Philippians respecting the obligations and the authority of presbyters and deacons; he is minute in his instructions respecting one individual presbyter, Valens by name, who had been guilty of some crime; but throughout the letter he never once refers to their bishop; and indeed its whole tone is hardly consistent with the supposition that they had any chief officer holding the same prominent position at Philippi which he himself held at Smyrna. We are thus led to the inference that episcopacy did not exist at all among the Philippians at this time, or existed only in an elementary form, so that the bishop was a mere president of the presbyteral council. At Thessalonica indeed, according to a tradition mentioned by Origen,[81] the same Gaius whom St. Paul describes as his host at Corinth was afterwards appointed bishop; but with so common a name the possibilities of error are great, even if the testimony were earlier in date and expressed in more distinct terms.

When from Macedonia we pass to Achaia, the same phenomena present themselves. At the close of the first century, Clement writes to Corinth, as at the beginning of the second century Polycarp writes to Philippi. As in the latter epistle, so in the former, there is no allusion to the episcopal office; yet the main subject of Clement's letter is the expulsion and ill-treatment of certain presbyters, whose authority he maintains as holding an office instituted by and handed down from the Apostles themselves. If Corinth however was without a bishop in the strict sense at the close of the first century, she cannot long have remained so. When some fifty years later Hegesippus stayed here on his way to Rome, Primus was bishop of this Church; and it is clear moreover from this writer's language that Primus had been preceded by several occupants of the see (*Hist. Eccles.* iv.22).[82] Indeed the order of his

---

[81]On Rom 16:23—'fertur sane traditione majoram' (iv. p. 86, ed. Delarue).
[82]At little further down he speaks of ἕκαστη διαδοχή, referring apparently to Corinth among the churches.

narrative, so far as we can piece it together from the broken fragments preserved in Eusebius, might suggest the inference, not at all improbable in
itself, that episcopacy had been established at Corinth as a corrective of the
dissensions and feuds which had called forth Clement's letter.[83]

Again Dionysius, one of the immediate successors of Primus, was the writer
of several letters of which fragments are extant[84] and at the close of the century
we meet with a later bishop of Corinth, Bacchyllus, who takes an active part
in the Paschal controversy (*Hist. Eccles.* v.22-23). When from Corinth we pass
on to Athens, a very early instance of a bishop confronts us, on authority that
seems at first sight good. Eusebius represents Dionysius of Corinth, who wrote
apparently about the year 170, as stating that his namesake the Areopagite,
'having been brought to the faith by the Apostle Paul according to the account
in the Acts, was the first to be entrusted with the bishopric (or supervision) of
the diocese (in the language of those times, the parish) of the Athenians' (*Hist.
Eccles.* iv.23). Now, if we could be sure that Eusebius was here reporting the
exact words of Dionysius, the testimony, though not conclusive, would be
entitled to great deference. In this case the easiest solution would be, that this
ancient writer had not unnaturally confounded the earlier and later usage of
the word bishop. But it seems not improbable that Eusebius (for he does not
profess to be giving a direct quotation) has unintentionally paraphrased and
interpreted the statement of Dionysius by the light of later ecclesiastical usages.
However Athens, like Corinth, did not long remain without a bishop. The
same Dionysius, writing to the Athenians, reminds them how, after the martyrdom of Publius their ruler (προεστοτά), Quadratus becoming bishop sustained the courage and stimulated the faith of the Athenian brotherhoods. If,
as seems more probable than not, this was the famous Quadratus who presented his apology to Hadrian during that emperor's visit to Athens, the existence of episcopacy in this city is thrown back early in the century; even
though Quadratus was not already bishop when Hadrian paid his visit.

6. The same writer from whom we learn these particulars about episcopacy
at Athens, also furnishes information on the Church in *Crete*. He writes

---

[83]Hegesippus mentioned the feuds in the Church of Corinth during the reign of Domitian, that had
occasioned the writing of this letter (*Hist. Eccles.* iii. 16), and then after some account of Clement's
epistle (in Euseb. *Hist. Eccles.* iv. 22). On the probable tenor of Hegesippus' work, see below.
[84]The fragments of Dionysius are found in *Hist. Eccles.* iv.23, see also Routh, *Rel Sacr.* I, p. 177sq.

letters to two different communities in this island, the one to Gortyna com-
mending Philip who held this see, the other to the Cnossians offering words
of advice to their bishop Pinytus (*Hist. Eccles.* iv.23). The first was author of a
treatise against Marcion (*Hist. Eccles. iv.25*); the latter wrote a reply to Dionysius, of which Eusebius has preserved a brief notice (*Hist. Eccles.* v.19). Of
episcopacy in Thrace, and indeed of the Thracian Church generally, we read
nothing till the close of the second century, when one Aelius Publius Julius
bishop of Debeltum, a colony in this province, signs an encyclical letter.[85] The
existence of a see at a place so unimportant implies the wide spread of episcopacy in these regions.

8. As we turn to *Rome*, we are confronted by a far more perplexing
problem than any encountered hitherto. The attempt to decipher the early
history of episcopacy here seems almost hopeless, where the evidence is at
once scanty and conflicting. It has been often assumed that in the metropolis
of the world, the seat of imperial rule, the spirit which dominated in the
State must by natural predisposition and sympathy have infused itself into
the Church also, so that a monarchical form of government would be developed more rapidly here than in other parts of Christendom. This supposition seems to overlook the fact that the influences which prevailed in
the early church of the metropolis were more Greek than Roman,[86] and that
therefore the tendency would be rather towards individual liberty than towards compact and rigorous government. But indeed such presumptions,
however attractive and specious, are valueless against the slightest evidence
of facts. And the most trustworthy sources of information which we possess
do not countenance the idea. The earliest authentic document bearing on
the subject is the Epistle from the Romans to the Corinthians, probably
written in the last decade of the first century. I have already considered the
bearing of this letter on episcopacy in the Church of Corinth, and it is now
time to ask what light it throws on the same institution at Rome.

Now we cannot hesitate to accept the universal testimony of antiquity that
it was written by Clement, the reputed bishop of Rome, and it is therefore

---

[85]The combination of three Gentile names in 'Aelius Publius Julius' is possible at this late epoch,
but, being a gross violation of Roman usage, suggests the suspicion that the signatures of three
distinct persons have got confused. The error, if error it be, does not affect the inference in
the text.
[86]See Lightfoot, *Philippians*, p. 20sq.

the more surprising that, if he held this high office, the writer should not only not distinguish himself in any way from the rest of the church (as Polycarp does for instance), but that even his name should be suppressed.[87] It is still more important to observe that, though he has occasion to speak of the ministry as an institution of the Apostles, he mentions only two orders and is silent about the episcopal office. Moreover he still uses the word 'bishop' in the older sense in which it occurs in the apostolic writings, as a synonym for presbyter,[88] and it may be argued that the recognition of the episcopate as a higher and distinct office would oblige the adoption of a special name and therefore must have synchronized roughly with the separation of meaning between 'bishop' and 'presbyter.' Again, not many years after the date of Clement's letter, St. Ignatius on his way to martyrdom writes to the Romans. Though this saint is the recognised champion of episcopacy, though the remaining six of the Ignatian letters all contain direct injunctions of obedience to bishops, in this epistle alone there is no allusion to the episcopal office as existing among his correspondents. The lapse of a few years carries us from the letters of Ignatius to the *Shepherd of Hermas*. And here the indications are equivocal. Hermas receives directions in a vision to impart the revelation to the presbyters and also to make two copies, the one for Clement who shall communicate with the foreign churches (such being his duty), the other for Grapte who shall instruct the widows. Hermas himself is charged to 'read it to this city with the elders who preside over the church' (*Vis.* ii.4). Elsewhere mention is made of the 'rulers of the church' (*Vis.* ii.2; iii.9). And again, in an enumeration of the faithful officers of the churches past and present, he speaks of the 'apostles and bishops and teachers and deacons' (*Vis.* iii.5). Here most probably the word 'bishop' is used in its later sense, and the presbyters are designated by the term 'teachers.' Yet this interpretation cannot be regarded as certain, for the 'bishops and teachers' in Hermas, like the 'pastors and teachers' in St. Paul, might possibly refer to the one presbyteral office in its twofold aspect. Other passages in which Hermas uses the same terms are indecisive. Thus he speaks of 'apostles and teachers' who preached to the whole world and taught with reverence

---

[87]See *St. Clement of Rome*, p. 252 sq. Appendix (and *Apostolic Fathers*, Part i. S. Clement of Rome I, p. 69sq).
[88]See Lightfoot, *Philippians*, p.26sq.

and purity the word of the Lord (*Sim.* ix.25); of 'deacons who exercised their diaconate ill and plundered the life of widows and orphans' (*Sim.* ix.26); of 'hospitable bishops who at all times received the servants of God into their homes cheerfully and without hypocrisy' 'who protected the bereaved and the widows in their ministrations without ceasing' (*Sim.* ix.27). From these passages it seems impossible to arrive at a safe conclusion respecting the ministry at the time when Hermas wrote. In other places he condemns the false prophet 'who, seeming to have the Spirit, exalts himself and would fain have the first seat' (*Mand.* xi); or he warns 'those who rule over the church' and 'those who hold the chief-seat,' bidding them give up their dissensions and 'live at peace among themselves' (*Vis.* iii.9);[89] or he denounces those who have 'emulation one with another for the first place or for some honor' (*Sim.* viii.7). If we could accept the suggestion that in this last class passages the writer condemns the ambition which aimed at transforming the presbyterian into the episcopal form of government[90] we should have arrived at a solution of the difficulty. But the rebukes are couched in the most general terms and apply at least as well to the ambitious pursuit of existing offices as to the arrogant assertion of hitherto unrecognized powers.[91] This clue failing us, the notices in the *Shepherd* are in themselves too vague to lead to any result. Were it not known that the writer's own brother was bishop of Rome, we should be at a loss what to say about the constitution of the Roman Church in his day.[92]

But while the testimony of these early writers appears at first sight and on the whole unfavorable to the existence of episcopacy in Rome when they wrote, the impression needs to be corrected by important considerations on the other side. Hegesippus, who visited Rome about the middle of the second century during the papacy of Anicetus, has left it on record that he drew up a list of the Roman bishops to his own time (in Eusebius, *Hist. Eccles.* iv.22). As the list is not preserved,[93] we can only conjecture its contents; but if we may judge from

---

[89]For the forms of the titles here see my note on Ignatius, *Ephes.* iii.

[90]So Ritschl, p. 403, 535.

[91]Comp. Matt 23:6 etc. When Irenaeus wrote, episcopacy was certainly a venerable institution, yet his language closely resembles the reproachful expressions of Hermas. 'Contumelis agunt reliquos et principalis consessionis tumore elate sunt.' (iv.26.3).

[92]See Lightfoot, *Philippians*, p. 168, note 9 and *St. Clement of Rome* p. 316, Appendix [*Apostolic Fathers Part I, St. Clement of Rome* I, p. 359sq.].

[93][It is probably preserved in Epiphanius, see *Apostolic Fathers Part I. St. Clement of Rome, I,*

the sentence immediately following, in which he praises the orthodoxy of this and other churches under each succession, his object was probably to show that the teachings of the Apostles had been carefully preserved and handed down, and he would therefore trace the episcopal succession back to apostolic times. Such at all events, is the aim and method of Irenaeus (see Iren. iii.33), who, writing somewhat later than Hegesippus and combating Gnostic heresies, appeals especially to the bishops of Rome, as depositaries of the apostolic tradition. The list of Irenaeus commences with Linus, whom he identifies with the person of this name mentioned by St. Paul, and whom he states to have been 'entrusted with the office of the bishopric' by the Apostles. The second in succession is Anencletus of whom he relates nothing, the third Clemens whom he describes as a hearer of the Apostles and as writer of the letter to the Corinthians. The others in order are Evarestus, Alexander, Xystus, Telesphorus, Hyginus, Pius, Anicetus, Soter, and Eleutherus during whose episcopacy Irenaeus writes. Eusebius in different works gives two lists, both agreeing in the order with Irenaeus, though not according with each other in the dates. Catalogues are also found in writers later than Irenaeus, transposing the sequence of the earliest bishops, and adding the name Cletus or substituting it for Anencletus.[94] These discrepancies may be explained by assuming two distinct churches in Rome—a Jewish and a Gentile community—in the first age; or they may have arisen from a confusion of the earlier and later senses of ἐπίσκοπος; or the names may have been transposed in the later lists owing to the influence of the Clementine Homilies, in which romance Clement is represented as the immediate disciple and successor of St. Peter. With the many possibilities of error, no more can be safely assumed of *Linus* (A.D. 68), and *Anencletus* (A.D. 80) than that they held some prominent position in the Roman Church.

p.327sq.] N.B. It is difficult to tell whether the square bracket notes are from Lightfoot correcting some of his earlier views as here, or later notices from Westcott, the final editor of this edition of 'The Christian Ministry.' It would appear to be the latter. (BW3)

[94]On this subject see Pearson's *Dissertationes duae de serie et successione primoriim Romae episcoporum* in his *Minor Theological Works* II, p. 296 sq. (ed. Churton), and especially the recent work of Lipsius, *Chronologie der romischen Bischofe*, Kiel 1869. The earliest list which places Clement's name first belongs to the age of Hippolytus. The omission of his name in a recently discovered Syriac list (*Ancient Syriac Documents*, p. 71) is doubtless due to the fact that the names Cletus and Clemens begin with the same letters. I have for convenience given the dates of the Roman bishops from the *Hist. Eccles.* of Eusebius without however attaching any weight to them in the case of the earlier names. See Lightfoot, *Philippians*, p. 169 [and *Apostolic Fathers, I, Part I, Clement of Rome*, I, p. 201sq].

But the reason for supposing *Clement* (A.D. 92) to have been a bishop is as strong as the universal tradition of the next ages can make it. Yet, while calling him a bishop, we need not suppose him to have attained the same distinct isolated position of authority which was occupied by his successors Eleutherus and Victor for instance, at the close of the second century, or even by his contemporaries Ignatius of Antioch and Polycarp of Smyrna. He was rather the chief *of* the presbyters than the chief *over* the presbyters. Only when thus limited, can the episcopacy of St. Clement be reconciled with the language of his own epistle or with the notice in his younger contemporary Hermas. At the same time the allusion in the *Shepherd*, though inconsistent with any exalted conception of his office, does assign to him as his special province the duty of communicating with foreign churches, which in the early ages was essentially the bishop's function, as may be seen by the instances of Polycarp, of Dionysius, of Irenaeus, and of Polycrates.

Of the two succeeding bishops, *Evarestus* (A.D. 100) and *Alexander* (A.D. 109), no authentic notices are preserved. Xystus (A.D. 119), who follows, is the reputed author of a collection of proverbs, which a recent distinguished critic has not hesitated to accept as genuine.[95] He is also the earliest of those Roman prelates whom Irenaeus, writing to Victor in the name of the Gallican Churches, mentions as having observed Easter after the western reckoning and yet maintained peace with those who kept it otherwise (Iren. In *Hist. Eccles.* v.24). The next, *Telesphorus* (A.D. 128) and *Hyginus* (A.D. 139), are described in the same terms. The former is likewise distinguished as the sole martyr among the early bishops of the metropolis.[96] The latter is mentioned as being in office when the peace of the Roman Church was disturbed by the presence of the heretics Valentinus Pius, and Cerdon.[97] With *Pius* (A.D. 142), the next in order, the office, if not the man, emerges into daylight. An anonymous writer, treating on the canon of Scripture, says that the *Shepherd* was written by Hermas 'quite lately while his brother Pius held the see of the

---

[95]Ewald, *Gesch. des V.* I. vii, p. 321 sq. On the other hand, see Zeller, *Philos. der Griechen* III. 1, p. 601 note, and Sanger in the *Judische Zeitschrift* (1867), p. 29 sq. It has recently been edited by Gildemeister, *Sextus Sententiae*, 1873.
[96]Irenaeus iii.3.3. At least Irenaeus mentions him alone as a martyr. Later stories convey the glory of martyrdom on others also.
[97]Irenaeus iii.4.3.

Church of Rome.[98] This passage, written by a contemporary, besides the testimony which it bears to the date and authorship of the *Shepherd* (with which
we are not here concerned), is valuable in its bearing on this investigation; for
the use of the 'chair' or 'see' as a recognised phrase, points to a more or less
prolonged existence of episcopacy in Rome, when this writer lived. To Pius
succeeds *Anicetus* (A.D. 157). And now Rome becomes for the moment the
centre of interest and activity in the Christian world.[99] During this episcopate
Hegesippus, visiting the metropolis for the purpose of ascertaining and re-
cording the doctrines of the Roman Church, is welcomed by the bishop.[100]
About the same time also another more illustrious visitor, Polycarp the venerable bishop of Smyrna, arrives in Rome to confer with the head of the
Roman Church on the Paschal dispute[101] and there falls in with and denounces the heretic Marcion.[102] These facts are stated on contemporary authority. Of *Soter* (A.D. 168), next in succession, a contemporary record is preserved. Dionysius of Corinth, writing to the Romans, praises the zeal of their
bishop, who in his fatherly care for the suffering poor and for the prisoners
working in the mines had maintained and extended the hereditary fame of
his church for zeal in all charitable and good works.[103] *Eleutherus* (A.D. 177),
who succeeds Soter, of an archdeacon. When Hegesippus paid his visit to the
metropolis, he found Eleutherus standing in this relation to the bishop Anicetus, and seems to have made his acquaintance while acting in this capacity
(*Hist. Eccles.* iv.22). Eleutherus however was a contemporary, not only of Hegesippus, but also of the great writers Irenaeus and Tertullian,[104] who speak
of the episcopal succession in the churches generally, and in Rome especially,
as the best safeguard for the transmission of the true faith from apostolic
times.[105] With *Victor* (A.D. 189) the successor of Eleutherus, a new era begins.
Apparently the first Latin prelate who held the metropolitan see of Latin

---

[98]See Lightfoot, *Philippians* p. 168, note 9, where the passage is quoted.
[99]See Westcott, *Canon* p. 191.
[100]Hegesippus in Euseb. *Hist. Eccles.* iv.23.
[101]See Irenaeus, in Euseb. *Hist. Eccles.* v.24.
[102]Irenaeus iii. 3.4; comp. iii.4.4.
[103]In Eusebius, *Hist. Eccles.* iv.23.
[104]He is mentioned by both Irenaeus iii.3.3 and Tertullian, *de Praescens.* 30 'sub episcopate Eleutheri benedicti.'
[105]Irenaeus iii.3.2; Tertullian, *de Praescens.* 32, 36; *adv. Marc.* iv.5.

Christendom,[106] he was moreover the first Roman bishop who is known to have had intimate relations with the imperial courts[107] and the first also who advanced those claims to universal dominion which his successors in later ages have always consistently and often successfully maintained.[108] 'I hear,' writes Tertullian scornfully, 'that an edict has gone forth, aye and that a peremptory edict; the chief pontiff, forsooth, I mean the bishop of bishops, has issued his commands.'[109] At the end of the first century the Roman Church was swayed by the mild and peaceful counsels of the presbyter-bishop Clement; the close of the second witnessed the autocratic pretensions of the haughty pope Victor, the prototype of a Hildebrand or an Innocent.

9. The Churches of *Gaul* were closely connected with and probably descended from the Churches of Asia Minor. If so, the episcopal form of government would probably be coeval with the foundation of Christian brotherhoods in this country. It is true we do not meet with any earlier bishop than the immediate predecessor of Irenaeus at Lyons, the aged Pothinus, of whose martyrdom an account is given in the letter of the Gallican Churches[110] this is also the first distinct historical notice of any kind relating to Christianity in Gaul.

10. *Africa* again was evangelized from Rome at a comparatively late date. Of the African Church before the close of the second century, when a flood of light is suddenly thrown upon it by the writings of Tertullian, we know absolutely nothing. But we need not doubt that this father represents the

---

[106]All the predecessors of Victor bear Greek names with two exceptions, Clemens and Pius; and even these appear not to have been Latin. Clement writes in Greek, and his style is wholly unlike what might be expected from a Roman. Hermas, the brother of Pius, not only employs the Greek language in writing, but bears a Greek name also. It is worth observing also that Tertullian (*de Praescr.* 30), speaking of the episcopate of Eleutherus, designates the church of the metropolis not 'ecclesia Romana,' but 'ecclesia Romanensis,' i.e. not the Church *of* Rome, but the Church *in* Rome. The transition from a Greek to a Latin Church was of course gradual; but, if a definite epoch must be named, the episcopate of Victor serves better than any other. The two immediate successors of Victor, Zephyrinus (202–219) and Callistus (219–223), bear Greek names, and it may be inferred from the account in Hippolytus that they were Greeks; but from this time forward the Roman bishops, with scarcely an exception, seem to have been Latins.

[107]Hippolytus, *Haer.* ix. 12, pp. 287, 288.

[108]See the account of his attitude in the Paschal controversy in Eusebius, *Hist. Eccles.* v.24.

[109]Tertullian, *de Pudic.* i. The bishop here mentioned will be either Victor or Zephyrinus; the passage points to the assumption of extraordinary titles by the Roman bishops about this time. See also Cyprian in the opening of the Council of Carthage (*Counc. Carth*, p. 158, ed. Fell) 'neque enim quisquam nostrum episcopum se episcoporum constituit' etc. doubtless in allusion to the arrogance of the Roman prelates.

[110]Cited in Eusebius, *Hist. Eccles.* v.1.

traditions and sentiments of his church, when he lays stress on episcopacy as an apostolic institution and on the episcopate as the depositary of pure Christian doctrine. If we may judge by the large number of prelates assembled in the African councils of a later generation, it would appear that the extension of the episcopate was far more rapid here than in most parts of Christendom.[111]

11. *The Church of Alexandria*, on the other hand, was probably founded in Apostolic times. Nor is there any reason to doubt the tradition that connects it with the name of St. Mark, though the authorities for the statement are comparatively recent. Nevertheless, of its early history we have no authentic record. Eusebius indeed gives a list of bishops beginning with St. Mark, which here, as in the case of the Roman see, is accompanied by dates;[112] but from what source he derived his information is unknown.[113] The first contemporary notice of church officers in Alexandria is found in a heathen writer. The emperor Hadrian, writing to the consul Servianus, thus describes the state of religion in this city: 'I have become perfectly familiar with Egypt, which you praised to me; it is fickle, uncertain, blown about by every gust of rumor. Those who worship Serapis are Christians, and those are devoted to Serapis who call themselves bishops of Christ. There is no ruler of a synagogue there, no Samaritan, no Christian presbyter, who is not an astrologer, a soothsayer, a quack. The patriarch himself whenever he comes to Egypt is compelled by some to worship Serapis, by others to worship Christ.'[114] In this letter, which seems to have been written

---

[111]At the African council convoked by Cyprian about 50 years later, the opinions of as many as 87 bishops are recorded; and allusion is made in one of his letters (*Epist.* 59) to a council held before his time, when 90 bishops assembled. For a list canonical and uncanonical of the African bishoprics at this time see Munter, *Primord. Eccl. Afric.* p. 31 sq. The enormous number of African bishops a few centuries later would seem incredible, were it not reported on the best authority. Dupin (*Optat. Milev.* p. lix) counts up as many as 690 African sees; compare also the Notitia in Runart's *Victor Vitensis*, p. 117sq. These last references I owe to Gibbon, c. xxxvii and c.xli.
[112]Eusebius, *Hist. Eccles.* ii.24; iii.14, etc. See Clinton's *Fasti Romani*, II, p. 544.
[113]Independently of the tradition relating to St. Mark, this may be inferred from canonical and uncanonical writings that appear to have emanated from Alexandria. The Epistle to the Hebrews, even if we may not ascribe it to that learned Alexandrian Apollos (Acts 23:24) at least bears obvious marks of Alexandrian culture. The so-called Epistle to Barnabas again, which may have been written as early as the reign of Vespasian, and can hardly date later than Nerva, must be referred to the Alexandrian school of theology.
[114]Preserved in Vopiscus, *Vit. Saturn.* 8. The Jewish patriarch (who resided at Tiberias) is doubtless intended; for it would be no hardship to the Christian bishop of Alexandria to be 'compelled to worship Christ.' Otherwise, the anachronism involved in such a title would alone have sufficed

in the year 134, Hadrian shows more knowledge of Jewish ecclesiastical polity than of Christian but, apparently without knowing the exact value of terms, he seems to distinguish the bishop and the presbyter in the Christian community.[115] From the age of Hadrian to the age of Clement no contemporary or nearly contemporary notices are found, bearing on the government of the Alexandrian Church. The language of Clement is significant; he speaks sometimes of two orders of the ministry, 'the presbyters and deacons,'[116] sometimes of three, 'the bishops, presbyters, and deacons.'[117] Thus it would appear that even as late as the close of the second century the bishop of Alexandria was regarded as distinct and yet not distinct from the presbytery.[118] And the language of Clement is further illustrated by the fact, which will have to be considered at length presently, that at Alexandria the bishop was nominated and apparently ordained by the twelve presbyters out of their own number. The episcopal office in this Church during the second century gives no presage of the worldwide influence to which under the prouder name of patriarchate it was destined in later ages to attain. The Alexandrian succession, in which history is hitherto most interested, is not the succession of the bishops but of the heads of the catechetical school. The first bishop of Alexandria, of whom

---

to condemn the letter as spurious. Yet Salamacius Casabon and the older commentators generally, agree in the supposition that the bishop of Alexandria is styled patriarch here. The manner in which the document is stated by Vopiscus to have been preserved ('Hadriani epistolam ex libriis Phlegontis liberti ejus proditam') is favorable to its genuineness; nor does the mention of Verus as the Emperor's 'son' in another part of this letter present any real chronological difficulty. Hadrian paid his visit to Egypt in the autumn of 130, but the letter is not stated to have been written there. The date of the third consulship of Servianus is A.D. 134, and the account of Spartianus (Ver. 3) easily admits of the adoption of Verus before or during this year, though Clinton (*Fast. Rom.* i. p. 124) places it as late as A.D. 135. Gregorovius (*Kaiser Hadrian* p. 71) suggests that 'filium meum' may have been added by Phlegon or by someone else. The prominence of the Christians in this letter is not surprising when we remember how Hadrian interested himself in their tenets on another occasion (at Athens). This document is considered genuine by such opposite authorities as Tillemont (*Hist. des Emp.* ii. p. 265) and Gregorovius (i.e. p. 41), and may be accepted without hesitation.

[115]At this time there appears to have been only one bishop in Egypt (see below). But Hadrian, who would have heard of numerous bishops elsewhere, and perhaps had no very precise knowledge of the Egyptian Church, might well indulge in this rhetorical flourish. At all events he seems to mean different offices when speaking of the bishop and the presbyter.

[116]*Strom.* vii.i (p. 830, Potter).

[117]*Strom.* vi.13 (p. 793) cf. *Strom.* iii.12, *Paed.* iii.12 (see the next note); see Kaye's *Clement of Alexandria* p. 463 sq.

[118]Yet in one passage he, like Irenaeus (see Lightfoot, *Philippians*, p. 98), betrays his ignorance that in the language of the New Testament, bishop and presbyter are synonyms. See *Paed.* Iii.12.

any distinct incident is recorded on trustworthy authority, was a contemporary of Origen.

The notices thus collected[119] present a large body of evidence establishing the fact of the early and extensive adoption of episcopacy in the Christian Church. The investigation however would not be complete, unless attention were called to such indirect testimony as is furnished by the tacit assumptions of writers living towards and at the close of the second century. Episcopacy is so inseparably interwoven with all the traditions and beliefs of men like Irenaeus and Tertullian, that they betray no knowledge of a time when it was not. Even Irenaeus, the earlier of these, who was certainly born and probably grown up before the middle of the century, seems to be wholly ignorant that the bishop had passed from a lower to a higher value since the apostolic times.[120] Nor is it important only to observe the positive though indirect testimony that they afford. Their silence suggests a strong negative presumption, that while every other point of doctrine or practice was eagerly canvassed, the form of Church government alone scarcely came under discussion.

But these notices, besides establishing the general prevalence of episcopacy, also throw considerable light on its origin. *They indicate that the solution suggested by the history of the word 'bishop' and its transference from the lower to the higher office is the true solution, and that the episcopate was created out of the presbytery.* They show that this creation was not so much an isolated act as a progressive development, not advancing everywhere at an uniform rate but exhibiting at one and the same time different stages of growth in different churches. They seem to hint also that, so far as this development was affected at all by national temper and characteristics, it was slower where the prevailing influences were more purely Greek, as at Corinth and Philippi and Rome, and more rapid where an oriental spirit predominated, as at Jerusalem and Antioch and Ephesus. Above all, they establish this result clearly, that its maturer forms are seen first in those regions where the latest surviving Apostles (more especially

---

[119]In this sketch of the episcopate, in the different churches, I have not thought it necessary to carry the list later than the second century, nor (except in a very few cases), has any testimony been accepted, unless the writer flourished before the close of this century. The Apostolic Constitutions would add several names to the list; but this evidence is not trustworthy, though in many cases, the statements doubtless rested on some traditional basis.

[120]See Lightfoot, *Philippians*, p. 98. The same is true of Clement of Alexandria.

St. John) fixed their abode, and at a time when its prevalence cannot be dissociated from their influence or their sanction.

The original relation of the bishop to the presbyter, which this investigation reveals, was not forgotten even after the lapse of centuries. Though offices not set over the presbyters, he was still regarded as, in some sense, one of them. Irenaeus indicates this position of the episcopate very clearly. In his language, a presbyter is never designated a bishop, while on the other hand he very frequently speaks of a bishop as a presbyter. In other words, though he views the episcopate as a distinct office from the presbytery, he does not regard it as a distinct order in the same sense in which the diaconate is a distinct order. Thus, arguing against the heretics he says, 'But when again we appeal against them to that tradition which is derived from the Apostles, which is preserved in the churches by successions of presbyters, they place themselves in opposition to it, saying that they, being wiser not only than the presbyters but even than the Apostles, have discovered the genuine truth.'[121] Yet just below, after again mentioning the Apostolic tradition, he adds, 'We are able to enumerate those who have been appointed by the Apostles bishops in the churches and their successors down to our own time';[122] and still further, after saying that it would take up too much space if he were to trace the succession in all the churches, he declares that he will confound his opponents by singling out the ancient and renowned Church of Rome founded by the Apostles Peter and Paul and will point out the tradition handed down to his own time by the 'succession of *bishops*,' after which he gives a list from Linus to Eleutherus.[123]

So again, in another passage, he writes, 'Therefore obedience ought to be rendered to the presbyters who are in the churches, who have the succession from the Apostles as we have shown, who with the succession of the episcopate have also received the sure grace of truth according to the pleasure of the Father,' after which he mentions some 'who are believed by many to be presbyters, but serve their own lusts and are elated with the pomp of the chief seat' and bids his readers shun these and seek such as 'together with the rank of the presbytery show their speech sound and their conversation void of offence,' adding of these latter, 'Such presbyters the Church nurtures

---

[121]Irenaeus iii.2.2.
[122]Irenaeus iii.3.1.
[123]Irenaeus iii.3.2-3.

and rears, concerning whom also the prophet saith, "I will give thy rulers in peace and thy bishops in righteousness."[124] Thus also writing to Victor of Rome in the name of the Gallican churches, he says, 'It was not so observed by the presbyters before Soter, who ruled the Church which thou now guidest, we mean Anicetus and Pius, Hyginus, and Telesphorus and Xystus.'[125] And the same estimate of the office appears in Clement of Alexandria, for, while he speaks elsewhere of the three offices in the ministry, mentioning them by name, he in one passage puts forward a twofold division, the presbyters whose duty it is to improve, and the deacons whose duty it is to serve, the Church.[126] The functions of the bishop and presbyter are thus regarded as substantially the same in kind, though different in degree, while the functions of the diaconate are separate from both. More than a century and a half later, this view is put forward with the greatest distinctness by the most learned and most illustrious of the Latin fathers. 'There is one ordination,' writes the commentator Hilary, 'of the bishop and the presbyter; for either is a priest, but the bishop is first. Every bishop is a presbyter, but every presbyter is not a bishop, for he is bishop who is first among the presbyters.'[127]

The language of St. Jerome, to the same effect, has been quoted elsewhere.[128] To the passages there given may be added the following: 'This has been said to show that with the ancients, presbyters were the same as bishops, but gradually all the responsibility was deferred to a single person, that the thickets of heresies might be rooted out. Therefore, as presbyters know that by the custom of the Church they are subject to him who shall have been set over them, so let bishops also be aware that they are superior to presbyters more owing to custom than to any actual ordinance of the Lord, etc. Let us see therefore what sort of person ought to be ordained presbyter or bishop.'[129]

---

[124]Irenaeus iv. 26.2-5.

[125]In Eusebius, *Hist. Eccles.* v. 24. In other places Irenaeus apparently uses πρεσβύτεροι to denote antiquity and not office, as in the letter to Florinus, Euseb. *Hist. Eccles.* v. 20 (comp. ii. 22. 5); in which sense the word occurs also in Papias (Euseb. *Hist Eccles.* iii.39; see *Contemporary Review*, Aug. 1875, p. 379sq. [*Essays on Supernatural Religion* p. 143 sq.]); but the passages quoted in the text decisive, nor is there any reason (as Rothe assumes, p. 414 sq.) why the usage of Irenaeus should throughout be uniform.

[126]See the anecdote of St. John in *Quis div. salv.* 42 p. 959 which shows that he too, like Irenaeus, regards the bishop as a presbyter, though the converse would not be true.

[127]Ambrosiaster on 1 Tim 3:10.

[128]See Lightfoot, *Philippians*, p. 98.

[129]On Titus 1:5 (vii, p. 696).

In the same spirit too the great Augustine, writing to Jerome says: 'Although according to titles of honor, the practice of which, the Church has now made valid, the episcopate is greater than the presbytery, yet in many things Augustine is less than Jerome.'[130] To these fathers this view seemed to be an obvious deduction from the identity of the terms 'bishop' and 'presbyter' in the apostolic writings; nor indeed, when they wrote, had usage entirely effaced the original connection between the two offices. Even in the fourth and fifth centuries, when the independence and power of the episcopate had reached its maximum, it was still customary for a bishop in writing to a presbyter to address him as fellow-presbyter thus bearing testimony to a substantial identity of order. Nor does it appear that this view was ever questioned until the era of the Reformation. In the western Church at all events it carried the sanction of the highest ecclesiastical authorities and was maintained even by popes and councils.[131]

Nor was it only in the *language* of the later Church that the memory of this fact was preserved. Even in her practice indications might here and there be traced, which pointed to a time when the bishop was still only the chief member of the presbytery. The case of the Alexandrian Church, which has already been mentioned casually, deserves special notice. St. Jerome, after denouncing the audacity of certain persons who 'would give to deacons the precedence over presbyters, that is over bishops,' and alleging scriptural proofs of the identity of the two, gives the following fact in illustration: 'At Alexandria, from Mark the Evangelist down to the times of the bishops Heraclas (A.D. 233-249) and Dionysius (A.D. 249-265), the presbyters always nominated as bishop one chosen out of their own body and placed in a higher grade, just as if an army were to appoint a general, or deacons were to choose from their own body one whom they knew to be diligent and call him archdeacon.'[132] Though the direct statement of this

---

[130]So for instance Cyprian, *Epistle* 14 writes 'compresbyteri nostri Donatus et Fortunatus,' and addressing Cornelius bishop of Rome (*Epist.* 45) he says, 'cum ad me talia de te et compresbyteris tecum considentibus scripta venissent.' Compare also *Epist.* 44, 45, 71, 76. Augustine writes to Jerome in the same terms, and in fact this seems to have been the recognized form of address. See the *Quaest. Vet. Et Novi Test.* ci (in Augustine Op. iii P.2, p. 93). 'Quid est enim episcopus nisi primus presbyter, hoc est summus sacerdos? Denique non aliter quam compresbyteros hic vocat et consacerdotes suos. Numquid et ministros condiaconos suos dicit episcopus' where the writer is arguing against the arrogance of the Roman deacons. See Lightfoot, *Philippians*, p. 96.
[131]See the references collected by Giesler, i. p. 105.
[132]*Epist.* cxlvi. *ad Evangel.* (i. p. 1082).

Father refers only to the appointment of the bishop, still it may be inferred that the function of the presbyters extended also to the consecration. And this inference is borne out by other evidence. 'In Egypt,' writes an older contemporary of St. Jerome, the commentator Hilary, 'the presbyters seal (i.e. ordain or consecrate), if the bishop be not present.'[133] This however might refer only to the ordination of presbyters, and not to the consecration of a bishop. But even the latter is supported by direct evidence, which though comparatively late deserves consideration, inasmuch as it comes from one who was himself a patriarch of Alexandria. Eutychius, who held the patriarchal see from A.D. 933 to A.D. 940, writes as follows: 'The Evangelist Mark appointed along with the patriarch Hananias twelve presbyters who should remain with the patriarch, to the end that, when the patriarchate was vacant, they might choose one of the twelve presbyters, on whose head the remaining eleven laying their hands should bless him and create him patriarch.' The vacant place in the presbytery was then to be filled up, that the number twelve might be constant.[134] 'This custom,' adds this writer, 'did not cease till the time of Alexander' (A.D. 313–326), patriarch of Alexandria. 'He however forbad that henceforth the presbyters should create the patriarch, and decreed that on the death of the patriarch the bishops should meet to ordain the (new) patriarch, etc.'[135] It is clear from this passage that Eutychius considered the functions of nomination and ordination to rest with the same persons.

---

[133]Ambrosiast. on Eph 4:12. So too in the *Quaest. Vet. Et Novo Test.* ci (falsely ascribed to St. Augustine), August. *Op.* III, P. 2, p. 93 'Nam in Alexandria et per totam Aegyptum si desit episcopus consecrate (v.1 consignat) presbyter.'

[134]Eutychii Patr. Alexandr. *Annales* i. p. 331 (Pococke, Oxon. 1656). The inferences in the text are resisted by Abraham Ecchellensis *Eutychius vindicatus* p. 22 sq. (in answer to Selden the translator of Eutychius), and by Le Quien, *Oriens Christianus* ii. p. 342, who urge all that can be said on the opposite side. The authority of a writer so inaccurate as Eutychius, if it had been unsupported, would have had no weight; but, as we have seen, this is not the case.

[135]Between Dionysius and Alexander four bishops of Alexandria intervene, Maximus (A.D. 265), Theonas (A.D. 283), Peter I. (A.D. 301), and Achillas (A.D. 312). It will therefore be seen that there is a considerable discrepancy between the accounts of Jerome and Eutychius as to the time when the change was effected. But we may reasonably conjecture (with Ritschl, p. 432) that the transition from the old state of things to the new would be the result of a prolonged conflict between the Alexandrian presbytery who had hitherto held these functions, and the bishops of the recently created Egyptian sees to whom it was proposed to transfer them. Somewhat later one Ischyras was deprived of his orders by an Alexandrian synod, because he had been ordained by a presbyter only: Athan. *Apol. c. Arian.* 75 (i. p. 152). From this time, at all events, the Alexandrian Church insisted as strictly as any other on episcopal ordination.

If this view however be correct, the practice of the Alexandrian Church was exceptional; for at this time the formal act of the bishop was considered generally necessary to give validity to ordination. Nor is the exception difficult to account for. At the close of the second century, when every considerable church in Europe and Asia appears to have had its bishop, the only representative of the episcopal order in Egypt was the bishop of Alexandria. It was Demetrius first (A.D. 190–233), as Eutychius informs us[136] who appointed three other bishops, to which number his successor Heraclas (A.D. 233–249) added twenty more. This extension of episcopacy to the provincial towns of Egypt paved the way for a change in the mode of appointing and ordaining the patriarch of Alexandria. But before this time it was a matter of convenience and almost of necessity that the Alexandrian presbyters should themselves ordain their chief.

Nor is it only in Alexandria that we meet with this peculiarity. Where the same urgent reason existed, the same exceptional practice seems to have been tolerated. A decree of the Council of Ancyra (A.D. 314) ordains that 'it be not allowed to country-bishops to ordain presbyters or deacons, nor even to city-presbyters, except permission be given in each parish by the bishop in writing.'[137] Thus while restraining the existing license, the framers of the

---

[136]Eutych. *Ann. 1.* c. p. 332. Heraclas, we are informed on the same authority (p. 335), was the first Alexandrian prelate who bore the title of patriarch, this designation being equivalent to metropolitan or bishop of bishops.

[137]*Council Ancrya.* can. l3 (See Routh, *Rel. Sacr.* iv. p. 121). The various readings and interpretations of this canon will be found in Routh's note. On the former p. 144 sq. Routh himself reads 'but on the one hand much less city elders' making the πρεσβύτερος πόλεως object of χειρότονειν, but to this there is a twofold objection: (1) he necessarily understands the former πρεσβύτερους to mean πρεσβύτερους χώρας though this is not expressed: (2) he interprets 'much less,' in a sense which seems to exclude and which is not borne out by his examples. The name and office of the 'country-bishop' appear to be a relic of the time when 'bishop' and 'presebyter' were synonyms. While the large cities had their college of presbyters, for the villages a single πρεσβύτερος would suffice; but from his isolated position he would be tempted, even if he were not obliged, to perform on his own responsibility certain *acta* which in the city would only be performed by the bishop properly so called, or at least would not be performed without his consent. Out of this position the office of the latter would gradually be developed; but the rate of progression would not be uniform, and the regulations affecting it would be determined by the circumstances of the particular locality. Hence, at a later date, it seems in some places to have been presbyteral, in others episcopal. In the Ancyran canon just cited a 'chorepiscopus' is evidently placed below the city presbytery; but in other notices he occupies a higher position. For the conflicting accounts of the 'country-bishop' see Bingham ii. xiv. Baur's account of the origin of the episcopate supposes that each Christian congregation was presided over, not by a college of presbyters, but by a single πρεσβύτερος or ἐπίσκοπος, i.e. that the constitution of the Church was from the first monarchical: see *Pastoralbriefe* p. 81 sq., *Ursprung des Episcopats* p. 84 sq. This

decree still allow very considerable latitude. *And it is especially important to observe that they lay more stress on episcopal sanction than on episcopal ordination.* Causes of the development of episcopacy is secured, they are content to dispense with the latter.

As a general rule however, even those writers who maintain a substantial identity in the offices of the bishop and presbyter reserve the power of ordaining to the former.[138] This distinction in fact may be regarded as a settled maxim of Church polity in the fourth and later centuries. And when Arius maintained the equality of the bishop and presbyter and denied the necessity of episcopal ordination, his opinion was condemned as heretical, and is stigmatized as 'frantic' by Epiphanius.[139]

It has been seen that the institution of an episcopate must be placed as far back as the closing years of the first century, and that it cannot, without violence to historical testimony, be dissevered from the name of St. John. But it has been seen also that the earliest bishops did not hold the same independent position of supremacy that was and is occupied by their later representatives. It will therefore be instructive to trace the successive stages by which the power of the office was developed during the second and third centuries. Though something must be attributed to the frailty of human pride and love of power, it will nevertheless appear that the pressing needs of the Church were mainly instrumental in bringing about the result, and that his development of the episcopal office was a providential safeguard amid the confusion of speculative opinion, the distracting effects of persecution, and the growing anarchy of social life, which threatened not only the extension but the very existence of the Church of Christ. Ambition of office in a society where prominence of rank involved prominence of risk was at least no vulgar and selfish passion.

This development will be conveniently connected with three great names, each separated from the other by an interval of more than half a century,

---

view is inconsistent alike with the analogy of the synagogue and with the notices in the apostolic and early ecclesiastical writings. But the practice which he considers to have been the general rule would probably hold in small country congregations, where a college of presbyters would be unnecessary as well as impossible.

[138]St Jerome himself (*Epist.* cxlvi.), in the context of the passage in which he maintains the identity of the two orders and alleges the tradition of the Alexandrian Church (see above), adds, 'Quid enim facit excepta ordinatione episcopus quod presbyter non faciat?' So also *Const. Apost.* viii. 28; Chrysost. *Hom.* xi. on 1 Tim 3:8. See Bingham ii. iii. 5, 6, 7, for other references.

[139]*Haer. lxxv.*3; comp. Augustine, *Haer.* § 53. See Wordsworth, *Theoph. Angl.* c.x.

and each marking a distinct stage in its progress. Ignatius, Irenaeus, and Cyprian, represent three successive advances towards the supremacy that was ultimately attained.

1. *Ignatius of Antioch* is commonly recognized as the staunchest advocate of episcopacy in the early ages. Even, though we should refuse to accept as genuine any portions that are not contained in the Syriac Version,[140] this view would nevertheless be amply justified. Confining our attention for the moment to the Syriac letters we find that to this father the chief value of episcopacy lies in the fact that it constitutes a *visible centre of unity* in the congregation. He seems in the development of the office to keep in view the same purpose that we may suppose to have influenced the last surviving Apostles in its institution. The withdrawal of the authoritative preachers of the Gospel, the personal disciples of the Lord, had severed one bond of union. The destruction of the original abode of Christendom, the scene of the life and passion of the Savior and of the earliest triumphs of the Church, had removed another. Thus deprived at once of the personal and the local ties which had hitherto bound individual to individual and church to church, the Christian brotherhood was threatened with schism, disunion, dissolution. 'Vindicate thine office with all diligence,' writes Ignatius to the bishop of Smyrna, 'in things temporal as well as spiritual. Have a care of unity, than which nothing is better' (*Polyc.* 1). 'The crisis requires thee, as the pilot requires the winds or the storm-tossed mariner a haven, so as to attain unto God' (*Polyc.* 2). 'Let not those who seem to be plausible and teach falsehoods dismay thee; but stand thou firm as an anvil under the hammer 'tis the part of a great athlete to be bruised and to conquer' (*Polyc.* 3). 'Let nothing be done without thy consent, and do thou nothing without the consent of God' (*Polyc.* 4). He adds directions also, that those who decide on a life of virginity shall disclose their intention to the bishop only, and those who marry shall obtain his consent to their union, that 'their marriage may be according to the Lord and not according to lust' (*Polyc.* 5). And turning from the bishop to the people he adds, 'Give heed to your bishop, that God also may give heed to

---

[140]In the earlier editions of this work, I assumed that the Syriac Version published by Cureton represented the Epistles of Ignatius in their original form. I am now convinced that this is only an abridgment and that the shorter Greek form is genuine; but for the sake of argument, I have kept the two apart in the text. I hope before long to give reasons for this change of opinion in my edition of this father [see Additional Note C, below].

you. I give my life for those who are obedient to the bishop, to presbyters, to deacons. With them may I have my portion in the presence of God' (*Polyc.* 6). Writing to the Ephesians also he says that in receiving their bishop Onesimus he is receiving their whole body, and he charges them to love him, and one and all to be in his likeness (*Ephes.* 1), adding, 'Since love does not permit me to be silent, therefore I have been forward in exhorting you to conform to the will of God' (*Ephes.* 4).

From these passages it will be seen that St. Ignatius values the episcopate chiefly as a security for good discipline and harmonious working in the Church. And, when we pass from the Syriac letters to the Short Greek, the standing ground is still unchanged. At the same time, though the point of view is unaltered, the Greek letters contain far stronger expressions than are found in the Syriac. Throughout the whole range of Christian literature, no more uncompromising advocacy of the episcopate can be found than appears in these writings. This championship indeed is extended to the two lower orders of the ministry,[141] more especially to the presbyters.[142] But it is when asserting the claims of the episcopal office to obedience and respect, that the language is strained to the utmost. 'The bishops established in the farthest parts of the world are in the counsels of Jesus Christ' (*Ephes.* 3). 'Every one whom the Master of the house sendeth to govern His own household we ought to receive, as Him that sent him; clearly therefore we ought to regard the bishop as the Lord Himself' (*Ephes.* 6). Those 'live a life after Christ' who 'obey the bishop as Jesus Christ' (*Trall.* 2). 'It is good to know God and the bishop; he that honors the bishop is honored of God; he that does anything without the knowledge of the bishop serveth the devil' (*Smyrn.* 9). 'He that obeys his bishop, obeys not him, but the Father of Jesus Christ, the Bishop of all.' 'On the other hand, he that practises hypocrisy towards his bishop, not only deceiveth the visible one, but cheateth the Unseen' (*Magn.* 3). 'As many as are of God and of Jesus Christ, are with the bishop' (*Philad.* 3). Those are approved who are 'inseparate [from God], from Jesus Christ, and from the bishop, and from the ordinances of the Apostles' (*Trall.* 7). 'Do ye all,' says this writer again, 'follow the bishop, as Jesus Christ followed the Father' (*Smyrn.* 8; comp. *Magn.* 7). The Ephesians

---

[141]*Polyc.* 5.5, *Magn.* 13, *Trall.* 3, 7, *Philad.* 4, 7, *Smyrn.* 8, 12.
[142]*Ephes.* 2, 20, *Magn.* 2, 6, *Trall.* 13.

are commended accordingly, because they are so united with their bishop 'as the Church with Jesus Christ and as Jesus Christ with the Father.' 'If,' it is added, 'the prayer of one or two hath so much power, how much more the prayer of the bishop and of the whole Church' (*Ephes.* 5). 'Wherever the bishop may appear, there let the multitude be, just as where Jesus Christ may be, there is the universal Church' (*Smyrn.* 8). Therefore 'let no man do any-thing pertaining to the Church without the bishop' (ibid. comp. *Magn.* 4; *Philad.* 7). 'It is not allowable either to baptize or to hold a love-feast without the bishop: but whatsoever he may approve, this also is well pleasing to God, that everything which is done may be safe and valid' (*Smyrn.* 8). 'Unity of God,' according to this writer, consists in harmonious co-operation with the bishop (*Polyc.* 8; comp. *Philad.* 3, 8).

And yet with all this extravagant exaltation of the episcopal office, the presbyters are not put out however of sight. They form a council[143] a 'worthy spiritual coronal' (*Magn.* 13) round the bishop. It is the duty of every indi-vidual, but especially of them, 'to refresh the bishop unto the honor of the Father and of Jesus Christ and of the Apostles' (*Trall.* 12). They stand in the same relation to him, 'as the chords to the lyre' (*Ephes.* 4 comp the metaphor in *Philad.* 1). If the bishop occupies the place of God or of Jesus Christ, the presbyters are as the Apostles, as the council of God (*Trall.* 2, 3; *Magn.* 6; *Smyrn.* 8). If obedience is due to the bishop as the grace of God, it is due to the presbytery as the law of Jesus Christ (*Magn.* 10).

It need hardly be remarked how subversive the true spirit of Christianity, in the negation of individual freedom and the consequent suppression this language of direct responsibility to God in Christ, is the crushing despotism with which this language, if taken literally, would invest the episcopal office. It is more important to bear in mind the extenuating fact, that the needs and distractions of the age seemed to call for a greater concentration of authority in the episcopate; and we might well be surprised, if at a great crisis the defence of an all-important institution were expressed in words carefully weighed and guarded.

Strangely enough, not many years after Ignatius asserted the claims of the episcopate as a safeguard of orthodoxy, another writer used the same

---

[143]The word πρεσβύτεριον which occurs in 1 Tim 4:14, is very frequent in the Ignatian Epistles.

instrument to advance a very different form of Christianity. The organization, which is thus employed to consolidate and advance the Catholic
Church, might serve equally well to establish a compact Ebionite community. I have already mentioned the author of the *Clementine Homilies* as
a staunch advocate of episcopacy. His view of the sanctions and privileges
of the office does not differ materially from that of Ignatius. 'The multitude
of the faithful,' he says, 'must obey a single person, that so it may be able to
continue in harmony.' Monarchy is a necessary condition of peace; this may
be seen from the aspect of the world around, at present there are many
kings, and the result is discord and war; in the world to come God has appointed one King only, that 'by reason of monarchy an indestructible peace
may be established: therefore all ought to follow some one person as guide,
preferring him in honor as the image of God; and this guide must show the
way that leadeth to the Holy City' (*Clem. Hom.* iii.61,62). Accordingly he
delights to speak of the bishop as occupying the place or the seat of Christ
(*Clem. Hom.* iii.60, 66, 70). Every insult, he says, and every honor offered
to a bishop is carried to Christ and from Christ is taken up to the presence
of the Father; and thus it is requited manifold (*Clem. Hom.* iii.66, 70). Similarly another writer of the Clementine cycle, if he be not the same, compares Christ to the captain, the bishop to the mate, and the presbyters to
the sailors, while the lower orders and the laity have each their proper place
in the ship of the Church (*Clem. Hom., Ep. Clem.* 5).

It is no surprise that such extravagant claims should not have been allowed
to pass unchallenged. In opposition to the lofty hierarchical pretensions thus
advanced on the one hand in the Ignatian letters on behalf of Catholicism and
on the other by the Clementine writer in the interests of Ebionism, a strong
spiritualist reaction set in. If in its mental aspect the heresy of Montanus must
be regarded as a protest against the speculative subtleties of Gnosticism, on its
practical side it was equally a rebound from the aggressive tyranny of hierarchical assumption. Montanus taught that the true succession of the Spirit, the
authorized channel of Divine grace, must be sought not in the hierarchical but
in the prophetic order. For a rigid outward system he substituted the free
inward impulse. Wildly fanatical as were its manifestations, this reaction nevertheless issued from a true instinct that rebeled against the oppressive yoke
of external tradition and did battle for the freedom of the individual spirit.

Montanus was excommunicated and Montanism died out; but though dead, it yet spake; for a portion of its better spirit was infused into the Catholic Church, which it leavened and refreshed and invigorated.

2. *Irenaeus* followed Ignatius after an interval of about two generations. With the altered circumstances of the Church, the aspect of the episcopal office has also undergone a change. The religious atmosphere is now charged with heretical speculations of all kinds. Amidst the competition of rival teachers, all eagerly bidding for support, the perplexed believer asks for some decisive test by which he may try the claims of the disputants. To this question, Irenaeus supplies an answer. 'If you wish,' he argues, 'to ascertain the doctrine of the Apostles, apply to the Church of the Apostles. In the succession of bishops tracing their descent from the primitive age and appointed by the Apostles themselves, you have a guarantee for the transmission of the pure faith, which no isolated, upstart, self-constituted teacher can furnish. There is the Church of Rome for instance, whose episcopal pedigree is perfect in all its links, and whose earliest bishops, Linus and Clement, associated with the Apostles themselves, there is the Church of Smyrna again, whose bishop Polycarp, the disciple of St. John, died only the other day' (see iii.2-4; iv.26-32; v.20.1-2). Thus the episcopate is regarded now not so much as *the center of ecclesiastical unity but rather as the depositary of apostolic tradition.*

This view is not peculiar to Irenaeus. It seems to have been advanced earlier by Hegesippus, for in a detached fragment he lays stress on the succession of the bishops at Rome and at Corinth, adding that in each church and in each succession the pure faith was preserved;[144] so that he seems here to be controverting that 'gnosis falsely so called' which elsewhere he denounces (*Hist. Eccles.* iii.32). It is distinctly maintained by Tertullian, the younger contemporary of Irenaeus, who refers, if not with the same frequency, at least with equal emphasis, to the tradition of the apostolic churches as preserved by the succession of the episcopate (*de Praescens.* 32).

3. As two generations intervened between Ignatius and Irenaeus, so the same period roughly speaking separates Irenaeus from *Cyprian.* If with Ignatius the bishop is the center of Christian unity, if with Irenaeus he is the

---

[144]In Eusebius, *Hist. Eccles.* iv.22.

depositary of the apostolic tradition, with Cyprian he is *the absolute vice-gerent of Christ* in things spiritual. In mere strength of language indeed it would be difficult to surpass Ignatius, who lived about a century and a half earlier. With the single exception of the sacerdotal view of the ministry which had grown up meanwhile, Cyprian puts forward no assumption that this father had not advanced either literally or substantially long before. This one exception however is all-important, for it raised the sanctions of the episcopate to a higher level and put new force into old titles of respect. Theoretically therefore it may be said that Cyprian took his stand on the combination of the ecclesiastical authority as asserted by Ignatius with the sacerdotal claim that had been developed in the half-century just past. But the real influence which he exercised in the elevation of the episcopate consisted not in the novelty of his theoretical views, but in his practical energy and success. The absolute supremacy of the bishop had remained hitherto a lofty title or at least a vague ill-defined assumption. It became through his exertions a substantial and patent and worldwide fact. The first prelate whose force of character vibrated throughout the whole of Christendom, he was driven not less by the circumstances of his position than by his own temperament and conviction to throw all his energy into this scale. And the permanent result was much vaster than he could have anticipated beforehand or realized after the fact. Forced into the episcopate against his will, he raised it to a position of absolute independence, from which it has never since been deposed. The two great controversies in which Cyprian engaged, though immediately arising out of questions of discipline, combined from opposite sides to consolidate and enhance the power of the bishops.[145]

The first question of dispute concerned the treatment of such as had lapsed during the recent persecution under Decius. Cyprian found himself on this occasion doing battle against a twofold opposition, against the confessors who claimed the right of absolving and restoring these fallen brethren, and against his own presbyters who in the absence of their bishop supported the claims of the confessors. From his retirement he launched his shafts

---

[145]The influence of Cyprian on the episcopate is ably stated in two vigorous articles by Kayser entitled *Cyprien ou l'Autonomie de l'Episcopat* in *Revue de Theologie* xv. pp. 138 sq., 242 sq. (1857). See also Rettberg, *Thascius Cacilius Cyprianus* p. 367 sq., Huther, *Cyprian's Lehre von der Kirche* p. 59 sq. For Cyprian's work generally see Smith's *Dict. of Christ. Biogr.* s.v.

against this combined array, where an aristocracy of moral influence was leagued with an aristocracy of official position. With signal determination and courage in pursuing his aim, and with not less sagacity and address in discerning the means for carrying it out, Cyprian had on this occasion the further advantage, that he was defending the cause of order and right. He succeeded moreover in enlisting in his cause the rulers of the most powerful church in Christendom. The Roman clergy declared for the bishop and against the presbyters of Carthage. Of Cyprian's sincerity, no reasonable question can be entertained. In maintaining the authority of his office he believed himself to be fighting his Master's battle, and he sought success as the only safeguard of the integrity of the Church of Christ. In this lofty and disinterested spirit, and with these advantages of position, he entered upon the contest.

It is unnecessary for my purpose to follow out the conflict in detail, to show how ultimately the positions of the two combatants were shifted, so that from maintaining discipline against the champions of too great laxity, Cyprian found himself protecting the fallen against the advocates of too great severity; to trace the progress of the schism and the attempt to establish a rival episcopate; or to unravel the entanglements of the Novatian controversy and lay open the intricate relations between Rome and Carthage.[146] It is sufficient to say that Cyprian's victory was complete. He triumphed over the church de-confessors, triumphed over his own presbyters, triumphed over the schismatic bishop and his party. It was the most signal success hitherto achieved for the episcopate, because the battle had been fought and the victory won on this definite issue. The absolute supremacy of the episcopal office was thus established against the two antagonists from which it had most to fear, against a recognised aristocracy of ecclesiastical office and an irregular but not less powerful aristocracy of moral weight.

The position of the bishop with respect to the individual church over which he ruled was thus defined by the first contest in which Cyprian engaged. The second conflict resulted in determining his relation to the Church

---

[146]The intricacy of the whole proceeding is a strong evidence of the genuineness of the letters and other documents that contain the account of the controversy. The situations of antagonists, varying and even interchanged with the change of circumstances, are very natural, but very unlike the invention of a forger who has a distinct side to maintain.

universal. The schism that had grown up during the first conflict created the difficulty which gave occasion to the second. A question arose whether baptism by heretics and schismatics should be held valid or not. Stephen, the Roman bishop, pleading the immemorial custom of his church, recognised its validity. Cyprian insisted on rebaptism in such cases. Hitherto, the bishop of Carthage had acted in cordial harmony with Rome, but now there was a collision. Stephen, inheriting the haughty temper and aggressive policy of his earlier predecessor Victor, excommunicated those who differed from the Roman usage in this matter. These arrogant assumptions were directly met by Cyprian. He summoned first one and then another synod of African bishops, who declared in his favor. He had on his side also the churches of Asia Minor, which had been included in Stephen's edict of excommunication. Thus the bolt hurled by Stephen fell innocuous, and the churches of Africa and Asia retained their practice.

The principle asserted in the struggle was not unimportant. As in the fomer conflict, Cyprian had maintained the independent supremacy of the bishop over the officers and members of his own congregation, so now he contended successfully for his immunity from any interference from without. At a later period indeed, Rome carried the victory, but the immediate result of this controversy was to establish the independence and enhance the power of the episcopate. Moreover, this struggle had the further and not less important consequence of defining and exhibiting the relations of the episcopate to the Church in another way.

As the individual bishop had been pronounced indispensable to the existence of the individual community, so the episcopal order was now put forward as the absolute indefeasible representative of the universal Church. Synods of bishops indeed had been held frequently before; but under Cyprian's guidance they assumed a prominence which threw all existing precedents into the shade. 'One undivided episcopate' was his watchword. The unity of the Church, he maintained, consists in the unanimity of the bishops.[147] In this controversy, as in the former, he acted throughout on the

---

[147]*De Unit. Eccl.* 2: 'Quam unitatem firmiter tenere et vindicare debemus maxime episcopi qui in ecclesia praesidemus, ut episcopatum quoque ipsum unum atque indivisum probemus' and again 'Episcopatus unus est, cujus a singulis in solidum pars tenetur, ecclesia quoque una est etc.' So again he argues (*Epist.* 43) that, as there is one Church, there must be only 'unum altare et unum sacerdotium (i.e. one episcopate).' Comp. also *Epist.* 46, 55, 67.

principle, distinctly asserted, that the existence of the episcopal office was
not a matter of practical advantage or ecclesiastical rule or even of apostolic
sanction, but an absolute incontrovertible decree of God. The triumph of
Cyprian therefore was the triumph of this principle.

The greatness of Cyprian's influence on the episcopate is indeed due to this
fact, that with him the statement of the principle precedes and necessitates the
practical measures. Of the sharpness and distinctness of his sacerdotal views
it will be time to speak presently; but of his conception of the episcopal office
generally thus much may be said here, that he regards the bishop as exclusively
the representative of God to the congregation and hardly, if at all, as the representative of the congregation before God. The bishop is the indispensable
channel of divine grace, the indispensable bond of Christian brotherhood. The
episcopate is not so much the roof as the foundation-stone of the ecclesiastical
edifice; not so much the legitimate development as the primary condition of
a church.[148] The bishop is appointed directly by God, is responsible directly to
God, is inspired directly from God. This last point deserves especial notice.
Though in words he frequently defers to the established usage of consulting
the presbyters and even the laity in the appointment of officers and in other
matters affecting the well-being of the community, yet he only makes the
concession to nullify it immediately. He pleads a direct official inspiration
'which enables him to dispense with ecclesiastical custom and to act on his
own responsibility.' Though the presbyters may still have retained the shadow
of a controlling power over the acts of the bishop, though the courtesy of
language by which they were recognised as fellow-presbyters[149] was not laid
aside, yet for all practical ends the independent supremacy of the episcopate
was completely established by the principles and the measures of Cyprian.

In the investigation just concluded I have endeavored to trace the changes
in the relative position of the first and second orders of the ministry, by
which the power was gradually concentrated in the hands of the former.

---

[148]*Epist.* 66: 'Scire debes episcopum in ecclesia esse et ecclesiam in episcopo, et si quis cum episcopo
non sit in ecclesia non esse'; *Epist.* 33: 'Ut ecclesia super episcopos constituatur et omnis actus
ecclesiae per eosdem praepositos gubernetur.' Hence the expression 'nec episcopum nec ecclesiam
cogitans,' (*Epist.* 41); hence also 'honor episcopi' is associated not only with 'ecclesiae ratio' (*Epist.*
33) even with 'timor Dei' (*Epist.* 15). Compare also the language (*Epist.* 59): 'Nec ecclesia istic
cuiquam clauditur nec episcopus alicui denegatur,' and again (*Epist.* 43), 'Soli cum episcopis non
sint, qui contra episcopos rebellarunt.'

[149]See especially *Epist.* 3, 43, 55, 59, 73 and above all 66 (*ad Pupianum*).

Such a development involves no new principle and must be regarded chiefly in its practical bearings. It is plainly competent for the Church at any given time to entrust a particular office with larger powers, as the emergency may require. And, though the grounds on which the independent authority of the episcopate was at times defended may have been false or exaggerated, no reasonable objection can be taken to later forms of ecclesiastical polity because the measure of power accorded to the bishop does not remain exactly the same as in the Church of the subapostolic ages.

Nay, to many thoughtful and dispassionate minds even the gigantic power wielded by the popes during the middle ages will appear justifiable in itself (though they will repudiate the false pretensions on which it was founded, and the false opinions which were associated with it), since only by such a providential concentration of authority could the Church, humanly speaking, have braved the storms of those ages of anarchy and violence. Now however it is my purpose to investigate the origin and growth of a new principle, which is nowhere enunciated in the New Testament, but which notwithstanding has worked its way into general recognition and seriously modified the character of later Christianity. The progress of the *sacerdotal* view of the ministry is one of the most striking and important phenomena in the history of the Church.

It has been pointed out already that the sacerdotal functions and privileges, which alone are mentioned in the Apostolic writings, pertain to all believers alike and do not refer solely or specially to the ministerial office. If to this statement it be objected that the inference is built upon the *silence* of the Apostles and Evangelists, and that such reasoning is always precarious, the reply is that an exclusive sacerdotalism (as the word is commonly understood)[150] contradicts the general tenor of the Gospel. But indeed the strength or weakness of an argument drawn from silence depends wholly on the circumstance under which the silence is maintained. And in this case it cannot be

---

[150]In speaking of sacerdotalism, I assume the term to have essentially the same force as when at a later date it was certainly applied to the Jewish priesthood. In a certain sense (to be considered hereafter) all officers appointed to minister 'for men in things pertaining to God' may be called priests; and sacerdotal phraseology when first applied to the Christian ministry, may have borne this innocent meaning. But at a later date, it was certainly so used to imply a substantial identity of character with the Jewish priesthood, i.e. to designate the Christian minister as one who offers sacrifices; and makes atonement for the, sins of others.

considered devoid of weight. In the Pastoral Epistles for instance, which are largely occupied with questions relating to the Christian ministry, it seems scarcely possible that this aspect should have been overlooked, if it had any place in St. Paul's teaching.

The Apostle discusses at length the requirements, the responsibilities, the sanctions, of the ministerial office: he regards the presbyter as an example, as a teacher, as a philanthropist, as a ruler. How then, it may well be asked, are the sacerdotal functions, the sacerdotal privileges, of the office wholly set aside? If these claims were recognised by him at all, they must necessarily have taken a foremost place. The same argument again applies with not less force to those passages in the Epistles to the Corinthians, where St. Paul asserts his apostolic authority against his detractors. Nevertheless, so entirely had the primitive conception of the Christian Church been supplanted by this sacerdotal view of the ministry, before the northern races were converted to the Gospel, and the dialects derived from the Latin took the place of the ancient tongue, that the languages of modern Europe very generally supply only one word to represent alike the priest of the Jewish or Heathen ceremonial and the presbyter of the Christian ministry.[151]

For, though no distinct traces of sacerdotalism are visible in the ages immediately after the Apostles, yet having once taken root in the Church it shot up rapidly into maturity. Towards the close of the second century we discern the first germs appearing above the surface, yet, shortly after the middle of the third, the plant has all but attained its full growth. The origin of this idea,

---

[151]It is a significant fact that in those languages which have only one word to express the two ideas, this word etymologically represents 'presbyterus' and not 'sacerdos,' e.g. the French *pretre*, the German *priester*, and the English priest; thus showing that the sacerdotal idea was imported and not original. In the Italian, where two words *prete* and *sacerdote* exist side by side, there is no marked difference in usage, except that *prete* is the more common. If the latter brings out the sacerdotal idea more prominently, the former is also applied to Jewish and Heathen priests and therefore distinctly involves this idea. Wiclif version of the New Testament naturally conforms to the Vulgate, in which it seems to be the rule to translate πρεσβύτεροι by 'presbyteri' (in Wiclif 'preestes') where it obviously denotes the second order in the ministry (e.g. Acts 24:23; 1 Tim 5:17, 19; Tit 1:5; James 5:14), and by 'seniores' (in Wiclif 'eldres' or 'elder men') in other passages, but if so, this rule is not always successfully applied (e.g. Acts 11:30; 21:18; 1 Pet 5:1). A doubt about the meaning may explain the anomaly that the word is translated 'presbyteri,' 'preestes,' Acts 15:2, and 'seniores,' 'elder men,' Acts 15:4, 6, 22; 16:4; though the persons intended are the same. In Acts 20:17, it is rendered in Wiclif's version 'the grettist men of birthe,' a misunderstanding of the Vulgate 'majores natu.' The English versions of the Reformers and the reformed church from Tyndale downwards translate πρεσβύτεροι uniformly by 'elders.'

the progress of its development, and the conditions favourable to its spread, will be considered in the present section of this essay.

A separation of orders, it is true, appeared at a much earlier date, and was in some sense involved in the appointment of a special ministry. This, and not more than this, was originally contained in the distinction of clergy and laity. If the sacerdotal view of the ministry engrafted itself on this distinction, it nevertheless was not necessarily implied or even indirectly suggested thereby. The term 'clerus,' as a designation of the ministerial office, did not owing to any existing associations convey the idea of sacerdotal functions. The word is not used of the Aaronic priesthood in any special sense that would explain its transference to the Christian ministry. It is indeed said of the Levites that they have no 'clerus' in the land, the Lord Himself being their 'clerus.'[152] But the Jewish priesthood is never described conversely as the special 'clerus' of Yahweh, while on the other hand the metaphor thus inverted is more than once applied to the whole Israelite people.[153] Up to this point, therefore the analogy of Old Testament usage would have suggested 'clerus' as a name rather for the entire body of the faithful than for the ministry specially or exclusively. Nor do other references to the *clerus* or lot in connection with the Levitical priesthood countenance its special application. The tithes, it is true, were assigned to the sons of Levi as their 'clerus,'[154] but in this there is nothing distinctive, and in fact the word is employed much more prominently in describing the lands allotted to the whole people. Again the courses of priests and Levites selected to conduct the temple-service were appointed by lot[155] but the mode adopted in distributing a particular set of duties is far too special to have supplied a distinctive name for the whole order. If indeed it were an established fact that the Aaronic priesthood at the time of the Christian era commonly bore the name of 'clergy' we might be driven to explain the designation in this or in some similar way, but apparently no evidence of

---

[152]Deut 10:9; 18:1, 2; comp. Num 26:62; Deut 12:12; 14:27, 29; Josh 14:3. Jerome (*Epist.* lii. 5, i. p. 258) says, 'Propterea vocantur clerici, vel quia de sorte sunt Domini, vel quia ipse Dominus sors, id est pars, clericorum est.' The former explanation would be reasonable, if it were supported by the language of the Old Testament. The latter is plainly inadequate.

[153]Deut 4:20. Comp. Deut 9:29 LXX.

[154]Num 18:22, 24, 26.

[155]1 Chron 24:5, 7, 21; 25:8, 9.

any such usage exists,[156] and it is therefore needless to cast about for an explanation of a fact which itself is only conjectural. The origin of the term clergy, as applied to the Christian ministry, must be sought elsewhere.

And the record of the earliest appointment made by the Christian Church after the Ascension of the Lord seems to supply the clue. Exhorting the assembled brethren to elect a successor in place of Judas, St Peter tells them that the traitor 'had been numbered among them and had received the lot (κλῆρος) of the ministry,' while in the account of the subsequent proceedings it is recorded that the Apostles 'distributed *lots*' to the brethren, and that 'the lot fell on Matthias and he was added to the eleven Apostles.'[157] The following therefore seems to be the sequence of meanings, by which κλῆρος the word arrived at this peculiar sense: (1) the lot by which the office was assigned; (2) the office thus assigned by lot; (3) the body of persons holding the office. The first two senses are illustrated by the passages quoted from the Acts; and from the second to the third the transition is easy and natural. It must not be supposed however that the mode of appointing officers by lot prevailed generally in the early Church. Besides the case of Matthias no other instance is recorded in the New Testament; nor is this procedure likely to have been commonly adopted. But just as in the passage quoted the word is used to describe the office of Judas, though Judas was certainly not selected by lot, so generally from signifying one special mode of appointment to office it got to signify office in the Church generally.[158]

If this account of the application of 'clerus' to the Christian ministry be correct, we should expect to find it illustrated by a corresponding progress in the actual usage of the word. And this is in fact the case. The sense 'clerical appointment or office' chronologically precedes the sense 'clergy.' The former

---

[156]On the other hand, λαός is used of the people as contrasted either with the rulers or with the priests. From this latter contrast comes λαϊκός 'laic' or 'profane,' and λαϊκόω 'profane' which, though not found in the LXX, occur frequently in the versions of Aquila, Symmachus, and Theodotion (λαϊκός, 1 Sam 21:4; 5:3; Ezek 48:15; λαϊκόω, Deut 20:6; 38:30; Ruth 1:12; Ezek 7:22) comp. Glem. Rome 40.

[157]Acts 1:17—κατηριθμημένος ἦν ἐν ἡμῖν καὶ ἔλαχεν τὸν κλῆρον τῆς διακονίας ταύτης. The use of the word in 1 Pet 5:3—ὡς κατακυριεύοντες τῶν κλήρων (i.e. the flocks assigned to them), does not illustrate this meaning.

[158]See Clem. Alex. *Quis div. salv.* 42, where κλῆρον is 'to appoint to the ministry'; and comp. Iren. iii. 3. 3. A similar extension of meaning is seen in this same word κλῆρος applied to land. Signifying originally a piece ground assigned by lot, it gets to mean landed property generally, whether obtained by assignment or by inheritance or in any other way.

meaning occurs several times in Irenaeus. He speaks of Hyginus as 'holding the ninth *clerus* of the episcopal succession from the Apostles' (Iren. i.21.1); and of Eleutherus in like manner he says, 'He now occupies the *clerus* of the episcopate in the tenth place from the Apostles' (Iren. iii.3.3).[159] On the other hand the earliest instance of 'clerus,' meaning clergy, seems to occur in Tertullian who belongs to the next generation.[160]

It will thus be seen that the use of 'clerus' to denote the ministry cannot be traced to the Jewish priesthood, and is therefore wholly unconnected with any sacerdotal views. The term does indeed recognise the *clergy* as an order distinct from the laity; but this is a mere question of ecclesiastical rule or polity, and involves no doctrinal bearings. The origin of sacerdotal phraseology and ideas must be sought elsewhere. Attention has been already directed to the absence of any appeal to sacerdotal claims in the Pastoral Epistles. The silence of the Apostolic fathers deserves also to be noticed. Though the genuine letters of all three may be truly said to hinge on questions relating to the ministry, no distinct traces of this influence are visible. St. Clement, as the representative of the Roman Church, writes to the Christian brotherhood at Corinth, offering friendly counsel in their disputes and rebuking their factious and unworthy conduct towards certain presbyters whom, though blameless, they had ejected from office. He appeals to motives of Christian love, to principles of Christian order. He adduces a large number of examples from biblical history condemnatory of jealousy and insubordination. He urges that men, who had been appointed directly by the Apostles or by persons themselves so appointed, ought to have received better treatment. Dwelling at great length on the subject, he nevertheless advances no sacerdotal claims or immunities on behalf of the ejected ministers. He does, it is true, adduce the Aaronic priesthood and the Temple service as showing that God has appointed set persons and set places and will have all things done in order. He had before illustrated this lesson by the

---

[159]In this passage, however, as in the preceding one, the word is explained by a qualifying genitive. In Hippolytus *Haers.* ix.12 it is used absolutely of 'clerical offices.' The Epistle of the Gallican Churches (Eusebius, *Hist. Eccles.* v.1) speaks more of the κλῆρος 'of the martyrs' i.e. the order or rank of the martyrs, Comp. Test. Xii Patriarchs Levi 8. See Ritschl, p. 390sq. to whom I am indebted for several of the passages quoted.

[160]E.g *de Monog.* 12 'Unde enim episcopi et clerus?' and again 'Extollimur et inflamur adversus clerum.' Perhaps however earlier instances may have escaped notice. In Clem. *Quis div. salv.* 42 the word seems not to be used in this sense.

subordination of ranks in an army, and by the relation of the different members of the human body. He had insisted on the duties of the strong towards the weak, of the rich towards the poor, of the wise towards the ignorant, and so forth. He had enforced the appeal by reminding his readers of the utter feebleness and insignificance of man in the sight of God, as represented in the Scriptures of the Old Testament; and then follows the passage which contains the allusion in question: 'He hath not commanded (the offerings and ministrations) to be performed at random or in disorder, but at fixed times and seasons; and where and through whom He willeth them to be performed, He hath ordained by His supreme will. They therefore who make their offerings at the appointed seasons are acceptable and blessed, since following the ordinances of the Master they do not go wrong. For to the high priest peculiar services are entrusted, and the priests have their peculiar office assigned to them, and on Levites peculiar ministrations are imposed. The layman is bound by lay ordinances. Let each of you brethren, in his own rank give thanks to God, retaining a good conscience, not transgressing the appointed rule of his service (λειτουργία)' etc.[161]

Here it is clear that in St. Clement's conception the sanction possessed in common by the Aaronic priesthood and the Christian ministry is not the sacerdotal consecration, but the divinely appointed order. He passes over in silence the numerous passages in the Old Testament which enjoin obedience to the priests; while the only sentence (§ 42) which he puts forward as anticipating and enforcing the authority of the Christian ministry is a misquoted and misinterpreted verse from Isaiah; 'I will establish their overseers (bishops) in righteousness and their ministers (deacons) in faith.'[162] Again a little later he mentions in illustration the murmuring of the Israelites that was rebuked by the budding of Aaron's rod (Clem. Rom., 43). But here too

---

[161]Clem. Rom. 40, 41. Neander, *Church History*, i. p. 272 note, Bohn's translation conjectures that this passage is an 'interpolation from a hierarchical interest,' and Dean Milman (*Hist. of Christianity*, III. p. 259) says that it is 'rejected by all judicious and impartial scholars.' At the risk of forfeiting all claim to judiciousness and impartiality one may venture to demur from this arbitrary criticism. Indeed the recent discovery of a second independent ms. and of a Syriac Version, both containing the suspected passage may be regarded as decisive on this point.

[162]Isaiah 60:7 where the A.V. correctly renders the original 'I will also make thy officers (literally magistrates) peace and thine exactors (i.e. task-masters) righteousness'; i.e. there shall be no tyranny or oppression. The LXX departs from the original and Clement has altered the LXX. By this double divergence, a reference to the two orders of ministry is obtained.

he makes it clear how far he considers the analogy to extend. He calls the sedition in the case 'jealousy concerning the priesthood' in the other 'strife concerning the honour of the episcopate.'[163] He keeps the names and the offices distinct. The significance of this fact will be felt at once by comparing his language with the expressions used by any later writer, such as Cyprian, who was penetrated with the spirit of sacerdotalism.

Of St. Ignatius, as the champion of episcopacy, much has been said already. It is sufficient to add here, that he never regards the ministry as a sacerdotal office. This is equally true, whether we accept as genuine the whole of the seven letters in the Short Greek, or only those portions contained in the Syriac version. While these letters teem with passages enjoining the strictest obedience to bishops, while their language is frequently so strong as to sound almost profane, this father never once appeals to sacerdotal claims,[164] though such an appeal would have made his case more than doubly strong. If it be ever safe to take the sentiments of an individual writer as expressing the belief of his age, we may infer from the silence which pervades these letters, that the sacerdotal view of the ministry had not yet found its way into the Christian Church.

When we pass on to the third Apostolic father, the same phenomenon is repeated. Polycarp, like Clement and Ignatius, occupies much space in discussing the duties and the claims of Christian ministers. He takes occasion especially to give his correspondents advice as to a certain presbyter who had disgraced his office by a grave offense.[165] Yet he again knows nothing, or at least says nothing, of any sacerdotal privileges which claimed respect, or of any sacerdotal sanctity which has been violated. Justin Martyr writes about a generation later. He speaks at length and with emphasis on the eucharistic offerings. Here at least we might expect to find sacerdotal views of the

---

[163]Contrast § 43 to § 44. The common feature which connects the two offices together is stated in the words, in §43—'in order that there not be ἀκαταστάσια.'

[164]Some passages are quoted in Greenwood, *Cathedra Petri* I. p. 73 as tending in this direction, e.g. *Philad.* 9. But rightly interpreted they do not favor this view. In the passage quoted for instance, the writer seems to be maintaining the superiority of the new covenant, as represented by the great High-Priest (ἀρχιερεύς) in and through whom the whole Church has access to God, over the old dispensation of the Levitical priesthood (ἱερωσύνη). If this interpretation be correct, the passage echoes the teaching of of the Epistle to the Hebrews and is opposed to exclusive sacerdotalism. On the meaning of θυσιαστήριον in the Ignatian Epistles, see below.

[165]See Lightfoot, *Philippians*, p. 63sq.

Christian ministry propounded. Yet this is far from being the case. He does indeed lay stress on sacerdotal functions, but these belong to the whole body of the Church, and are not in any way the exclusive right of the clergy. 'So we,' he writes, when arguing against Trypho the Jew, 'who through the name of Jesus have believed as one man in God the maker of the universe, having divested ourselves of our filthy garments, that is our sins, through the name of His first-born Son, and having been refined (πυρωθέντες) by the word of His calling, are the true high-priestly race of God, as God Himself also beareth witness, saying that in every place among the Gentiles are men offering sacrifices well-pleasing unto Him and pure (Mai. i.11). Yet God doth not receive sacrifices from any one, except through His priests. Therefore God, anticipating all sacrifices through this name, that Jesus Christ ordained to be offered, I mean those offered by the Christians in every region of the earth with (ἐπί) the thanksgiving (the eucharist) of the bread and of the cup, beareth witness that they are well-pleasing to Him; but the sacrifices offered by you and through those your priests He rejects, saying, "And your sacrifices I will not accept from your hands" etc. (Mai. i. 10).'[166] The whole Christian people therefore (such is Justin's conception) have not only taken the place of the Aaronic priesthood, but have become a nation of high-priests, being made one with the great High-Priest of the new covenant and presenting their eucharistic offerings in His name.

Another generation leads us from Justin Martyr to Irenaeus. When Irenaeus writes, the second century is very far advanced. Yet still the silence that has accompanied us hitherto remains unbroken. And here again it is important to observe that Irenaeus, if he held the sacerdotal view, had every motive for urging it, since the importance and authority of the episcopate occupy a large space in his teaching. Nevertheless he not only withholds this title as a special designation of the Christian ministry, but advances an entirely different view of the priestly office. He recognises only the priesthood of moral holiness, the priesthood of apostolic self-denial. Thus commenting on the reference made by our Lord to the incident in David's life where the king and his followers eat the shew-bread, 'which it is not lawful to eat save for the priests alone,' Irenaeus remarks (*Haers*. iv.8.3): 'He excuses His disciples by the

---

[166]*Dialogue with Trypho*, c.116, 117, p. 344.

words of the law, and signifies that it is lawful for priests to act freely. For David had been called to be a priest in the sight of God, although Saul carried on a persecution against him; for all just men belong to the sacerdotal order.[167] Now all apostles of the Lord are priests, for they inherit neither lands nor houses here, but ever attend on the altar and on God. "Who are they," he goes on, "that have left father and mother and have renounced all their kindred for the sake of the word of God and His covenant, but the disciples of the Lord?" Of these Moses says again, "But they shall have no inheritance; for the Lord Himself shall be their inheritance," and again, "The Priests, the Levites, in the whole tribe of Levi shall have no part nor inheritance with Israel, the first-fruits (*fructificationes*) of the Lord are their inheritance, they shall eat them." For this reason also Paul says, "I require not the gift, but I require the fruit." The disciples of the Lord, he would say, were allowed when hungry to take food of the seeds (they had sown): for "The laborer is worthy of his food.'"

Again, striking upon the same topic in a later passage (*Haers.* v.34.3), and commenting on the words of Jeremiah (Jer 31:14), 'I will intoxicate the soul of the priests the sons of Levi, and my people shall be filled with my good things,' he adds, 'we have shown in a former book, that all disciples of the Lord are priests and Levites: who also profaned the Sabbath in the temple and are blameless.' Thus Irenaeus too recognizes the whole body of the faithful under the new dispensation as the counterparts of the sons of Levi under the old. The position of the Apostles and Evangelists has not yet been abandoned.

A few years later, but still before the close of the century, Polycrates of Ephesus writes to Victor of Rome. Incidentally he speaks of St. John as 'having been made a priest' and 'wearing the mitre,'[168] and this might seem to be a distinct expression of sacerdotal views, for the 'mitre' to which he alludes is doubtless the tiara of the Jewish high-priest. But it may very reasonably be questioned if this is the correct meaning of the passage. Whether St. John did actually wear this decoration of the high-priestly office, or

---

[167]This sentence is cited by John Damascene and Antonius . . . but the words were quoted doubtless from memory by the one writer and and borrowed by the other from him. βασιλεύς is not represented in the Latin and does not suit the context. The close conformity of their quotations from the Ignatian letters is a sufficient proof that these two writers are not independent authorities; see the passages in Cureton's *Corp.* Ignat. p. 180sq.

[168]In Euseb. *Hist. Eccles.* v. 24, Comp. Tertullian, *adv. Jud.* 14 'exornatus podere et mitra'; Test. xii. Patr. *Levi* 8. See also, as an illustration of the metaphor, Tertull. *Monog.* 12 'Cum ad peraequationem disciplinae sacerdotalis provocamur, *deponimus infulas.*'

whether Polycrates has mistaken a symbolical expression in some earlier writer for an actual fact, or whether lastly his language itself should be treated as a violent metaphor, I have had occasion to discuss elsewhere.[169] But in any case the notice is explained by the language of St. John himself, who regards the whole body of believers as high-priests of the new covenant;[170] and it is certain that the contemporaries of Polycrates still continued to hold similar language.[171] As a figurative expression or as a literal fact, the notice points to St. John as the veteran teacher, the chief representative, of a pontifical race. On the other hand, it is possible that this was not the sense which Polycrates himself attached to the figure or the fact, and if so, we have here perhaps the earliest passage in any extant Christian writing where the sacerdotal view of the ministry is distinctly put forward.

Clement of Alexandria was a contemporary of Polycrates. Though his extant writings are considerable in extent and though they are largely occupied with questions of Christian ethics and social life, the ministry does not hold a prominent place in them. In the few passages where he mentions it, he does not betray any tendency to sacerdotal or even to hierarchical views. The bias of his mind indeed lay in an opposite direction. He would be much more inclined to maintain an aristocracy of intellectual contemplation than of sacerdotal office. And in Alexandria generally, as we have seen, the development of the hierarchy was slower than in other churches. How far he is from maintaining a sacerdotal view of the ministry and how substantially he coincides with Irenaeus in this respect, will appear from the following passage: 'It is possible for men even now, by exercising themselves in the commandments of the Lord and by living a perfect gnostic life in obedience to the Gospel, to be inscribed in the roll of the Apostles. Such men are genuine presbyters of the Church and true deacons of the will of God, if they practice and teach the things of the Lord, being not indeed ordained by men nor considered righteous because they are presbyters, but enrolled in the presbytery because they are righteous: and though here on earth they may not be honored with a chief seat, yet shall they sit on the four and twenty thrones judging the peoples' (*Strom.* vi.13, p. 793). It is quite consistent with this truly

---

[169]*Dissertations on the Apostolic Age*, p. 121, note.
[170]Rev 2:17, see the commentators.
[171]So Justin in *Dialog. w. Tryph.* § 116. See also the passage of Origen quoted below.

spiritual view, that he should elsewhere recognise the presbyter, the deacon, and the layman, as distinct orders (*Strom.* iii.90, p. 552). But on the other hand he never uses the words 'priest', 'priestly', 'priesthood', of the Christian ministry. In one passage, indeed, he contrasts laity and priesthood, but without any such reference. Speaking of the veil of the temple and assigning to it a symbolical meaning, he describes it as 'a barrier against laic unbelief', behind which 'the priestly ministration is hidden' (Strom. v.33sq. p. 665sq.).[172] Here the laymen and the priests are respectively those who reject and those who appropriate the spiritual mysteries of the Gospel. Accordingly in the context, St. Clement, following up the hint thrown out in the Epistle to the Hebrews, gives a spiritual meaning to all the furniture of the holy place.

His younger contemporary Tertullian is the first to assert direct sacerdotal claims on behalf of the Christian ministry. Of the heretics he complains that they impose sacerdotal functions on laymen.[173] 'The right of giving baptism', he says elsewhere, 'belongs to the chief priest (*summus sacerdos*), that is, the bishop' (*de Baptismo* 17). 'No woman', he asserts, 'ought to teach, baptize, celebrate the eucharist, or arrogate to herself the performance of any duty pertaining to males, much less of the sacerdotal office' (*de Virg. Vel.* 9). And generally he uses the words *sacerdos, sacerdotium, sacerdotalis,* of the Christian ministry. It seems plain moreover from his mode of speaking, that such language was not peculiar to himself but passed current in the churches among which he moved. Yet he himself supplies the true counterpoise to this special sacerdotalism in his strong assertion of the universal priesthood of all true believers. 'We should be foolish', so he writes when arguing against second marriages, 'to suppose that a latitude is allowed to laymen which is denied to priests. Are not we laymen also priests? It is written, "He hath also made us a kingdom and priests to God and His Father." It is the authority of the Church that makes a difference between the order (the clergy) and the people—this authority and the consecration of their rank by the assignment of special benches to the clergy. Thus where there is no bench of clergy, you present the eucharistic offerings and baptize and are your own sole priest. For where three are gathered together, there is a church, even though they be

---

[172]Kaye (*Clement of Alexandria* p. 464) incorrectly adduces this passage as an express mention of 'the distinction between the clergy and laity.'

[173]*De Praescr. Haer.* 41 'Nam et laicis sacerdotalia munera injungunt.'

laymen. Therefore if you exercise the rights of a priest in cases of necessity, it is your duty also to observe the discipline enjoined on a priest, where of necessity you exercise the rights of a priests.'[174]

And in another treatise he writes in bitter irony, 'When we begin to exalt and inflame ourselves against the clergy, then we are all one; then we are all priests, because, "He made us priests to God and His Father," but when we are required to submit ourselves equally to the priestly discipline, we throw off our fillets and are no longer equal.'[175] These passages, it is true, occur in treatises probably written after Tertullian had become wholly or in part a Montanist, but this consideration is of little consequence, for they bear witness to the fact that the scriptural doctrine of an universal priesthood was common ground to himself and his opponents, and had not yet been obscured by the sacerdotal view of the Christian ministry.[176]

An incidental expression in Hippolytus serves to show that a few years later than Tertullian sacerdotal terms were commonly used to designate the different orders of the clergy. 'We,' says the zealous bishop of Pontus, 'being successors of the Apostles and partaking of the same grace both of high-priesthood and of teaching and accounted guardians of the Church, do not close our eyes drowsily or tacitly suppress the true word, etc.' (*Haers. proem* p. 3).

The march of sacerdotal ideas was probably slower at Alexandria than at Carthage or Rome. Though belonging to the next generation, Origen's views are hardly so advanced as those of Tertullian. In the temple of the Church, he says, there are two sanctuaries: the heavenly, accessible only to Jesus Christ, our great High-Priest; the earthly, open to all priests of the new covenant, that is, to all faithful believers. For Christians are a sacerdotal race and therefore have access to the outer sanctuary. There they must present their offerings, their holocausts of love and self-denial. From this

---

[174]*De Exh. Cast.* 7. See Kaye's *Tertullian* p. 211 whose interpretation of 'honor per ordinis consessum sanctificatus' I have adopted.

[175]*De Monog.* 12. I have taken the reading 'impares' for 'pares,' as required by the context.

[176]Tertullian regards Christ our great High-Priest, as the counterpart under the new dispensation of the priest under the old, and so interprets the text 'Show thyself to the priest'; *adv. Marc.* iv. 9, *adv. Jud.* 14. Again, he uses 'sacerdos' in a moral sense, *de Spectac.* 16 'sacerdotes pacis,' *de Cult. Fem.* ii.12 'sacerdotes pudicitiae,' *ad Uxor.* i. 6 (comp. 7) 'virginitatis et viduitatis sacerdotia.' On the other hand in *de Pall.* 4 he seems to compare the Christian minister with the heathen priests but too much stress must not be placed on a rhetorical image.

outer sanctuary our High-Priest takes the fire, as He enters the Holy of Holies to offer incense to the Father (see Lev 16:12).[177] Very many professed Christians, he writes elsewhere (I am here abridging his words), occupied chiefly with the concerns of this world and dedicating few of their actions to God, are represented by the tribes, who merely present their tithes and first-fruits. On the other hand 'those who are devoted to the divine word, and are dedicated sincerely to the sole worship of God, may not unreasonably be called priests and Levites according to the difference in this respect of their impulses tending thereto.' Lastly 'those who excel the men of their own generation perchance will be high-priests.' They are only high-priests however after the order of Aaron, our Lord Himself being High-Priest after the order of Melchizedek.[178] Again in a third place he says, 'The Apostles and they that are made like unto the Apostles, being priests after the order of the great High-Priest, having received the knowledge of the worship of God and being instructed by the Spirit, know for what sins they ought to offer sacrifices, etc.'[179] In all these passages Origen has taken spiritual enlightenment and not sacerdotal office to be the Christian counterpart to the Aaronic priesthood. Elsewhere however he makes use of sacerdotal terms to describe the ministry of the Church;[180] and in one place distinguishes the priests and the Levites as representing the presbyters and deacons respectively.[181]

Hitherto the sacerdotal view of the Christian ministry has not been held apart from a distinct recognition of the sacerdotal functions of the whole Christian body. The minister is thus regarded as a priest, because he is the mouthpiece, the representative, of a priestly race. Such appears to be the conception of Tertullian, who speaks of the clergy as separate from the laity

---

[177] *Hom. ix. in Lev.* 9, 10 (II. p. 243 Delarue).

[178] *In Joann.* i. § 3 (iv. p. 3).

[179] *De Orat.* 28 (i. p. 255). See also *Hom. iv. in Num* 3 (ii. p. 283).

[180] *Hom. v. in Lev* 4 (ii. p. 208 sq.) 'Discant sacerdotes Domini qui ecclesiis praesunt,' and also ib. *Hom.* ii. 4 (ii. p. 191) 'Cum non erubescit sacerdoti Domini indicare peccatum suum et quaerere medicinam' (he quotes James 5:14 in illustration). But *Hom.* x in Num 1, 2 (II, p. 302) quoted by Redepenning (*Origenes* II, p.417) hardly this sense, for the 'pontifex' applies to our Lord, and it is clear from *Hom. in Ps.* xxxvii. § 6 (ii. p. 688) that in Origen's opinion the confessor to the penitent need not be an ordained minister. The passages in Redepenning's *Origenes* bearing on this subject are i, p. 357, ii. pp. 250, 417, 436 sq.

[181] *Hom. xii. in Jerem.* 3 (iii. (ii. p. 196) 'If any one therefore, among these priests (I mean us, the presbyters) or among these Levites who stand about the people (I mean the deacons)' etc.

only because the Church, in the exercise of her prerogative, has for convenience entrusted to them the performance of certain sacerdotal functions
belonging properly to the whole congregation, and of Origen, who, giving a
moral and spiritual interpretation to the sacerdotal office, considers the
priesthood of the clergy to differ from the priesthood of the laity only in
degree, in so far as the former devote their time and their thoughts more
entirely to God than the latter. So long as this important aspect is kept in
view, so long as the priesthood of the ministry is regarded as springing from
the priesthood of the whole body, the teaching of the Apostles has not been
directly violated. But still it was not a safe nomenclature which assigned the
terms *sacerdos*, ἱερεύς, and the like, to the ministry, as a special designation.
The appearance of this phenomenon marks the period of transition from the
universal sacerdotalism of the New Testament to the particular sacerdotalism of a later age.

   If Tertullian and Origen are still hovering on the border, Cyprian has
boldly transferred himself into the new domain. It is not only that he uses
the terms *sacerdos, sacerdotium, sacerdotalis*, of the ministry with a frequency hitherto without parallel. But he treats all the passages in the Old
Testament that refer to the privileges, the sanctions, the duties, and the responsibilities of the Aaronic priesthood, as applying to the officers of the
Christian Church. His opponents are profane and sacrilegious; they have
passed sentence of death on themselves by disobeying the command of the
Lord in Deuteronomy to 'hear the priest';[182] they have forgotten the in-
junction of Solomon to honor and reverence God's priests;[183] they have de-
spised the example of St. Paul who regretted that he 'did not know it was the
high priest';[184] they have been guilty of the sin of Korah, Dathan, and
Abiram.[185] These passages are urged again and again. They are urged
moreover, as applying not by parity of reasoning, not by analogy of circumstance, but as absolute and immediate and unquestionable. As Cyprian
crowned the edifice of episcopal power, so also was he the first to put forward
without relief or disguise the sacerdotal assumptions; and so uncompromising

---

[182]Deut 17:12; see *Epist.* 3, 4, 43, 59, 66.
[183]Though the words are ascribed to Solomon, the quotation comes from Ecclus. vii. 29, 31; see
   Epist. 3.
[184]Acts 23:4; see *Epist.* 3, 59, 66.
[185]*De Unit. Eccl* p. 83 (Fell), *Epist.* 3, 67, 69, 73.

was the tone in which he asserted them, that nothing was left to his successors but to enforce his principles and reiterate his language.[186]

After thus tracing the gradual departure from the Apostolic teaching in the encroachment of the sacerdotal on the pastoral and ministerial view of the clergy, it will be instructive to investigate the causes to which this divergence from primitive truth may be ascribed. To the question whether the change was due to Jewish or Gentile influences, opposite answers have been given. To some it has appeared as a reproduction of the Aaronic priesthood, due to Pharisaic tendencies, such as we find among St. Paul's converts in Galatia and at Corinth, still lingering in the Church. To others, as imported into Christianity by the ever-increasing mass of heathen converts who were incapable of shaking off their sacerdotal prejudices and appreciating the free spirit of the Gospel. The latter view seems correct in the main, but requires some modification. At all events so far as the evidence of extant writings goes, there is no reason for supposing that Jewish sacerdotalism was especially rife among the Jewish Christian converts. The Testaments of the Twelve Patriarchs may be taken to represent one phase of Judaic Christianity; the Clementine writings exhibit another. In both alike there is an entire absence of sacerdotal views of the ministry. The former work indeed dwells at length on our Lord's office, as the descendant and heir of Levi and alludes more than once to His institution of a new priesthood; but this priesthood is spiritual and comprehensive. Christ Himself is the High-Priest (*Reuben* 6; *Symeon* 7; *Levi* 18), and the sacerdotal office is described as being 'after the type of the Gentiles, extending to all the Gentiles' (*Levi* 8). On the Christian ministry the writer is silent. In the Clementine Homilies the case is somewhat different, but the inference is still more obvious. Though the episcopate is regarded as the backbone of the Church, though the claims of the ministry are urged with great distinctness, no appeal is ever made to priestly sanctity as the ground of this exalted estimate. Indeed the hold of the Levitical priesthood on the mind of the pious Jew must have been materially weakened at the Christian era by the development of the synagogue organization on the one hand, and by the ever-growing influence of the learned and literary classes, the scribes and rabbis, on the other. The points

---

[186]The sacerdotal language in the *Apostolical Constitutions* is hardly less strong, while it is more systematic; but their date, is uncertain and cannot well be placed earlier than Cyprian.

THE EPISTLES OF 2 CORINTHIANS AND 1 PETER

on which the Judaizers of the Apostolic age insist are the rite of circumcision, the distinction of meats, the observance of sabbaths, and the like. The necessity of the priesthood was not, or at least is not known to have been, part of their programme. Among the Essene Jews especially, who went so far as to repudiate the temple sacrifices, no great importance could have been attached to the Aaronic priesthood[187] and after the Apostolic age at all events, the most active Judaizers of the Dispersion seem to have belonged to the Essene type. But indeed the overwhelming argument against ascribing the growth of sacerdotal views to Jewish influence lies in the fact, that there is a singular absence of distinct sacerdotalism during the first century and a half, when alone on any showing Judaism was powerful enough to impress itself on the belief of the Church at large.

It is therefore to Gentile feeling that this development must be ascribed. For the heathen, familiar with auguries, lustrations, sacrifices, and depending on the intervention of some priest for all the manifold religious rites of the state, the club, and the family, the sacerdotal functions must have occupied a far larger space in the affairs of everyday life, than for the Jew of the Dispersion who of necessity dispensed, and had no scruple at dispensing, with priestly ministrations from one year's end to the other. With this presumption drawn from probability the evidence of fact accords. In Latin Christendom, as represented by the Church of Carthage, the germs of the sacerdotal idea appear first and soonest ripen to maturity. If we could satisfy ourselves of the early date of the Ancient Syriac Documents lately published, we should have discovered another centre from which this idea was propagated. And so far their testimony may perhaps be accepted. Syria was at least a soil where such a plant would thrive and luxuriate. In no country of the civilized world was sacerdotal authority among the heathen greater. The most important centers of Syrian Christianity, Antioch and Emesa, were also the cradles of strongly-marked sacerdotal religions which at different times made their influence felt throughout the Roman empire.[188] This being

---

[187]*Dissertations on the Apostolic Age*, pp, 79, 82sq. 350; *Colossians* p. 89. In the syzygies of the *Clementine Homilies* (ii. 16, 33) Aaron is opposed to Moses, the high-priest to the lawgiver as the bad to the good, the false to the true, like Cain to Abel, Ishmael, to Isaac, etc. In the *Recognitions* the estimate of the High-Priest's position is still unfavourable (i. 46, 48). Compare the statement in Justin, *Dial. c. Tryph*, 117.

[188]The worship of the Syrian goddess of Antioch was among the most popular of oriental superstitions

so, it is a significant fact that the first instance of the term 'priest' applied to a Christian minister, occurs in a heathen writer. At least I have not found any example of this application earlier than Lucian *de Morte Peregrine*, 11.

But though the spirit, which imported the idea into the Church of Christ and sustained it there, was chiefly due to Gentile education, yet its form was almost as certainly derived from the Old Testament. And this is the modification which needs to be made in the statement, in itself substantially true, that sacerdotalism must be traced to the influence of Heathen rather than of Jewish converts.

In the Apostolic writings we find the terms 'offering,' 'sacrifice,' applied to certain conditions and actions of the Christian life. These sacrifices or offerings are described as spiritual (1 Pet 2:5), they consist of praise (Heb 13:15), of faith (Phil 2:17), of almsgiving (Acts 24:17; Phil 4:18; comp. Heb 13:16), of the devotion of the body (Rom 13:1), of the conversion of unbelievers (Rom 15:16), and the like. Thus whatever is dedicated to God's service may be included under this metaphor. In one passage also the image is so far extended, that the Apostolic writer speaks of an altar (Heb 13:10) pertaining to the spiritual service of the Christian Church. *If on this noble Scriptural language a false superstructure has been reared, we have here only one instance out of many, where the truth has been impaired by transferring statements from the region of metaphor to the region of fact.*

These 'sacrifices' were very frequently the acts not of the individual Christian, but of the whole congregation. Such for instance were the offerings of public prayer and thanksgiving, or the collection of alms on the first day of the week, or the contribution of food for the *agape*, and the like. In such cases, the congregation was represented by its minister, who thus acted as its mouthpiece and ministers, was said to 'present the offerings' to God. So the expression is used in the Epistle of St. Clement of Rome.[189] But in itself it involves no sacerdotal view. This ancient father regards the sacrifice or offering as the act of the whole

---

under the earlier Caesars; the rites of the Sun-god of Emesa became fashionable under Elagabalus.
[189]Clem. *Rom.* 44. What sort of offerings are meant, may be gathered from other passages in Clement's Epistle; e.g. § 35,§ 52 § 41 Comp. Heb 13:10, 15, 16—Ἔχομεν θυσιαστήριον ἐξ οὗ φαγεῖν οὐκ ἔχουσιν ἐξουσίαν οἱ τῇ σκηνῇ λατρεύοντες ... δι' αὐτοῦ οὖν ἀναφέρωμεν θυσίαν αἰνέσεως διὰ παντὸς τῷ Θεῷ, τοῦτ' ἔστιν καρπὸν χειλέων ὁμολογούντων τῷ ὀνόματι αὐτοῦ. τῆς δὲ εὐποιΐας καὶ κοινωνίας μὴ ἐπιλανθάνεσθε· τοιαύταις γὰρ θυσίαις εὐαρεστεῖται ὁ Θεός. The doctrine of the early Church respecting 'sacrifice' is investigated by Hofling, *die Lehre der altesten Kirche vom Opfer* (Erlangen 1851).

Church performed through its presbyters. The minister is a priest in the same sense only in which each individual member of the congregation is a priest. When St. Clement denounces those who usurp the functions of the presbyters, he reprobates their conduct not as an act of sacrilege but as a violation of order. He views the presbytery as an Apostolic ordinance, not as a sacerdotal caste.

Thus when this father speaks of the presbytery as 'presenting the offerings,' he uses an expression that, if not directly scriptural, is at least accordant with the tenor of Scripture. But from such language the transition to sacerdotal views was easy, where the sacerdotal spirit was rife. From being the act of the whole congregation, the sacrifice came to be regarded as the act of the minister who officiated on its behalf.

And this transition was moreover facilitated by the growing tendency to apply the terms 'sacrifice' and 'offering' exclusively or chiefly to the eucharistic service. It may be doubted whether, even as used by St. Clement, the expression may not have a special reference to this chief act of Christian dedication.[190] It is quite certain that writers belonging to the generations next following, Justin Martyr and Irenaeus for instances employ the terms very frequently with this reference. We may here reserve the question in what sense the celebration of the Lord's supper may or may not be truly called a sacrifice. The point to be noticed at present is this—that the offering of the eucharist, being regarded as the one special act of sacrifice and appearing externally to the eye as the act of the officiating minister, might well lead to the minister being called a priest and then being thought a priest in some exclusive sense, where the religious bias was in this direction and as soon as the true position of the minister as the representative of the congregation was lost sight of.

But besides the metaphor or the analogy of the sacrifice, there was another point of resemblance also between the Jewish priesthood and Christian ministry, which favoured the sacerdotal view of the latter. As soon as the episcopate and presbytery ceased to be regarded as sub-orders and were looked upon as distinct orders, the correspondence of the threefold ministry with the three

---

[190]On the whole however the passage from the Epistle Hebrews alluded to in the last note seems to be the best exponent of St. Clement's meaning, as he very frequently follows this Apostolic writer. If it has any special reference to the holy eucharist, as it may have, δωρά will nevertheless be the alms and prayers and thanksgivings that accompanied the celebration of it. Comp. *Const. Apostl.* ii.25 §27, §34.

ranks of the Levitical priesthood could not fail to suggest itself.[191] The solitary bishop represented the solitary high-priest; the principal acts of Christian sacrifice were performed by the presbyters, as the principal acts of Jewish sacrifice by the priests; and the attendant ministrations were assigned in the one case to the deacon, as in the other to the Levite. Thus the analogy seemed complete. To this correspondence however there was one grave impediment. The only High-Priest under the Gospel recognised by the Apostolic writings, is our Lord Himself. Accordingly in the Christian remains of the ages next succeeding this title is reserved as by right to Him,[192] and though belonging to various schools, all writers alike abstain from applying it to the bishop. Yet the scruple was at length set aside. When it had become usual to speak of the presbyters as '*sacerdotes*,' the designation of '*pontifex*' or '*summus sacerdos*' for the bishop was far too convenient and too appropriate to be neglected.

Thus the analogy of the sacrifices and the correspondence of the threefold order supplied the material on which the sacerdotal feeling worked. And in this way, by the union of Gentile sentiment with the ordinances of the Old Dispensation, the doctrine of an exclusive priesthood found its way into the Church of Christ.

How far is the language of the later Church justifiable? Can the Christian ministry be called a priesthood in any sense, and if so, in what sense? The historical investigation, which has suggested this question as its proper corollary, has also supplied the means of answering it.

Though different interpretations may be put upon the fact that the sacred writers throughout refrain from applying sacerdotal terms to the Christian ministry, I think it must be taken to signify this much at least, that this ministry, if a priesthood at all, it is a priesthood of a type essentially different from the Jewish. Otherwise we shall be perplexed to explain why the earliest Christian teachers should have abstained from using those terms that alone would adequately express to their hearers the one most important aspect of the ministerial office. It is often said in reply, that we have here a question

---

[191]The chief passages in these fathers related to Christian oblations are Justin *Apol.* I 13 (p. 60), 65-67 (p. 97sq.), *Dial.* 28, 29 (p. 246), 41 (p. 259sq.), 116, 117 (p. 344 sq.), Iren. *Haer.* iv. cc. 17, 18, 19, v.2.3, Fragm. 38 (Stieren). The place occupied by the eucharistic elements in their view of sacrifice will only be appreciated by reading the passages continuously.

[192]See Clem. Rom. 36, 58, Polyc. *Phil.* 129, Ignat. *Philad.* 7, Test. xii. Patr. *Rub.* 6, *Sym.* 7 etc., Clem. *Recogn.* i.48.

not of words, but of things. This is undeniable, *but words express things*, and the silence of the Apostles still requires an explanation.

However the interpretation of this fact is not far to seek. The Epistle to the Hebrews speaks at great length on priests and sacrifices in their Jewish and their Christian bearing. It is plain from this epistle, as it may be gathered also from other notices, Jewish and Heathen, that the one prominent idea of the priestly office at this time was the function of offering sacrifice and thereby making atonement. Now this Apostolic writer teaches that all sacrifices had been consummated in the one Sacrifice, all priesthoods absorbed in the one Priest. The offering had been made once for all, and, as there were no more victims, there could be no more priests.[193] All former priesthoods had borne witness to the necessity of a human mediator, and this sentiment had its satisfaction in the Person and Office of the Son of Man. All past sacrifices had proclaimed the need of an atoning death, and had their antitype, their realization, their annulment, in the Cross of Christ. This explicit statement supplements and interprets the silence elsewhere noticed in the Apostolic writings.

Strictly accordant too with the general tenor of his argument is the language used throughout by the writer of this epistle. He speaks of Christian sacrifices, of a Christian altar; but the sacrifices are praise and thanksgiving and well-doing, the altar is apparently the Cross of Christ.[194] If the Christian

---

[193]The epistle deals mainly with the office of Christ as antitype of the High-Priest, offering the annual sacrifice of atonement: and it has been urged that there is still room for a sacrificial priesthood under the High-Priest. The whole argument however is equally applicable to the inferior priests, and in one passage at least it is directly so applied (Heb 10:11, 12), 'And every priest stands daily (καθ' ἡμέραν) ministering and offering the same sacrifices, etc.'; where the Heb 10:1. ἀρχιερεύς for ἱερεύς seems to have arisen from the desire to bring the verse into more exact conformity with what has gone before. This passage, it should be remembered, is the summing-up and generalization of the previous argument.

[194]It is surprising that some should have interpreted θυσιαστήριον in Heb 13:10 of the Lord's table. There may be a doubt as to the actual significance of the term in this passage, but an actual altar is plainly not intended. This is shown by the context both before and after, e.g. Heb 13:9 the opposition of χάριτι and βρώμασιν, Heb 13:15 the contrast implied in the mention of θυσίαν αἰνέσεως and καρπὸν χειλέων and Heb 13:16 the naming of εὐποιΐας καὶ κοινωνίας as the kind of sacrifice with which God is well pleased. In my former editions I interpreted the θυσιαστήριον of the congregation assembled for worship, having been led to this interpretation by the Christian phraseology of succeeding ages. So Clem. Alex. *Strom.* vii.6, p. 848. The use of the word in Ignatius also, though less obvious, appears to be substantially the same, *Ephes.* 5, *Trall.* 7, *Philad.* 4 (but in *Magn.* 7 it seems to be a metaphor for our Lord Himself); see Hofling, *Opfer* etc. p. 32 sq. Similarly too Polycarp (§ 4) speaks of the body of widows as θυσιαστήριον θεοῦ. [See notes on these passages in *Apostolic Fathers*, Part ii. S. Ignatius, S. Polycarp.] But I have since been convinced that the context points to the Cross of Christ spiritually regarded, as the true interpretation. Since my first

ministry were a sacerdotal office, if the holy eucharist were a sacerdotal act, in the same sense in which the Jewish priesthood and the Jewish sacrifice were sacerdotal, then his argument is faulty and his language misleading. Though dwelling at great length on the Christian counterparts to the Jewish priest, the Jewish altar, the Jewish sacrifice, he omits to mention the one office, the one place, the one act, which on this showing would be their truest and liveliest counterparts in the every-day worship of the Church of Christ. He has rejected these, and he has chosen instead moral and spiritual analogies for all these sacred types. Thus in what he has said and in what he has left unsaid alike, his language points to one and the same result.

If therefore the sacerdotal office be understood to imply the offering of sacrifices, then the Epistle to the Hebrews leaves no place for a Christian priesthood. If on the other hand the word be taken in a wider and looser acceptation, it cannot well be withheld from the ministry of the Church of Christ. Only in this case the meaning of the term should be clearly apprehended, and it might have been better if the later Christian vocabulary had conformed to the silence of the Apostolic writers, so that the possibility of confusion would have been avoided. According to this broader meaning, the priest may be defined as one who represents God to man and man to God.

---

edition appeared, a wholly different interpretation of the passage has been advocated by more than one writer. It is maintained that ἔχομεν θυσιαστήριον should be understood as 'we Jews have an altar,' and that the writer of the epistle is here bringing an example from the Old Dispensation itself (the sin-offering on the day of atonement) in which the sacrifices were not eaten. This interpretation is attractive, but it seems to me inadequate to explain the whole context (though it suits parts well enough), and is ill adapted to individual expressions (e.g. θυσιαστήριον where θυσία would be expected, and τῇ σκηνῇ λατρεύοντες which thus becomes needlessly emphatic), not to mention that the first person plural and the present tense ἔχομεν seem unnatural where the author and his readers are spoken of, not as actual Christians, but as former Jews. In fact the analogy of the sacrifice on the day of atonement appears not to be introduced till the next verse, ὧν γὰρ εἰσφέρεται ζῴων τὸ αἷμα περὶ ἁμαρτίας εἰς τὰ ἅγια διὰ τοῦ ἀρχιερέως, τούτων τὰ σώματα κατακαίεται ἔξω τῆς παρεμβολῆς. Some interpreters again, from a comparison of 1 Cor 9:13 with 1 Cor 10:18, have inferred that St. Paul recognises the designation of the Lord's table as an altar. On the contrary, it is a fact, that in both passages he avoids using this term of the Lord's table, though the language of the context might readily have suggested it to him, if he had considered it appropriate. Nor does the argument in either case require or encourage such an inference. In 1 Cor 9:13, 14, the Apostle writes 'Know ye not that they who wait at the altar are partakers with the altar? Even so hath the Lord ordained that they which preach the gospel should live of the gospel.' The point of resemblance in the two cases is the holding of a sacred office; but the ministering on the altar is predicated only of the former. So also in 1 Cor 10:18 sq., the altar is named as common to Jews and Heathens, but the table only as common to Christians and Heathens; i.e. the holy eucharist is a banquet, but it is not a sacrifice (in the Jewish or heathen sense of the word).

It is moreover indispensable that he should be called by God, for no man 'taketh this honor to himself.' The Christian ministry satisfies both these conditions. Of the fulfilment of the latter the only evidence as having within our cognisance is the fact that the minister is called according to a divinely appointed order. If the preceding investigation be substantially correct, the threefold ministry can be traced to Apostolic direction; and short of an express statement we can possess no better assurance of a divine appointment or at least a divine sanction. If the facts do not allow us to unchurch other Christian communities differently organized, they may at least justify our jealous adhesion to a polity derived from this source.

And while the mode of appointment satisfies the one condition, the nature of the office itself satisfies the other; for it exhibits the doubly representative character which is there laid down. The Christian minister is God's ambassador to men. He is charged with the ministry of reconciliation; he unfolds the will of heaven; he declares in God's name the terms on which pardon is offered; and he pronounces in God's name the absolution of the penitent. This last mentioned function has been thought to invest the ministry with a distinctly sacerdotal character. Yet it is very closely connected with the magisterial and pastoral duties of the office, and is only priestly in the same sense in which they are priestly. As empowered to declare the conditions of God's grace, he is empowered also to proclaim the consequences of their acceptance. But throughout his office is representative and not vicarial.[195] He does not interpose between God and man in such a way that direct communion with God is superseded on the one hand, or that his own mediation becomes indispensable on the other.

Again, the Christian minister is the representative of man to God—of the congregation primarily, of the individual indirectly as a member of the congregation. The alms, the prayers, the thanksgivings of the community are offered through him. Some representation is as necessary in the Church as it is in a popular government: and the nature of the representation is not affected by the fact that the form of the ministry has been handed down from Apostolic times and may well be presumed to have a divine sanction. For here again it must be borne in mind that the minister's function is

---

[195]The distinction is made in Maurice's *Kingdom of Christ* ii. p. 216.

representative without being vicarial. He is a priest, as the mouthpiece, the delegate, of a priestly race. His acts are not his own, but the acts of the congregation. Hence too it will follow that, viewed on this side as on the other, his function cannot be absolute and indispensable. It may be a general rule, it may be under ordinary circumstances a practically universal law, that the highest acts of congregational worship shall be performed through the principal officers of the congregation. But an emergency may arise when the spirit and not the letter must decide. The Christian ideal will then interpose and interpret our duty. The higher ordinance of the universal priesthood will overrule all special limitations. The layman will assume functions which are otherwise restricted to the ordained minister.[196]

Yet it would be vain to deny that a very different conception prevailed for many centuries in the Church of Christ. The Apostolic ideal was set forth, and within a few generations forgotten. The vision was only for a time and then vanished. A strictly sacerdotal view of the ministry superseded the broader and more spiritual conception of their priestly functions. From being the representatives, the ambassadors, of God, they came to be regarded as His vicars. Nor is this the only instance where a false conception has seemed to maintain a long-lived domination over the Church. For some centuries, the idea of the Holy Roman Empire enthralled the minds of men. For a still longer period the idea of the Holy Roman See held undisturbed sway over Western Christendom. To those who take a comprehensive view of the progress of Christianity, even these more lasting obscurations of the truth will present no serious difficulty. They will not suffer themselves to be blinded thereby to the true nobility of Ecclesiastical History. They will not fail to see that, even in the seasons of her deepest degradation, the Church was still the regenerator of society, the upholder of right principle against selfish interest, the visible witness of the Invisible God; they will thankfully confess that, notwithstanding the pride and selfishness and dishonor of individual rulers, notwithstanding the imperfections and errors of special institutions and developments, yet in her continuous history, the Divine promise has been signally realized, 'Lo I am with you always, even unto the end of the world.'

---

[196]For the opinion of the early church, see especially the passage of Tertullian quoted above.

A. ADDITIONAL NOTES TO THE DISSERTATION UPON
THE CHRISTIAN MINISTRY.

The following extracts from Bishop Lightfoot's works illustrate his view of the Christian Ministry over and above the particular scope of the Essay in his Commentary on the Philippians. He felt that unfair use had been made of that special line of thought which he there pursued, and soon after the close of the Lambeth Conference of 1888 he had this collection of passages printed. It is felt by those who have the best means of knowing that he would himself have wished the collection to stand together simply as his reply to the constant imputation to him of opinions for which writers wished to claim his support without any justification.

1. Commentary on *the Epistle to the Philippians* (Essay on the Christian Ministry, 1868). (i) p. 199, ed. 1; p. 201, later ed. 'Unless we have recourse to a sweeping condemnation of received documents, it seems vain to deny that early in the second century the episcopal office was firmly and widely established. Thus during the last three decades of the first century, and consequently during the lifetime of the latest surviving Apostle, this change must have been brought about.' (ii) p. 212, ed. 1; p. 214, later ed. 'The evidence for the early and wide extension of episcopacy throughout proconsular Asia, the scene of St. John's latest labors, may be considered irrefragable.' (iii) p. 225, ed. 1 ; p. 227, later ed. 'But these notices, besides establishing the general prevalence of episcopacy, also throw considerable light on its origin. . . . Above all, they establish this result clearly, that its maturer forms are seen first in those regions where the latest surviving Apostles (more especially St. John) fixed their abode, and at a time when its prevalence cannot be dissociated from their influence or their sanction.' (iv) p. 232, ed. 1; p. 234, later ed. 'It has been seen that the institution of an episcopate must be placed as far back as the closing years of the first century, and that it cannot, without violence to historical testimony, be dissevered from the name of St. John.' (v) p. 265, ed. 1; p. 267, later ed. 'If the preceding investigation be substantially correct, the three-fold ministry can be traced to Apostolic direction; and short of an express statement we can possess no better assurance of a divine appointment or at least a divine sanction. If the facts do not allow us to unchurch other Christian communities differently organized, they may at least justify our jealous adhesion to a polity derived from this source.'

2. *Commentary on the Epistle to the Philippians* (Preface to the Sixth Edition), 1881. 'The present edition is an exact reprint of the preceding one. This statement applies as well to the "Essay on the Threefold Ministry" as to the rest of the work. I should not have thought it necessary to be thus explicit, had I not been informed of a rumor that I had found reason to abandon the main opinions expressed in that Essay. There is no foundation for any such report. The only point of importance on which I have modified my views, since the Essay was first written, is the authentic form of the letters of St. Ignatius. Whereas, in the earlier editions of this work I had accepted the three Curetonian letters, I have since been convinced (as stated in later editions) that the seven letters of the Short Greek are genuine. This divergence however does not materially affect the main point at issue, since even the Curetonian letters afford abundant evidence of the spread of episcopacy in the earliest years of the second century. But on the other hand, while disclaiming any change in my opinions, I desire equally to disclaim the representations of those opinions which have been put forward in some quarters. The object of the Essay was an investigation into the origin of the Christian Ministry. The result has been a confirmation of the statement in the English Ordinal, "It is evident unto all men diligently reading the Holy Scripture and ancient authors that from the Apostles' time there have been these orders of Ministers in Christ's Church, Bishops, Priests, and Deacons." But I was scrupulously anxious not to overstate the evidence in any case; and it would seem that partial and qualifying statements, prompted by this anxiety, have assumed undue proportions in the minds of some readers, who have emphasized them to the neglect of the general drift of the Essay.'

3. Sermon preached before the Representative Council of the Scottish Episcopal Church in St. Mary's Church at Glasgow, October 10, 1882. ('Sermons preached on Special Occasions,' p. 182 sq.) 'When I spoke of unity as St. Paul's charge to the Church of Corinth, the thoughts of all present must, I imagine, have fastened on one application of the Apostolic rule which closely concerns yourselves. Episcopal communities in Scotland outside the organization of the Scottish Episcopal Church—this is a spectacle which no one, I imagine, would view with satisfaction in itself, and which only a very urgent necessity could justify. Can such a necessity be pleaded? "One body" as well as "one Spirit," this is the Apostolic rule. No natural interpretation can be put on these words

which does not recognize the obligation of external, corporate union. Circumstances may prevent the realisation of the Apostle's conception, but the ideal must be ever present to our aspirations and our prayers. I have reason to believe that this matter lies very near to the hearts of all Scottish Episcopalians. May God grant you a speedy accomplishment of your desire. You have the same doctrinal formularies; you acknowledge the same episcopal polity; you respect the same liturgical forms. "Sirs, ye are brethren." Do not strain the conditions of reunion too tightly. I cannot say, for I do not know, what faults or what misunderstandings there may have been on either side in the past. If there have been any faults, forget them. If there exist any misunderstandings, clear them up. "Let the dead past bury its dead." While you seek unity among yourselves, you will pray likewise that unity may be restored to your Presbyterian brothers. Not insensible to the special blessings which you yourselves enjoy, clinging tenaciously to the threefold ministry as the completeness of the Apostolic ordinance and the historical backbone of the Church, valuing highly all those sanctities of liturgical office and ecclesiastical season, which, modified from age to age, you have inherited from an almost immemorial past, thanking God, but not thanking Him in any Pharisaic spirit, that these so many and great privileges are continued to you which others have lost, you will nevertheless shrink, as from the venom of a serpent's fang, from any mean desire that their divisions may be perpetuated in the hope of profiting by their troubles. *Divide et impera* may be a shrewd worldly motto; but coming in contact with spiritual things, it defiles them like pitch. *Pacifica et impera* is the true watchword of the Christian and the Churchman.'

4. *The Apostolic Fathers, Part ii. S. Ignatius: S. Polycarp*, Vol. i. pp. 376, 377, 1885 (pp. 390, 391, 1889). 'The whole subject has been investigated by me in an Essay on "The Christian Ministry"; and to this I venture to refer my readers for fuller information. It is there shown, if I mistake not, that though the New Testament itself contains as yet no direct and indisputable notices of a localized episcopate in the Gentile Churches, as distinguished from the moveable episcopate exercised by Timothy in Ephesus and by Titus in Crete, yet there is satisfactory evidence of its development in the later years of the Apostolic age; that this development was not simultaneous and equal in all parts of Christendom; that it is more especially connected with the name of St. John; and that in the early years of the second century the episcopate was

widely spread and had taken firm root, more especially in Asia Minor and in Syria. If the evidence on which its extension in the regions east of the Aegean at this epoch be resisted, I am at a loss to understand what single fact relating to the history of the Christian Church during the first half of the second century can be regarded as established; for the testimony in favor of this spread of the episcopate is more abundant and more varied than for any other institution or event during this period, so far as I recollect.'

5. Sermon preached before the Church Congress at Wolverhampton, October 3, 1887. ('Sermons preached on Special Occasions,' p. 259 sq.) 'But if this charge fails, what shall we say of her isolation? Is not this isolation, so far as it is true, much more her misfortune than her fault? Is she to be blamed because she retained a form of Church government which had been handed down in unbroken continuity from the Apostolic times, and thus a line was drawn between her and the reformed Churches of other countries? Is it a reproach to her that she asserted her liberty to cast off the accretions which had gathered about the Apostolic doctrine and practice through long ages, and for this act was repudiated by the Roman Church? But this very position,—call it isolation if you will—which was her reproach in the past, is her hope for the future. She was isolated because she could not consort with either extreme. She was isolated because she stood midway between the two. This central position is her vantage ground, which fits her to be a mediator wheresoever an occasion of mediation may arise. But this charge of isolation, if it had any appearance of truth seventy years ago, has lost its force now.'

6. Durham Diocesan Conference. Inaugural Address, October, 1887. 'When I speak of her religious position I refer alike to polity and to doctrine. In both respects the negative, as well as the positive, bearing of her position has to be considered. She has retained the form of Church government inherited from the Apostolic times, while she has shaken off a yoke, which even in medieval times our fathers found too heavy to bear, and which subsequent developments have rendered tenfold more oppressive. She has remained stedfast in the faith of Nicaea, but she has never compromised herself by any declaration which may entangle her in the meshes of science. The doctrinal inheritance of the past is hers, and the scientific hopes of the future are hers. She is intermediate and she may become mediatorial, when

the opportunity occurs. It was this twofold inheritance of doctrine and polity that I had in view, when I spoke of the essentials which could under no circumstances be abandoned. Beyond this, it seems to me that large concessions might be made. Unity is not uniformity. On the other hand it would be very short-sighted policy—even if it were not traitorous to the truth—to tamper with essentials and thus to imperil our mediatorial vantage ground, for the sake of snatching an immediate increase of numbers.'

7. Address on the Reopening of the Chapel, Auckland Castle, August 1st, 1888. ('Leaders in the Northern Church,' p. 145.) 'But, while we "lengthen our cords," we must "strengthen our stakes" likewise. Indeed this strengthening of our stakes will alone enable us to lengthen our cords with safety, when the storms are howling around us. We cannot afford to sacrifice any portion of the faith once delivered to the saints; we cannot surrender for any immediate advantages the threefold ministry that we have inherited from Apostolic times, and which is the historic backbone of the Church. But neither can we on the other hand return to the fables of medievalism or submit to a yoke which our fathers found too grievous to be borne—a yoke now rendered a hundredfold more oppressive to the mind and conscience, weighted as it is by recent and unwarranted impositions of doctrine.'

8. Extract from Preface to the Didache [*Apostolic Fathers*, pp. 215, 216]. 'The work is obviously of very early date, as is shown by the internal evidence of language and subject-matter. Thus for instance the itinerant prophetic order has not yet been displaced by the permanent localized ministry, but exists side by side with it as in the lifetime of St. Paul (Eph 4:11; 1 Cor 12:28). Secondly, episcopacy has apparently not yet become universal; the word "bishop" is still used as synonymous with "presbyter" and the writer therefore couples "bishops" with "deacons" (§ 15) as St. Paul does (1 Tim 3:1-8; Phil 1:1) under similar circumstances. Thirdly, from the expression in § 10 "after ye have been filled" it appears that the *agape* still remains part of the Lord's Supper. Lastly, the archaic simplicity of its practical suggestions is only consistent with the early infancy of a church. These indications point to the first or the beginning of the second century as the date of the work in its present form.'

9. The Ignatian Question. In the following passage in his later work, *The Apostolic Fathers, Part ii. S. Ignatius, S. Polycarp*, I. p. 407 sq. (1st edit 1885), i. p. 422 sq. (2nd edit. 1889), Dr Lightfoot sums up his reasons for the change

of opinion upon the Ignatian question announced above. The facts then are these: (1) No Christian writings of the second century, and very few writings of antiquity, whether Christian or pagan, are so well authenticated as the Epistles of Ignatius. If the Epistle of Polycarp be accepted as genuine, the authentication is perfect; (2) The main ground of objection against the genuineness of the Epistle of Polycarp is its authentication of the Ignatian Epistles. Otherwise there is every reason to believe that it would have passed unquestioned. (3) The Epistle of Polycarp itself is exceptionally well authenticated by the testimony of his disciple Irenaeus. (4) All attempts to explain the phenomena of the Epistle of Polycarp, as forged or interpolated to give color to the Ignatian Epistles, have signally failed. (5) The external testimony to the Ignatian Epistles being so strong, only the most decisive marks of spuriousness in the epistles themselves, as for instance proved anachronisms, would justify us in suspecting them as interpolated or re-jecting them as spurious. (6) But so far is this from being the case that one after another the anachronisms urged against these letters have vanished in the light of further knowledge. Thus, the alleged refutation of the Valen-tinian doctrine of aeons in *Magn.* 8 depends on a false reading which re-cently discovered materials for the text have corrected. The supposed anachronism of 'the leopards' (*Rom.* 5) has been refuted by the production of passages overlooked by the objector. The argument from the mention of the 'Catholic Church' (*Smyrn.* 8) has been shown to rest on a false interpre-tation which disregards the context. (7) As regards the argument which Daille calls 'palmary'—the prevalence of episcopacy as a recognized insti-tution—we may say boldly that all the facts point the other way. If the writer of these letters had represented the Churches of Asia Minor as under pres-byteral government, he would have contradicted all the evidence, which without one dissentient voice points to episcopacy as the established form of Church government in these districts from the close of the first century. (8) The circumstances of the condemnation, captivity, and journey of Ig-natius, which have been a stumbling-block to some modern critics, did not present any difficulty to those who lived near the time and therefore knew best what might be expected under the circumstances; and they are suffi-ciently borne out by examples, more or less analogous, to establish their credibility. (9) The objections to the style and language of the epistles are beside the purposė. In some cases they arise from a misunderstanding of the writer's meaning. Generally they may be said to rest on the assumption that an apostolic father could not use exaggerated expressions, overstrained images, and the like—certainly a sandy foundation on which to build an argument. (10) A like answer holds with regard to any extravagances in sentiment or opinion or character. Why should Ignatius not have exceeded the bounds of sober reason or correct taste? Other men in his own and immediately succeeding ages did both. As an Apostolic Father he was not exempt from the failings, if failings they were, of his age and position. (11) While the investigation of the contents of these epistles has yielded this negative result, in dissipating the objections, it has at the same time had a high positive value, as revealing indications of a very early date, and therefore presumably of genuineness, in the surrounding circumstances, more especially in the types of false doctrine which it combats, in the ecclesiastical status which it presents, and in the manner in which it deals with the evangelical and apostolic documents. (12) Moreover we discover in the personal environments of the assumed writer, and more especially in the notices of his route, many subtle coincidences which we are constrained to regard as undesigned, and which seem altogether beyond the reach of a forger. (13) So likewise the peculiarities in style and diction of the epistles, as also in the representation of the writer's character, are much more capable of explanation in a genuine writing than in a forgery. (14) While external and internal evidence thus combine to assert the genuineness of these writings, no satisfactory account has been or apparently can be given of them as a forgery of a later date than Ignatius. They would be quite purposeless as such; for they entirely omit all topics which would especially interest any subsequent age. On these grounds we are constrained to accept the Seven Epistles of the Middle Form as the genuine work of Ignatius.

Appendix F

J. B. Lightfoot as
Biblical Commentator[1]

C. K. Barrett

I FIND MY TASK IN GIVING THIS LECTURE on Lightfoot in at least one respect an embarrassment. Eighteen years ago, here in Durham, I gave to the Lightfoot Society a paper on Lightfoot; I touched other aspects of his work, but to a great extent the paper was devoted to his commentaries. It was published in the *Durham University Journal* in the following year, 1972.[2] I am not embarrassed because I am under the illusion that my hearers today have turned up their copies of the *DUJ* and perused my paper; that is in the highest degree unlikely, I am embarrassed simply by the prospect of inevitable repetition, which I should prefer to avoid. I shall avoid it as far as I can, and this paper will follow a different line than its predecessor. But to some extent I shall be obliged to repeat myself. It will be necessary to give a certain amount of necessary information, and the basic facts about Lightfoot's life

---

[1]This essay first appeared in the special issue of the *Durham University Journal* in 1992. It was given at the conference at Durham celebrating the centenary of Lightfoot's death in 1889. This special issue of the journal no longer exists, and we are happy to make it available here. [(BW3)] This essay and the one by J. D. G. Dunn that follows in the next appendix are reprinted by kind permission of the University of Durham.
[2]*Durham University Journal* 64, no 33 (1972): 193-204.

and work do not change, though we are now better aware of Lightfoot's manuscripts preserved in the Chapter Library at Durham;[3] these provide some biographical material and throw additional light on Lightfoot's work and thought.[4] My earlier lecture was, on the whole,—there were a few exceptions—laudatory. This is because it was in the main descriptive of Lightfoot's work, and what there is to describe is very good indeed. What Lightfoot set out to do he did with very great skill and very great thoroughness. In his own chosen line he has perhaps no equal in the English-speaking world. There is however room for more critical examination. His own work suggests questions to which it does not, at least on the surface, provide answers. Did he do everything that may rightly be expected of a commentary? Were the methods he used the right methods? Should his methods be replaced, or perhaps supplements by others? Did he take his own methods as far as they would go? Did he draw from them all the conclusions to which they pointed?

We shall see as we proceed how these questions, or some of them, are raised, and what answers Lightfoot himself can supply. The result will not detract from our estimate of Lightfoot; he is great enough to abide our question. In any case, repetition or not, we must begin with some facts.

Most of the biographical details may be found in my earlier lecture.[5] Lightfoot gained his equipment as a commentator in the first instance at King Edward's School, Birmingham, under James Prince Lee, later Bishop of Manchester, not only a thorough training in Greek and Latin, and wide reading in classical literature and history, but in a firm Christian faith and a devotion to hard work. He learned the meaning of Prince Lee's own motto, *Virtus constat in agendo.* Thence to Cambridge, where he worked with Westcott, who had by three years preceded him from Prince Edward's to Trinity. Having taken a first in mathematics he took the Classical Tripos in 1851 and came out as Senior Classic. The legend that he wrote all his Tripos papers without a single mistake is perhaps credible as far as language papers are concerned. It cannot have been easy to find passages of classical Greek

---

[3] I gladly take this opportunity to express my gratitude to Roger Norris of the University and Chapter Libraries, who helped me in every possible way.
[4] See especially the identification by G. R. Treloar and B. N. Kaye of Lightfoot's Norrisian Prize Essay, *Durham University Journal* 79 (1987): 165-200.
[5] See also the late J. A. T. Robinson's 1981 Durham Cathedral lecture, "Joseph Barber Lightfoot."

and Latin that were truly unseen to him, and composition presented few problems. Inevitably he was elected to a fellowship at Trinity, and proceeded to improve his linguistic knowledge yet further by the best of all methods—teaching the language to others. Theology he was now learning in his spare time; that is, after others had gone to bed at night and before they got up in the morning. The same diligence that he had applied to reading the classics he applied to patristic literature, with results that appear not only in the editions of Clement, Ignatius and Polycarp but in his contributions to the great Dictionaries, of Christian Antiquities and Christian biography.[6]

In an even earlier lecture than that on Lightfoot, to which I have already referred, I described the way in which Lightfoot, Westcott and Hort divided up the New Testament with a view to writing commentaries on the whole. Lightfoot was to take Paul, and, as everyone knows, he wrote commentaries on Galatians (1865), Philippians (1868) and in one volume Colossians and Philemon (1875). Each contains an introduction, dealing with the usual questions; the Greek text, edited by Lightfoot, in consultation but not in complete agreement with Westcott and Hort (who, as we all know, were drawing up their text of the whole New Testament); notes on the text, which included brief explanatory paraphrases, which restate in English the meaning of the text; longer notes on special points of interest and difficulty; and dissertations on larger topics related to the content of the several epistles. A summary such as this cannot do justice to the width and detail of Lightfoot's work; a brief outline is called for.

In *Galatians* there are extended notes on St. Paul's sojourn in Arabia, St. Paul's first visit to Jerusalem, the name and office of an apostle, various readings in Galatians 2:5, the later visit of Paul to Jerusalem, patristic accounts of the collision in Antioch, the interpretation of Deuteronomy 21:23, the words denoting 'faith,' the faith of Abraham, St. Paul's infirmity in the flesh, the various readings in Galatians 4:25, the meaning of Hagar in Galatians 4:25, Philo's allegory of Hagar and Sarah, the various readings in Galatians 5:1, and the patristic commentaries on this epistle. In addition, there are dissertations on 'Were the Galatians Celts or Teutons?' and 'The Brethren of the Lord' and 'St. Paul and the Three.'

---

[6]Notably, the great essay on Eusebius of Caesarea, in *A Dictionary of Christian Biography, Literature, Sects, and Doctrines*, 2:308-48.

In *Philippians* there are extended notes on the synonyms *bishop* and *presbyter*, the meaning of *praetorium* in Philippians 1:13, the synonyms μορφή and σχῆμα, different interpretations of οὐχ ἁρπαγμὸν ἡγήσατο, lost epistle to the Philippians?, 'Clement my fellow laborer,' and Caesar's household. There are dissertations on 'The Christian Ministry' and 'St. Paul and Seneca,' the latter with additional notes on the letters of Paul and Seneca.

In *Colossians* there are extended notes on some various readings in the epistle (Colossians), on the meaning of πλήρωμα, and on the epistle from Laodicea. There are no dissertations, but the introduction contains seventy-two pages on the churches of the Lycus and forty-one pages on the Colossian heresy, with an additional sixty-six pages on some points connected with the Essenes.

It has seemed worthwhile to read rapidly through these titles, which, taken together, give some impression of Lightfoot's wide-ranging learning. There is scarcely one that does not reveal such patristic learning as probably no living New Testament scholar could claim. Jewish material, in the original languages, is called on when it is needful, and the extended note on Hagar and Sarah required the Cambridge University Press have not only a Syriac but also an Arabic font.

The three commentaries were published in Lightfoot's lifetime. He left lecture notes, and other notes, on other epistles which doubtless he would have used in published work had he lived, and had his interest not become absorbed in what must be regarded as his greatest work, that on the text of 1 Clement and the Epistles of Ignatius (with 2 Clement and Polycarp added for full measure)—not to mention his conscientious, time-consuming work as bishop of Durham. The notes were edited after his death for his trustees and published under the title *Notes on Epistles of St. Paul from Unpublished Commentaries* (1895). Here we have notes, similar to but less full than those of the finished commentaries, on 1 Thessalonians; 2 Thessalonians; 1 Corinthians 1–7; Romans 1–7; and Ephesians 1:1-14. We may note here that the trustees did not publish all the available material. The Chapter Library at Durham contains a quantity of manuscript material which is interesting in that it shows both how probably the most popular teacher of theology at Cambridge in his time prepared and presented his material, and also how the finished commentaries took shape.

It will no doubt be proper to attempt a brief characterization of the commentaries that have a finished form. The first characteristic that the reader is likely to observe is their beautiful clarity. Except in the extended notes and dissertations, which are in the style of monographs rather than of commentary, there are no footnotes, and the reader takes in Lightfoot's exposition, and the grounds on which he bases it, without distraction. It would be difficult to find a sentence that does not immediately tell the reader the author's meaning. Of course, some of the arguments are complex because the text on which Lightfoot is commenting is difficult, but even in such passages the meaning is not in doubt. This appears pre-eminently in the explanatory paraphrases, of which I quote, more or less at random, that on Colossians 1:15-17:

> He is the perfect image, the visible representation, of the unseen God. He is the Firstborn, the absolute Heir of the Father, begotten before the ages; the Lord of the Universe by virtue of primogeniture, and by virtue also of creative agency. For in and through Him the whole world was created, things in heaven and things on earth, things visible to the outward eye and things cognizable to the inward perception. His supremacy is absolute and universal. All powers in heaven and on earth are subject to Him. This subjected extends even to the most exalted and most potent of angelic beings, whether they be called Thrones, or Dominions or Princedoms or Powers, or whatever title of dignity men may confer upon them. Yes; He is the First and He is the Last. Through Him, as the mediatorial Word, the universe has been created; and unto Him as the final goal, it is tending. In Him is no before or after. He is pre-existent and self-existent before all the worlds. And in Him, as the binding and sustaining power, universal nature coheres and consists.[7]

But this general note is followed by details, and here too, though the details are followed out at length, there is comparable clarity. Thus the note on εἰκών, which is far too long to quote in full, runs in outline thus:

> This expression is used repeatedly by Philo, as a description of the Logos [six quotations follow]. . . . Still earlier than Philo . . . the term was used of the divine σοφία personified in Wisdom vii.26. . . . St. Paul himself applies the term to our Lord in an earlier epistle, 2 Cor. iv.4. . . . Closely allied to εἰκών also is χαρακτήρ . . .

---

[7] J. B. Lightfoot, *St. Paul's Epistles to the Colossians and to Philemon* (London: Macmillan, 1875), p. 210.

So much for usage. Now meaning:

Beyond the very obvious notion of *likeness* the word εἰκών involves two other ideas: 1) Representation. In this respect it is allied to χαρακτήρ, and differs from ὁμοίωμα. In ὁμοίωμα the resemblance may be accidental, as one egg is like another; but εἰκών implies an archetype of which it is a copy [quotations of and references to Gregory Nazianzen, Philo, Trench, Basil, 1 Corinthians, 1 Clement, Clementine Homiles follow]. The use which was made of the expression and especially of this passage in the Christological controversies of the fourth and fifth centuries may be seen from the patristic quotations in Perav. *Theol. Dogm. De Trin.* Ii.11.9sq.; vi. 5, 6. 2) Manifestation. This idea comes from the implied contast to τοῦ ἀοράτου Θεοῦ. St. Chrysostom indeed mantains the direct opposite, arguing that, as the archetype is invisible, so the image must be invisible also [quotation]. So too Hilary [quotation]. And this was the view of the Nicene and post-Nicene fathers generally. But the underlying idea of the εἰκών, and indeed of the λόγος generally, is the manifestation of the hidden [quotations from Philo, Tertullian, Hippolytus, Origen, Basil, John follow . . .].[8]

The example I have chosen to illustrate the clarity of Lightfoot's exposition and argumentation can and must serve other purposes also and illustrate other characteristics, notably his knowledge of the Fathers and his independence. He always has at hand the right quotation to bring out the meaning of a passage and to support the interpretation that he offers; but he can also declare that on a point of considerable importance the Nicene and post-Nicene Fathers were mistaken. Naturally he is no less independent of— and hardly less well read in—the works of his contemporaries. There is a characteristic note early in the description of the Christian ministry.[9]

The origin of the Christian ministry is ably investigated in Rothe's *Anfänge der Christlichen Kirche etc.* (1837), and Ritschl's, *Entstehung der Altkatholischen Kirche,* (2nd ed. 1857). These are the most important of the recent works on the subject with which I am acquainted, and to both of them I wish to acknowledge my obligations, though in many respects I have arrived at results different from either.

Lightfoot's knowledge and use of patristic material can be illustrated by his account of patristic commentaries on Galatians.[10] He knows Origen, Ephraem

---

[8]Ibid., pp. 210-12.
[9]J. B. Lightfoot, *St. Paul's Epistle to the Philippians* (London: Macmillan, 1868), p. 187.
[10]J. B. Lightfoot, *St. Paul's Epistle to the Galatians* (London: Macmillan, 1865), pp. 227-36.

Syrus, Eusebius of Emesa, Chrysostom, Severianus, Theodore of Mopsuestia, Theodoret, Euthalius, Gennadius, Photius, Victorinus, Hilary, Jerome, Augustine, Pelagius, Cassiodorus, John of Damascus, the *Catena* published by Cramer, Oecumenius, Theophylact, Primasius, Sedulius, Claudius, Florus, Rabanus Maurus, Walafrid, Strabo and Haymo; Atto, Lanfranc, Bruno and Herveus are added.

Equally striking and characteristic but equally difficult to illustrate briefly and effectively is Lightfoot's feeling for a Greek phrase or sentence, acquired over many years of familiarity with Greek literature of all kinds. For brevity, take these words, which provide a familiar problem in Galatians 1:19, εἰ μὴ Ἰάκωβον.

> Is James here styled an Apostle or not? Are we to translate 'I saw no other Apostle save James' or 'I saw no other Apostle, but only James?' It will be seen that the question is not whether εἰ μὴ retains its *exceptive* force or not, for this it seems always to do . . . , but whether the exception refers to the whole clause or to the verb alone . . . the latter is quite a possible construction. . . . But on the other hand the sense of ἕτερον naturally links it with εἰ μὴ, from which it cannot be separated without harshness, and ἕτερον carries the ἀποστόλων with it. It seems then that James is here called an Apostle. [11]

Lightfoot was perhaps even greater as a historian than as a grammarian. He has especially in Galatians a set of historical problems as difficult as any the New Testament presents. His treatment of them is clear and in the main satisfying. His identification of the meeting described in Galatians 2 with council of Acts 15 is surely correct, and Lightfoot defends it with great force, though he labors under the difficulty that his principles made it impossible for him to answer adequately the two chief objections to it. He mentions them fairly.[12] How is it that Paul passes from his first Jerusalem visit to his third without a hint of the second (described in Acts 11:30; 12:25)? And how is it that Paul in Galatians makes no mention of the decree decided at the council, according to Acts 15:29? These difficulties can be readily disposed of if one is prepared to say that the second and third visits in Acts are doublets and that the decree was promulgated in Paul's absence and without his

---

[11]Ibid., pp. 84f.
[12]Ibid., p.127.

consent. Lightfoot would not have felt free to adopt these explanations, which impugn the veracity of Acts. This sets a very serious limit to the value of his historical work, illustrated by his discussion of Acts 15, in which he settles the historical trustworthiness of the Acts narrative by confronting it with Galatians after, not before, reaching his decision.[13] Lightfoot was inhibited in his work as an historian by a false understanding of inspiration and authority; it is for this reason that his work on the apostolic fathers is even better, and is of more permanent value, than his work on the New Testament. Apart however from this defect he works out the historical relations of Galatians with reference to every scrap of evidence that the epistle affords, with great skill.[14]

The story of the council points forward to Lightfoot's long dissertation on St. Paul and the Three. It would not be proper to take this up in this lecture, for it will probably be dealt with in another of this week's lectures. In any case I dealt with it in some detail in my earlier Lightfoot lecture and brought out its strengths and weaknesses.[15] Lightfoot recognized as clearly as F. C. Baur ever did the conflict that lies at the heart of early Christian history and indeed treats it, or begins to treat it, even more radically than Baur in that he places the documents of strife and reconciliation at earlier dates than Baur. But he seems never quite to see how radical his understanding of early Christian development is, or, if he sees it, he shies away from it, stepping back from the brink of recognizing that the uneasy diversity, which he does clearly see, is part of the New Testament itself.

Let me add here, with a view to taking up the theme later, that Lightfoot did not neglect that other part of a commentator's duty, the theological evaluation of the text. Of this I shall give one example.[16] Lightfoot's treatment of the notorious problem in Galatians 3:16—οὐ λέγει καὶ τοῖς σπέρμασιν, ὡς ἐπὶ πολλῶν, ἀλλ' ὡς ἐφ' ἑνός καὶ τῷ σπέρματί σου, ὅς ἐστιν Χριστός. First he deals with the language with a near quotation from Plato (Laws, 9, 853c) to show that the plural σπέρμασι is not impossible, and the argument that the point Paul is making is that where a plural (e.g., τέκνα) might have been

---

[13]I have drawn attention to this in New Testament Studies 28 (1982): 314.
[14]As an example of historical knowledge that goes beyond the New Testament, see, e.g., the discussion of the meaning of πραιτώριον (Lightfoot, Philippians, pp. 99-104).
[15]Durham University Journal 64, ns 33 (1972): 199-203.
[16]It is given less fully in ibid., p. 197.

used the Old Testament in fact has a singular. 'The singular collective noun, if it admits of plurality (as it is interpreted by St. Paul himself, Rom. iv.18; ix.7) at the same time involves the idea of unity.' At this point Lightfoot takes the important step. 'The question therefore is no longer one of grammatical accuracy, but of theological interpretation. Is this a legitimate sense to apply to the seed of Abraham?' Lightfoot goes on to show that the Christ 'was the true seed of Abraham?' 'In Him the race was summed up, as it were. In Him it fulfilled its purpose and became a blessing to the whole earth. . . . He was not only the representative, but the embodiment of the race.'[17]

I have deliberately ended this sketch of Lightfoot's achievement as a commentator with a reference to theology because it is at this point that he has been attacked, and if this lecture is to be a critical discussion, as it must, it is here that we must begin. There cannot be many theologians still resident in Cambridge who remember Charles Smyth's provocative University Sermon.[18] It was in one of its less provocative parts that he referred, as Cambridge men often do,—or did—to the three great figures of Cambridge theology. His hearer expected him to name them: Lightfoot, Westcott and Hort. He said Westcott, Hort and Hoskyns. To take up the positive aspect of his substitution is a temptation I must firmly thrust aside. The negative aspect is relevant. Smyth of course was not denigrating Lightfoot the exponent of classical and sacred philology.[19] He had used the word *theologian*, and it was theologians of whom he was thinking. Lightfoot was a great man; was he a great theologian? Was he a theologian at all?

Disparagement of Lightfoot as a theologian goes back at least to the year in which his *Galatians* was published and to his old friend and colleague Hort. Some passages in Hort's letters must be quoted.[20] He writes (2.35) to John Ellerton on 7 May 1865:

> The main purpose of the volume [*Galatians*] is to determine precisely the nature of the Apostolic *history*, to which Galatians is the key, and that is its distinctive merit. . . . Doctrinal questions are almost entirely avoided, as Lightfoot means to keep them for Romans. However, that is certainly the

[17]Lightfoot, *Galatians*, pp. 142-43.
[18]Printed with suitable omissions in *The Cambridge Review* 68, no. 1661 (February 1, 1947): 269-71.
[19]I borrow the apt title of the journal that Lightfoot helped to found and, through its short life, to edit.
[20]*Life and Letters of Fenton John Anthony Hort*, by his son, A. F. Hort, 2 vols. (London: Macmillan, 1896).

weakest point of the book; and Jowett's notes and essays, with all their perversities, are still an indispensable supplement.

I have been unable to find where Lightfoot expresses the intention that Hort ascribes to him—of dealing almost exclusively with the apostolic history and saving the Pauline theology for the commentary on Romans (of which we only have the imperfect fragment in *Unpublished Commentaries*). This is not to say that Hort was mistaken; Lightfoot may have said these things in conversation with his friend, or written them in a letter now lost.

Nearly two years later (21 February 1867) Hort was writing again to Ellerton, who evidently had asked Hort's opinion of several books which he, Ellerton, had not read. Hort writes:

> Touching Lightfoot's *Galatians* . . . [21] Certainly his doctrinal comments are far from satisfying me. They belong far too much to the mere Protestant version of St. Paul's thoughts, however Christianized and rationalized. One misses the real attempt to fathom St. Paul's own mind, and to compare it with the facts of life which one finds in Jowett. On the other hand, he is surely always admirable on historical grounds, and especially in interpreting passages which afford indirect historical evidence, so also all matters of grammar and language and such like essential externalities.

As myself a mere Protestant I find myself wondering what is the mere Protestant version of Paul's thoughts; also how it may be, or needs to be, Christianized and rationalized. It seems that, having resisted the temptation to digress to Hoskyns, we shall be obliged to turn aside for a few moments to Hort, though I shall do my best to keep the digression within narrow limits, recognizing that a full account of Hort's own theological position is matter for another occasion. It must suffice to quote two letters, both written to Westcott. The first was written on 23 September 1864 (2.30f):

> I believe Coleridge was quite right in saying that Christianity without a substantial Church is vanity and dissolution; and I remember shocking you and Lightfoot not so very long ago by expressing a belief that 'Protestantism' is only parenthetical and temporary. In short, the Irvingite creed (*minus* the belief in the superior claims of the Irvingite communion) seems to me unassailable in

---

[21]The running dots are in the *Life and Letters*, presumably indicating an omission made by the editor. Of what? Of something too uncomplimentary to repeat?

things ecclesiastical. Yet that is not after all the essential aspect of sacred things. If we may take St. Paul's life and work for our guidance (and St. Peter's 'Of a truth I perceive that God is no respecter of persons' goes even further) we may well be content to put up with comparative formlessness for I know not how many generations than go back to 'the elements of the world.'

Westcott must have replied, for five days later (September 28) Hort wrote again (2.31f.):

> We must not be tempted into discussing the Church and the Churches in the opening line of a letter. I must take the chance of your misunderstanding me for the present, and merely state one comprehensive belief—that perfect Catholicity has been nowhere since the Reformation (strictly, indeed, it was cruelly injured long before by the *Filoque* and the Athanasian Creed), and that since then we have had the pre-eminence of the constitutional Catholicity and (not 'Rome' but) the Churches that hold to Rome in historical Catholicity.

Looking at the matter from the outside, and without adequate discussion, Hort, it seems, has all the appearance of a good middle-of-the-road Anglican. The Reformation was a regrettable necessity, called for by errors and excesses in the medieval church; it should have been carried out with greater tact and moderation. Luther was 'a great and good man,' but 'he was sometimes violent and unwise.'[22]

It is interesting to reflect that of the three, Hort was the only one who did not become a bishop; he seems to have been the likeliest candidate. One is almost disposed to see divine providence in the system of appointment by royal prerogative. Westcott was saved by his mystical piety and his profound sympathy with the unfortunate, Lightfoot by the fact that he was an historian, a fact that made him too much of an antisacerdotal presbyterian for Hort. Or was even this strong enough to save him? The question will lead to a further development in the critical assessment of Lightfoot.

No more than any other commentator did Lightfoot come to his work without presuppositions. What were they? I have said a little about theology, and I shall return to the theme. Two other kinds of presuppositions call for consideration: philosophical and institutional.

---

[22]2.306, a letter of November 17, 1883.

In one of my earlier papers[23] I compared Lightfoot and F. C. Baur. I pointed out, what is now generally recognized, that Baur did not impose a Hegelian view of history on the New Testament documents, but recognized, as is certainly true, that Baur was a Hegelian; this Hegelianism had in fact a far more powerful, and I would add, harmful—effect on his theology than on his history. 'Lightfoot in contrast,' I said (p. 316), 'was not a philosopher and showed no interest in a theory of history.' He said himself,[24] 'I brought to the task nothing more than ordinary sense.' I went on however to say (p. 317), 'Lightfoot's presuppositions were theological or religious, but it may be that behind them we should recognize a way of apprehending reality. . . . Does his "ordinary sense" represent a kind of empiricism?' B. N. Kaye, in an important article,[25] with most of which I can heartily agree, takes issue with this. In a paragraph of conclusions he writes:

> The conflict between Baur and Lightfoot on early Christianity is really about the question of the origins of Christianity. It seems to me that in broad terms they agree about the importance of history and theology being related to each other. Their approach to historical method is very similar and they are both convinced that there is a vital connection between contemporary Christianity and its origins. . . . They differ, however, as to the particular and precise definition of the character of that connection; Baur thinking in dynamic and developmental terms, Lightfoot in terms of a 'given' in the incarnation and the struggle to maintain the truth of that 'given' through the subsequent life of the Church with the aid of the institution of the Christian ministry. It seems to me therefore not at all the case that Lightfoot has no philosophy of history. Rather, he appears to me to represent not just an empiricist philosophy but a fairly traditional Anglican point of view, such as might be found in the writings of Richard Hooker, whom Lightfoot is wont on occasion to quote. It appears to me most certainly to be the case that Lightfoot is very importantly involved, in his New Testament writings, in English church problems.

With most of this I agree—indeed with more of it than Dr. Kaye appears to think I do, though I cannot but observe that a concern with English church problems is not the same as a philosophical standpoint. I return

---

[23]C. K. Barrett, 'Quomodo historia conscribenda sit,' *New Testament Studies* 28 (1982): 303-20.
[24]J. B. Lightfoot, *Essays on the Work Entitled Supernatural Religion* (London: Macmillan, 1889), 180.
[25]B. N. Kaye, 'Lightfoot and Baur on Early Christianity,' *Novum Testamentum* 26 (1984): 193-224; the quotation is on p. 223.

however to my suggestion that Lightfoot's 'ordinary sense' might be thought of in philosophical terms as 'empiricism'; and if an outsider may be permitted to express an opinion on such a matter, few things seem to me more characteristic of a 'fairly traditional Anglican point of view' than a devout empiricism.[26] I am inclined to think, though here in particular I would defer to the specialists, that this is by no means uncharacteristic of Hooker.[27]

It may be worthwhile to dwell briefly upon the last sentence in the paragraph that I have quoted from Dr. Kaye. 'Lightfoot is very importantly involved, in his New Testament writings, in English church problems.' It is arguable that increasing involvement in these problems led to changes in critical attitude. Probably his most radical, most Baurian, work is to be seen in his earliest commentary, that on Galatians. I give one quotation only.[28] 'The systematic hatred of St. Paul is an important fact, which we are too apt to overlook but without which the whole history of the Apostolic ages will be misread and misunderstood.' Lightfoot does not, I think, return to this vehement expression of the turbulent and disunited apostolic age. His language in *Philippians*, though firm, is more moderate:

> If these sectarians resolutely opposed St. Paul they were hardly less zealous in preaching Christ. The incentive of rivalry goaded them on to fresh exertions. Their Gospel was dwarfed and mutilated; it ignored the principle of liberty which was a main feature of the true Gospel; but though their motives were thus unworthy and their doctrine distorted, still 'Christ was preached'; and for this cause, smothering all personal feeling, the Apostle constrained himself to rejoice. (p. 18)

Most important, however, is the fact that Lightfoot found it necessary, after he had become bishop of Durham, not to retract his long dissertation on the Christian ministry,[29] but to point out that it had been misunderstood. In this dissertation it is plainly stated that 'the functions of the Apostle and the bishop differ widely.' Originally, the terms *bishop* and *presbyter* were

---

[26]Cf. the references in *New Testament Studies* 28, page 317, to J. W. Rogerson's phrase 'a Lockian sort of supernaturalism.'

[27]Lightfoot quotes Hooker perhaps less frequently than this suggests; in rereading for this lecture, I have noticed only one example, though doubtless there are more.

[28]From page 311 from the dissertation on 'St. Paul and the Three.' There is more to this effect in *Durham University Journal* 64: 199-203.

[29]Lightfoot, *Philippians*, pp. 181-269.

synonymous (argued in a special note, *Philippians*, pp. 95-99), hence it is deduced that 'the episcopate was formed not out of the apostolic order by localization but out of the presbyteral by elevation; and the title, which was originally common to all, came at length to be appropriated to the chief among them.' This is worked out in detail in the following pages. The last part of the dissertation (pp. 244-69) is devoted to an attack on sacerdotalism, defined (p. 245) as the view that designates 'the Christian minister as one who offers sacrifices and makes atonement for the sins of others.' This, though it subsequently developed rapidly, is not to be found in the New Testament.

Lightfoot on the origins of the episcopate is radical enough; but he can go farther. I allow myself to quote again passages I used in the past.[30]

This then is the Christian ideal; a holy season extending the whole year round—a temple confined only by the limits of the habitable world—a priesthood coextensive with the human race. (*Philippians*, p. 183f.)

It may be a general rule, it may be under ordinary circumstances a practically universal law, that the highest acts of congregational worship shall be performed through the principle officers of the congregation. But an emergency may arise when the spirit and not the letter must decide. The Christian ideal will then interpose and interpret our duty. The higher ordinance of the universal priesthood will overrule all special limitations. The layman will assume functions which are otherwise restricted to the ordained minister. (*Philippians*, p. 268)

A pity, one may think, ever to live by the letter, rather than by the Spirit, by the lower rather than the higher ordinance. That Lightfoot never said; but he had said more than enough for some of his readers.

It would seem that partial and qualifying statements . . . have assumed undue proportions in the minds of some readers, who have emphasized them to the neglect of the general drift of the Essay.[31]

The general drift was that from the apostles' time there have been these orders of ministers in Christ's church, bishops, priests and deacons. But

---

[30]*Durham University Journal* 64: 203f.
[31]Lightfoot, *Philippians*, 6th ed., p. x. The dissertation was reprinted separately (London: Macmillan, 1910) [see appendix above, [146-92] in this volume]. In the reprint the quotation is on p. 138.

Lightfoot had made it clear that in the apostles' time, bishops were the same as priests (or presbyters) and that priests were to be understood in an entirely unsacerdotal sense. These were not the points that he now, in 1881, wished to bring out.

No one could accuse Lightfoot, whose integrity was beyond question, of springing to the defense of an order simply because he had entered it. But it is probably true that he did, in the last decade of his life, feel greater responsibility for the traditions and order of the Church of England.

Apart from such considerations, before perhaps they began to weigh heavily with him, how did Lightfoot understand the business of a commentator, and how did he set about carrying it out? To answer these questions I shall draw upon two sources.

The first is the introductory lecture to his course, given several times in Cambridge, on the Acts of the Apostles.[32] Systems of interpretation (he says) depend on views of inspiration—a statement that can be made *a priori* and is confirmed by the history of biblical criticism. There are two extreme views, which stress either the human element in Scripture or the divine, each to the exclusion of the other. The latter stress is irrational, the former rationalistic. Neither is satisfactory. It is essential to give due weight to each element; this method only is in accord with the highest reason and the fullest faith. In modern times the irrational method came first. It reduced Scripture to featureless uniformity and falls immediately to the assaults of criticism; in falling it has carried with it the faith of some. The rationalist method arises by reaction. The divine element is virtually, if not actually, denied, and inspiration is lowered because it is claimed not only for Scripture but also for writers such as Homer, Aeschylus, Pythagoras and Plato.

The combination of divine and human elements is of fundamental importance; it makes it possible to recognize those differences in natural gifts and circumstances which enable us to understand how Paul saw the gospel as the abrogation, James the fulfillment of the law. It is when the human element is lost sight of that criticism and grammar are disregarded in a loose system of interpretation. Such indolence has not disappeared in England;

---

[32]Durham Chapter Library manuscripts. Since my lecture was written and delivered, Lightfoot's lecture has been published, with introductions by B. N. Kaye and G. R. Treloar, in *Durham University Journal* (1990): 161-75.

and Lightfoot illustrates it. 'I see no ground whatever for supposing that the language of the inspired writers is careless or ungrammatical.' It is not 'pure' but it is 'exact.' Aristotle himself is not more exact in his use of terms than St. Paul. With precise study of language must go the attempt to reproduce the historical circumstances under which the gospel was first preached.

The irrational method of interpretation is to be avoided, but at least it is better than the rationalistic, which boasts that it approaches Scripture free from prepossessions. But is this possible? Is it desirable? There are two kinds of prepossession. There are those which result from outward circumstances, such as education and social position. These must be resigned. There are also those which come from the inward dictates of the heart, from God speaking within us. These we must cling to.

The human indeed must be tried in *foro rationis*. The text must be discussed, the interpretation fixed, historical questions decided before this tribunal. But there is a higher court of appeal—the conscience. Spirtual things are spiritually discerned; spirituality is necessary in the interpreter.

One specific piece of advice follows; young students should avoid German criticism, or at least approach it 'in a spiritual frame of mind.' This is not a wholesale condemnation. There is much to learn from German scholars; they have done so much work, there must be something of value in their results. 'Then and then only shall we as a nation have a right to inflict this indiscriminating censure when we have spent as much time and pains over the sacred writings as they have, and produced results as considerable.'

Finally Lightfoot stresses the importance of prayer. If you study a historian such as Thucydides or Tacitus you must transport yourself into his time so as to think and feel as he did. In regard to the Bible this means the Spirit. Lightfoot does not say, though he probably meant, you must also learn to live in the biblical history.

A profound belief in the divine element in Scripture; a readiness to study its vocabulary, grammar and history with the whole of a senior classic's resources; a devout spirit of prayer and readiness to hear the word of God. We cannot doubt that Lightfoot brought these to his lectures and his commentaries.

My second source is Lightfoot's essay[33] on 'Recent Editions of St. Paul's Epistles,' in which he reviews the commentaries of Ellicott, Stanley and Jowett.

---

[33]In *Journal of Classical and Sacred Philology* 3 (1857; repr., 1970): 81-121.

Ellicott is soon dismissed; he offers grammatical criticism only. Evidently Lightfoot, for all his stress on grammar, regarded this as no more than preliminary to a commentary. The treatment of Stanley can only be described as savage. Stanley has 'taken upon himself a task for which he was unfitted either by his intellectual constitution or by his previous training. . . . he seems to be entirely wanting in that habit of strict accuracy, which is the first, second and third requisite for a successful critic' (p. 90). Examples dealing with text exegesis, lexicography, grammar and history follow. 'The treatment of tenses . . . in these volumes is so hopelessly confused and contradictory that any attempt to analyze it would be vain' (p. 96f.). 'If our belief in Mr. Stanley's efficiency as a commentator has not received its death-blow already, it will scarcely survive his self-contradictions' (p. 98). So much for Mr. Stanley.

Jowett was a different matter and had to be taken seriously, though 'his greatness appears in the Essays rather than in the commentary' (p. 102). Here are discussed the questions which (I suspect) the mere Protestant in Lightfoot did not bring into commentaries, though he was capable of understanding and appreciating them when he met them. 'How has this or that metaphysical question presented itself to different minds or to the same mind at different times? Under what contradictory aspects may a particular religious sentiment or moral truth be viewed? What phenomena does an individual mind exhibit at different stages in its growth? What contrasts do we find in the ancient and modern world of thought?' (p. 117f). These are not improper questions. It is Jowett's exegetical methods that evoke criticism. 'He applies entirely different principles of interpretation to the language of St. Paul from those by which he would investigate Sophocles or Xenophon. He removes him beyond the pale of ordinary grammatical considerations. We cannot argue therefore from these volumes what treatment he would adopt with a classical writer' (p. 102). He exaggerates the changes in the Greek language since the days of Pericles (p. 106) and—worse—makes the unwarranted assumption that degeneracy in a language implies indefiniteness. 'It is impossible that Prof. Jowett's views of the language of St. Paul should not to a great extent vitiate the character of his commentary' (p. 109). Lightfoot gives examples, but is also able to say that Jowett's 'practice is better than his theory' (p. 103).

The charge of inexact scholarship (which if put into reverse tells us much about Lightfoot's understanding of the commentator's task) may be taken a little further. It will bring us back to Hort, who joined in the criticism of Jowett. There was much in Jowett's work that he liked; much also that he disliked. One quotation will suffice. In November 1855 Hort wrote to Gerald Blunt:

> About Jowett, I don't think you could go beyond me in enjoying and praising him. His wonderful sympathy, depth of insight into men, and thorough love of truth and fact are above praise; but alas! his theological *conclusions* seem to me blank atheism, though *he* is anything but an atheist. Even the learning and scholarship of the book you must not accept on trust. It is nearly always second-hand, and often quite wrong.[34]

It is not surprising that criticism such as Lightfoot had published and Hort had written privately were brought into the controversy at Oxford over the endowment and remuneration of the Greek professorship which Jowett held. It was probably Jowett's contribution to *Essays and Reviews* that precipitated the trouble, but the adequacy of his Greek scholarship was brought into it. It is surprising that Hort leapt into it. It is surprising that Hort leapt to Jowett's defense in a letter to *The Record*.[35] It is too long to quote, but Hort makes the point that Lightfoot (in the *Journal of Classical and Sacred Philology*) had referred to a disagreement in opinion, not to lack of knowledge, and that Jowett had in any case not been asked to lecture on the New Testament. 'Marcus'[36] replies that Lightfoot had referred to confusion of the perfect and aorist tenses, and that if Oxford had not asked Jowett to lecture on the New Testament there may have been good reason for the omission. I find it impossible to acquit Hort of a measure of disingenuousness. This however is not a point that I may allow myself at present to pursue. Strictly relevant to a consideration of Lightfoot's biblical commentaries is the disagreement between him and Jowett about biblical Greek. We have already seen something of Lightfoot's crirticism of Jowett. Let Jowett now speak for himself. He is right when he complains that 'There is a danger of a making words mean too much; refinements of signification are drawn out of them, perhaps contained in their etymology, which are lost in common use and parlance.'[37] This might have been written by James Barr!

---

[34]Hort, *Life and Letters of Fenton John Anthony Hort*, 1:315.
[35]F. J. A. Hort, *The Record*, supplement, Wednesday evening, April 27, 1884, p. 4.
[36]I do not know who hides behind this pseudonym.
[37]Benjamin Jowett, Frederick Temple and Mark Pattison, *Essays and Reviews* (London: Parker, 1860), p. 391.

When he asks for a lexicon not of the entire Greek New Testament but of significant theological words (he mentions πίστις, χάρις, δικαιοσύνη, ἁγιασμός, νόμος, πνεῦμα, παράκλητος, ἀπόστολος, ἐπίσκοπος, πρεσβύτερος, ἀγαπη, Ὁ και η δίκαιος [?], ἡ κυριακῇ ἡμέρᾳ), he is anticipating Kittel. But to him the language of the New Testament was simply degenerate.

> The degeneracy of the Greek language is traceable in the failure of syntactical power; in the insertation of prepositions to denote relations of thought, which classical Greek would have expressed by the case only; in the omission of them when classical Greek would have required them; in the incipient use of ἵνα with the subjunctive for the infinitive; in the confusion of ideas of cause and effect; in the absence of the article in the case of an increasing number of words which are passing into proper names; in the loss of the finer shades of difference in the negative particles; in the occasional confusion of the aorist and perfect; in excessive fondness for particles of reasoning or inference; in various forms of apposition, especially that of the word to the sentence; in the use, sometimes emphatic, sometimes only pleonastic, of the personal and demonstrative pronouns. These are some of the signs of that the language is breaking-up and losing its structure.[38]

Lightfoot knew better. The language was developing, and the New Testament was part of the development. It is possible to be too nice in the handling the language of the New Testament,[39] but it is also possible to be not nice enough, and it can usually be assumed that the New Testament writers, not least Paul, said what they meant to say, even though by classical standards they did not say it in the most elegant, in the most 'correct' way. Lightfoot's insight in anticipating the papyrus discoveries of 'everyday' Greek has often been celebrated,[40] but the words must not be made to mean too much. He writes explicitly:

> We do not believe that St. Paul can be said in any strict sense to have written in the Greek of every day life. He wrote perhaps in the religious Greek of the day. A language formed partly by the influence of the LXX version, and partly by other traditional influences, but in many respects very different in color from the language spoken every day at Athens or Antioch, or even Alexandria.[41]

---

[38]Ibid., p. 398.
[39]Perhaps Westcott was.
[40]E.g., by J. A. T. Robinson in *Lightfoot of Durham*, ed. G. R. Eden and F. C. MacDonald (Cambridge: Cambridge University Press, 1932), p. 126.
[41]J. B. Lightfoot, *Journal of Classical and Sacred Philology* 4 (1859): 107-8.

This seems to me well observed. Comparison with Jowett that illuminates some of Lightfoot's basic principles may also serve to bring us to the last section of this sketch of Lightfoot as commentator. After dealing in *Essays and Reviews* with the language of Scripture, that is, with interpretation in the narrow sense, Jowett turns to application (p. 404). This is partly a matter of recognizing ourselves, especially in the parables, which speaks immediately to 'well-satisfied Pharisees; repentant Publicans' (p. 414), partly selection.

> It is impossible to gather from a few fragmentary and apparently not always consistent expressions, how the Communion was celebrated, or the Church ordered, what was the relative position of Presbyters and Deacons, or the nature of the gift of tongues, as a rule for the Church in after ages—such inquiries have no certain answer, and at the best, are only the subject of honest curiosity. But the words 'Charity never faileth' and 'Though I speak in the tongues of men and of angels, and have not charity, I am nothing'—these have a voice which reaches to the end of time.[42]

Over against this, Lightfoot has only one method of interpretation and application: the historical-critical method. The primary and inescapable task of exegesis is to determine the precise meaning of the words in question in the context in which they were first spoken or written. This task Lightfoot achieved with unsurpassed success. 'Lightfoot's strength lay in the historical interpretation of the documents which he handled.'[43] The New Testament commentaries set out to state, with the utmost accuracy and clarity, what Paul wished to say to the Galatians, to the Philippians, to the Colossians and to Philemon. There is a tacit assumption that this is also what Paul wished to say to Galatians, to the Philippians, to the Colossians and to Philemon. There is a tacit assumption that this is also what Paul would have wished to say to Christian Englishmen in the nineteenth century. This assumption comes, I believe pretty near to what Hort meant by 'mere Protestantism,' though whether Hort had found the best terms for denoting it is questionable. It is also questionable whether the assumption is justified; it is our last question in regard to Lightfoot as commentator. Does he complete his task? Does there not remain untouched a hermeneutical process which Lightfoot owed to his readers, but did not give them?

---

[42]Jowett, *Essays and Reviews*, p. 415.
[43]F. F. Bruce, in *New Testament Interpretation*, ed. I. H. Marshall (Exeter, UK: Paternoster, 1977), p. 45.

It goes without saying that nothing will be found in Lightfoot's work of modern linguistic or semantic theory. It also goes without saying that we shall not be fair to Lightfoot if we do not study along with his commentaries, his many sermons, many published and many more that are still available to us in manuscript. These are interesting and instructive in their form; and in what they say and do not say. I take one, preached in St. Paul's on Septuagesima Sunday 1877, on 2 Corinthians 3:6, 'The Letter Killeth, but the Spirit Giveth Life.' It begins with matter that could have been used in a lecture or commentary. The contrast of spirit and letter was coined by Paul; it occurs in three places in his letters; each passage is given straight-forward historical exegesis.[44] Then comes the turning point.

> This is the primary sense in which the Apostle speaks of the letter killing and the spirit giving life. But, like many another maxim of St. Paul, the saying is far too full to be exhausted by its primary meaning. It has applications as wide as human life is wide, as human thought is wide. On one such application—perhaps the most important of all—I shall venture to dwell for a few moments.[45]

Lightfoot then goes on to deal with the way in which the practical moral conclusions are to be drawn from difficult sayings such as 'Give to him that asketh thee.' In other words, a general truth was given to the Corinthians in a particular context. This context, reached by the skill of the historian and helped out by parallels, enables us to determine the precise meaning of the general truth. The general truth may then be applied to other contexts that were not in Paul's mind when he wrote to Corinth. Thus historical exegesis has not only the negative function[46] of saying to the modern theologian or moralist, 'No, you may not base your proposition on that text,' but the positive function of providing solid ground for inferences relevant to ages long after the original truth was stated. Lightfoot assumes—and if the assumption is valid he may be vindicated not only as a philologist and historian but also as a theologian—that the language and the historical circumstances of Scripture have a quality of universality that gives them a perennial applicability. Lightfoot's extraordinary familiarity with the Fathers is enough to show

[44]See appendix C in this volume, which has this sermon in full. (BW3)
[45]J. B. Lightfoot, *Sermons Preached in St. Paul's Cathedral* (London: Macmillan, 1891), pp. 206-17, quote on p. 214.
[46]R. Morgan with S. Barton, *Biblical Interpretation* (Oxford: Oxford University Press, 1988), p. 181.

that he was by no means unmindful of the postbiblical tradition and its value. It helped him in exegesis and provided examples of the way in which scriptural truth had been applied to postbiblical situations earlier than his own. He speaks also with admiration of Luther as well as of post-Enlightenment biblical scholars in Germany and elsewhere. There remains for him however an absolute qualitative distinction between the words of Scripture and all other words, and it is this, together of course with his splendid scholarly equipment, that places him securely in the line of great biblical expositors, from Origen and Chrysostom to Calvin and Bengel.

Appendix G

LIGHTFOOT IN RETROSPECT[1]

J. D. G. Dunn

1. LIGHTFOOT—A CLASSIC EXPONENT OF
HISTORICAL CRITICAL INVESTIGATION

Lightfoot is probably the best example of what might be called the classical route into the study of early Christian writings. I will not elaborate the now familiar accounts of his formidable philological prowess or amazingly detailed knowledge of classical and patristic texts.[2] His command of Greek is nicely illustrated by the magisterial rebuke delivered to the unfortunate anonymous author of *Supernatural Religion*, who had had the temerity to chastise his older colleague and friend B. F. Westcott for an alleged mistake in translation. The unknown author, he points out scathingly, 'is quite unconscious of the difference between the infinitive and the indicative,' that is, between indirect and direct speech.[3] And he proceeds to criticize him for equal

---

[1]This was the last of the lectures given at the Lightfoot centenary conference in Durham in 1989, published as part of a special issue of the *Durham University Journal* in 1992. I have omitted the opening paragraph that refers to the conference itself and the order of the papers presented. Again, it is reprinted by permission of Durham University and the author himself, who requested it be included here. (BW3)
[2]See George R. Eden and F. C. MacDonald, eds., *Lightfoot of Durham: Memories and Appreciations* (Cambridge: Cambridge University Press, 1932), p. 5.
[3]J. B. Lightfoot, *Essays on the Work Entitled Supernatural Religion* (London: Macmillan, 1889, 1893), p. 5.

incompetencies in Latin and German.[4] And when the latter replied with indignation that Lightfoot's criticism 'scarcely rises above the correction of an exercise or the conjungation of a verb,' Lightfoot simply observes, with mild irony, 'I cannot help thinking this language unfortunate from his own point of view.'[5] His chaplain, J. R. Harmer, commenting on Lightfoot's knowledge of languages, recalls on one occasion Lightfoot saying to him 'in the simplest manner: Does it not sometimes happen to you that when you have read a book you forget in what language it is written?' Harmer reckoned that Lightfoot had mastery of seven languages (French, German, Italian and Spanish, as well as English, Latin and Greek), and a considerable or at least working knowledge of Hebrew, Syriac, Arabic and Ethiopic.[6]

Such stories, however, will be familiar to any who have read the various reminiscences and lectures on Lightfoot that have appeared at infrequent intervals over the last hundred years.[7] Here I wish to focus attention more on Lightfoot's *commitment to historical inquiry* and its importance for understanding the Christian texts he handled. It was the use of his formidable linguistic and philological knowledge in the course of his historical inquiry which proved their value.

Lightfoot's commitment to rigor of historical investigation is a feature of his work from the beginning. His earliest extant writing is the recently published essay on D. F. Strauss and Christian origins, written probably in 1853 as the Norrisian Prize Essay.[8] There he makes it clear that the object of his attack is 'the mythicizer (who dismisses) all search after history as hopeless (and who finds) in the biblical records merely a collection of legends, and spontaneous product of national feelings and expectations'[9]—a not entirely

[4]Ibid., p. 19.
[5]Ibid., p. 128.
[6]Eden and MacDonald, *Lightfoot of Durham*, pp. 118-19. [Not to mention Armenian, which he picked up in later life. (BW3)]
[7]Among most recent materials see in particular C. K. Barrett, 'Joseph Barber Lightfoot,' *Durham University Journal* (1972): 193-204; J. A. T. Robinson, 'Joseph Barber Lightfoot,' Durham Cathedral Lecture, 1981; H. E. Savage, 'Bishop Lightfoot's Influence: His Trust in Young Men,' *Durham University Journal* 76 (1984): 1-6; G. R. Treloar, 'J.B. Lightfoot and St. Paul: 1854-65,' *Lucas* 7 (1989): 5-34.
[8]G. R. Treloar and B. N. Kaye, 'J. B. Lightfoot on Strauss and Christian Origins: An Unpublished Manuscript,' *Durham University Journal* 79 (1987): 165-200. [While this essay is undoubtedly important, it is probably a later recension of the original essay, which is presented in the appendix above. (BW3)]
[9]Ibid., p. 176.

accurate characterization of Strauss's treatment of Jesus,[10] but close enough for the purpose of his essay. His response is what we may call Lightfoot's first attempt to demonstrate the historical basis of Christianity. His theological rationale is that if the divine has become genuinely incarnated, that is, in history, then the study of that history is fundamental for the understanding and defense of Christian origins.[11]

In unpublished lecture notes headed 'Greek Testament Lectures, Lent Term 1855' he sets out his position clearly.

> The timidity, which shrinks from the application of modern science or criticism to the interpretation of Holy Scripture evinces a very unworthy view of its character. If the Scriptures are indeed true, they must be in accordance with every true principle of whatever kind. It is against the wrong application of such principles, and against the presumption which pushes them too far that we must protest. It is not much knowledge but little knowledge that is the dangerous thing, here as elsewhere. From the full light of science and criticism we have nothing to fear.[12]

Lightfoot did not depart from this claim or objective. For example, thirteen years later, in his essay on 'The Christian Ministry' Lightfoot makes it clear that for him the only way to deal with the disputed issue of the origin of the threefold ministry is by looking at the actual history as it has been recorded. 'In this clamor of antagonistic opinions history is obviously the sole upright, impartial referee; and the historical mode of treatment will therefore be strictly adhered to in the following investigation.'[13]

Let me try to illustrate what this commitment to historical inquiry meant for Lightfoot. In the first place, an obvious point, but one that nevertheless should be made: Lightfoot had no doubts as to the *primacy of the original source*. One cannot but be impressed, for example, by the way in which in his massive study of the Ignatian epistles he marshals nearly one hundred pages of documentation in the original languages from Polycarp (early second century) to Gregory Barhebraeus (late thirteenth century).[14] What

---

[10]D. F. Strauss, *The Life of Jesus Critically Examined*, trans. George Eliot (1846; reprint).
[11]Treloar and Kaye, 'J.B. Lightfoot on Strauss and Christian Origins,' p. 176.
[12]Cited by B. N. Kaye, 'Lightfoot and Baur on Early Christianity,' *Novum Testamentum* 26 (1984): 219.
[13]'The Christian Ministry,' in *Saint Paul's Epistle to the Philippians* (London: Macmillan, 1868), p. 187.
[14]J. B. Lightfoot, *The Apostolic Fathers Part II, St. Ignatius, S. Polycarp* (London: Macmillan, 1885), pp. 127-221.

is particularly impressive in Lightfoot's case, of course, is his phenomenal knowledge of these sources, and his ability to pull together all the relevant evidence on a point from a wide range of classical and early Christian texts. Where modern students seem often more concerned to demonstrate their knowledge of secondary sources, Lightfoot's texts and notes are crammed with detailed reference to related material, inscriptional as well as literary, all marshaled with such a thoroughness that the reader is usually ready to concede the point well before the display of evidence has been completed.

Not that he ignored secondary literature. By no means. He was thoroughly familiar with the contemporary debate, and at one point makes a special note of his debt to the German scholar Neander. One of his most devastating chapters in his reply to *Supernatural Religion* is on Ignatius, where he examines several of the impressive lists of 'authorities' which the anonymous writer put together to support particular claims, and which gave that book much of its credibility. In each case, Lightfoot is able to show, from his own knowledge of these writers, that many of the said authorities had been misunderstood or misappropriated.[15] But for the most part, Lightfoot is rightly concerned to demonstrate that claims about early Christian texts hang or fall on a proper knowledge and appreciation of these texts themselves.

In the second place, Lightfoot demonstrates the *importance of setting the language of a text in its historical context if its meaning is to be understood.* He would have found great difficulty with the suggestion that the words of a text somehow exist in a world of their own, the world of the text. Of course they belong in the context of the text itself, but they belong also within a world of meaning of contemporary usage that informs in greater or lesser degree their meaning in that particular text. Contemporary usage informs particular usage. It is important, as he indicates in rebuke to the writer of *Supernatural Religion,* that one should know how 'men in actual life do speak and write now, and might be expected to speak and write sixteen or seventeen centuries ago.'[16]

So for example when he comes to inquire what Paul might mean by the distinction between μορφῇ and σχῆμα ('form') in Philippians 2:6-7 he naturally makes careful inquiry of classical and Christian writings including

---

[15]Lightfoot, *Essays on the Work Entitled Supernatural Religion,* chap. 3.
[16]Ibid., p. 9.

Philo[17] scrutinizing the usage of a total of twenty-three authors, as C. K. Barrett has noted.[18] How else might one be able to weigh words which occur only once or twice in Paul? Similarly, when he wants to know the force of πλήρωμα ('fullness') in Colossians, where the survey includes particularly Gnostic writers as well.[19] And in his 'Notes on Romans' he is able to shed light on Paul's somewhat puzzling claim—'Only rarely will someone die for a righteous man, though perhaps for a good man someone will dare even to die' (Rom 5:7)—by noting that the distinction between δίκαιος and ἀγαθός is well enough known in classical and Christian thought and is very much the same as the Aristotelean distinction between the 'the man who is scrupulously just and the man who is prepared to make allowances'[20]—an insight from historical usage which undercuts a good deal of more recent attempts to make sense of the passage.

In the third place, it is equally important for Lightfoot that *a text cannot be properly understood unless it is set within and related to a particular context.* Thus, in dealing with the seeming inconsistencies in the different ways Paul comports himself before others, he points out that Paul's tone would be 'graduated according to the temper and character of his hearers,' and goes on to cite an apposite parallel.

> Luther denouncing the Pope for idolatry and Luther rebuking Carlstadt for iconoclasm writes like two different persons. He bids the timid and gentle Melanchthon 'sin and sin boldly'; he would cut off his right hand sooner than pen such words to the antinomian rioters of Munster. It is not that the man or his principles were changed; but the same words addressed to persons of opposite tempers would have conveyed a directly opposite meaning.[21]

Once again a pertinent reminder that text read in neglect of context is likely to result in text misread. Likewise to be noted is the care with which Lightfoot gathers together all the available information on the destinations to which Paul wrote his letters, recognizing that occasional letters as they were, their meaning is bound to be determined in greater or lesser degree by the situations

---

[17]Lightfoot, *Philippians*, pp. 127-33.
[18]Barrett, 'Joseph Barber Lightfoot,' p. 197.
[19]J. B. Lightfoot, *Epistle to the Colossians* (London: Macmillan, 1875), pp. 255-71.
[20]J. B. Lightfoot, *Notes on the Epistles of St. Paul* (London: Macmillan, 1895), pp. 286-87.
[21]J. B. Lightfoot, *Saint Paul's Epistle to the Galatians* (London: Macmillan, 1865), pp. 349-50.

addressed—an innovation in the exegesis of the nineteenth century.[22] So too Ignatius's 'intensity of passion . . . for doing and suffering' cannot be fairly appreciated without some awareness of the atmosphere of persecution and martyrdom which the repressive policies of Domitian and Trajan engendered in the years preceding his arrest.[23] Or again in his lectures on John he notes that the key to the meaning of the conversation in John 6, the great bread of life discourse, is contemporary Jewish expectation. The point is that

> The inference is unexpressed. The expectation, which explains all, is left to be inferred, because it would be mentally supplied by men brought up among the ideas of the time. We ourselves have to get it by the aid of criticism and research from rabbinical authorities. But when we have grasped it, we can unlock the meaning of the whole chapter.[24]

Some of the best examples of Lightfoot's priorities and method come as usual from his reply to the author of *Supernatural Religion*. For example, the latter had argued that when Eusebius fails to mention an allusion to a canonical book in any of the earlier writers whom he cites, it must mean that the earlier writer himself was silent on the point. In typical fashion, Lightfoot examines what Eusebius himself says about his purpose on this matter, and then reviews the earlier writers one by one, providing another devastating rebuttal of a grossly misapplied argument from silence. What might have been arguable when Eusebius was taken on his own as regards his meaning becomes incredible when the claims of Eusebius are related to the historical evidence of the earlier writers he refers to.[25] Or again the author of *Supernatural Religion* found it incredible that Ignatius could have received visitors and written letters while under close arrest on his way to Rome. And if we confined ourselves only to the letters of Ignatius, and to their world of meaning, the seeming inconsistency might carry some weight. But Lightfoot is able to provide a complete answer to the issue by referring to what we know of Roman remand and arrest at the time. By relating the text to its context the meaning becomes clear.[26]

[22]Eden and MacDonald, *Lightfoot of Durham*, pp. 124-25, 177.
[23]Lightfoot, *Ignatius*, pp. 2ff.
[24]J. B. Lightfoot, *Biblical Essays* (London: Macmillan,1893), p. 24.
[25]Lightfoot, *Essays on the Work Entitled Supernatural Religion*, chap. 2.
[26]Ibid., pp. 74-78; also Lightfoot, *Ignatius*, pp. 342-47.

Finally we might simply note the care with which Lightfoot tried to *avoid speculation that went beyond the available evidence.* To the author of *Supernatural Religion* he points out: 'In the land of the unverifiable there are no efficient critical police. When a writer expatiates amidst conjectural quotations from conjectural Apocryphal Gospels, he is beyond the reach of refutation.'[27] In referring to the Judean church which reformed at Pella he simply observes: 'Its history in the ages following is a hopeless blank; and it would be vain to attempt to fill in the picture with conjecture.'[28] And in responding with his usual meticulously detailed examination to the hypotheses of Frankel regarding the origin of the name 'Essenes,' Lightfoot concludes:

> It would be a reversal of all established rules of historical criticism to desert the solid standing-ground of contemporary history for the artificial combinations and shadowy hypotheses that Frankel would substitute in its place.

Complementary to this is the description by a visitor to Auckland, one Robert Barbour, ancestor of Robin Barbour, until recently NT Professor in Aberdeen, who comments on the fineness of Lightfoot's judgment: 'He always speaks with a pair of balances in his hands, like Justice, only he is not blindfolded like her.'[29]

In all this Lightfoot clearly demonstrates *the importance of reading a historical text within its historical context, that the meaning of the text does not arise out of the text alone, but out of the text read in context, and that the original context and intention of the author is a determinative and controlling factor in what may be read or heard from such a text.* Of course one would have to qualify this observation in a number of ways. The debates in which he engaged were primarily about historical issues; were the Ignatian epistles authentic, that is, authored by Ignatius of Antioch in the circumstances indicated in the epistles, and if so, how many? And such like. He never addresses the question of whether an historical text read in a different and later context might be heard to resonate with a different meaning, because it was being read within a different context. Moreover, the texts he focused his

---

[27]Lightfoot, *Essays on the Work Entitled Supernatural Religion*, p. 36.
[28]Lightfoot, *Galatians*, p. 313.
[29]Eden and MacDonald, *Lightfoot of Durham*, pp. 35-36.

attention most closely on were all epistles, occasional letters written to particular situations. In these cases historical context is bound to place a more substantial constraint on the meaning of the text than texts less tightly tied to particular historical contexts—for example, wisdom sayings and parables—the biblical material on which, for that very reason, modern literary criticism has been most fruitful. But Lightfoot would certainly have approved a referential theory of meaning; *that that to which the language of a text refers determines and controls the meaning of that text.* His absorption with historical issues and his commitment to historical inquiry is simply a particular example of that, but it surely demonstrates beyond question the importance of historical context in the case of such historical texts at least.

Lightfoot is also conspicuously free of the philosophical baggage which has so often been associated with 'the historical critical method.' Although a man of the nineteenth century his historical critical work was not controlled by the prevailing scientific paradigm, that the four dimensions of time and space are a closed continuum of cause and effect. On the contrary, however, there is a certain naivete or fond optimism, particularly in assessment of the historical value of John and Acts, which equally dates his work tremendously, in contrast with the perennial value and often remarkably fresh character of his exegesis of the Pauline letters. But his concern to defend Christianity is fully matched by his concern for truth, for historical truth—and that means historical and critical study of the historical data. It was Harnack who paid him the appropriate compliment by noting that 'he never defended a tradition for the tradition's sake.'[30] To this we must return later.

Nor, presumably, does it need to be said that new evidence uncovered since Lightfoot's time requires many minor, some major revisions to his particular conclusions—for example his rather unsatisfactory note on the difficult verse Colossians 2:18, and his essays on the Essenes which were without peer prior to the discovery of the Dead Sea Scrolls. Lightfoot would have been the first to insist that his findings, arguments and conclusions be revised in the light of the new evidence. Witness the considerable use he made of recent inscriptional evidence in shedding light on the use of names in Romans 16 and in his Ignatius.[31] This too would have been a fundamental

---

[30]Ibid., p. 133.
[31]Lightfoot, *Philippians*, pp. 174-77; *Ignatius*, e.g., 1:477-85.

part of the historical method for him—the recognition that *meaning of language and text derives from historical context and that our confidence regarding that meaning is in direct proportion to our knowledge of that context.* In all this I dare to hold out Lightfoot as a mentor to be followed. Christianity is a religion whose truth claims are irrevocably tied to a period of history nearly twenty centuries ago. It cannot dispense with historical inquiry and frees its foundations from that period at its peril. Whatever other contexts these constitutional documents may be read within, the period covered by Lightfoot's researches remains their primary context, and Lightfoot's mode of inquiry into them remains a model for all who come after him.

2. The Importance of the Jewish/Christian Debate and the Key to Understanding Earliest Christianity and Its Initial Development

If, in our threefold division, Cambridge stands for Lightfoot's classic English analytical textual and historical scholarship, Tübingen speaks more of a debate about Christian origins which played a major part in shaping Lightfoot's concerns from the beginning to the end of his career as a scholar.[32] This dialogue of Lightfoot with Tübingen has usually been thought as solely a dialogue with F. C. Baur and the Tübingen school to which Baur gave birth. But the recent publication of Lightfoot's Norissian Essay reveals that the first Tübingener with whom Lightfoot did battle was D. F. Strauss, stretching back his interaction with Tübingen a further ten years.[33] What is interesting for us here, however, is the way he tackles Strauss.

Strauss's *Life of Jesus* consists of a massive and very detailed analysis of the Gospel traditions, particularly the miracle stories. In it he subjects to merciless and penetrating criticism the attempts of his rationalizing predecessors to save the historical character of these accounts by rationalizing away the miraculous element in them. Strauss points out that again and again such a procedure flies in the face of what the text actually says and clearly intends. The only solution he can see is to recognize that the accounts

---

[32]Kaye, 'Lightfoot and Baur,' however, cautions against the common assumption that rebuttal of the Tübingen school was the all-important aim of Lightfoot's scholarly work (p. 223). But see also the article by Hengel [reprinted in an appendix in volume two of The Lightfoot Legacy (BW3)].
[33]Treloar and Kaye, 'J. B. Lightfoot on Strauss and Christian Origins,' p. 170.

of the miracles are myths—that is, in his definition, the clothing of an idea or religious conception in the literary form by means of which such an idea would have come to expression in those days. In this case, the idea is of Jesus as Messiah. Given the impression Jesus actually made on his disciples and the Jewish expectations regarding the Messiah, the literary form by means of which this idea came to expression in the minds of his followers included especially the miracle story.

What is striking about Lightfoot's reply is that he makes no attempt whatsoever to meet Strauss on the ground of the Gospel traditions, the almost exclusive focus of Strauss's work. Instead, he seeks to answer what he sees to be the central thrust of Strauss's basic thesis—that the mythical view attributes the emergence of Christianity to natural processes and denies the character as revealed religion. Lightfoot's response is simple: let us see whether the cause is sufficient to explain the effect.[34] That is to say, he proposes to answer the mythical view of Christianity's emergence by a study of the history of Christianity's emergence. The mythicizing thesis must be brought to the bar of history and subjected to historical scrutiny. And the examination proceeds, be it noted, by a series of studies on 'The Jews of Palestine and the Dispersion,' 'the Messiah' and 'the Judaizing Christians.' In this early essay, the concerns which were to mark the rest of his scholarly career are already clear, and the essay is really the first draft, imperfect in many details, he would have been the first to recognize, of arguments he was to extend and deepen in his subsequent writings. And the key issue, as Lightfoot clearly indicates, is how to explain the emergence of Christianity from within its original Jewish context.

His early response to Strauss then was the first phase of a lifelong enterprise. But thereafter the principal protagonist was certainly F. C. Baur. Baur had begun to develop his own explanation of Christian origins more than twenty years earlier in his article on the Christ party in the Corinthian congregation.[35] His central thesis is already clear in the second part of the title of that article—'the opposition between Petrine and Pauline Christianity in the earliest church.' That is to say, earliest Christianity was characterized by

---

[34]Ibid., p. 177.
[35]F. C. Baur, 'Die Christuspartei in der korinthischen Gemeinde, der Gegensatz des petrinischen und paulinischen Christentums in der ältesten Kirche, der Apostel Petrus in Rom,' *Tübinger Zeitschrift für Theologie* 4 (1831): 61-206.

a conflict between two factions, one with marked Jewish tendencies, and the other Pauline Christianity. From this initial observation Baur's reconstruction of earliest Christian history evolves inexorably. For example, the historical value of Acts cannot be defended, since it shows Paul and Peter are closely similar in message and conviction, that is, a Paul who is manifestly different from the Paul of the Epistles. The Acts of the Apostles must derive, therefore, from a later period in which attempts were being made to reconcile the conflicting views of the Petrine and Pauline factions.[36] And the epistles of Ignatius and Polycarp could not be authentic simply because a date for them in the second decade of the second century did not fit within this paradigm of a sustained conflict between these factions which was reconciled only later in the second century.

Baur's overarching schema is most clearly articulated in his *Church History*, published in the same year that Lightfoot wrote his Norrisian essay.[37] In its simplest terms, Christianity for Baur is the highest expression of the religious consciousness of mankind, because its spirituality, expressed quintessentially in the first beatitude, is far more free than any other religion from everything merely external, sensuous or material. The characteristic feature of the Christian principle is that 'it looks beyond the outward, or accidental, the particular and rises to the universal, the unconditioned, the essential.' This refusal to regard true religion as a thing bound down to special ordinances and localities is at the heart of universalism. The dispute between the Petrine and Pauline parties is thus a dispute between Jewish particularism and Christian universalism. The problem was that this absolute moral and spiritual insight could only enter the stream of history in a particular form—the cramping and narrow form of the Jewish national messianic idea. It was not surprising then that one set of Jesus' followers should hold to the national aspect of his appearance and miss the moral and spiritual universalism of the morality and spirituality that he inculcated. But Paul must have the credit for delivering Christianity from the status of a mere Jewish sect and liberating 'the all-commanding universalism of its spirit and aims.'[38] The analysis also

---

[36]See particularly the Introduction to Baur's *Paul, The Apostle of Jesus Christ* (1845; Eng. trans., London: Williams and Norgate, 1873).

[37]F. C. Baur, *The Church History of the First Three Centuries* (1853; Eng. trans., London: Willams and Norgate, 1878–1879).

[38]See ibid., pp. 5-6, 27-29, 33, 38-39, 43, 49-50, etc.

enables Baur to make a point of more contemporary polemical application: the Catholicism which became the compromise between the Petrine and Pauline factions is like Judaism in its attachment to the formal and external; whereas Protestantism is like Pauline Christianity in its attachment to the inner and 'spiritual.'[39]

It is the systematic tendentiousness of Baur's development of this schema to which Lightfoot objected. There was no disagreement on the importance of the period, or the need to subject it to historical scrutiny. The difference was one of method. Baur extrapolated from the, to him, clear evidence of the undisputed Pauline letters to the whole history of Christian beginnings, read through the lenses of the overarching philosophical schema. Lightfoot replied with a rigorous historical analysis of language and context; how these terms would have been understood, given the usage as we know it in the world of the time, how these claims or episodes fit into what we know of the history of the period.[40] Far from flying from the task of historical reconstruction, Lightfoot commits himself wholeheartedly to it, and, as we shall remind ourselves shortly, his criticism of the Tübingeners is that they have abused the principles of sound historical criticism.

It is sometimes maintained that for Lightfoot, Baur's theory of Christian beginnings stood or fell on the issue of the genuineness of the Clementine and Ignatian epistles.[41] And it is certainly true that Lightfoot recognized the particular importance of these documents for settling the issue. Already in 1875, in the third of his replies to *Supernatural Religion*, he had noted that 'If the Ignatian letters . . . are allowed to be genuine, the Tübingen views of early Christian history fall to the ground. It was therefore a matter of life and death to this school to condemn them wholly.'[42] Hence, of course, the massive expenditure of his critical energies on these epistles. But just as important for Lightfoot was the fact that other early Christian documents were being forced into an unnatural mold. The pseudo-Clementine Homilies have no right to be treated as the missing link between

---

[39]Kaye, 'Lightfoot and Baur,' p. 201.
[40]See particularly C. K. Barrett, 'Quomodo historia conscribenda sit,' *New Testament Studies* 28 (1982): 303-20, particularly p. 318.
[41]Cf. particularly S. Neill, *The Interpretation of the New Testament* (Oxford: Oxford University Press, 1964), p. 56-59.
[42]Lightfoot, *Essays on the Work Entitled Supernatural Religion*, p. 64; also *Ignatius*, 1:270.

the Judaism of the Christian era and the Catholicism of the late second century.[43] The genuiness of the epistle of Polycarp is equally fatal to the Tübingen school—a genuineness questioned only because it provided such strong testimony regarding Ignatius.[44]

Hence also, as Professor Hengel reminded us, Lightfoot's concern to argue for the authenticity, that is, apostolic authorship of the Fourth Gospel; if the Fourth Gospel is authentic, the Tübingen theory must be abandoned. Even the Apocalypse of John, Lightfoot observes in a footnote, is sufficient to furnish ample refutation of 'the peculiar views' of the Tübingen school.[45] Above all it is important to realize that for Lightfoot as well as Baur, the issue hung on the interpretation of Paul. It is at the point at which Baur had his most secure basis in history for his claims that Lightfoot joins decisive battle. Hence the first Pauline letter to which Lightfoot turned his attention was Galatians—as he himself readily acknowledged: 'it is felt by both sides that the Epistle to the Galatians is the true key to the position.'[46] And hence the importance of his lengthy essay in that volume on 'St. Paul and the Three,' in which Lightfoot deliberately set himself to undercut the central plank of Baur's reconstruction.[47]

At the same time it should not be assumed that Lightfoot was the polar opposite of Baur on every point or that he forced Baur to abandon the field entirely. Not only did Lightfoot accept that the crucial field of battle was the one designated by Baur—namely the Pauline literature; for though he read Acts much more straightforwardly as history, Lightfoot could not be content with an exegesis which was not scrupulously determined by what Paul actually wrote. But also when we read Paul, he could not deny some merit to Baur's interpretation. Thus, in reading Galatians 2:3ff., Paul's report of how Titus was not compelled to be circumcised on his visit to Jerusalem even though a Greek, Lightfoot does not resist an implication in Paul's language that the pillar apostles (James, Peter and John) were sympathetic to the conservative or Judaizing 'false brothers.'

---

[43]Lightfoot, *Galatians*, p. 341.
[44]Lightfoot, *Essays on the Work Entitled Supernatural Religion*, p. 96; *Ignatius*, 1:407.
[45]Lightfoot, *Galatians*, p. 363n2.
[46]Ibid., p. 293.
[47]So particularly Kaye, 'Lightfoot and Baur,' pp. 215-16.

On the whole it seems probable that they (the pillar apostles) recommended
St. Paul to yield the point. . . . The counsels of the Apostles of the Circumcision
are the hidden rock on which the grammar of the sentence is wrecked.[48]

And in his essays on 'St. Paul and the Three' he does not hesitate to speak
of 'The systematic hatred of St. Paul (as) an important fact, which we are too
apt to overlook, but without which the whole Apostolic age will be misread
and misunderstood.'[49] 'Pharisaic Ebionism' (as he calls it) 'was a disease in
the Church of the Circumcision from the first.'[50] Moreover, far from elabo-
rating the account of Acts into a portrayal of the apostolic age as one of idyllic
peace and unity, Lightfoot ends the same essay with the sobering conclusion:

> However great may be the theological differences and religious animosities of
> our time, they are far surpassed in magnitude by the distractions of an age
> which, closing our eyes to the facts, we are apt to invest with an ideal excel-
> lence. In the early Church was fulfilled, in its inward dissensions no less than
> its outward sufferings, the Master's warning that He came 'not to send peace
> on earth but a sword.'[51]

No wonder then that Barrett can speak of Lightfoot's 'modified Baurian
position' and sees 'the total effect' of Lightfoot's debate with Baur as the
destruction of the *chronology* of the Tübingen school.[52] As Lightfoot
himself claimed:

> The great battle with this form of error seems to have been fought out at an early
> date, and in the lifetime of the Apostles themselves and in the age [by which I
> presume he means the generation—J. D. G. D.] immediately following.[53]

Not of least importance, and this is the point I wish most to emphasize
here, Baur and Lightfoot were agreed on the importance of Christianity's

---

[48]Lightfoot, *Galatians*, pp. 105-6; similarly, p. 350: 'St. Paul's language leaves the impression (though
the inference cannot be regarded as certain), that they, (the pillar apostles), had not offered a
prompt resistance to the Judaizers in the first instance, hoping perhaps to conciliate them.'
[49]Ibid., p. 311.
[50]Ibid., pp. 322-23.
[51]Ibid., p. 374.
[52]Barrett, 'Quomodo,' pp. 310, 313-14. In his earlier essay Barrett had noted that the frank picture
in the immediately preceding quotation from Lightfoot is not easy to parallel in English writers
of the period, and sums up: 'It might not be too inaccurate to say that Baur asked the right questions and that Lightfoot set them in the right historical context.'
[53]Lightfoot, *Galatians*, p. 336.

emergence from Judaism as the key issue in understanding both the early history of Christianity and the character of Christianity itself. Thus Baur writes at the beginning of his *Paul:*

> how Christianity, instead of remaining a mere form of Judaism . . . asserted itself as a separate, independent principle, broke loose from it, and took its stand as a new enfranchised form of religious thought and life, essentially different from all the national peculiarities of Judaism is the ultimate, most important point of the primitive history of Christianity.[54]

And in his *Church History* he confirms:

> There can be no question that the purely moral element which lies at its first source has ever been (Christianity's) unchangable and substantial foundation. Christianity has never been removed from this foundation without denying its true and proper character.[55]

But Lightfoot is equally convinced of the seriousness of the issues at stake:

> If the primitive Gospel was, as some have represented it, merely one of many phases of Judaism, if those cherished beliefs which have been the life and light of many generations were afterthoughts, progressive accretions, having no foundation in the Person and Teaching of Christ, then indeed St. Paul's preaching was vain and our faith is vain also.[56]

The point I wish to make is that *the issues outlined here as matters of debate between Baur and Lightfoot are still among the most fundamental issues in our understanding of Christian origins and in our understanding of Christianity itself.* These issues were obscured for the next three generations of NT scholarship. This was principally because of the emergence of the history-of-religions perspective on the whole period, at the end of the nineteenth century and beginning of the twentieth century, a perspective that quickly came to dominate the debate on Christian origins. What this meant was that, on the Jewish side of the equation, apocalyptic (eschatology) became the major preoccupation, as a factor influencing Jesus, but also as a mythical clothing of his enduring message, able to be sloughed off to leave a moral core, or demythologized into existential demand for decision to

---

[54]Baur, *Paul*, p. 3.
[55]Baur, *Church History*, p. 37.
[56]Lightfoot, *Galatians*, p. xi; see also p. 293.

authentic existence. At the same time, on the Hellenistic side of the equation, the major preoccupation became the pursuit of the phantom of a pre-Christian Gnostic Redeemer myth. One could say that the period between Lightfoot and today has been a huge parenthesis between those on either side of that parenthesis who recognize the central importance of Christianity's Jewish matrix and the earliest phase of Christian development as the growing out of and increasing detachment from the matrix—a process fundamental to the shaping, and the shape of Christianity.[57]

Only in the last decade or decade and a half has the issue reemerged, but it has done so with considerable force. Partly because, on the one hand, with the discovery of the Dead Sea Scrolls and the substantial reassessment of Jewish literature of the period and the subsequent rabbinic traditions, we are now in a position to gain a 'fix' on first-century Judaism in a way and to an extent which was simply not possible before. And partly because, on the other hand, the Holocaust has forced Christian scholars to a painful reassessment of Christianity's relationship and attitude toward Judaism, its parent faith. Particularly important has been the overwhelming movement in favor of setting Jesus within the context of first-century Judaism, not least as 'Jesus the Jew.' What is now being designated a 'third quest of the historical Jesus' has as its common theme the reassertion in various ways of the Jewishness of Jesus.[58] Equally vigorous has been the debate about Paul's relationship with his parent faith, particularly on the question of the Jewish law.[59]

However, the corollaries and implications of the various theses are only beginning to be faced. For example, is the Christianity which actually emerged divorced from or continuous with the Jewish Jesus? Was the earliest form of Christianity *simply* a form of first-century Judaism and nothing more? Is Paul the real founder of Christianity as we (Gentiles) know it? In short, is the Christianity we know today something essentially different from and at odds with the teaching of Jesus and the earliest form of Christianity? But *these were the very issues which were posed by Baur and addressed by Lightfoot.*

---

[57]See further my *The Parting of the Ways* (London: SCM Press, 1991), chap. 1.

[58]The phrase has been given wide currency by N. T. Wright in his revision of Neill's *Interpretation* (Oxford: Oxford University Press, 1988), pp. 379-403. See those listed in my *Unity and Diversity in the New Testament*, 2nd ed. (London: SCM Press, 1990), p. xxxiii n. 9.

[59]See, e.g., my review of and contribution to the debate in *Jesus, Paul and the Law* (London: SPCK, 1990).

Regrettably, Lightfoot is less helpful here than we might have hoped. He never really addressed the question of the Jewishness of Jesus, not more in his subsequent work than in his earlier reply to relate the teaching of Jesus to the gospel of Paul. Nor does he betray any real appreciation of the startling contrast between the Jesus of the Synoptics and the Jesus of John. Here we may say that his strengths as an historian betray something of his weaknesses as a theologian, a point first noted by Hort[60] as we were reminded in [the lectures by Barrett and Hengel].[61] The immense knowledge and abilities which he applied so powerfully to the historical questions regarding letters addressed to and presupposing particular historical situations was much less well fitted to handling the complexities of the Gospel tradition. The nearest he comes is the brief comment in his essay on 'St Paul and the Three' that Jesus 'had discredited the law, but He had not deposed or abolished it.'[62] And in his treatment of the continuing tensions within Christianity following Paul and between Christianity and Judaism he evidently does not see the possibility of drawing in evidence Matthew or John (or Acts), despite the fact that they were all written in that period, and despite the prominence they gave to Jewish themes.

Some of this criticism is not entirely fair; we can hardly find fault with Lightfoot for being a child of his times; critical assessment of the Gospels was still at a very early stage in the second half of the nineteenth century. The primary issue at that stage was whether the first phase of Christianity was a purely Jewish phenomenon, so that the development under Paul resulted in a fundamental breach. And on this Lightfoot's counter to and modification of Baur is of lasting value, particularly in terms of the character and force of his exegesis.

Even more important is the underlying issue as to the character of Christianity. To what extent is its Jewish origins and heritage integral to Christianity? To what extent has the category 'Israel' been completely taken over by Christianity, and to what extent does it still 'belong to the Jews'? Are Christians alone 'the people of God,' or Jews alone, or only Jewish Christians? Is

---

[60]Hort, *Life and Letters of Fenton John Anthony Hort*, pp. 34, 79.
[61][See the preceding appendix in this volume and the Hengel article in the appendix in volume two. (BW3)]
[62]Lightfoot, *Galatians*, p. 295.

the most fundamental schism within the people of God not that between
Catholic and Protestant, or between East and West, but rather that between
Christian and Jew? Can the assembly of God's worshiping people, the *qahal
Israel*, the ἐκκλησίᾳ τοῦ Θεοῦ, be complete without the (other) seed of
Abraham—complete either in their worship or in their self-understanding?
These are issues which have only recently reemerged on the stage and only
recently been recognized by the World Council of Churches.[63] But they are
fundamental to any definition of Christianity, past, present or future. Here
not least the discussion needs to go back to Baur and Lightfoot, whose debate
in no little measure both clears the ground and allows the fundamental issue
to emerge in sharper focus.

3. LIGHTFOOT AS CHRISTIAN TEACHER

If Cambridge speaks to us of Lightfoot as the meticulous scholar, and Tübingen
speaks to us of the single most sustained preoccupation of his scholarly career,
then Durham speaks to us of Lightfoot the scholar of firm Christian convic-
tions and ecclesiastical commitment. The invitation to Durham in 1879 caused
him much heart searching, and while his acceptance was greeted with universal pleasure so far as the episcopal appointment was accepted, there was
widespread concern expressed lest his scholarly work be cut short—as indeed
was the case.[64] But the tug of the north—his father was a Yorkshireman and
his mother's family came from Newcastle—and the challenge of the great
northern diocese with its tradition of Christian scholarship in the past and its
pressing industrial problems in the present together made a compelling call
he could not refuse.

   As bishop he threw himself into the work with characteristic vigor. He
saw through the creation of the Newcastle diocese, and in ten years oversaw
the building of forty-five churches and mission halls, presided at 456 confirmation services (often with 250 or three hundred candidates at a service),
and trained nearly seventy ordinands at Auckland Castle at his own expense.
And yet even as bishop he never ceased to be a scholar; and not merely of
Christian beginnings in the first and second centuries. He was one of the

---

[63]H. G. Link, ed., *Apostolic Faith Today*, Faith and Order Paper no. 124 (Geneva: World Council
of Churches, 1985), pp. 259-60.
[64]Eden and MacDonald, *Lightfoot of Durham*, p. 107.

first to recognize and assert the importance of Northumbria in the seventh-century evangelization of England; and he was familiar with every detail of the ecclesiastical antiquities in both Durham and Northumberland. His sermons on *Leaders of the Northern Church*,[65] incomplete at his death, were the fruit of his own natural curiosity about the history of his diocese. And wholly typical is the painstaking detail with which he investigated the history of the chapel at Auckland itself, demonstrating beyond dispute that the present chapel had been converted to its present purpose from the old hall of the castle by Bishop Cosin.[66] In the midst of such labor, the three great volumes on Ignatius were finished in 1885.

All this was possible only because of Lightfoot's amazing memory and intense power of concentration. Regularly he would take work in hand while on holiday; and there is more than one reminiscence of Lightfoot sailing on a stormy sea or being driven down some precipitous path calmly correcting the proofs of Ignatius, albeit recalled through an 'idealizing haze,' in Dr. Thompson's words.[67] Even after a hard day he would try to find some time for study, often into the early hours of the morning. One of his 'sons' (the ordinands who trained at Auckland) recalls with pleasure that the preface to the Ignatius volumes is dated St. Peter's Day 1885—a day on which it was Lightfoot's custom to give himself fully and unstintingly to his 'sons' on their annual reunion. And part of the legend is the parallel with the Venerable Bede, writing to the last, till the pen fell from his fingers shortly before his death.[68]

Such bare details and reminiscences speak volumes of the man and the impression he made, but the point I wish to develop here is one which emerges from all this: the fact that Lightfoot was able to hold together his historical critical scholarship with his firm Christian conviction, and the extent to which he was successful in doing so. I have already spoken sufficiently of Lightfoot's commitment to critical historical scholarship. Here I want to focus attention on the other side of the dialectic in Lightfoot's

---

[65]J. B. Lightfoot, *Leaders of the Northern Church* (London: Macmillan, 1890).

[66]J. B. Lightfoot, *Historical Essays* (London: Macmillan, 1895), pp. 182-210.

[67]Dunn is referring to an essay by David Thompson on 'Lightfoot as a Victorian Churchman,' which, although it was included in the original centenary of Lightfoot *Durham University Journal* special issue in 1992, is not included here, since its focus is beyond the parameters of these three volumes. (BW3)

[68]Details from Eden and MacDonald, *Lightfoot of Durham*, passim; another summary in Robinson, 'Joseph Barber Lightfoot,' pp. 14-15.

scholarship. The matter is put strongly and perhaps somewhat unwisely in his earliest work, the Norrisian Prize Essay. There in his concluding defense of revealed religion, he maintains stoutly:

> There is a testimony which it is not in the power of historical criticism to grasp; the testimony of the heart which finds in Christianity its deepest aspirations realized and its fondest hopes fulfilled. . . . If then the Christian is asked whether his books are not to be tried by the same standard as all other writings, he will fearlessly answer that they are not; he will not shrink indeed in the investigation from any of the aids of philosophy or criticism, for, as the truth is, he believes that his Faith, will be found to be ever one in accordance with the strictest criticism and the highest philosophy, but he will deprecate an avowed determination on the part of those who approach this question, to divest themselves of the inward influences of Christianity.[69]

The passage rings slightly awkwardly when we recall Lightfoot's outspoken commitment to historical criticism, already documented in the first section of this paper. But the point is clear enough. There is a truth dimension in earliest Christian texts and traditions which is not wholly subject to historical criticism, a truth, we might say, whose perception involves a personal engagement with the subject matter of the text. Lightfoot had no fear of historical criticism because he saw truth as undivided. The truth of the Christian faith was attested both by personal experience and by a critical study of history. He did not see faith and criticism as incompatible. He did not fall into the trap of thinking that a wholly objective assessment of historical data was possible. He did not think criticism was possible without presuppositions. His fiercest criticisms, indeed, were

---

[69]Treloar and Kaye, 'J. B. Lightfoot on Strauss and Christian Origins,' p. 198. [I must note that this presents a text-critical problem. The actual Norissian Prize essay ends as follows—'For there is a testimony which it is not in the power of historical criticism to grasp; the testimony of the heart which finds in Christianity its deepest aspirations realized and its fondest hopes fulfilled— the testimony of the conscience smitten and pierced as by a sharp two-edged sword, by the record of His words "who spake as no man spake," the testimony of experience which reminds the Christian that in proportion as he has cultivated his best faculties and highest feelings of his nature, the clouds of doubt and difficulty have been dispersed before the "light of the Spirit which bears witness to his spirit," and have only gathered again when he has been betrayed into spiritual carelessness or moral ambiguity.' This is followed by several extraneous and out-of-place paragraphs on Philo and an apology. I *suspect* that Treloar and Kaye found an adapation of Lightfoot's original essay for a *later* purpose—namely as a response to the essayists referred to in Hengel's article in volume two of this series. The original essay did not end as cited above. (BW3)]

leveled at those who seemed to him to be imposing their ideas or faith uncritically on the text. 'We Christians,' he comments in one place, in a passage also cited by Professor Hengel,

> are constantly told that we must expect to have our records tested by the same standards which are applied to other writings. That is exactly what we desire, and what we do not get. It is not easy to imagine the havoc which would ensue, if the critical principles of the Tübingen school and their admirers were let loose on the classical literature of Greek and Rome.[70]

And while he did not hesitate to bring his own faith presuppositions into play, he was more than ready to let his findings react back critically on his presuppositions—even if we judge that he did not always do so successfully. So in the preface to *Galatians* he recalls the words of Hooker—'A number there are who think they canot admire, as they ought, the power of the Word of God, if in things divine they should attribute any force to man's reason' and continues:

> The caution is equally needed (in the present day). The abnegation of reason is not the evidence of faith but the confession of despair. Reason and reverence are natural allies, though untoward circumstances may sometimes interpose and divorce them.[71]

As John Robinson justifiably notes in his Cathedral Lecture on Lightfoot: 'Lightfoot would have been horrified to think that serious scholarship could by-pass the historical questions or suppose they could be settled *a priori* by the theological.'[72]

The extent to which Lightfoot was successful in holding together his faith commitment and his critical scholarship in fruitful interaction is probably nowhere more clearly illustrated than in his lengthy essay on 'The Christian Ministry' in his commentary on *Philippians*[73]—the Christian teacher writing ten years after his own ordination as priest and nine years before he became bishop, and looking, appropriately, at the historical roots and origin of his own office and ministry.

---

[70]Lightfoot, *Essays on the Work Entitled Supernatural Religion*, p. 82.
[71]Lightfoot, *Galatians*, pp. xi-xii.
[72]Robinson, 'Joseph Barber Lightfoot,' p. 16.
[73]Lightfoot, *Philippians*, pp. 181-269.

He begins with a remarkable description of 'the Kingdom of Christ,' which Professor Barrett also cited.

> It has no sacred days or seasons, no special sanctuaries, because every time and every place alike are holy. Above all it has no sacerdotal system. It interposes no sacrificial tribe or class between God and man, by whose intervention alone God is reconciled and man forgiven. Each individual member holds personal communion with the Divine Head. To Him immediately he is responsible, and from Him directly he obtains pardon and draws strength.

Having thus stated what appears to him as the ideal, he goes on at once to qualify it.

> Yet the broad statement, if allowed to stand alone, would suggest a false impression, or at least would convey only a half-truth. It must be evident that no society of men could hold together without officers, without rules, without institutions of any kind; and the Church of Christ is not exempt from this universal law. The conception in short is strictly an *ideal*, which we must ever hold before our eyes, which should inspire and interpret ecclesiastical polity, but which nevertheless cannot supersede the necessary wants of human society, and, if crudely and hastily applied, will lead only to signal failure. As appointed days and set places are indispensable to her efficiency, so also the Church could not fulfil the purposes for which she exists, without rulers and teachers, without a ministry of reconciliation, in short, without an order of men who may in some sense be designated a priesthood.[74]

Here indeed is a striking vision: the kingdom of God as a society without hierarchy and priesthood; an ideal that should inspire and interpret ecclesiastical polity; ecclesiastical orders and priesthood as a *social* rather than a *theological necessity.*

This two-handed emphasis—on the necessity of the historical development, and the distinction from that of the theological ideal—is illustrated on what follows. The main section of the essay is given over to tracing the emergence of the threefold order of ministry—deacon, presbyter, bishop, with particular attention paid to the latter. In a wide geographical and historical sweep he observes clear 'evidence for the early and wide extension of episcopacy throughout proconsular Asia' in the second century; but he also

---

[74]Ibid., pp. 181-82.

notes that the striking silence of Ignatius and Polycarp on the subject so far as Philippi and Rome itself are concerned. He goes on to argue that the episcopate emerged out of the presbyterate, a progressive development slower in the West and faster in the East, and concludes:

> Though something must be attributed to the frailty of human pride and love of power, it will nevertheless appear that the pressing needs of the Church were mainly instrumental in bringing about the result, and that this development of the episcopal office was a providential safeguard amid the confusion of speculative opinion, the distracting effects of persecution, and the growing anarchy of social life, which threatened not only the extension but the very existence of the Church of Christ.[75]

To be noted again is his clear distinction of episcopacy as of the *bene esse* (the well-being) of the church, and not of the *esse* (the essence) of the church.

Having thus traced the historical development, Lightfoot proceeds to measure this historical reality against the theological ideal sketched out in the opening paragraph. He reserves some particularly critical comments for Ignatius: 'Throughout the whole range of Christian literature, no more uncompromising advocacy of the episcopate can be found than appears in his writings.' He speaks of 'this extravagant exaltation of the episcopal office,' and adds:

> It need hardly be remarked how subversive of the true spirit of Christianity, in the negation of individual freedom and the consequent suppression of direct responsibility to God in Christ, is the crushing despotism with which this language, if taken literally, would invest the episcopal office.[76]

The heresy of Montanus, he suggests was:

> A rebound from the aggressive tyranny of hierarchial assumption—Wildly fanatical as were its manifestation, this reaction nevertheless issued from a true instinct which rebelled against the oppressive yoke of external tradition and did battle for the freedom of the individual spirit.[77]

Such words, from one who was hardly a low churchman or pietest, reveal the striking ability of genuine Christian scholarship to be self-critical about

---

[75]Ibid., p. 234.
[76]Ibid., pp. 236-37.
[77]Ibid., pp. 238-39.

its roots and tradition. His final conclusion on the subject demonstrates a marvelous ecumenical openness that is heartening to hear from one who was himself to become a bishop within the historic episcopate: 'If the facts do not allow us to unchurch other Christian communities differently organized, they may at least justify our jealous adhesion to a polity derived from this source' (divine sanction).[78]

Lightfoot's other main preoccupation in the essay is a sustained polemic against the ideal of sacerdotal priesthood. He had already sketched out the Christian ideal—'as individuals, all Christians are priests alike.'

> The Apostles never lost sight of (this idea) in their teaching. . . . For communicating instruction and for preserving public order, for conducting religious worship and for dispensing social charities, it became necessary to appoint special officers. But the priestly functions and privileges of the Christian people are never regarded as transferred or even delegated to these officers . . . the sacerdotal title is never once conferred upon them. The only priests in the Gospel, designated as such in the New Testament, are the saints, the members of the Christian brotherhood.[79]

The subsequent emergence of the *sacerdotal* view of ministry he attributes to Gentile and heathen influence and, within the Christian community, particularly to the influence of Cyprian.

> The only High Priest under the Gospel recognized by the apostolic writings is our Lord Himself. . . . (But) by the union of Gentile sentiment with the ordinances of the Old Dispensation, the doctrine of an exclusive priesthood found its way into the Church of Christ.[80]

As a New Testament specialist myself, I can find nothing to fault in these statements. It remains something of a wonder to me, as evidently also to Lightfoot, that the successors of the NT Christians could so easily go back on the firm conviction of the NT writers that the old distinction between priest and people had been left behind once and for all—a failure, it would appear, of eschatological perspective and spiritual nerve.

As already noted, however, Lightfoot had also recognized the historical

---

[78]Ibid., p. 267.
[79]Ibid., pp. 183-86.
[80]Ibid., pp. 258-64.

and social inevitability of the emergence of 'an order of men who may in some sense be designated a priesthood.' The way Lightfoot saw to resolve the resulting tension between apostolic ideal and historical outworking was for the minister to be regarded as a priest only:

> As the mouthpiece, the representative, of a priestly race. . . . So long as this important aspect is kept in view, so long as the priesthood of the ministry is regarded as springing from the priesthood of the whole body, the teaching of the Apostles has not been directly violated.[81]

Nor does he hesitate to draw the appropriate corollary in the closing paragraphs:

> the minster's function is *representative* without being vicarial. He is a priest, as the mouthpiece, the delegate, of a priestly race. His acts are not his own, but the acts of the congregation. Hence too it will follow that . . . his function cannot be absolute and indispensable. It may be a general rule . . . that the highest acts of congregational worship shall be performed through the principal officers of the congregation. But an emergency may arise when the spirit and not the letter must decide. The Christian ideal will then interpose and interpret our duty. The higher ordinance of the universal priesthood will overrule all special limitations. The layman will assume functions which are otherwise restricted to the ordained minister.[82]

Such were Lightfoot's views on Christian ministry. His essay caused much unhappiness in those of a more Catholic persuasion. His friend Hort could find little to fault in the historical account, but as 'a staunch sacerdotalist' could not agree on the doctrinal.[83] And as late as July 1889, on a visit to Auckland, H. P. Liddon tried 'to get him to reconsider his position regarding the Christian Ministry in his celebrated Essay,' without apparent success, though Lightfoot evidently regretted some of the 'inferences which Dissenters and others drew from his Essay.'[84] But Lightfoot himself had allowed the essay to remain unaltered through repeated editions of *Philippians*, explicitly denying in the preface to the sixth edition that he had

---

[81]Ibid., pp. 257-58.
[82]Ibid., p. 268.
[83]Hort, *Life and Letters of Fenton John Anthony Hort*, 2:86 (a letter to Lightfoot, dated October 26, 1867).
[84]J. O. Johnston, *Life and Letters of Henry Parry Liddon* (London: Longmans, Green, 1904), pp. 369-70.

abandoned the main opinions expressed therein, and reaffirming, both explicitly that the threefold ministry was of divine sanction, the point on which he evidently felt he had been misrepresented, and implicitly that his views on sacerdotal priesthood and lay ministry remained the same.

Lightfoot, then, would have questioned sharply the prevailing Catholic view, expressed in the Second Vatican Council, that 'there is an *essential difference* between the faithful's priesthood in common and the priesthood of the ministry or the hierarchy, and not just a difference of degree,'[85] with its clear echo in the ARCIC statement on Ministry and Ordination.[86] Contrast Lightfoot commenting on Clement: 'The Minister is a priest in the same sense only in which each individual member of the congregation is a priest.'[87] On the other hand, he would almost certainly have welcomed the Dominican Edward Schillebeeckx's study of ecclesiastical ministry which, in effect, takes up from Lightfoot to show that in the early centuries priesthood was thought to be vested primarily in the community and only secondarily and derivatively in the ordained.[88] And he would have welcomed too, no doubt, those within his own tradition, like Anthony Harvey, who take up the same question as to whether presidency of the Eucharist need always be confined to the priestly ordained, with a clear negative answer.[89] We should note also that during his time as bishop, Lightfoot was a pioneer in the advocacy and promotion of lay ministry—giving lay people a new and effective voice in the church councils and calling into being a trained body of lay readers, lay preachers and lay evangelists. In 1885 he was calling for a generative representative assembly in the Church of England.[90] To similar effect John Robinson notes Lightfoot's commendation of women deacons—'As I read my New Testament—Phoebe is as much a deacon as Stephen or Philip is a deacon—and he gave her a place in the window of Trinity Chapel a century before the College admitted women!'[91]

In all this Lightfoot was a hundred years ahead of his time. The emphases which characterized his teaching on the Christian ministry have only recently

---

[85]*Lumen Gentium* 10 (emphasis mine).
[86]Anglican Roman Catholic International Commission, *The Final Report* (CTS/SPC, 1982), p. 36.
[87]Lightfoot, *Philippians*, p. 262.
[88]Edward Schillebeeckx, *Ministry: A Case for Change* (London: SCM Press, 1981), chap. 2.
[89]A. E. Harvey, *Priest or President* (London: SPCK, 1975).
[90]Eden and MacDonald, *Lightfoot of Durham*, pp. 63-68.
[91]Robinson, 'Joseph Barber Lightfoot,' p. 14.

come to general prominence in the rediscovery of the ministry of the whole people of God.[92] But the attempts to relate that to the much more deeply established concepts of ordained ministerial priesthood have so far proved singularly unsuccessful, undermined, it would appear, by a combination of appeal to tradition, professional pride and vested interest. But Lightfoot's resolution of the conflict between NT Scripture and subsequent tradition, in terms of a *priestly ministry which is competent as such only insofar as it is representative of the priestly people*, seems to provide a way forward on issues like lay presidency and women ministry which respects both Scripture and tradition. For if the priesthood of the individual is a function of the priesthood of the congregation, then it would seem to follow that those who are recognized as representative of the congregation need no further justification in essence in order to exercise a priestly ministry on behalf of the congregation. And even if that observation might be regarded as overhasty by some, at the very least, it would seem desirable for the church, and the Church of England in particular, to go back to one of its most distinguished writers on the subject of Christian ministry and sit once again at his feet. He being dead, yet speaketh.

With such thoughts these all too personal reflections on Lightfoot come to an end. Having returned to Lightfoot after many years it has been fascinating to begin to realize how much of my own concerns, a century later, have mirrored his and no doubt have been influenced by him. It is a debt I am more than happy to own. How could one who has written on *Unity and Diversity in the New Testament*[93] not warm to the words of Lightfoot's sermon on Paul's idea of unity, cited by Dr. Thompson: 'A moment's reflection will show, that uniformity is impoverishment, and that diversity is absolutely necessary, if there is to be anything like fullness in the final result.'[94] Lightfoot as critical historian and Lightfoot as Christian teacher is a model I cherish. And his debate with Baur takes us to the heart of the question, more pertinent than ever, regarding the relation of Christianity and Judaism and the emergence of Christianity's distinctive features. I find also that I have followed his advice given to the future dean of Wells: 'Begin to write as soon

---

[92]See particularly *Baptism, Eucharist, and Ministry* (Geneva: World Council of Churches, 1982), 'Ministry' sections 1-6.

[93]J. D. G. Dunn, *Unity and Diversity in the New Testament* (London: SCM Press, 1977).

[94]J. B. Lightfoot, *Sermons Preached on Special Occasions* (London: Macmillan, 1891), pp. 8-9.

as you possibly can. That was what Prince Lee always said to us. That is the way to learn. Almost all I have learnt has come from writing books. If you write a book on a subject, you have to read everything that has been written about it.[95] Good advice still for postgraduate and aspiring scholar, even if, as Professor Hengel reminded us, it is less realistic in the twentieth century than it was in the nineteenth.

But let me close with the description of Lightfoot's funeral, on 26th December 1889, by his lifelong friend, Edward Benson, then archbishop of Canterbury, which I first discovered written out in the flyleaf of Lightfoot's *Galatians*, a volume which I bought from the library of a Church of Scotland minister living next door in 1960, to become one of the foundation stones of my own library. Benson recalls:

> The rite at Durham and Auckland most beautiful. Late yestreen he was brought and laid eastward in the middle of the Chapel of the Nine Altars with tapers at head and foot, and the red Cross overlying him on the purple pall. Clergy watched through the night in relays. Next morning the choir perfectly filled with clergy and the nave with people. I was on the North side of the Sanctuary and his coffin now before the Altar. It was borne by Auckland students in relays. The great people of the County and all manner of 'representatives' followed him—and poor miners are getting confirmed because 'he told them and they didn't mind, but now that he is gone they must.' There is no class of men that the scholar has not touched. The simple, the sincere, unpretending heart of him was greater than his greatest criticism.[96]

---

[95]Eden and MacDonald, *Lightfoot of Durham*, p. 135.
[96]A. C. Benson, *The Life of Edward White Benson, Sometime Archbishop of Canterbury* (London: Macmillan, 1899), 2:291. See also the description by another of his long-term friends, F. J. A. Hort, in *Life and Letters of Fenton John Anthony Hort*, pp. 409-10.

PUBLISHED WORKS BY LIGHTFOOT IN CHRONOLOGICAL SEQUENCE

Compiled by Benjamin J. Snyder

Abbreviations

BE	*Biblical Essays* (1893)
BL	Westcott, *Bishop Lightfoot* (1894)
CS	*Cambridge Sermons* (1890)
CUL	Cambridge University Library
DAA	*Dissertations on the Apostolic Age* (1892)
EWSR	*Essays on the Work Entitled Supernatural Religion* (1889)
HE	*Historical Essays* (1895)
LNC	*Leaders of the Northern Church* (1890)
OFR	*On a Fresh Revision of the English New Testament* (1871)
SSO	*Sermons Preached on Special Occasions* (1891)
TCC	Wren Library, Trinity College, Cambridge

"Hyperides." *Journal of Classical and Sacred Philology* 1 (1854): 109-24.

Review of P. Schaff, *History of the Apostolic Church, with a General Introduction to Church History. Journal of Classical and Sacred Philology* 2 (1855): 119-20.

Review of E. Falkener, *A Description of Some Important Theatres and Other Remains in Crete. Journal of Classical and Sacred Philology* 2 (1855): 120.

"The Mission of Titus to the Corinthians." *Journal of Classical and Sacred Philology* 2 (1855): 194-205. [= BE 271-84]

Review of C. O. Müller, *Denkmaler der Alten Kunst, Nach der Auswahl und Anordnung. Journal of Classical and Sacred Philology* 2 (1855): 240-41.

Review of W. Webster and W. F. Wilkinson, *The Greek Testament, with Notes Grammatical and Exegetical. Journal of Classical and Sacred Philology* 2 (1855): 360-61.

Review of American Bible Union, *The Second Epistle of Peter, the Epistles of John and Judas, and the Revelation: Translated from the Greek, on the Basis of the Common English Version, with Notes. Journal of Classical and Sacred Philology* 2 (1855): 361-63.

Review of W. Blew, *Agamemnon the King: A Tragedy from the Greek of Aeschylus.* *Journal of Classical and Sacred Philology* 2 (1855): 363-64.

"Recent Editions of St Paul's Epistles." *Journal of Classical and Sacred Philology* 3 (1856): 81-121.

Review of F. A. Paley, *The Tragedies of Aeschylus. Re-edited with an English Commentary. Journal of Classical and Sacred Philology* 3 (1856): 238.

"On the Style and Character of the Epistle to the Galatians." *Journal of Classical and Sacred Philology* 3 (1856): 289-327.

"They That Are of Caesar's Household." *Journal of Classical and Sacred Philology* 4 (1857): 57-79.

Review of W. J. Conybeare and J. S. Howson, *The Life and Epistles of St Paul. Journal of Classical and Sacred Philology* 4 (1857): 107-9.

On the Celibacy Question. Privately printed, October 26, 1857.

"Notes on Some Corrupt and Obscure Passages in the *Helena* of Euripides." *Journal of Classical and Sacred Philology* 4 (1858): 153-86.

Two flysheets on the Minor Scholarships proposed to be created at Trinity College. Privately printed, March 17 and 31, 1859 [copies in *College Notices*, vol. 1, TCC].

"On the Long Walls at Athens." *Journal of Classical and Sacred Philology* 4 (1859): 294-302.

On the Report of the Syndicate Appointed to Regulate the Examinations of Students Not Members of the University. Privately printed, March 6, 1860.

"I have just received Mr Roberts' second paper, and I hasten to reply to it . . ." Privately printed, March 8, 1860. [copy among the Cambridge University Papers ET 61, CUL]

Christian Progress. A Sermon Preached in the Chapel of Trinity College, Cambridge, at the Commemoration of Benefactors, December 15, 1860. London: Macmillan, 1861.

The Increasing Purpose of God. A Sermon, Preached in the Church of St Olave, Hart Street. On Trinity Monday, May 27, 1861, Before the Corporation of Trinity House. London: Rivingtons, 1861.

"Romans, The Epistle to the," "Thessalonians, First Epistle to the," and "Thessalonians, Second Epistle to the." In *A Dictionary of the Bible*, ed. W. Smith, 3:1053-58, 1477-81, 1481-84. London: John Murray, 1863.

St Paul's Epistle to the Galatians. A Revised Text with Introduction, Notes, and Dissertations. London: Macmillan, 1865.

"The New Professorship." Privately printed, February 6, 1866.

In Memory of William Whewell. A Sermon Preached in the College Chapel on Sunday, March 18, 1866. London: Macmillan, 1866.

The Mustard Seed and the Leaven. A Sermon Preached on Tuesday, September 18, at St. Paul's Church, Bedford, on Behalf of the Society for the Propagation of the Gospel in Foreign Parts. London: Macmillan, 1866.

"Papias of Hierapolis." *Contemporary Review* 5 (1867): 397-417.

"Caius or Hippolytus?" *Journal of Philology* 1 (1868): 98-112.

"Two Neglected Facts Bearing on the Ignatian Controversy." *Journal of Philology* 1 (1868): 47-55.

St Paul's Epistle to the Philippians. A Revised Text with Introduction, Notes and Dissertations. London: Macmillan, 1868.

Review of J. Bleek, *An Introduction to the Old Testament. Cambridge University Gazette* 23 (1869): 184-85.

S. Clement of Rome. London: Macmillan, 1869.

"Heading of the Paris MS of the Ignatian Epistle to the Romans." *Journal of Philology* 2 (1869): 157.

"M. Renan On the Epistle to the Romans." *Journal of Philology* 2 (1869): 264-95. [= BE 287-320]

Review of E. Renan, *Saint-Paul. Academy* 1 (1869): 10-11, 37-38.

Untitled fly-sheet on "the Report of the Great St Mary's Pulpit Syndicate." February 14, 1871. [copy among the Cambridge University Papers FA 8592, CUL]

"The Evidences of Christianity in Relation to the Current Forms of Scepticism." *Report of the Church Congress* (1871): 76-84.

"The Epistle to the Romans." *Journal of Philology* 3 (1871): 193-214. [= BE 352-74]

On a Fresh Revision of the English New Testament. London: Macmillan, 1871, 1891.

Letter to the editor. *Guardian*, April 10, 1872.

"Professor Lightfoot on Divinity Degrees." *Guardian*, May 22, 1872.

Review of J. G. Müller, *Erklärung des Barnabasbriefes. Academy* 3 (1872): 206-7.

Letter to the editor. *Guardian*, October 9, 1872.

Strength Made Perfect in Weakness. A Sermon Preached in St Paul's Cathedral on Sunday, December 22, 1872, at the Bishop of London's Ordination. London: Macmillan, 1873.

ΠΑΝΤΑ ΎΜΟΝ: *A Sermon Before the University Church Society.* Cambridge: privately printed, n.d. [1873]. [= SSO 1-20]

Except It Die. A Sermon Preached in the Chapel of Trinity College, Cambridge, on Sexagesima Sunday, February 16, 1873. London: Macmillan, 1873. [= CS 63-79]

Letter to the editor. *Times*, May 23, 1873.

"The Drama." In *"The Use and Abuse of the World." Six Sermons Preached . . . in the Church of St James's, Piccadilly*, ed. J. E. Kempe. London: SPCK, 1873. Reprinted as *The Drama.* London: SPCK, 1898. [= SSO 21-37]

Review of H. J. Holtzmann, *Kritik der Epheser- und Kolosserbriefe auf Grund einer Analyse ihres Verwandtschaftsverhältnisses. Academy* 4 (August 1, 1873): 287-89.
"The Present Need and the Best Means of Quickening Interest in Theological Thought." *Report of the Church Congress* (1873): 227-33.
The Three Temples. An Address Delivered in the Temporary Church of S. Luke's, New Chesterton, Cambridge, on S. Luke's Day, October 18th, 1873, . . . On the Occasion of Setting the Memorial Stone of the First Portion of a Permanent Church for S. Luke's District by the Bishop of the Diocese. Cambridge: privately printed, 1873.
Cynaphloyntec: An Address to the University Church Society. Edited by Brooke F. Westcott and J. B. Lightfoot. Cambridge: C. J. Clay, 1873.
Comparative Progress of Ancient and Modern Missions. A Paper Read at the Annual Meeting of the Society for the Propagation of the Gospel in Foreign Parts, April 29, 1873. London: Clay, 1874. [= HE 71-92]
"The Egyptian and Coptic Versions." In *A Plain Introduction to the Criticism of the NT*, edited by Fredrick H. Scrivener, 319-57. Cambridge, 1874.
"Supernatural Religion. (First Article)." *Contemporary Review* 25 (1874): 1-22. [= EWSR 1-31]
"Supernatural Religion (No. II): The Silence of Eusebius." *Contemporary Review* 25 (1875): 169-88. [= EWSR 32-58]
"Supernatural Religion (No. III): The Ignatian Epistles." *Contemporary Review* 25 (1875): 337-59. [= EWSR 59-88]
"Supernatural Religion (No. IV): Polycarp of Smyrna." *Contemporary Review* 25 (1875): 827-66. [= EWSR 89-141]
"Supernatural Religion (No. V): Papias of Hierapolis." *Contemporary Review* 26 (1875): 377-403. [= EWSR 142-77]
"Supernatural Religion (No. VI): Papias of Hierapolis." *Contemporary Review* 26 (1875): 828-56. [= EWSR 178-216]
Editor of H. L. Mansel, *The Gnostic Heresies of the First and Second Centuries.* London: John Murray, 1875.
Saint Paul's Epistle to the Colossians and Philemon. A Revised Text, with Introductions, Notes, and Dissertations. London: Macmillan, 1875.
"Supernatural Religion (No. VII): The Later School of St John." *Contemporary Review* 27 (1876): 471-96. [= EWSR 217-50]
"The New MS of Clement of Rome." *Academy* 9 (1876): 486.
Review of *Patrum Apostolicorum Opera. Recensuerunt Oscar de Gebhardt, Adolfus Harnack, Theodorus Zahn. Academy* 10 (1876): 113-14.
"Supernatural Religion (No. VIII): The Churches of Gaul." *Contemporary Review* 28 (1876): 405-20. [= EWSR 251-71]

The Father of Missionaries. A Sermon Preached on S. Andrew's Day, 1876, Before the Members of the University, in S. Michael's Church, Cambridge. Cambridge: C. J. Clay, 1877. [= SSO 38-54]

On the Proposed Grace for Abolishing Compulsory Attendance at Professors' Lectures. Cambridge University Press, 1877.

S. Clement of Rome, an Appendix Containing the Newly Recovered Portions with Introductions, Notes, and Translations. London: Macmillan, 1877.

All Things to All Men. A Sermon Preached in St Paul's Cathedral on St Mark's Day, at the Consecration of the First Bishop of Truro. London: Macmillan, 1877. [= SSO 55-70]

"Supernatural Religion (No. IX): Tatian's Diatessaron." *Contemporary Review* 29 (1877): 1132-43. [= EWSR 272-88]

Letter to the editor. *Guardian*, July 4, 1877.

"Donne the Poet-Preacher." In *The Classic Preachers of the English Church. Lectures Delivered at St James' Church in 1877*, series 1, edited by J. E. Kempe, 1-26. New York: E. P. Dutton, 1877. [= HE 221-45]

Articles on Abibas, Ablabius, Aburgius, Acacius (x 4), Achillas, Agapetus (x 2), Alypius, Amphilochius, Anastasius (x 4), Anthimus, Antipater, Antonius, Apion, Apostolic Fathers, Arabianus, Archelaus, Arinthaeus, Asclepiades, Asterius, Atarbius, and Athanasius (bishop of Ancyra); and Eusebius of Cae-sarea. In *A Dictionary of Christian Biography, Literature, Sects, and Doctrines,* edited by W. Smith and H. Wace, 1:7, 11-12, 14-17, 58, 88, 103-8, 110, 119, 122, 125, 128-30, 147-49, 151, 153, 159, 175, 178-79, 203-4; 2:308-48. London: John Murray, 1877–1887.

"Illustrations of the Acts from Recent Discoveries." *Contemporary Review* 32 (1878): 288-96. [= EWSR 291-302]

Address on the Distribution of Scholarships and Prizes of the Liverpool Council of Education in the Concert Room, St George's Hall, Liverpool, January 16, 1879. London: William Tegg, 1879.

Bought with a Price. Cambridge: Macmillan, 1879. [= CS 283-99]

"The Bishop of Durham and the 'Quicumque.'" *Guardian*, August 27, 1879, 1216.

"The Colossian Heresy (1879)." in *Conflict at Colossae: A Problem in the Inter-pretation of Early Christianity Illustrated by Selected Modern Studies*, edited by Fred O. Francis and Wayne A. Meeks, 13-59. Atlanta: SBL, 1975.

"Bishop Lightfoot on Temperance." *Church of England Temperance Chronicle*, March 20, 1880.

Inaugural Address. Delivered at the Co-operative Congress, Held at Newcastle-On-Tyne, May 17th, 1880. Manchester: The Central Co-operative Board, 1880.

The Unity of the Church. A Paper Read at the Leicester Church Congress, September 29, 1880. Durham: Andrews, 1880.

"The Last Petition of the Lord's Prayer." *Guardian*, September 7, 14, and 21, 1881. [= OFR 269-323]

"Inaugural Address." *Report of the Church Congress* (1881): 12-19.

The Right Rev. The Lord Bishop of Durham, Rev. Canon Ellison, and Mark Knowles . . . on Church Temperance Work, with Speech of the Rev. E. H. Perowne, D.D., Vice Chancellor, Chairman at an University Meeting at Cambridge, 22 October, 1881. London: Church of England Temperance Publication Depot, n.d.

"The Cambridge Mission to Delhi." Reprinted from *The Cambridge Review*, November 23, 1881. [copy in Cambridge University Papers MD5, CUL]

"Living Oracles." A Sermon Preached in St Paul's Cathedral at the Anniversary of the British and Foreign Bible Society, by the Right Rev. the Lord Bishop of Durham, Vice President of the Society, on Tuesday, May 2, 1882. London: The Bible House, 1882.

"Many Members and One Body." A Sermon Preached Before the Representative Council of the Scottish Episcopal Church . . . on Tuesday, October 10, 1882. Edinburgh: R. Grant & Son, 1882. [= SSO 174-90]

Primary Charge. Two Addresses Delivered to the Clergy of Durham in December 1882. London: Macmillan, 1884.

An Address to Friends of the White Cross Movement, Delivered in St Mary's Church, Gateshead, May 20, 1883. White Cross series. London: Hatchards, 1884.

An Address to Members of the White Cross Army. Delivered at the Lightfoot Institute, March 20th, 1884. White Cross series. London: Hatchards, 1885.

An Address Delivered to the Durham Junior Clerical Society by the Bishop (S. Michael and All Angels, 1884). Cambridge, privately printed, n.d.

"Results of Recent Historical and Topographical Research upon the Old and New Testament Scriptures." *Report of the Church Congress* (1884): 227-32.

"What Disestablishment Would Involve: A Warning." Address of the Lord Bishop of Durham at the Annual Meeting of the Church Defence Institution, Held on June 19, 1885. London: Printed for the Church Defence Institution, 1885.

"The White Cross." *Contemporary Review* 48 (1885): 262-68.

Durham Diocesan Church Conference. Manifesto on Disestablishment. Inaugural Address by the Right Rev. the Lord Bishop of Durham. Newcastle-Upon-Tyne: Andrew Reid, 1885.

The Apostolic Fathers, Part 2: S. Ignatius. S. Polycarp. Revised Texts with Introductions, Notes, Dissertations, and Translations. 3 vols. London: Macmillan, 1885–1889.

"Paul and Festus—A Contrast." In *Expository Sermons in the New Testament*, 139-42. London: Hodder & Stoughton, 1885.

"The Vision of God." In *The Anglican Pulpit of Today*, 27-34. London: Hodder & Stoughton, 1886.

The Bishop of Durham on the Sunday Closing Bill. Speech in the House of Lords, May 11, 1886. Sunday Closing Tracts. New series 17, n.d.

Bishop Auckland, to W. A. Knight. July 12, 1886.

"Inaugural Address." *Journal of the British Archaeological Association* 43 (1887): 1-12.

Lay Evangelists, an Address Delivered by the Bishop of Durham, on Friday, October 22nd, 1886, in Bishopwearmouth Parish Church, When Seven Persons Were Set Apart for This Office. Sunderland, 1887.

A Charge Delivered to the Clergy of the Diocese of Durham, November 25, 1886. London: Macmillan, 1887.

"The Earliest Papal Catalogue." *Academy* 785 (1887): 362-63.

The Sermon by the Lord Bishop of Durham, Preached Before the Church Congress, in the Collegiate Church of St Peter, Wolverhampton, on Monday, October 3rd, 1887. London: SPCK, 1887. [= SSO 248-64]

"The Bishop's Inaugural Address." *Durham Diocesan Gazette* 1 (1887): 2-10.

The Threefold Ministry. (From the Writings of the Bishop of Durham). Privately printed, 1888. [= DAA 241-46 & BL 129-39]

An Address, on the Reopening of the Chapel, Auckland Castle, August 1, 1888, by the Bishop of Durham. Bishop Auckland: Cummins, n.d. [= LNC 139-57]

"The Bishop of Durham, Writing to His Diocesan Conference from Bournemouth Yesterday Week." *Guardian*, February 27, 1889.

"The Lost Catalogue of Hegesippus." *Academy* 785 (1889): 363-63.

"The Muratorian Fragment." *Academy* 907 (1889): 186-88.

Essays on the Work Entitled Supernatural Religion. London: Macmillan, 1889, 1893.

The Apostolic Fathers, Part 1. S. Clement of Rome. A Revised Text, with Introductions, Notes, Dissertations, and Translations. 2 vols. London: Macmillan, 1890.

Cambridge Sermons. London: Macmillan, 1890.

"Internal Evidence for the Authenticity and Genuineness of St John's Gospel." *The Expositor* fourth series 1 (1890): 1-21, 81-92, 176-88 [= BE, 1-44]. Reprinted in Ezra Abbot, Andrew P. Peabody and Joseph Barber Lightfoot, *The Fourth Gospel, Evidences External and Internal of Its Johannean Authorship; Essays by Ezra Abbot, Andrew P. Peaboy and Bishop Lightfoot.* New York: C. Scribner's Sons, 1891.

Leaders of the Northern Church. London: Macmillan, 1890, 1891, 1899, 1907.

Ordination Addresses and Counsels to Clergy. London: Macmillan, 1890.

Sermons. Contemporary Pulpit Library. London: Swan Sonnenschein, 1890.

The Apostolic Fathers, Abridged. Revised Texts with Short Introductions and English Translations. Edited and completed by J. R. Harmer. London: Macmillan, 1891.

Sermons Preached in St Paul's Cathedral. London: Macmillan, 1891.

Sermons Preached on Special Occasions. London: Macmillan, 1891.

Dissertations on the Apostolic Age. Reprinted from Editions of St Paul's Epistles. London: Macmillan, 1892.

"Acts of the Apostles." In *A Dictionary of the Bible*, edited by W. Smith and J. M. Fuller, 24-43. 2nd ed. London: John Murray, 1893.

Biblical Essays. London: Macmillan, 1893.

The Apostolic Fathers Comprising: The Epistles (Genuine and Spurious) of Clement of Rome, the Epistles of S. Iognatius, the Epistle of S. Polycarp, the Martyrdom of S. Polycarp, the Teaching of the Apostles, the Epistle of Barnabas, the Shepherd of Hermas, the Epistle to Diognetus, the Fragments of Papias, the Reliques of the Elders Preserved in Irenaeus. London: Macmillan, 1893. Coauthored with J. R. Harmer.

Notes on the Epistles of St Paul from Unpublished Commentaries. Edited with an introductory note by J. R. Harmer. London: Macmillan, 1895.

Historical Essays. London: Macmillan, 1895. By Joseph Barber Lightfoot, J. R. Harmer, and Alfred Plummer.

Later Editions of Lightfoot's Writings

*Lightfoot, J. B., M. R. James, Henry Barclay Swete and J. Armitage Robinson. *Excluded Books of the New Testament.* E. Nash & Grayson, 1927.

Biblical Essays. With an introduction by P. E. Hughes. Grand Rapids: Baker Book House, 1979.

The Christian Ministry. Edited with an introduction by P. E. Hughes. Wilton, CT: Morehouse-Barlow, 1983.

Treloar, G. R., and B. N. Kaye. "J. B. Lightfoot on Strauss and Christian Origins: An Unpublished Manuscript." *Durham University Journal* 79 (1987): 165-200.

Kaye, B. N., and G. R. Treloar. "J. B. Lightfoot and New Testament Interpretation: An Unpublished Manuscript of 1855." *Durham University Journal* 82 (1990): 161-75.

The Apostolic Fathers. Translated by J. B. Lightfoot and J. R. Harmer. Edited by M. W. Holmes. 2nd ed. Grand Rapids: Baker Book House, 1990.

TRANSLATIONS OF LIGHTFOOT'S WRITINGS

Analysis of Certain of St. Paul's Epistles. Reprinted from Bishop Lightfoot's Commentaries. London, 1906.

Balslev, V., J. S. Fibiger Jørgensen, H. Hagerup and J. B. Lightfoot. *Apostlen Paulus Breve til Menighederne i Galatien, Filippi, Kolossæ og Filemon.* København: Karl Schønberg, 1884–1888. [Danish]

Chen, Xizeng, C. J. Ellicott, J. B. Lightfoot and Qun Jiang. *Feilimen Shu Mian Mian Guan.* Taibei shi: Huo dao chu ban she, 2005. [陳希曾埃特科特, and J. B Lightfoot. 腓利門書面面觀. 臺北市: 活道, 2005.]

Correspondence of J.B. Lightfoot, 1862–1897.

Die Didaché : Die Onderwysing van Die Twaalf Apostles : In Afrikaans Vertaal Uit Die Hersiene Griekse Teks van J.B. Lightfoot, Met Kantaantekenige En 'N Kerkhistoriese Verkenning van Die Belang En. 1ste uitg. Kaapstad: N. G. Kerk, 1980.

Kirisuto Kyōkai Kyōshokuron. Tōkyō: Kyōbunkan, 1899.

Los Padres Apostólicos. Barcelona: CLIE, 1990.

Soksado Kyobudŭl [속사도 교부들]. Ch'op'an. Sŏul-si: Taehan Kidokkyo Sŏhoe, 1994.

Monographs on Lightfoot
or His Works

Compiled by Benjamin J. Snyder

Arthur, T. *The Good Bishop: A Poem*. Newcastle-Upon-Tyne, 1890.

Barbour, R. W. *Auckland Castle 1882. Letters of the Rev. R. W. Barbour to His Wife from the Bishop's Palace*. Privately printed, n.d.

Browne, G. F. *A Description of the Series of Stained Glass Windows to Be Placed in the Church of S. Ignatius the Martyr, Sunderland, Built by the Late Bishop of Durham, the Right Rev. J. B. Lightfoot, D.D., As a Thank-Offering for God's Mercies Vouchsafed to Him During Seven Years of His Episcopate, 1879–86*. Sunderland, n.d.

Bullock, C. *The Two Bishops: A Welcome and a Memory*. London: Home Words, 1890.

Caldcleugh, Thomas, J. B. Lightfoot and A. N. L. Munby. *Catalogue of Books Bequeathed to the University of Durham by Joseph Barber Lightfoot, D.D., Late Lord Bishop*. Durham, 1891.

Cassels, W. R. *A Reply to Dr. Lightfoot's Essays by the Author of "Supernatural Religion."* London: Longmans, 1889.

———. *Supernatural Religion: An Inquiry into the Reality of Divine Revelation*. 4th ed. 3 vols. London: Longmans, Green, 1874–1877.

Dunn, James D. G., ed. *The Lightfoot Centenary Lectures to Commemorate the Life and Work of Bishop J. B. Lightfoot (1828–89). Durham University Journal*, extra complementary number for subscribers (January 1992). [Introduction / James D. G. Dunn—Lightfoot as Victorian Churchman / David M. Thompson— Bishop Lightfoot and the Tübingen School on the Gospel of John and the

Second Century / Martin Hengel—J. B. Lightfoot as Biblical Commentator / C. K. Barrett—Lightfoot in Retrospect / James D. G. Dunn]

———. *The Partings of the Ways: Between Christianity and Judaism and Their Significance for the Character of Christianity.* 2nd ed. London: SCM Press, 2006.

Eden, George R., and Fredrick C. Macdonald, eds. *Lightfoot of Durham. Memories and Appreciations.* Cambridge: Cambridge University Press, 1932.

Gasque, W. Ward. *A History of the Criticism of the Acts of the Apostles.* Grand Rapids: Eerdmans, 1975.

Hopkins, E. *The White Cross Army. A Statement of the Bishop of Durham's Movement.* London: Hatchard's, 1883.

Killen, William P. *The Ignatian Epistles Entirely Spurious. A Reply to the Right Rev. Dr Lightfoot.* Edinburgh: T&T Clark, 1886.

Lake, W. C. *Bishop Lightfoot. A Sermon Preached in Durham Cathedral on Sunday, Dec 29th, 1889.* Durham: Andrews, 1890.

Leary, T. H. L. *A Critical Examination of Bishop Lightfoot's Defence of the Last Petition in the Lord's Prayer.* London: The Christian Opinion & Revisonist Office, 1882.

MacDonald, Fredrick Charles. *The Story of St Peter's Chapel, Auckland Castle, with an Appendix Describing the Windows and Other Features of Interest, Being the Original Draft Manuscript of the Late Frederick Charles MacDonald . . . Hon. Canon of Durham.* Revised and completed by H. F. MacDonald. West Hartlepool: G. R. Todd, 1937.

Memorial to Bishop Lightfoot. Account of the Meeting Held on the 18th February, 1890, in the Chapter House of Durham Cathedral. [copy among the Cambridge University Papers, CUL]

Moule, H. C. G. *My Cambridge Classical Teachers.* Durham: Andrews, 1913.

———. *"Wise Men and Scribes." A Commemoration Sermon Preached in the Chapel of Trinity College, Cambridge, December 10th, 1907.* Cambridge: Bowes & Bowes, 1907.

Neill, S. *The Interpretation of the New Testament 1861–1961.* Oxford: Oxford University Press, 1964.

Newsome, D. *Godliness and Good Learning. Four Studies on a Victorian Ideal.* London: John Murray, 1961.

The Nineteenth Century Painted Glass Windows in St Peter's Chapel Auckland Castle. n.d. [copy in the Dean & Chapter Library, Durham Cathedral]

Presentation of a Pastoral Staff to the Bishop of Durham (with Description and Plate). Durham: Andrews, 1890.

Roberts, John. *"To the Members of the Senate" . . . A Short Reply to Mr. Lightfoot on the Cambridge Local Examinations.* Cambridge, 1860.

Robinson, John A. T. *Joseph Barber Lightfoot, Durham Cathedral Lecture.* Durham: Dean & Chapter of Durham, 1981.

S. Ignatius the Martyr, Hendon, Sunderland. Service of Consecration. Services and Sermons of the Octave, and Other Matters with Regard to the Church and District of S. Ignatius the Martyr. Consecration by the Right Rev. the Lord Bishop of Durham, D.D., on Tuesday, the 2nd July, 1889. Sunderland, 1889.

See of Durham, 15th May, A.D. 1879: Enthronement, Installation, and Induction of the Right Reverend Bishop Lightfoot. Durham: County Advertiser Office, 1879.

The Society of Christ and the Blessed Mary the Virgin (Durham Diocesan Church Workers) Jubilee Book 1887–1937. 1937.

Treloar, Geoffrey R. *Lightfoot the Historian: The Nature and Role of History in the Life and Thought of J. B. Lightfoot (1828–1889) as Churchman and Scholar.* Wissenschaftliche Untersuchungen zum neuen Testament, 2.103. Tübingen: Mohr Siebeck, 1998.

Tyson, Joseph B. *Marcion and Luke-Acts: A Defining Struggle.* Columbia: University of South Carolina Press, 2006.

Watkins, H. W. *Bishop Lightfoot. Reprinted from the Quarterly Review, with a Prefatory Note by B. F. Westcott.* London: Macmillan, 1894.

Westcott, Brooke Foss. *Bishop Lightfoot.* London: Macmillan, 1894.

———. *From Strength to Strength: Three Sermons on Stages in a Consecrated Life.* London: Macmillan, 1890.

Wordsworth, C. *Some Remarks on Bishop Lightfoot's Dissertation on the Christian Ministry.* Edinburgh: Blackwood, 1884.

Articles or Essays on Lightfoot or His Works

Compiled by Benjamin J. Snyder

Asmus, J. Review Of *Historical Essays*. *Historische Zeitschrift* 77 (1896): 274-76.

Barnard, L. W. "Bishop Lightfoot and the Apostolic Fathers." *Church Quarterly Review* 161 (1960): 423-35.

Barrett, C. K. "How History Should Be Written." In *History, Literature, and Society in the Book of Acts*, edited by Ben Witherington, 33-57. Cambridge: Cambridge University Press, 2007.

———. "J. B. Lightfoot as Biblical Commentator." In *The Lightfoot Centenary Lectures to Commemorate the Life and Work of Bishop J.B. Lightfoot (1828–89)*, edited by James D. G. Dunn, 53-70. *Durham University Journal* extra complementary number for subscribers (January 1992).

———. "Joseph Barber Lightfoot." *Durham University Journal* 64 (1972): 193-204.

———. "Joseph Barber Lightfoot." In *Oxford Dictionary of National Biography*, edited by H. C. G Matthew, 757-62. Oxford: Oxford University Press, 2004.

———. "Quomodo Historia Conscribenda Sit." *New Testament Studies* 28 (1982): 303-20.

Behlmer, Heike. "Paul de Lagarde and the Coptic New Testament: A Short Note on Archival Material in the Lagarde Papers." *Arc* 33 (2005): 23-31.

Benson, A. C. "Bishop Lightfoot." *Cornhill Magazine* 103 (1911): 672-87.

"Bishop Lightfoot." *Durham Directory* (1891): 49-52.

"Bishop Lightfoot on the New Testament in the Second Century." *Church Quarterly Review* 30 (1890): 134-59.

"Bishop Lightfoot's Apostolic Fathers." *Edinburgh Review* 164 (1886): 100-137.

"Bishop Lightfoot's St Clement of Rome." *Church Quarterly Review* 32 (1891): 49-68.

"Bishop of Durham, The." *Times*, December 23, 1889. Reprinted in *Eminent Persons, Biographies Reprinted From The Times*, 4:203-10. London: Macmillan, 1893.

Black, Matthew. "J.B. Lightfoot." In *Religion in Geschichte und Gegenwart*, edited by K. Galling, 4:376. 3rd ed. Tübingen, 1957–1965.

Browning, W. R. F. "Joseph Barber Lightfoot (1828–1889)." In *A Dictionary of the Bible*, 236. 2nd. ed. Oxford: Oxford University Press, 2009.

Bruce, F. F. "J.B. Lightfoot (died 1889): Commentator and Theologian." *Evangel* 7 (1989): 10-12.

Buck, Charles H. "The Date of Galatians." *Journal of Biblical Literature* 70 (1951): 113-22.

Butler, E. C. "Bishop Lightfoot and the Early Roman See." *Dublin Review* 4th series 4 (1893): 497-514.

———. "Bishop Lightfoot and the Early Roman See." *Dublin Review* fourth series 4 (1893): 836-57.

Byrom, J. K. "They Were Not Divided." *Theology* 77 (1974): 536-37.

Cadwallader, Alan H. "Male Diagnosis of the Female Pen in Late Victorian Britain: Private Assessments of Supernatural Religion." *Journal of Anglican Studies* 5 (2007): 69-88.

———. "What's in a Name? The Tenacity of a Tradition of Interpretation." *Lutheran Theological Journal* 39 (2005): 218-34.

Conder, Paul C. N. "They Were Not Divided." *Theology* 77 (1974): 422-31.

Cox, Michael. "Joseph Barber Lightfoot (1828–1889)." In *Who Wrote What? A Dictionary of Writers and Their Works*, 182. 3rd ed. Oxford: Oxford University Press, 2002.

Cross, F. L., and E. A. Livingstone, eds. "Joseph Barber Lightfoot." In *The Oxford Dictionary of the Christian Church*, 823. 3rd ed. Oxford: Oxford University Press, 2005.

Cross, J. A. "The Acts of the Apostles. I. A Criticism of Lightfoot and Headlam." *Journal of Theological Studies* 1 (1899): 64-75.

Cunningham, R. T. "The Second Epistle of Clement." *British and Foreign Evangelical Review* 28 (1879): 368-85.

Curteis, G. H. "Cardinal Newman and Bishop Lightfoot." *Edinburgh Review* 178 (1893): 248-65.

Daube, David. "Jesus and the Samaritan Woman: The Meaning of συγχράομαι." *Journal of Biblical Literature* (1950): 137-47.

"Death of the Bishop of Durham." *Newcastle Daily Chronicle*, December 23, 1889.

"Death of the Bishop of Durham." *Guardian*, December 24, 1889.

"Death of the Bishop of Durham." *Record*, December 27, 1889.

Dehandschutter, Boudewijn. "Ignatius, Letter to the Magnesians 8:2 Once Again." In *Jesus, Paul, and Early Christianity: Studies in Honour of Henk Jan de Jonge*, edited by Rieuwerd Buitenwerf, Harm W. Hollander and Johannes Tromp, 89-99. Leiden: Brill, 2008.

Dimock, Nathaniel. "The Apostolic Fathers and Christian Ministry: A Review." *Churchman* 1 (1887): 505-19.

Dunn, James D. G. Introduction to *The Lightfoot Centenary Lectures to Commemorate the Life and Work of Bishop J.B. Lightfoot (1828–89)*, edited by James D. G. Dunn, 1-2. *Durham University Journal* extra complementary number for subscribers (January 1992).

———. "Lightfoot in Retrospect." In *The Lightfoot Centenary Lectures to Commemorate the Life and Work of Bishop J. B. Lightfoot (1828–89)*, edited by James D. G. Dunn, 71-94. *Durham University Journal* extra complementary number for subscribers (January 1992).

———. "J(oseph) B(arber) Lightfoot (1828–1889)." In *Dictionary of Major Biblical Interpreters*, edited by Donald K. McKim, 661-65. Downers Grove, IL: IVP Academic, 2007.

Eden, George R. "Joseph Barber Lightfoot. A Sermon Preached in Durham Cathedral at the Commemoration of Founders and Benefactors on January 28th, 1926, by the Right Reverend the Lord Bishop of Wakefield." *Durham University Journal* 5 (1926): 408-12.

"'Edinburgh Review' on Newman, The." *Spectator*, August 5, 1893.

Edwards, D. L. "Lightfoot and Westcott." In *Leaders of the Church of England 1828–1944*, 207-22. London: Oxford University Press, 1971.

Edwards, W. T., Jr. "Joseph Barber Lightfoot as an Interpreter of the New Testament." ThD thesis, Southern Baptist Theological Seminary, 1958.

Elgie, W. F., and G. W. "Dr Lightfoot and His Reviewer." *Churchman* (September 14, 1865): 1099.

———. "Your Reviewer." *Churchman* (September 21, 1865): 1122.

Elliott, E. B. "The Rev. E. B. Elliott on Prophetic Articles in the Third Volume of Dr Smith's Dictionary of the Bible." *The Christian Observer* (March 1864): 199-221.

Fairbairn, A. M. "Some Recent English Theologians: Lightfoot, Westcott, Hort, Jowett, Hatch." *Contemporary Review* 71 (1897): 341-65.

Farrar, F. W. "Bishop Lightfoot." *Contemporary Review* 57 (1890): 170-82.

Faulkner, John Alfred. "Essayist Benson on Lightfoot on the Early Episcopate." *Methodist Review* 96 (1914): 622-24.

Fuller, J. M. "The Bishop of Durham on the Ignatian Epistles." *Quarterly Review* 162 (1886): 467-500.

Fuller, Reginald H. "Historical Criticism and the Bible." In *Anglicanism and the Bible*, edited by Frederick Houk Borsch, 143-68. Wilton, CT: Morehouse Barlow, 1984.

Funk, Franz X. "The Apostolic Fathers II." *Literatur Rundschau* 12 (1886): 99-101.

G., D. S. "Lightfoot of Durham." *Modern Churchman* 22 (November 1932): 463-66.

Gasque, W. Ward. "Nineteenth-Century Roots of Contemporary New Testament Criticism." In *Scripture, Tradition and Interpretation*, edited by W. Ward Gasque and W. S. LaSor, 146-56. Grand Rapids: Eerdmans, 1978.

Gibb, J. "Theologians of the Day." *Catholic Presbyterian* (1882): 177-86.

Glaswell, M. E. "Joseph Barber Lightfoot (1828–1889)." In *Theologische Realenzyklopädie*, edited by Gerhard Krause and Gerhard Müller, 21:196-98. Berlin: de Gruyter, 1991.

———. "Joseph Barber Lightfoot (1828–1889)." In *Dictionary of Biblical Interpretation*, edited by John H. Hayes, 2:76-77. Nashville: Abingdon, 1999.

Goranson, Stephen. "'Essenes': Etymology from 'šh." *Revue Qumran* 11 (1984): 483-98.

Gregory, Caspar R. "J.B. Lightfoot." In *Realencyklopädie für protestantische Theologie und Kirche*, edited by J. J. Herzog, 11:487-89. 3rd ed. Leipzig: J. C. Hinrichs, 1896–1913.

Gwatkin, H. "Review of *Historical Essays*." *English Historical Review* 11 (1896): 600-601.

Harnack, Adolf von. "The Apostolic Fathers II." *Theologische Literaturzeitung* 14 (1886): 315-19.

———. "Bishop Lightfoot's Ignatius and Polycarp." *Expositor* third series 2 (1885): 401-14.

———. "Lightfoot on the Ignatian Epistles." *Expositor* third series 3 (1886): 9-22, 175-92.

Harris, J. Rendel. "Tatian and the Date of the Fourth Gospel." *Contemporary Review* 64 (1893): 800-810.

Headlam, A. C. "Lightfoot's Apostolic Fathers." *Quarterly Review* 182 (1895): 369-98.

Heard, R. G. "Cambridge Biblical Scholarship. Westcott, Lightfoot, and Hort." *Cambridge Review* (February 15, 1947): 321-22.

Hengel, Martin. "Bishop Lightfoot and the Tubingen School on the Gospel of John and the Second Century." In *The Lightfoot Centenary Lectures to Commemorate the Life and Work of Bishop J. B. Lightfoot (1828-89)*, edited by James D. G. Dunn, 23-51. *Durham University Journal* extra complementary number for subscribers (January 1992).

———. "Bischof Lightfoot und die Tübinger Schule." In *Theologische, historische und biographische Skizzen*, 448-79. Tübingen: Mohr Siebeck, 2010.

Henson, H. H. "Bishop Lightfoot." In *Bishoprick Papers*, 133-40. London: Oxford University Press, 1946.

Hincks, Edward Young. "From Strength to Strength: Three Sermons on Stages in a Consecrated Life." *Andover Review* 13 (1890): 699-700.

Holman, Susan R. "Lightfoot's 'Woman': Scribal Transmission and the Victorian Reporter." *Anglican Theological Review* 84 (2002): 251-68.

Hoover, Jesse A. "False Lives, False Martyrs: Pseudo-Pionius and the Redating of the Martrydom of Polycarp." *Vigiliae Christianae* 67 (2013): 471-98.

Hort, Fenton J. A. "Joseph Barber Lightfoot." In *Dictionary of National Biography, 1885–1900*, 33:232-40. London: Smith, Elder, 1893.

Howard, Wilbert F. "The Cambridge Triumvirate." In *The Romance of New Testament Scholarship*, edited by Wilbert Francis Howard, 55-83. London: Epworth, 1949.

Jackson, F. Foakes. "Books Recommended by Bishop Lightfoot." In *A History of Church History*, 170-82. Cambridge: Heffer, 1939.

Kaye, Bruce N. "Lightfoot and Baur on Early Christianity." *Novum Testamentum* 26 (1984): 193-224.

Killen, William P. "The Ignatian Epistles Entirely Spurious. A Reply to the Right Rev. Dr Lightfoot." *Journal of Higher Criticism* 8 (2001): 91-143. Reprinted from W. D. Killen, *The Ignatian Epistles Entirely Spurious. A Reply to the Right Rev. Dr Lightfoot*. Edinburgh: T&T Clark, 1886.

Lambton, J. G. "Lord Durham on Bishop Lightfoot." *Illustrated Church News* (October 29, 1892).

Livingstone, E. A. "Joseph Barber Lightfoot (1828–1889)." In *The Concise Oxford Dictionary of the Christian Church*, 981. 3rd. ed. Oxford: Oxford University Press, 2013.

Loane, M. L. "Joseph Barber Lightfoot Bishop of Durham." In *Three Faithful Servants*, edited by Marcus Lawrence Loane and Geoffrey C. Bingham, 89-119. Blackwood, Australia: New Creation Publications, 1991.

Malden, R. H. "Bishop Lightfoot 1828–1889." In *Great Christians*, edited by R. S.

Forman, 335-47. London: Nicholson & Watson, 1933.

Morgan, R. "Historical Criticism and Christology: England and Germany." In *England and Germany. Studies in Theological Diplomacy*, edited by S. Sykes, 80-112. Frankfurt am Main: Peter D. Lang, 1982.

———. *"Non angli sed angeli:* Some Anglican Reactions to German Gospel Criticism." In *New Studies in Theology 1*, edited by S. Sykes and J. D. Holmes, 1-30. London: Duckworth, 1980.

Moss, Candida R. "Nailing Down and Tying Up: Lessons in Intertextual Impossibility from the Martyrdom of Polycarp." *Vigiliae Christianae* 67 (2013): 117-36.

Muir, A. F. "Ignatius and Polycarp: Last Links with the Apostolic Age." *British and Foreign Evangelical Review* 35 (1886): 298-325.

Nordell, Philip. "Review of *Dissertations on the Apostolic Age.*" *Biblical World* 1 (1893): 236.

Painter, John. "ARCIC on Mary: An Historical Consideration of the Use of Early Church Evidence in the Seattle Statement." *Journal of Anglican Studies* 4 (2006): 59-80.

Parks, J. L. "Bishop Lightfoot's Theory of Episcopate." *Sewanee Review* 2 (1894): 425-48.

Parochus. "The Bishop of Durham on the Athanasian Creed." *Guardian*, August 20, 1879.

Pelland, Gilles. "Le dossier des lettres d'Ignace d'Antioche: à propos d'un livre récent." *Science et Esprit* 32 (1980): 261-97.

Perriman, Andrew. "The Pattern of Christ's Sufferings: Colossians 1:24 and Philippians 3:10-11." *Tyndale Bulletin* 42 (1991): 62-67.

Petersen, W. L. "Patristic Biblical Quotations and Method: Four Changes to Lightfoot's Edition of Second Clement." *Vigiliae Christianae* 60 (2006): 389-419.

Picirelli, R. E. "The Meaning of *Epignosis.*" *Evangelical Quarterly* 47 (1975): 85-93.

Pointer, Steven R. "J. B. Lightfoot." In *Historians of the Christian Tradition: Their Methodology and Influence on Western Thought*, edited by Michael Bauman and Martin I. Klauber, 331-50. Nashville: Broadman & Holman, 1995.

———. "J. B. Lightfoot as a Christian Historian of Early Christian Literature." *Christian Scholar's Review* 23 (June 1994): 426-44.

Poole, R. S. "Modern Commentaries on the Bible." *Macmillan's Magazine* 13 (1865): 143-52.

———. "Modern Commentaries on the Bible." *Macmillan's Magazine* 14 (1866): 196-205.

R. A. "Joseph Barber Lightfoot, Bishop of Durham." *Cambridge Review* (January 16, 1890): 134-36.

———. "Joseph Barber Lightfoot, Bishop of Durham." *Cambridge Review* (January 23, 1890): 150-52.

Ramsay, W. M. "Bishop Lightfoot." *Theology* (February 1933): 75-82.

"Reminiscences." *Guardian*, January 1, 1890.

"Report of the Meeting for Procuring a Memorial in Cambridge of the Late Joseph Barber Lightfoot Lord Bishop of Durham." *Cambridge University Reporter* 820 (1890): 406-20.

"Review of Essays on the Work Entitled *'Supernatural Religion.'*" Reprinted from *Contemporary Review* by J. B. Lightfoot. *Old and New Testament Student* 9 (1898): 315.

"Review of *Galatians.*" *Athenaeum* 2039 (November 24, 1866): 675-76.

"Review of *Galatians.*" *Churchman* (September 7, 1865): 1070-71.

"Review of *Galatians.*" *Christian Advocate and Review* 5 (1865): 362-65.

"Review of *Galatians.*" *Literary Churchman* 40 (1865): 279-83.

"Review of *Galatians.*" *London Review* (November 4, 1865): 493-94.

"Review of *Galatians.*" *Nonconformist* (May 17, 1865): 405-6.

"Review of *Philippians.*" *Athenaeum* 2129 (August 15, 1868): 202.

"Review of *Philippians.*" *Contemporary Review* 9 (1868): 444.

"Review of *Philippians.*" *Literary Churchman* (November 28, 1868): 487-89.

"Review of *St. Clement of Rome.*" *Academy* 1 (1870): 255.

"Review of *St. Clement of Rome.*" *Cambridge University Gazette*, December 8, 1869.

"Review of *St. Clement of Rome.*" *Nonconformist*, September 15, 1869.

"Review of *St. Clement of Rome: Appendix.*" *Athenaeum* 2602 (1877): 296.

"Review of *St. Clement of Rome: Appendix.*" *Guardian*, November 28, 1877.

"Review of *St. Clement of Rome: Appendix.*" *Literary Churchman* (July 14, 1877): 273-74.

Richards, P. H. "J. B. Lightfoot as a Biblical Interpreter." *Interpretation* 8 (1954): 50-62.

Robinson, John A. T. "J. B. Lightfoot. The Champion of Critical Scholarship." MS sermon preached at St. Botoiph's Church, Cambridge, on November 7, 1976.

———. "Joseph Barber Lightfoot." In *The Roots of a Radical*, 155-61. London: SCM Press, 1980.

Rodd, Cyril S. "Commentator Supreme." *Expository Times* 104 (1993): 128.

Sanday, W. "Bishop Lightfoot." *Expositor* third series 4 (July 1886): 13-29.

———. "Bishop Lightfoot." *Academy* 922 (1890): 9-10.

————. "Bishop Lightfoot as an Historian." *English Historical Review* 5 (1890): 208-20.

————. "The Bishop of Durham." *Athenaeum* 3244 (1889): 894-95.

Savage, H. E. "'Bishop Lightfoot's Influence: His Trust in Young Men.' A Paper by the Very Rev. H.E. Savage (Dean of Lichfield, 1909-39). Edited with an introductory note by B. S. Benedikz." *Durham University Journal* 77 (1984): 1-6.

Selwyn, E. G. "The University Sermon." *Cambridge Review* (November 11, 1938): 89-90.

Silva, Moisés. "The Place of Historical Reconstruction in New Testament Criticism." In *Hermeneutics, Authority, and Canon*, edited by D. A. Carson and John D. Woodbridge, 109-33. Grand Rapids: Zondervan, 1986.

Smith, A. J., ed. "Joseph Barber Lightfoot, 1877." In *John Donne: The Critical Heritage*, 485-86. New York: Routledge, 1995.

Smyth, Egbert Coffin. "Apostolic Fathers, Pt 2: S Ignatius, S Polycarp: Revised Texts with Introductions, Notes, Dissertations, and Translations." *Andover Review* 5 (1886): 218-20.

————. "Biblical Essays." *Andover Review* 19 (1893): 778-79.

————. "The Results of Recent Historical and Geographical Research: Papers Before the Church Congress at Carlisle." *Andover Review* 2 (1884): 498-501.

Starbuck, Charles C. "The Apostolic Fathers: Revised Texts, with Introduction and English Translation, Edited and Completed." *Andover Review* 18 (1892): 111.

"Supernatural Religion." *Inquirer*, November, 7, 1874.

Thompson, David M. "Bishop Lightfoot and the Northern Church." In *Life and Thought in the Northern Church c. 1100–c. 1700*, 549-61. Woodbridge, UK: Boydell, 1999.

————. "Lightfoot as Victorian Churchman." In *The Lightfoot Centenary Lectures to Commemorate the Life and Work of Bishop J. B. Lightfoot (1828–89)*, edited by James D. G. Dunn, 3-21. *Durham University Journal* extra complementary number for subscribers (January 1992).

Treloar, Geoffrey R. "The Cambridge Triumvirate and the Acceptance of New Testament Higher Criticism in Britain 1850–1900." *Journal of Anglican Studies* 4 (2006): 13-32.

————. "J. B. Lightfoot and St. Paul, 1854–65: A Study of Intentions and Method." *Lucas* 7 (1989): 5-33.

Treloar, Geoffrey R., and Bruce N. Kaye. "J. B. Lightfoot on Strauss and Christian Origins: An Unpublished Manuscript," *Durham University Journal* 79 (1987): 165-200.

Tuckett, C. M. "Lightfoot's Text of 2 Clement: A Response to W. L. Peterson." *Vigiliae Christianae* 64 (2010): 501-19.

V., C. W. Review of *Notes on Epistles of St. Paul from Unpublished Commentaries by J. B. Lightfoot*. *Biblical World* 6 (1895): 312-13.

Watkins, H. W. "Bishop Lightfoot." *Quarterly Review* 176 (1893): 73-105.

Webster, Alan B. "Lightfoot's Ordination Addresses." *Church Quarterly Review* 166 (1965): 65-74.

Wiersbe, W. W. "Lightfoot: A Devoted Scholar." *Moody Monthly* 76 (1976): 127-31.

Wilson, D. J. "The Life of J.B. Lightfoot (1828–89), with Special Reference to the Training for the Ministry." PhD diss., Edinburgh University, 1956.

Wilson, J. C. "The Problem of the Domitianic Date of Revelation." *New Testament Studies* 39 (1993): 587-605.

Wilson, R. "Lightfoot, Savage and Eden—Sidelights on a Great Episcopate." *Theology* 55 (1952): 294-99.

Witherington, Ben. "Text Archaeology: The Finding of Lightfoot's Lost Manuscripts." *Biblical Archaeology Review* 40 (2014): 28.

Wright, N. T. "Ἁρπαγμός and the Meaning of Philippians 2:5-13." *Journal of Theological Studies* 37 (1986): 321-52.

AUTHOR INDEX

SCRIPTURE INDEX

THE LIGHTFOOT LEGACY SET

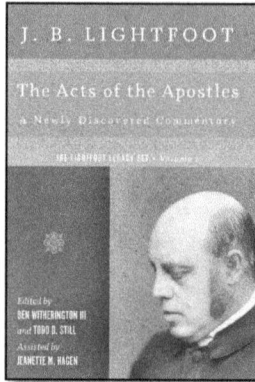

The Acts of the Apostles:
A Newly Discovered Commentary
978-0-8308-2944-6

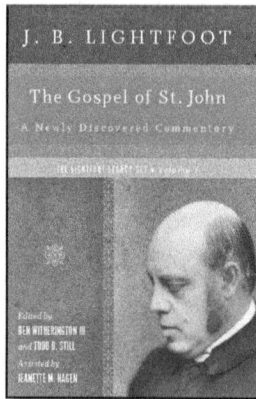

The Gospel of St. John:
A Newly Discovered Commentary
978-0-8308-2945-3

www.ingramcontent.com/pod-product-compliance
Lightning Source LLC
Chambersburg PA
CBHW030946150426
42814CB00031B/398/J